"The methodology and practices espoused by Tannenb[...] quickly find business-critical information that is easily l[...] book will help any team begin the process of reenginee[...] [im]prove its maintenance and accessibility to all consumers both inside and outside an organization. Any company contemplating large-scale data integration, consolidation, or migration should consider this book required reading."

—Jon S. Stumpf, *Vice President, Emerging Technology Office of the CIO, American International Group*

"In the mid-1990s, there was only one text containing authoritative information on repository implementation. Now Adrienne Tannenbaum has done it again with *Metadata Solutions.* Incorporating the latest technological advances with decades of experience, this book offers the most comprehensive treatment of the subject that is available. My copy is already getting worn!"

—Peter Aiken, *Institute for Data Research Virginia Commonwealth University*

"It's great to see a book by one of the world's leading metadata experts that explains the complexities of metadata technology from first principles and how to apply it in the real world."

—Philip A. Bernstein, *Senior Researcher (formerly Architect of Microsoft Metadata Services), Microsoft Corporation*

"Metadata is extremely important as businesses become more and more connected, yet there is a tremendous lack of knowledge on the topic. Adrienne, a thought leader in the field, has created a practical "how-to" book with examples that both novice and experienced developers should be able to use to successfully guide their metadata efforts."

—Peter Brooks, *Business Consultant, NerveWire*

"Tannenbaum's second book conducts a further exploration into the often confusing world of metadata and its architecture and management. As an expert in this field, Adrienne endeavors to explain metadata to the manager as well as the technician, and this text will be a useful reference for this complex subject."

—Anne Marie Smith, *Information Management Consultant and Assistant Professor, LaSalle University*

"Tannenbaum offers multiple realistic approaches to managing data as a corporate asset via metadata. She uses a simple framework to tie together the complex topic of developing a metadata solution that will stand the test of time."

—Mary Doerr, *Data Administration Management, Morgan Stanley*

"Adrienne Tannenbaum's new book attempts to clarify the role of metadata in overall database design, and to expand the understanding of this important topic. This book will serve as both an introduction for nonspecialists, and as a guide to good metadata design for specialists."

—Capers Jones, *Chief Scientist, Software Productivity Research, Inc.*

Metadata Solutions

Using Metamodels, Repositories, XML, and Enterprise Portals to Generate Information on Demand

Adrienne Tannenbaum

Addison-Wesley

Boston • San Francisco • New York • Toronto • Montreal
London • Munich • Paris • Madrid
Capetown • Sydney • Tokyo • Singapore • Mexico City

The publisher offers discounts on this book when ordered in quantity for special sales. For more information, please contact:

Pearson Education Corporate Sales Division
One Lake Street
Upper Saddle River, NJ 07458
(800) 382-3419
corpsales@pearsontechgroup.com

Visit AW on the Web: *www.awl.com/cseng/*

Library of Congress Cataloging-in-Publication Data
Tannenbaum, Adrienne
     Metadata solutions : using metamodels, repositories, XML, and enterprise portals to generate information on demand / Adrienne Tannenbaum.
          p.   cm.
     Includes bibliographical references and index.
     ISBN 0-201-71976-2
     1. Information technology. 2. Metadata.   I. Title

T58.5 .T37 2001
005.7—dc21

                                                                                2001031646

ISBN 0-201-71976-2
Text printed on recycled paper
1 2 3 4 5 6 7 8 9 10 –CRS– 0504030201
First printing, August 2001

To my family, Jim, Chris, and Nicole
for living through another
book creation process

Contents

PART II   Metadata as Part of the Solution   85

PART III   Entering Meta-Meta Land   175

PART V   Sample Metadata Solutions   347

Foreword

Most people who deal with information systems, as either information technology professionals or end users, would agree that metadata should be a critical component of nearly every application environment that is built and deployed. Who would argue that comprehensive, plain-language explanations of data elements isn't desirable? And who would take a stand that at-your-fingertips information that traced end-to-end flows of data across environments wouldn't be essential to maintenance of applications and systems?

However, if you were to take a look at 100 real-world information systems, chosen at random, chances are that only a handful, if any, of those environments would be equipped with anywhere near the metadata capabilities envisioned by their designers and the user community. If awarded an academic grade, 95 or 98 or even 100 systems of that sample would receive at best a C— and, very often, an F for "failure."

The obvious question is, "So what happened to the metadata?" The answer: You name it! From project schedules to budget constraints to inadequate metadata management tools, the excuses for inadequate metadata have been coming fast and furiously since the mid-1970s.

But among the most common—and valid—reasons for metadata implementation failure has been, quite simply, that many key concepts of metadata haven't been adequately understood by system developers and end users. Beyond the simplistic definitions of user-oriented metadata as "plain-language descriptive information about data elements" or system-oriented metadata as "end-to-end traceability that describes transformations, shows when jobs have been run, etc." lies an incredibly complex—yet very powerful—set of concepts and their implementation that tremendously enhance the usability and maintainability of information systems . . . when managed correctly throughout the development and operations life cycle.

Back in the 1980s, Nike ran a series of advertisements featuring football and baseball star Bo Jackson trying a variety of other sports, with the tag line of "Bo knows hockey" or "Bo knows golf." Borrowing from the theme of those ads, Adrienne Tannenbaum knows metadata, and Adrienne Tannenbaum knows metadata systems. In *Metadata Solutions,* Adrienne guides the reader through the business models, technology, and implementation alternatives for metadata with a unique combination of explanation and detail. This book is an easy-to-understand guided tour that covers this critical topic as comprehensively as has ever been done.

Adrienne Tannenbaum is, arguably, the industry's leading authority on metadata and its treatment. From her first book almost a decade ago, in which she provided highly practical guidance for implementing and maintaining corporate repository environments, she has provided readers, seminar and conference attendees, and consulting clients with the most practical recommendations for achieving what has been envisioned in the area of metadata management since the mid-1970s.

The technology evolves; metadata standards come and go (more frequently than real-world practitioners appreciate!); and products for data warehousing, software engineering, and other IS disciplines increasingly provide more robust metadata capabilities. Making sense of metadata in such a volatile environment, with so many interdependencies, can be a full-time job. Fortunately, Adrienne Tannenbaum has taken on that assignment and the book you are about to read is the essential guide for once and for all making metadata management an intrinsic, immutable part of today's and tomorrow's information systems.

Alan Simon
Deloitte Consulting
Data Warehousing Solutions Group

Preface

I remember when dealing with *data* became a specialty of its own. No longer viewed as simply being supportive of the processes in an organization, data became an asset that led to solid decision making and improved processes. Data, which had been collected sometimes in haphazard ways, became so valuable that people were trying to find logical connections between sporadic and isolated data. While attempting to unify data, we all realized that its locations, characteristics, definitions, sources, and access were becoming equally important. Hence, the "birth" of metadata.

Associating metadata solely with data does not do it justice. In fact, there are so many aspects to the world of information that metadata needs to embrace each and every one of them. Whether we realize it or not, metadata is already everywhere. What we are missing is an organized view of today's metadata, despite its origin. The current world of information needs an associated *metadata solution*.

Many people already know that metadata is everywhere, but despite this discovery, they have created more of it, in more places. It is time to make an honest assessment of metadata efforts and focus on metadata as the gateway to information. To do so, we must understand what metadata is, where it comes from, and how to expand its role in the world of automated intelligence.

Few will debate the importance of metadata. It is time, then, for a book that tackles metadata in a way that will clearly turn the focus toward a metadata solution.

Intended Audience

If you have been assigned the task of managing an organization's information, this book is clearly for you. Likewise, if you are wondering why today's "data dictionaries" or "repositories" just don't seem to serve their intended roles, this book will clearly explain what should have been accomplished. Because metadata is potentially so broad, this book provides an excellent backbone for those who are charged with building a full metadata solution. The individuals who will benefit the most from this approach include:

- *Chief information and/or technology officers* who are responsible for assessing their organization's metadata situation with the objective of beginning a full, practical, metadata solution implementation process
- *Business users* who have experienced data inaccuracy, lack of metadata, and general inability to find necessary information
- *Information technology project managers* who are responsible for overseeing the design and development of any data-intensive application. Examples include a data warehouse, integrated database, decision support application, customer relationship management application, reengineered series of legacy databases, or any type of project that requires assessment of "what is" with the objective of planning an improvement
- *Data management professionals* who are responsible for the administration, standardization, sharing, and organization of corporate data, especially those who have had experiences in unsuccessful repository or metadata solution implementations
- *Developers,* especially those who are faced with integrating or analyzing existing corporate applications
- *Software vendors* who are struggling with a need to supply standard metadata to consumers while integrating their own software into a metadata-accessible result
- *Consulting professionals,* particularly those who have faced issues at client companies that resulted from the lack of readily available and accurate metadata

This book provides information and content that will enlighten all of these groups. Some aspects of the book may appear to be quite technical, as clarified in the next section.

How This Book Is Organized

Consider *Metadata Solutions: Using Metamodels, Repositories, XML, and Enterprise Portals to Generate Information on Demand* the first book to address the metadata situation from the beginning through a practical solution and into its maintenance and enhancement. As such, the book has been divided into the following parts:

Part I: Today's Information prepares readers for the book's subsequent discussion of metadata. This part provides an overview and information from several perspectives that may be new to many people. It then discusses the information problems that have surfaced. Finally, the part reviews the information solutions that have been tried (and for the most part still exist) and explain where they fell short. At the conclusion of Part I, the reader should be ready to discuss metadata. Many experienced information practitioners may skip this part, but even with information integration experience, some eyes may still be opened.

Part II: Metadata as Part of the Solution begins the discussion of metadata. First, a solid definition of today's buzzword focuses on the effects of tunnel vision even on cross-application concepts such as metadata. Part II begins the metadata requirements process. By stepping the reader through a methodology that first identifies metadata beneficiaries, determines metadata requirements, and then begins a categorization process, Part II gets the reader used to metamodels. Metadata stores, the physical storage locations for metadata, are also discussed, giving various ways to implement metamodels. As a reminder that metadata solutions are much more than the storage of metamodels, the metadata solution architecture is the last topic discussed in this part.

Part III: Entering Meta-Meta Land moves inside the metadata solution. To deal with the fact that metadata is everywhere, the true metadata solution needs to address the location and access requirements of existing metadata. In addition, metadata solutions process and display their metadata differently based on the type of metadata. Designers and developers of true metadata solutions must be able to treat metadata with a software perspective. Part III focuses on what metadata means to a tool, and discusses the meta-metamodel. Once this basic understanding is covered, metadata-based technologies such as repositories, the Web, XML, and file management systems are all discussed. Aspects of Part III may be too technical for the casual reader, but the chapters do clearly explain the internals of metadata solution technology.

Part IV: Beginning the Metadata Solution Process discusses implementation-specific aspects other than the metadata and its associated metamodels.

Nontechnical factors such as readiness, scoping, and internal environment changes are addressed at the beginning of the part. The discussion then moves to technical factors such as the multitool architecture, metadata update and exchange, and metadata presentation. A chapter is dedicated to metadata solution technical support, specifically metadata and repository administration. Part IV ends with advice on determining the right solution.

Part V: Sample Metadata Solutions begins with a case study, "A Typical Metadata Disaster," which portrays a common metadata situation in corporate America. Succeeding chapters present metadata solution implementations, all focused on solving the identified disaster. Illustrated solutions, often including actual program code, metamodels, and architectural diagrams, include a centralized repository, an integrated metadata solution architecture, an information directory, metadata interexchange using XML, a standalone metadata store, and an enterprise portal. Although some aspects of this part are quite technical, I strongly urge all readers at least to browse the various solutions.

Part VI: Maintaining the Metadata Solution deals with how the metadata solution stays alive. One way is by ensuring that it meets the requirements of its targeted beneficiaries. This final part discusses the organizational responsibilities that go with such a task. It also focuses on how to ensure the livelihood of the metadata itself by discussing metadata quality. The book closes by pointing out where metadata meets the business strategy, now and into the future.

Reading Paths

Implementing a metadata solution involves a variety of skills, from business analysis all the way through technical application and interface development. Accordingly, the chapters in this book range in terms of audience and interest level. The chapters that are geared purely to those responsible for hands-on metadata solution delivery because they contain sample code or metadata solution internals have been labeled *Technical* in the upper left corner of the first page of the chapter.

To accommodate the different backgrounds of this book's readers, I have set up the following reader categories and noted the chapters of interest to them:

- *Information systems managers* who need to be aware of the intricacies of metadata solutions, but have not planned hands-on involvement:
  - ◆ Part I—all chapters
  - ◆ Part II—all chapters
  - ◆ Part III—Chapters 15, 16
  - ◆ Part IV—all chapters
  - ◆ Part V—Chapters 21, 24, 25
  - ◆ Part VI—all chapters

- *Business users* who crave a well-implemented metadata solution:
  - ◆ Part I—all chapters
  - ◆ Part II—Chapters 7, 8, 9
  - ◆ Part III—Chapters 15, 16
  - ◆ Part IV—Chapters 17, 20
  - ◆ Part V—Chapter 21
  - ◆ Part VI—all chapters

- *Technical analysts and developers* who are familiar with database technology:
  - ◆ Part I—Chapters 1, 2, 6
  - ◆ Part II— all chapters
  - ◆ Part III—all chapters
  - ◆ Part IV—all chapters
  - ◆ Part V—all chapters
  - ◆ Part VI—all chapters

- *Data management professionals* who are familiar with metadata and its current treatment:
  - ◆ Part I—Chapters 1, 4, 5, 6
  - ◆ Part II—all chapters
  - ◆ Part III—Chapter 12, 14, 15, 16
  - ◆ Part IV—all chapters
  - ◆ Part V—all chapters
  - ◆ Part VI—all chapters

Model Legend

Various models throughout the book illustrate metadata relationships, metamodels, and metadata flows. Because there is no uniform way to depict models these days, Figure P-1 shows the symbols that you will see in the models in this book.

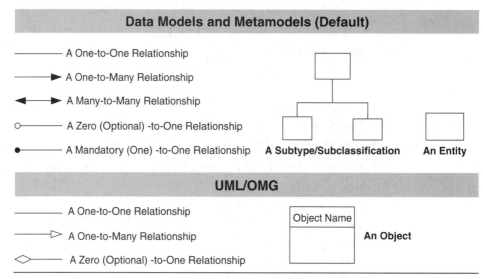

Figure P-1 **A modeling legend**

Most of the illustrations in this book follow my default modeling characteristics, as represented at the top of Figure P-1. However, because other illustrations and models have been brought in from other sources, it is important to understand their notations, as depicted. The Unified Modeling Language (UML) is the standard followed by the Object Management Group (OMG).

What Is Your Objective?

As you read this book, it will be helpful to correlate the described metadata situations with your own. Case studies, submitted by large organizations that have lived through metadata-related situations, are used throughout the book. Consider how a renewed metadata perspective like the one discussed here can revitalize your organization's metadata. You should expect to gain enough knowledge to move forward on a hands-on metadata solution implementation of any scope.

Acknowledgments

When people asked me back in 1994 when my second book was coming out, I always said, "Never." Of course, at the time, I forgot about all of the capable and willing individuals who are always there to help. I truly have to thank each and every one of them, for without them, I never would have undertaken the book-writing task (again!). As metadata enters the limelight, so too does my gratitude, both spoken and unspoken to all of the following individuals:

- The clients of Database Design Solutions, Inc., for giving me the experiences that led to the publication of this book. I would like to say a special Thank You to Bill Stolte for coming up with a great title for this book.
- My case study suppliers, most of them clients, for being willing to share these experiences.
- My contributors, for taking a bite off the workload that comes with composing a publication of this size
- Database Design Solutions consultants, some of them contributors, for supplying, reviewing, and commenting on manuscript pieces. Many of these consultants always remind me what professional relationships are all about, and I want to take this time to thank those who took their personal time to contribute to the book's completion:
  - ◆ Patricia Cupoli, for her continued expertise in data management support and organization
  - ◆ David Mellen, for his professional reputation in the database arena, and his ability to transfer that experience into the world of metadata solutions

- ◆ Richard Triano, for his unsurpassed organization and research skills and his ability to support metamodel development over and over again
- ◆ Linh Nguyen, for writing an entire chapter from a two-line outline

- ■ Database Design Solutions staff, most notably Monika Vehse, for compiling and organizing the manuscript and its illustrations during all phases of its creation. I would also like to thank Lisa Koenig for her tips on book marketing and cover design.

Others provided additional insight into certain areas of the book: Charles Betz, Donna Burbank, Bob Newell, Capers Jones, Elton Stokes, Dan Sullivan, and Jim Holmes.

Finally, I extend my deepest thanks to my immediate family—Jim, Chris, and Nicole. Without all of them, this book would never have come to be.

About the Author

Adrienne Tannenbaum is the founder and president of Database Design Solutions, Inc. in Bernardsville, New Jersey. She has worked in all facets of database and application development, concentrating since 1990 on the design, development, and implementation of metadata solutions. Knowing back then that it would be just a matter of time before the world would be crying for metadata and an organized approach to its creation, access, and management, she authored the first book on metadata solutions, *Implementing a Corporate Repository: The Models Meet Reality* (1994). Adrienne, who holds an MBA from Rutgers Graduate School of Management, has spoken at major industry conferences and lectured internationally.

Database Design Solutions (www.dbdsolutions.com) was founded in 1989 as a vendor-neutral consultancy geared toward the revitalization of corporate data. Adrienne recognized that most Fortune 500 organizations had no idea what data they had, what it meant, or how to optimally access and use it. She has dedicated her career and the firm to services and products that correct this deficiency. The firm's specialties include:

- Metadata solutions, including metadata gateways
- Web-based data access and distribution
- E-commerce initiatives with data integration objectives
- Data analysis
- Data management strategies
- Logical and physical database design
- Database tuning and administration
- Data warehousing

Part I
Today's Information

Why has metadata become the buzzword of the new millennium? Simply stated, today's information is not all that it is cracked up to be. As we spend more and more money trying to get to more and more information, we still seem to suffer the same age-old problem—we are never quite sure if the numbers are correct. But because we never seem to be able to validate these numbers, we are often forced to "run with them."

We all have suffered repercussions as a result of incorrect or unavailable data, and we have confused data with information. Only when we feel comfortable with accumulated reams of supportive information can we honestly say that we have the knowledge we need to function effectively in today's business environment. Why is everything always so hard? Surely, technology is here to provide *information on demand*.

It is time to answer these questions. Part I addresses information in ways you may not have considered. It begins by discussing the history of information—how did collecting it start, and where did businesses go wrong? What is information supposed to be used for? Is the role of information one we can all agree upon? Why is there such confusion over whose responsibility it is to create and maintain information?

Any discussion about information cannot be restricted to that which we can control within our own organizations. Clearly, external information is also a player in today's world. With so much information at our fingertips, careers are dedicated to its management and integration.

Part I focuses on the highlights of the efforts of IT professionals during the 1990s. At the end of this part, you will know the state of information in today's businesses. More important, you will also realize how IT got where it is and why a new approach is necessary. . . and yes, that new approach should involve a metadata solution.

Chapter 1

The Business Is Information

It is the best of times, it is the worst of times, it is the age of wisdom, it is the age of foolishness.[1] Most of us think of this as a variation of a quote from Charles Dickens, yet in today's information technology (IT) world, the quote could not be more appropriate. Information is everywhere and we all wish information were good. In fact, we now have so much information that most of us cannot separate what is good from what is irrelevant. Technology, coupled with wisdom and experience, makes yesterday's unreachable information available with the click of a mouse. Once we have what we thought we were looking for, we often spend an inordinate amount of time foolishly trying to "reapproach" the definition, accessibility, and maintenance of the information so that next time we won't have to go through the same motions to get and interpret *the right stuff*.

Information has become a full-time career. We spend so much of our professional lives looking for just the right numbers to support such things as hunches, marketing strategies, business proposals, and downsizing decisions. Because, however, we usually have no clear means of culling the good from the bad, the process is always more than just finding information; it is also validating it and being able to *prove* its validity to our downward information recipients. Is this a specialty that requires technical know-how? Does the responsibility fit within IT? How does information fuel a business's bottom line? When does its

---

1. A variation of a quote from Charles Dickens, *A Tale of Two Cities* (London & New York: G. P. Putnam's Sons, 1849).

correct or incorrect interpretation become recognized as an essential business function?

During IT's evolution, the focus has been on software, or those bundles of program code that *created* information. The interpretation of the information was not a typical concern of programmers. Information was created for use and analysis by business users. If incorrect or inadequate business decisions were based on the information that was supplied on IT-generated reports, IT was involved or held responsible only if the information was incorrect. At that time, the only way IT information was seen as "incorrect" was due to a "programming bug." Back in the 1960s, programming bugs were never associated with anything other than "errors in logic."

Today, dealing with the inadequacy of information seems to begin as an IT responsibility. In fact, the IT part of an organization often forgets *its reason for existence*. More important, this reason for existence consistently seems to miss the mark in terms of information delivery. Often, the vicious cycle of inadequate information becomes a finger-pointing episode with the business customer being told to take some, if not all, of the blame.

In this chapter our sights are set on today's information. As you read, consider how you work (or struggle) with your organization's information, and think about why things just don't seem to be "clicking." Sit back, it's going to be a long and painful ride; but at the end of Part I you will be ready to do something about it.

Information Defined

How confusing can it get? People interchange the terms *data, knowledge,* and *information* all the time. It is really important to consider how and when they connect. Consider the following simple analogy:

> A 10-year-old child walks to the corner deli with a dollar bill. Practically tasting that chocolate bar during the whole walk, he arrives, makes his selection, and puts the dollar on the counter. The delicatessen owner takes the dollar, rings up the transaction on his manual cash register, and the child walks home with his sweet tooth satisfied.
>
> The delicatessen owner knows that transactions like this one form a substantial portion of his walk-in business. He has no idea exactly how much, however, because he has no process in place to identify the data that surrounds each transaction.

Here we have the difference between data and information—and the delicatessen owner's knowledge and experience, no matter how great, could never turn that transaction into a piece of reusable information.

Data that is not captured may become information, but based only on external factors, such as a delicatessen owner's experience. If the data *is* captured, its role as information (or potential information) depends on how it is identified in the context of related data and processes. Collected and processed information often becomes *knowledge*.

Let's take our analogy to corporate America:

A major manufacturing organization is very process driven when it comes to meeting manufacturing quotas of quantity, quality, and time. Plant management exists to verify daily, weekly, and monthly results and compare them to quotas. Manufacturing reports are generated routinely as the primary means of identifying potential problems and plants that perform both adequately and inadequately.

A new product line is being considered. The new product line differs slightly from a current product in that it will contain a different product stamp and have different packaging. To establish manufacturing quotas for this new product line, management needs data on previous plant performance with respect to:

- Time and cost to create a new product stamp
- The amount of time it takes to stamp products
- How much time is spent assembling a similar product's packaging
- The additional time needed to insert this product into the packaging for final inspection

All of this data exists. Where is it? How is it calculated? How do we get to it?

This data has already been captured; however, its identity is not easily ascertained. Nor are its location and accessibility. Without this key *metadata,* the data cannot easily become information. In corporate America, however, an IT professional would be assigned the task of locating the data and analyzing it within the realm of this problem. The result would be a set of numbers, perhaps delivered on a report of sorts—eventual one-time information.

How information is defined in an organization often leads to questions like these:

- How much time and money was spent locating the data?
- How much additional time would have been spent making sure the located data was ready to support additional *information* requests?
- What is the cost of first-time information and how often do we incur the same expense?

A Purist Definition of *Information*

The purist definition of *information* is "something told, knowledge."[2] In business, most information still comes from "something told." And why is that? The answer to the question is obvious: *If what IT creates is not easily available for investigation, study, or second-party instruction, IT does not create information.* To truly create information, its creation must encompass its practical management.

> ❖ **Information**   The set of available data, whether internal or external, numeric, textual, graphic, visual, audio, and so on, that, when combined with any set of manual or mechanized processes and integrated with preexisting information, assists the decision maker.

Such definitions are merely baselines that attempt to point one in the right direction. When considering information as a standalone concept, it is essential to relate the concept to its application in today's decision-making environment.

As Figure 1-1 shows, data must be combined with numerous processes, both manual and mechanized, before it becomes information. Bits of information are then combined with preexisting information, accumulated knowledge, and the ability to conclude. The result is increased knowledge. This iterative process requires *real* information.

---

2. *The Oxford Dictionary and Thesaurus* (New York: Oxford University Press, 1996), p. 765.

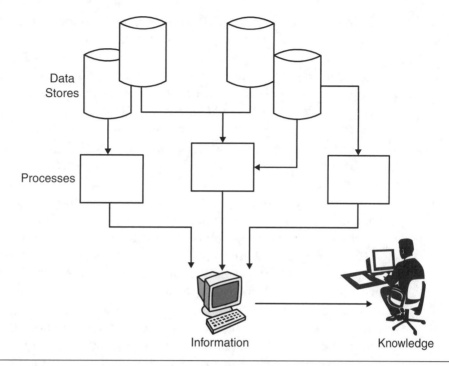

Figure 1-1   **The process of transforming data into information**

Evolution of Information

Consider where information originated, and how it ended up in its current state. Most people in the IT world have always considered information to be the bits and bytes that reside in data stores. In the early days of IT, these "data stores" were often magnetic tapes, or at best, they were sequential files stored on a mainframe computer. The information was never available for analysis, other than on paper reports—each report being the result of a programmatic effort to summarize and present the data that existed. The interesting aspect of original information is its embedded definition within its creating application. During the initial days of data, the terms *information* and *data* were virtually interchangeable—rarely would information created in an application be used for analyses that did not include the same processes. Common examples of data include insurance claims, bank loan payments, and telephone bills.

Early data was transactional. Processes were computerized to apply speed, efficiency, and accuracy to the data-accumulation routine; and data storage became more and more efficient. Hierarchical databases, designed for streamlined information access, gave programmers the opportunity to begin the separation of data and process. It was at this point in the information evolution that nontransactional data could be related, via a predefined path, to the transactions themselves. For example, all transactions that involved a particular customer were much easier to find by using a customer identifier as the means of accessing the full set of transactions. No longer did all records have to be read in order to figure out which ones were relevant. But these customer records were still tracked in the context of their transactional applications, and not intended to be shared across applications.

When multiple processes craved the same data, separate storage of common data—for potential use by several applications—began; hence the beginnings of the "customer master," "product master," and so on. This led to *data administration,* which focused primarily on managing and standardizing the names and values of corporate and common data elements, as opposed to the usage of the resulting information or the actual *values* of the common data.

With the advent of relational database management in the 1970s, data started to become more closely associated with the resulting information. For the first time, the data processing (DP) organization became known as information systems (IS). Data was now "modeled" based on its business relationships rather than its processing requirements. The same data could evolve into different types of information, depending on the context in which it was accessed and subsequently processed. Standard query languages such as Structured Query Language (SQL) allowed different applications to access the same databases. The separation of data and information began in that data was organized and related based on its *potential* role as information. Relational models considered every relationship that could be identified between data entities—people, places, things, or events about which data is stored.

The new applications of the 1970s and 1980s used relational databases as their underpinnings. As the database management system (DBMS) software became more and more efficient, transactional applications also moved to relational backbones. Transactions could now be organized and related for follow-up analysis, thereby forming the data that could eventually become information.

Figure 1-2 illustrates a simple relational model with elements of a database in logical arrangement according to the ways they interact, not according to the space they require. Unfortunately, data management went astray with the advent of the relational model. In the first place, the relational model was sel-

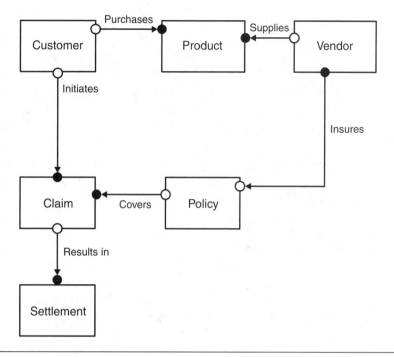

Figure 1-2   **A relational model**

dom implemented faithfully, which sacrificed data access flexibility. Second, it eventually became much easier to design and access databases and business users began to create their own "private databases," in many cases using data that was extracted from main corporate databases. The advent of the personal computer (PC) then made it amazingly simple for the slightly savvy business user to set up a standalone database and fill it with a series of extracts from several production applications. The information systems (IS) organization was renamed information technology (IT) and it began to focus on the overall technological infrastructure, as opposed to the systems themselves.

As PCs became more and more of a desktop commodity, client/server applications became the rule rather than the exception. IT focused its design efforts on architectures that included the desktop PC. Not only did application processing move there, but in many cases, so too did the data. With the advent of client/server architectures, IT followed the philosophy of keeping the data where it is needed; data management was no longer a consideration, nor a requirement. Processing and hardware were becoming inexpensive, so IT personnel temporarily forgot what data management was all about. Silos and silos of information were created on virtually every departmental server and every user desktop, each silo put there to serve a particular purpose.

The early 1990s found IT suffering from its own ignorance. Again, IT people seemed to forget how data eventually becomes information, and that *IT's business is information*. Many user organizations began to take the information goal into their own hands. Data stewards were assigned within business user areas as an attempt to standardize *data* before it became information. Data webs were everywhere, and in many organizations IT controlled the main, common data, but had no real indication as to how many places it had been extracted. Worse than that, they were often unaware that the IT versions were becoming inaccurate based on the user updates occurring outside the IT domain.

The Role of Information

Remember that data and processes come together to form information. What information is used for—that is, its role—depends greatly on how well organizations adhere to some basic information rules. The rules are listed, and then discussed.

Rules about Information

The rules about information that follow form the essence of successful information management. Each rule evolved from the history that resulted in today's information abundance and suboptimal relevance. Having gone down "memory lane," it is essential to consider how data history has affected the need for these rules.

1. Information can take on virtually any format, as long as it is identifiable, storable, and retrievable by its identifiers.

2. The creation of information should not be restricted to its role within the framework of its creating process(es).

3. Not all data is intended initially to be information, but it could very easily become information as the business climate changes.

4. The process of deriving information from other information should be discouraged; that is, information should always be derived from data.

5. Information is everywhere, but its usability is related directly to its relationship to basic data.

6. When information is needed, the average information consumer will go to extreme lengths to find it, get it, and apply it.

7. Unless the information consumer is aware of the existence of information, it is unlikely that even the best information will be used optimally.

Rule 1: *Information can take on virtually any format, as long as it is identifiable, storable, and retrievable by its identifiers.* This rule is perhaps the simplest, and often the most ignored. Information without metadata is useful only to those who understand its creation history. But more important, the metadata should serve a purpose other than clarification and definition—it should *get you to the information*. Simply stated, if the best information exists with excellent business rules and documented sources, it does no one (person, application, tool, or database) any good if it is not easily identifiable and accessible via its simple metadata. *Just as there is no room for useless data, there is no room for useless metadata.*

Rule 2: *The creation of information should not be restricted to its role within the framework of its creating process(es).* For example, if information is being put together to support the creation of an annual report, it is essential to "think outside the box" so that the information can be reaccessed and reused. Reconsider the corner delicatessen example.

Converting the chocolate bar transaction data into information requires a series of steps, including analysis of the requirements surrounding the planned creation, maintenance, and interpretation of this data. But limiting the scope to that of the corner deli could prevent this delicatessen from interfacing with suppliers, establishing multiple stores, and perhaps expanding the inventory to include items other than packaged food. True information would be flexible enough to support future processes, as Figure 1-3 begins to represent.

Rule 3: *Not all data is intended initially to be information, but it could very easily become information as the business climate changes.* As with the corner delicatessen, one never knows what type of processes will evolve. For example, a transaction like the sale of a chocolate bar might be combined with existing invoicing processes to help determine its profitability in comparison to other products the corner deli sells.

Rule 4: *The process of deriving information from other information should be discouraged; that is, information should always be derived from data.* This rule is an important point, and one that IT has not quite embodied.

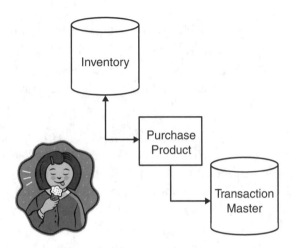

Figure 1-3 **The corner deli from an information perspective**

When information exists, it is the intersection of data and process. Taking that information and revising it to support a totally different process forms the beginnings of information webs. Soon, the source of the various information renditions will not be identifiable, and all existing information will begin losing the same characteristics that made it information in the first place.

For example, consider massive data marts,[3] which are built of information extracted from operational production application databases. The result is used to support a particular informational need. Another informational need arises, and the same information is extracted, perhaps from the resulting data mart, but in a different way, for a different purpose. Over time, massive information webs result. Many organizations have decided to implement raw "staging areas" as a means of keeping "data," as opposed to information, available for extraction. Figure 1-4 illustrates the semblance of sanity that data versus information extracts bring to datamart creation.

Rule 5: *Information is everywhere, but its usability is related directly to its identifiable relationship to basic data.* What good is a set of delicatessen transactions, each a unique conglomeration of data being combined with the delicatessen owner's knowledge to form information, if all the resulting information cannot be tied together? This is where the basic data comes in. If the delicatessen owner knows something about each customer as he or she makes the purchase, this basic data needs to be standardized, available, and shared.

---

3. Data marts and data warehousing are discussed in Chapter 4.

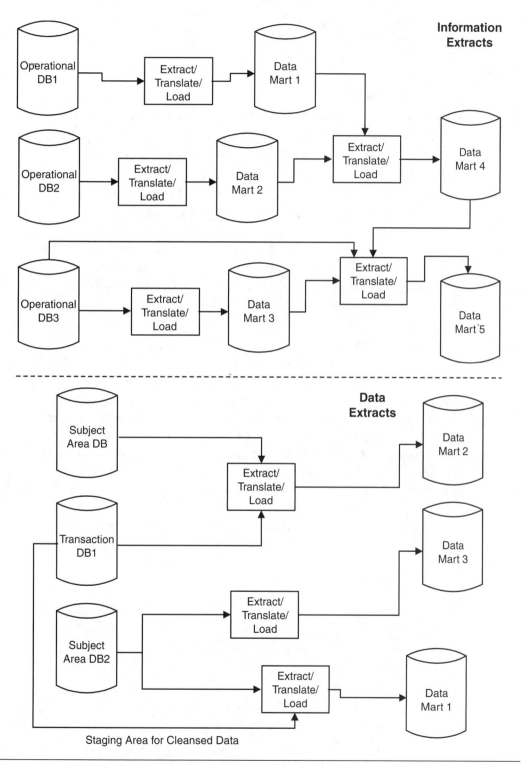

Figure 1-4 Information versus data extracts

Rule 6: *When information is needed, the average information consumer will go to extreme lengths to find it, get it, and apply it.* Today's information dilemma is proof of this basic rule. Surfing the Web is a modernized version of the rule's relevance. A successful information management environment eliminates the need for massive effort.

Rule 7: *Unless the information consumer is aware of the existence of information, it is unlikely that even the best information will be used optimally.* This rule is the most obvious but the most minimized in terms of its impact on the way in which we define information. The best of products and services are virtually useless unless the world knows about them. Fortunately, information awareness is not the result of market penetration or expensive marketing campaigns—it is the result of an easily accessible directory that points the information consumer in the right direction.

Information Tunnels

Many organizations struggle with the results of poorly created information environments. As they reengineer processes, they reengineer information. The impact of this reengineering ranges from well-received information subsets (tunnels) to data or information marts (organized sets of separate tunnels) to major data warehouses. An information tunnel gets you where you want to go, as long as you know where to start. If you don't know where to start, or if you are at the entrance to one tunnel but want to go elsewhere (want to use the information for another purpose), you'll be out of luck.

The information is only as usable as the consumer's awareness of its availability. Let's look at the realities of information in today's organizations.

Chapter 2

The Information in Today's Organization

Now that we have reviewed the history and evolution of information, we will assess its current situation. In this chapter, we focus specifically on the information over which today's organization has control. Usually we can control information that we create. Controlling and managing are two different processes, however. Ideally, we should control our information gracefully, and always for the benefit of those who need it most.

Information is often "managed" without regard to "today"—today being not a date, but a condition. It represents the state of information not only in terms of its actual availability, accuracy, and accessibility, but also in terms of its perceived characteristics. Because "today" is the result of "yesterday," many information management professionals are often quite focused on establishing a framework that will bypass today and get us to the "future." Let's look at how information is treated in today's organizations.

Information in Practice

The biggest disease affecting information practice today is tunnel vision. Many of us readily admit to tunnel vision in the past, but we hesitate to realize that we blindly follow the same philosophy and practices at the beginning of the third millennium. Despite reengineered business processes, streamlined application development, Web-based electronic commerce, and business-to-business partnerships, we don't seem to see the commonality of the information that spans these efforts. Worse, we never consider that locating and identifying information is very often more important than interpreting it. Obviously, if we can't find and identify information, we can't use it.

We are organized and often reimbursed based on the "tunnel" with which we are associated (e.g., accounting, product development, customer). It is only natural, therefore, that supporting information is in line with that perspective. As Figure 2-1 illustrates quite simply, information tunnels are typically based on processing requirements. Even though the same data may be required in more than one tunnel, it is usually not easy to go from one tunnel to another. In any case, data is typically converted to tunnel-resident information, reflective of a limited set of requirements.

Organizations vary in their awareness of today's information situation. For the most part, upper management and executives rarely have to deal with the issues of information redundancy and integration. In fact, many large organizations have "information dissemination" functions created solely to respond to information requests from executives. People spend "as long as it takes," work-

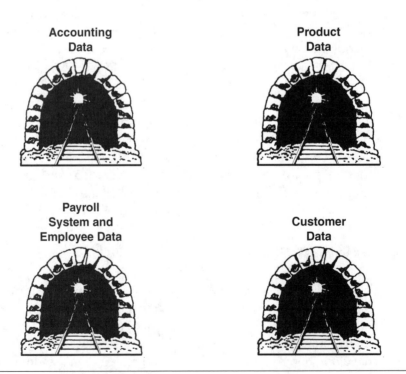

Figure 2-1   Information tunnels

ing nonstop if a deadline hangs over them to combine, interpret, sort, extract, and present the information known to address "enterprise" questions such as, Who are our five largest customers? In any organization with multiple billing systems, answering this question (if it is answerable!), for example, could be a major task involving the combination and comparison of sales facts that might contain conflicting and/or redundant customer identification. To prevent the constant repetition of the work required to massage this information, many data warehouses[1] and data marts have been built to satisfy the need for information to support executive decisions.

The simple question about customer size, which came from a consulting client more than 10 years ago, could not be answered without a major overhaul of the client's data. The company, a chemical compound manufacturer, sold chemicals at various stages of production and mixed them with compounds that were often processed to create finished goods. As a result, many customers were also resellers, distributors, and manufacturing partners, depending of course on what was purchased, and its chemical state at the time of purchase, as represented on the invoice. It was virtually impossible to identify the company's five largest customers without a down-to-earth data modeling session and a redesign of the company's various databases.

Many companies have survived or are currently living through a similar crisis. The dilemma, of which many organizations are unaware, is that they are often nowhere near as sure as they should be of the exact location, span, and penetration of the information they are seeking.

Figure 2-2 depicts a typical manufacturing scenario. Customers are identified inconsistently across applications, and some customers are also manufacturing partners. Given the information as it stands, how would we surmise who the customers are?

The 5 Questions

Based on the condition of most corporate information environments, I remain amazed that many organizations spend millions of dollars to reengineer data and process structures without considering the need for an organized information picture. Data warehouses, ERP systems, CRM initiatives, and e-commerce applications, to name a few, are the results of redesigning systems to make information analysis easier. I and my fellow consultants have yet to meet an

---

1. Data warehousing is discussed in Chapter 4.

Reseller Tracking System		Invoice Tracking System	
Products	*Customers*	*Invoice No.*	*Customer*
AL413	General Aluminum	13678	GA-MS
MGN	Building Products, Inc.	13679	GA-Corp
MGFP	Building Products, Inc.	13680	Smith 06
	Universal Building Products	13681	Smith 07
	Telekinetics, Inc.	13682	HousELM
	Housing Elements	13683	HouseElm 02
	Smith Factory Products		
	Wallace Insulation		

Distribution Tracking		Manufacturing Partners	
Product	*Distributor*	*Partner*	*Product*
FG123	Smith FP	SmithFP	FG061
FG017	BP-WASH	SmithFP	FG707
CP076	GA-MS	GeneralAL	FG001
CP077	Smith FP	Insulation, Inc.	FG701
MGFP	GA-DC	Sheetrock Dist.	FG017
		Brown Bricks	CH078

Figure 2-2   **A conflicting and redundant customer/product information scenario**

organization, with or without these improvements, that can answer our trademarked 5 Questions:[2]

1. What data do we have?

2. What does it mean?

3. Where is it?

4. How did it get there?

5. How do I get it (go get it for me!)?

At best, organizations can answer these questions within a limited scope. For example, in the world of desktop computers, we can instantly get a list of the files on one or more hard drives (What data do we have?). We also, by clicking on the filenames, can instantly open them (How do I get it?). Of course, the information we desire must exist in a file, and must be part of the immediate

---

2. The 5 Questions is a trademark of and the questions and method are copyrighted by Database Design Solutions, Inc., Bernardsville, New Jersey.

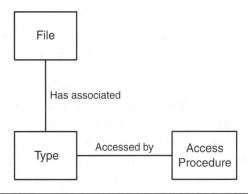

Figure 2-3 **A file system model**

file environment. But the way to get to the file is so inherently simple that the rules for obtaining and guaranteeing this simplicity are even simpler. Note the model in Figure 2-3. To accomplish this simplicity, all files must be named and associated with a file type, and that file type has one and only one access procedure. Why isn't it this easy with all of our data? To answer this question, we will refer to this example throughout the book.

In today's information environments, the answers to these five questions, when and if they can be answered, reflect tunnel vision (e.g., one data warehouse, one decision support tool display, one program library). More and more tunnels lead haphazardly to partial answers to one or more of these questions.

Today's Answers

How the 5 Questions are answered in today's world of corporate information varies to some degree based on the emphasis an organization places on the information. For example, organizations that place substantial priority on research and its resulting product development, inventions, and/or industry breakthroughs always make research data, its conclusions, and the required documentation well organized and available. Generally, these organizations have research libraries that are managed and controlled by librarians well versed in the cataloging and retrieval of research data. Even when the research data is in a variety of formats (e.g., text documents, statistical studies, and application databases), the librarians generally know where everything is, and have search mechanisms including at least a company intranet.

Answers to the 5 Questions get a bit more complicated once a research effort results in product development. The types of data that we track and the reasons that we track them vary immensely. Using the pharmaceutical industry as an example, no longer are the scientific experiments the sole domain of the scientists, but the results now move into clinical trials and may become part of a drug's marketing package. Federal law requires specific information (e.g., type of research, profiles of participants, length of trials, and specific results) to support the drug approval process and to be available for inclusion in packaging of approved drugs. Consider the twist of purpose for the research data once the resulting drug (pharmaceutical product) is manufactured and marketed. Consider also how the original research data looks when it becomes part of the marketing information collection. Finally, consider how easy or hard it would be to include this information as part of the answer to Question 1— What data do we have? Most pharmaceutical organizations recreate the data, or minimally copy it over with each phase of the drug development process— new purpose, new software, new database, . . . new metadata?

What about organizations that do not have a research arm? Consider retailers without manufacturing, whose products are acquired from wholesalers or are only packaged within the retail organization. The eventual product line may not represent the items purchased from the supplier (wholesaler, distributor, manufacturer). The typical order-entry system contains the full array of products, with variations (colors, sizes, shapes, etc.) and pricing options (single unit, altered unit, customized unit, bulk orders, etc.). If an item is for sale, the data surrounding the sale is available . . . or is it? In the domain of the order-entry system, the data a user or customer wants is available. Again, remember that information and data can be distinct and variable. If the results of this order-entry system were going to be captured for the purposes of decision support, however, some of the required information (e.g., answers to the remaining four questions) would not be obvious. Furthermore, depending on the purpose of the information gathering, some *information* requirements may constitute information above and beyond the data itself (consider the fourth question, How did it get there?). What if I am a developer looking for the specifics on how to translate order-entry data to meet the needs or demands of the customer, whether an individual or a commercial customer?

Generally, answers to the 5 Questions share similar qualities. They are narrowly focused and address the perspective of the individual or group that supplied the answers. Even within data management organizations, the answers to these questions reflect a narrowed scope based usually on the inability to physically address specific islands of data (depending on, for example, their physical platforms or surrounding software packages). Ironically, even data management organizations that implemented metadata repositories, data dictionaries, or information directories[3] restricted the boundaries of coverage in most cases. These efforts, originated in the IT department, are usually not geared toward business users' requirements, access, or relevance.

Tunnel vision is also obvious when we address the answers to each question from the viewpoint of today's information implementations.

What Data Do We Have?

A true answer to this question would result in a card catalog of an organization's data organized by major subject area. In today's common implementations, business users are forced to go right to the data they seek via shortcuts on their screens. But if there is a need to go beyond that immediate scope (and there always is), generally phone calls are the only way to find out exactly what other data is available.

What Does It Mean?

If an organization is progressive and methodical, a "data dictionary" is created by documenting each data element at the time it is defined, which typically happens during a data modeling phase,[4] but this represents an ideal situation. Many organizations purchase data processing or information management software and have no data planning or data management function associated with its installation. Likewise, the definition of the data elements within the package is left to off-the-shelf vendor values. The majority of organizations, however, do not have data dictionaries. In these scenarios, the details behind the data elements are typically tracked individually (e.g., by the business users or by the developers). Many databases start springing up, each containing a miniworld of metadata, ranging from data element names and definitions to data tracking documentation, many of which include substantial information about the source of the data. In reality, many organizations do not have official databases that track these things; as a result, many "databases" are implemented, each of which represents a particular perspective of the data's meaning, and none of them maintained from a global or central framework.

Where Is It?

The answers to this question depend directly on what "it" is that we are looking for, and who we are. The answers also depend on what organizations are

---

3. Specific details surrounding metadata repository case studies are supplied in Chapter 5.

4. Data models are discussed in Chapter 4.

aware of in terms of data and how easy it is to find it. Since client/server computing took the reigns off controlled data definition and storage, it is virtually impossible to locate all of it. For example, if "policy" data is not associated with a "policy" term, the only way to find all policy data is to look for it after all data has been categorized manually. Of course, computer search engines will find instances of the word *policy* in all kinds of data stores, *but they have to be there*. In today's corporate world, the answers to the question can vary depending on the type, location, and name of the data.

Type of data   Ironically, it is fairly easy to find nonoperational data such as documents, application programs, and presentation graphics, *assuming the names are reasonable and/or the contents contain the main qualifier*. Operational data, which is generated by transactions and the supporting processing, is typically located based on its identity. Unfortunately, the names of these data elements can range from accurate logical business names to short, programmer/DBA-developed identifiers to software package vendor identifiers. Based on this common problem, many "scanners" now exist that search physical data stores based on contents.

Location of data   Where data is determines how easy it is to find. If it exists in a structured database that has its own metadata-based directory and that is accessible via a shortcut on everyone's desktop, then sure enough it will be found. If it is sitting in a privately developed desktop database that resulted from one business user's design and requirements, it may never show up in anyone's search. If it is on another server that can be remotely accessed and it has a common term as part of its name, it may turn up in an access query. Finally, if it is a specific type of file with its own access procedure, as populated in a standard model (see Figure 2-3), it will be located. Only you know how likely these situations are in your organization, but *unfortunately, not everyone who looks for data understands that even though data exists, it may never be found*.

Data association/data naming   Of course, if the data you are looking for concerns customer addresses and it is named "Party Location," how likely is it that you will find it? Without predicting odds, organizations geared toward data location and fulfillment usually offer sets of standard names and aliases as well as standard subject-area categories to help identify data that may not have obvious names. Again, if the rules exist but they are not followed, or people are not even aware of them, the effort results in more harm than good. One of the worst things that can happen is the return of a subset of information when the receiver is not aware that he or she is seeing a subset.

How Did It Get There?

The answer to this question can be extremely simple or very broad. What one will never know, however, is whether a simple answer should really be broader. The advent of data warehousing began to put much emphasis on the "source" of data, yet in most major corporations "data webs" have existed for quite some time, in many cases unbeknown to the data analyst or documenter. The answer to this question is often restricted to the amount of information capable of fitting into a predetermined and presized Source field. If a particular data element has more than one source, it is up to the documentation specialist to determine how to report all of them or, in most cases, to choose the most recent source of that data element. In neither scenario does the information do any good for the data recipient because the true beginnings of the data are never documented. As a result, the business analyst will never know, for example, that "Gross Income" started from the Accounting System, and was then massaged three times through three different accounting spreadsheets before it reached the report being documented

How Do I Get It (Go Get It for Me)?

Because information gathered in response to this question is often either supplied by a technical person or is a "freebie" (i.e., software provides the capability), this is probably the only question that appears to be answered accurately on all accounts. As mentioned earlier, operating systems are typically based on an underlying model that provides point-and-click access to anything that has been defined consistently and in conformance with certain rules (see Figure 2-3). Ironically, however, the more accurate this answer is, the less likely it is to be of service. This is the reason the question is answered to begin with. Historically, if someone looked for and actually *found* data, the way it was found was important. In today's world, however, someone can receive data without any idea how it was accessed. In fact, the route to the data is often "hidden" or "included" as part of the software being used to locate the data. Only when we cannot find the data or, more often, have no choice as to what data to use or what software to assist with the location process, do we *always* make a point of learning how to access it. More and more organizations and vendors are focusing on documenting the path to and method of obtaining data. Nevertheless, in most scenarios, the resulting documentation represents an isolated subset of the 5 Questions, or all of the 5 Questions for an isolated group of data (see Figure 2-4).

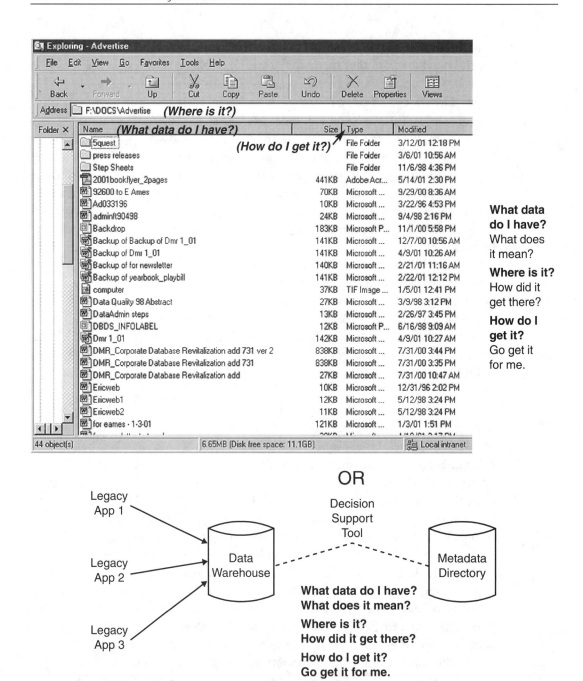

Figure 2-4   Viewing the 5 Questions™ in isolation

Information Sharing and Redundancy

Remember from Chapter 1 that *information is merely a frame of mind;* it is often impossible to assess what we are actually sharing and whether it is a redundant representation of pieces that exist elsewhere. Also because frames of mind are temporary, what is information today may not be information tomorrow or what is information to me is not necessarily information to you. As esoteric as these statements may appear, their translations into IT reality result in the actual way information is shared today. For example, consider the objective of standardizing customer information. In a well-planned scenario, the information to be shared would not only be the values themselves (e.g., the names and addresses of the customers), but also the qualities (characteristics) of these values; the rules surrounding the creation, maintenance, and deletion of values; and the means of accessing these values, as discussed (remember the 5 Questions). Depending on the implemented database architectures as well as the processing platforms that require access, controlled replication is often necessary.

Unfortunately, despite the fact that people who "standardize" have the best intentions, the implementations often lose sight of these intentions. To establish true standardized sharing requires planning, analysis, and forethought. The consideration that is often neglected or minimized during standardization plans is the focus on today and why today is the way it is. How often do we hear, "Never mind today, and let's plan for tomorrow so that today does not repeat itself"? *Ignoring the current state of information and why it exists almost always guarantees the repetition of this state even with the best-laid plans.*

Let's return to our original objective, that of standardizing the customer information, this time using a major bank for illustration. Most of us immediately think of taking existing customer tables, masters, and databases and using them as the source for one clean, standard, *corporate* version. In fact, most data management projects start with tasks such as this. Figure 2-5 is a simplified example of the beginnings of the customer standardization effort in a major financial institution.

At first glance, it is clear that one person (Patrick Anderson) is listed in all three of the major applications, as a customer according to each type. Original standardization efforts focused primarily on the data—its qualities as well as its official values (hence the term *customer of record*). The objectives may not have been the elimination of redundancy (depending of course on the size and number of occurrences of related customer instances), but instead, in preparation for the future, the standardization of "what it will take" (from now on) to

Residential Mortgage System

Account Number	× (8)	AN4632
Loan Number	× (20)	RZ163-AND
Primary Borrower	× (20)	ANDERSON, PATRICK
Secondary Borrower	× (20)	SMITH, JOANNE

.
.
.

Source A

Savings Account Statement Generation

Account Number	× (10)	1010367217
Primary Account Holder	× (30)	ANDERSON, PATRICK
Joint Account Holder	× (30)	ANDERSON, PATRICK JR.
Street	× (30)	43 MORRISTOWN BLVD. EAST
City	× (20)	MORRISTOWN
State	× (2)	NJ
Zip	× (9)	079601076

Source B

Commercial Checking Accounts

Account Number	× (10)	39046218
Commercial Account Holder	× (30)	ANDERSON, PATRICK
Commercial DBA	× (50)	CORNER SUB SHOP
Commercial Address Line 1	× (30)	14 E. SECOND AVENUE
Commercial Address Line 2	× (30)	BLDG 22
City	× (20)	FLORHAM PARK
State	× (2)	NJ
Zip	× (9)	07932

Figure 2-5   **A simple system for managing customer identification**

define a bank customer (regardless of the service or product the bank provides to him or her).

Consider the fact that the bank sees the commonality among the various application-focused customer renditions to be the customer's relationship to the product, specifically the *primary point of contact*. Approaching the future from a common point of view would therefore result in the need for a "contact" standard, rather than a "customer" standard, for example. Because the same individual can serve as the *primary* contact in various scenarios, the relationships in which the individual participates would dictate the type of information to be tracked. A simple data model appears in Figure 2-6.

Most standardization efforts began by reorganizing data and defining commonality based on various relationships and perspectives. Once that was done,

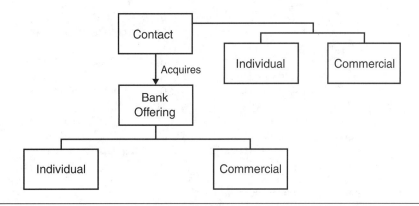

Figure 2-6 A simple bank contact data model

in our simple example the objective would have been the identification of future customers in conformance with the new model. The difficulties arise when we consider the fact that existing applications deal with the old way of viewing things while data analysts need to bridge the old to the new in order to get a full base for customer-related queries. Enter *information redundancy and conflict*.

Revisit Figure 2-5 to see the way things are, and consider the common scenarios for getting where we want to go (a common set of contact information). In most logical scenarios, the data model becomes a blueprint for future systems. As such, new applications would define contacts instead of customers and relate them to the application-specific products or services as needed. Accessing new contacts and old customers would require new and old access routines, and comparing the new to the old would not be an easy task. In fact, in Figure 2-7, we see that all that really has been accomplished is the addition of yet another source of information about possibly redundant contacts/customers, this time identified by a *contact number*.

To support *information sharing,* the access to both existing and reconfigured information has to be a part of the plan. In the best situations, not only is the data itself standardized, but so too is its access. To facilitate this simple philosophy, a model such as the one in Figure 2-8 must be followed.

With a model that includes the answer to Question 5 (How do I get it?), information sharing becomes feasible. Consider that for this model to have a positive impact all data beneficiaries will need access to the common procedures. The answers to the 5 Questions will come from this model's implementation. Many may consider this approach "object oriented," yet it is totally practical within a relational framework, as modeled.

Contact Number	× (20)	14639
Contact Name	× (30)	ANDERSON, PATRICK
Contact Type	× (1)	I
Contact Address Line 1	× (30)	43 MORRISTOWN BLVD. EAST
Contact Address Line 2	× (30)	
Contact Address City	× (20)	MORRISTOWN
Contact Address State	× (2)	NJ
Contact Address Zip		079601076

Figure 2-7   **The contact perspective**

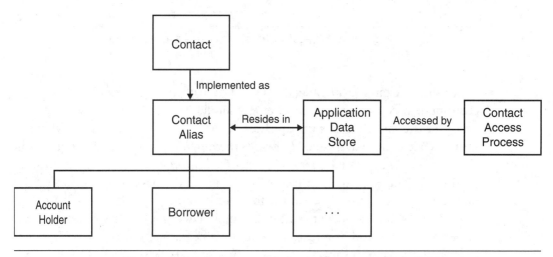

Figure 2-8   **A common information access model**

Supporting Intraorganization Information

When we discuss the practical model that will allow information sharing, we are still discussing things from the viewpoint of software. As long as our software, whether purchased or custom developed, is equipped to follow the blueprint that requires adherence to a structure such as the one in Figure 2-8, information redundancy and conflict can be dealt with from the point of view of identification and access. But software obviously does not accomplish the whole job; identification and access assume that information exists. How should we support this objective when we create information? How should our information usage procedures be modified? Where do the boundaries on information get drawn, if at all? Is information that is used in an IT organization different from and subject to the same rules as information that is used outside the IT organization? How does all of this meet the needs of the business?

Information redundancy is a never-ending situation unless the creation of information is directly connected to that which already exists. How do we determine the need to create information? Is it based on the fact that I tried to find it and could not . . . or is it based on the fact that the accuracy of my information access showed me that the information truly is not available? People in data management strive for the latter, but in many organizations "new" information is created hourly often by those who use identical existing information. To avoid such redundancy, a firm and practical set of information-based practices has to support the information-sharing framework that we model and implement.

Inside Information Technology

It is ironic when developers are guilty of breaking their own rules and it is usually rationalized via the old saying, "Rules are meant to be broken." If an information-sharing framework becomes only a picture on somebody's wall, the entire process should be revisited. Successful information sharing means it is easier to use that which exists than to create another rendition of it. Basic rules surround the successful support of an IT information environment:

1. The supported information should be desired.
2. It should be easier to use the supported information than it is to create new information.
3. Accessing the existing information via existing data access routines should make the developer's job easier, not harder.

These rules seem like common sense, but lack of common sense causes many data management organizations to be ridiculed.[5] Generally, the creation of data, or any new framework element, should require adherence to and population of one model-based framework. Remember the 5 Questions, and consider the type of information required by IT personnel to be able to answer them:

- The desired data
- The identifiers associated with the desired data

---

5. Data management is discussed in Chapter 4.

- The definitions, business meaning, and rules surrounding the desired data
- The location of the desired data
- The rules surrounding the creation and/or duplication of the desired data
- Access procedures required to obtain the desired data (yes this is software!)

To some degree, the ability to support these rules results in an immediate ability to answer the 5 Questions. Consider these questions, and their answers, the beginning of a *metadata framework*. And consider a metadata framework the prerequisite to *information on demand.*

Outside Information Technology

Information sharing and controlled information redundancy is more important outside than inside IT. In fact, despite the fact that the frameworks, models, and associated enforcement software are developed and maintained within IT, the world outside IT is the ultimate beneficiary. IT developers make the information *desired* by the world outside IT. Likewise, the identifiers are established to make the world outside IT *aware* of the existence of the desired data. Definitions are created in the terms of the business user, again for the use of the ultimate beneficiary. Creating new data should happen only within a well-developed framework, of course, since all data created by the business user reflects business production via the input into operational systems. And getting to this data should be the easiest part of the whole information experience.

Chapter 3

Information Outside the Organization

Information is no longer generated solely within the realm of those responsible for its access. Many organizations use outside data to validate, supplement, or substantiate internal information. Before the widespread use of the Internet, data suppliers were in business for just that purpose. The data suppliers usually offered a choice of formats, and customers purchased data extracts according to their requirements. A supplier's ability to provide customer-specific data formats was often a market standout, for which customers were willing to pay a slight premium. Today, however, much outside information is free.

That Famous Download

"I'll check the Web." It is so much easier to check the Web for information than to check the company's data sources that this statement has become a staple of corporate English. The type of information downloaded from the Web ranges from publication names (in support of a particular searchable topic) to Web site names (companies or organizations that provide products or services that support a search topic) to bits and pieces of the information itself (the document topics and the associated documents, application software upgrades, clip art and other graphics, pirated videos, pirated music, etc.).

What happens to this information? With today's Web browsers, the majority of it stays in the domain of the browser tool. Each tool, designed with a

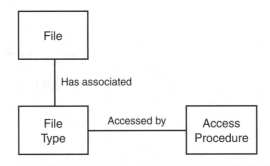

Figure 3-1   A file system metamodel

great appreciation of the 5 Questions,[1] makes it easy for the returning user to get metadata-driven definition and access to all previous Web-based information sets. As each new Web-based query is attempted, the metadata framework is invisibly populated in the same manner.

Once the results of a download are saved or moved off the browser, the rules of the metadata framework usually are no longer applicable. At this point, all the problems and perspectives discussed in Chapters 1 and 2 apply. Furthermore, the type of information probably complicates the scenario, especially if it relates (or should be related) to existing corporate information. Revisit our simple initial metamodel in Figure 3-1.

Many Internet-originating files have Internet-specific file types (.htm, .com, .xml, etc.), and in and of themselves, they generally cause Web-specific software to open and display the files. However, subtle differences depend on whether the accessing client is connected to the Web and the type of software used to open these files. For example, regardless of whether the client is connected at the moment of request, a browser will open a downloaded file and display the results in much the same way as it would a live browse of local files (of course if the client is not connected, the assumption is that this requested item was previously downloaded and can now be opened locally). If, on the other hand, the file has not been downloaded, it is essential that the browser be connected in order to display or execute its contents. What if the accessing software is not a Web browser? Here different results depend on the original purpose of the accessing software and the ease with which modifications could have been made to support a new file type (see Figure 3-1) and its associated access procedure.

---

1. The 5 Questions is a trademark of and the questions and method are copyrighted by Database Design Solutions, Inc., Bernardsville, New Jersey.

Web development tools are designed to access Web-specific file types, regardless of whether the access is live or based on a downloaded file. Other tools originally developed to create and/or access non-Internet files (e.g., word processors) have been slowly accommodating these file types by allowing the conversion of non-Internet files to publishable Web formats (e.g., html format). The ability to display these Web formats and the visual qualities inherent in these displays seems to have been a progressive set of attributes over time. For example, in the early versions, viewing a file in a format conducive to Web-browsing and access meant seeing command-level language. As the Web became more popular, Web publishing became easier, and traditional word-processing tools became able to display graphically pleasing Web-formatted files.

We can make those downloaded files fit into our basic file system metamodel by associating specific access procedures with Web-based file types. But now, we begin to see what happens when technologies arrive before standards. Many software tools address the access of these files in a different way, some able to create or change them, others merely able to display them. The decision as to which software product and/or executable to associate with a particular Internet file type is left to the person responsible for populating this metamodel, in most cases the workstation user. So far, so good.

Our file system metamodel (Figure 3-1) very simply addresses the accessing of file-based information. But this access is restricted to file-name–based access, and requires the file's name and type to get to the file's contents. If file names are neither indicative of their contents nor identifiable, this metamodel's weaknesses start to unfold. Consider the recently identified need to access files that are part of another realm, in this case, the Internet. Problems could ensue. The model could now require additional location-specific information. Information beyond a file's name and type will be needed to get us there. The sample model now must expand to include network and protocol specifics, as Figure 3-2 shows.

The Data Vendors

When searching or buying data, to some extent we are deciding which files to select, their inherent file types being part of the package deal. In most situations, we can access the files we find, either because they represent a generic format or because they come with accessing software. The rules may be slightly different when we are shopping for vendors rather than specific data.

Consider one of the most common subjects for which we have data suppliers—*customer data*. Before the advent of the Internet and the free download,

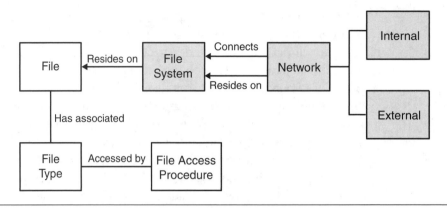

Figure 3-2   An expanded file system metamodel

many organizations functioned as the primary suppliers of customer and/or prospect data, sliced in any fashion and created based on custom requests. For example, a call to a major vendor in this area would typically result in the following requirements from the requestor:

- All customers with net incomes above 5 million dollars AND
- All customers headquartered in the tristate area (New York, New Jersey, Pennsylvania) AND
- All customers with at least 1,000 employees AND
- All customers with their own manufacturing facility AND
- Full customer identification information including:
  - Company name
  - Company headquarters address
  - Primary company contact info (address, phone, e-mail, fax)
  - Primary product line
  - Year of incorporation

With the ability to meet all of these specifications, choosing the format and order of the records in the customer extract was not always an option when data vendors monopolized the availability of external data. Generally, the vendor indicated what the file would look like, and the data buyer prepared to load it to an internal database. In addition, in many scenarios customers were forced to use the vendor's primary identifiers (which were usually internally generated numbers) in case, for example, they wanted to receive updates on a regular basis. There were not many complaints at the time, since most of us were used to thinking from the viewpoint of one application, one database, one purpose. In fact, some purchasing companies were actually grateful for the data vendors' rules and regulations because they provided (perhaps the only) standard format to their corporate data as a whole!

A Data Vendor's Story

A specific situation always stands out when the issue of data vendors comes up. A very large organization, with billions of dollars in revenue, close to one million employees, thousands of field sites, and who knows how much data, had started to "cross analyze." In other words, for perhaps the first time, there was a need to compare data that originated from and was stored in different applications. As was to be expected, one of the most frustrating issues with performing this type of analysis was the inability to link or combine information about the same (or what appeared to be the same) customer, since the same customer was not always identified or even named consistently across applications. Another complication was presented when a group of individuals in the Marketing Department decided to purchase external data as a means of test-marketing upcoming products.

Efforts to deal with the complications included the establishment of an IT-based Data Management function[2] and Business Area Data Stewards, who all attempted to standardize customer information, but were not successful. In contrast, the individual responsible for direct interface with the data vendor (based on requests from Marketing) was constantly talking about how efficiently the data vendor identified the customers (in many cases this being the reason that the vendor was used to begin with). Of course, the vendor's business was based on this; the receiving organization could not even come close to consistent customer identification. Discussions continued, constantly comparing internal data management processes (or lack thereof) with those that were perceived to exist in the IT organization of the data vendor. Users in the Marketing Department were unable to combine purchased data information with internal customer data, and the supporting IT personnel eventually admitted their inability to help.

In an attempt to solve several problems, of both the Marketing and the internal Data Management groups, a joint decision was made to use the data vendor as a means of consolidating their own internal customer data. As amazing as this may seem, the Data Management group now not only purchased data from this

---

2. Data management and the supporting organization are discussed in Chapter 4.

vendor, but also supplied it. Their internal customer names and addresses were now sent to the data vendor monthly in order to receive them back in a standard, consolidated fashion, each with a new *vendor-supplied customer identification number*. Once received, the Data Management group stored the full customer set, and used the vendor-supplied number as a means of accessing any customer that had been so identified. Marketing was now able to cross analyze and, if necessary, get additional information about their own customers.

This true story reflects an admitted incompetence, that is, the Data Management group's inability to enforce or begin any type of customer standardization, and the solution resulted in payment to an *external data vendor* in order to be able to identify the company's own customers.

Data Vendor Maturity

The era of the monopolistic data vendors began to subside once other players joined the market and once the Internet became an easy way to obtain and download external data. Today it is unlikely that anyone would conform to a specific vendor's primary identifiers, unless of course these identifiers permit access to the one and only of some particular data occurrence, or more commonplace, the vendor supplies extremely functional software along with the data so that the data recipient can begin analysis without the participation of an internal development organization.

As data became more and more of a commodity, more and more vendors began to offer it. Organizations no longer had to conform to vendor standards (unless of course the vendor was offering something that was well worth this effort), and the consumer was put in charge, to a limited extent. Many committees resulted, specifically geared to keep the data consumer in the better bargaining position; most of the committees, however, were financed and populated by representative software vendors. As a result, minimal "standards" began to arise in specific industries. For example, the SKU (Stock Keeping Unit) number was an attempt to standardize retail item identification; it facilitates a retail organization's connection between inventory control and the external commerce associated with it. In addition to such standard identifiers, some industries adopted exchange formats to allow intercompany commerce both within and between specific countries.

As with most standards,[3] the regulatory side of data management always seems to be "catching up." The regulations are often reactive, based on an

---

3. Today's metadata standards are discussed in Chapter 16.

industry member or coalition's pioneering journey into unknown or unrestricted areas. As a result, the forerunners usually have the opportunity to "call the shots" when it comes to determining the initial public data characteristics.

Information Exchange

Data flows in and out of every major corporate conglomerate. In many cases, those who create the data are not deciding what it should look like or how it should be associated with what already exists. If something becomes a requirement, however, it establishes the format to which data exchange must adhere. Without a standard format, information exchanges would be quite similar to the corporate application environment portrayed in Figure 3-3.

To assist data travel, standards have been developed; most address the content and/or format of the extracts, typically the data itself in terms of its value

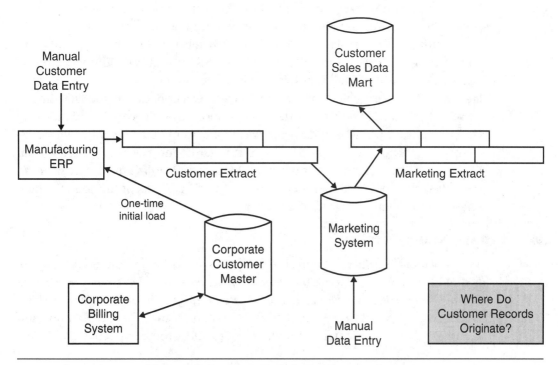

Figure 3-3   Chaotic information exchange

display and order. Standards do not cover all possible situations, so I find it helpful to create three categories for today's exchange standards:

- *Format*—the order, length, and style of the data entries
- *Content*—what data is to be included, and the value(s) it should take on
- *Processing*—what should happen to the data, and how

What Is a Standard Format?

The simplest way to describe a standard format is to think of the various things we can export or copy data onto at a PC workstation—floppy disk, CD-ROM, zip-drive, cassette tape, file (and the various file types). Each of these formats is perceived to be standard; that is, no matter what type of PC we use, we should be able to read a floppy disk that was created with another. Take it one step further and ask if this statement holds true regardless of the operating system installed on each PC. Finally, take this step further and ask if this statement still applies if a PC-created floppy needs to be read by a server or a minicomputer instead of another client. If the format is truly standard, all of these situations should make no difference in the target processor's ability to read the disk. What happens, however, may depend on the source and target circumstances; hence the standards usually need to clarify more than format.

To bring the example a bit down to earth, let us revisit the SKU and compare it to the UPC (Uniform Product Code). SKU numbers, although unique, are restricted to the retail industry and indicate such things as the style, color, and size of an item. Their format does not apply as broadly as the later implemented UPC code. The UPC code is much more descriptive, is 12 digits long (following the UCC-12 standard, anyway),[4] and is in fact universal (across industries). Yes, both SKUs and UPCs are standards, and yes, there exist several UPC standards! A standard format would imply that *no matter what is being described*, the code is always a certain length and consists of the specific identifiable components in a specified order.

What Is Standard Content?

Taking standards to the next level, we look at what is being described or identified. With a standard content, *the item being described is described in the same manner regardless of where, when, how, or why it is being identified*. Of course, we always add a tinge of practicality when creating these definitions, and recognize that tunnel vision has a tendency to affect the perspective and objec-

---

4. Beginning in 2005, however, an extra digit will be added.

tive for which things are identified. Hence, standard content also is often restricted not only to a particular industry (e.g., retail) but also to a particular function (e.g., inventory) within that industry. For example, our UPC code is targeted toward the description of finished products, with the objective of supporting international commerce. Standard content implies that each UPC component is valued consistently as long as the same product is being described *anywhere for any retail purpose*. Of course, there are bound to be exceptions.

When we consider the retail industry, we often think of items being sold in the four walls of a store; with e-commerce, however, many stores are virtual. But virtual commerce still requires a product's integration with the physical stores and outlets. Therefore, UPC codes are bound to be a fact of life. Remember how we consistently think of item identification standards as somewhat narrowly focused even within a particular industry? Unfortunately, this is not always true. In the retail industry, for example, the standard becomes less firmly defined when the product is an over-the-counter (OTC) medication. Enter the NDC (National Drug Code), provided by the Food and Drug Administration. In some scenarios, an OTC drug has an NDC instead of a UPC, in others it has both codes, and in yet others the UPC reigns. Perhaps part of the dilemma stems from the fact that the NDC originated in the U.S. Food and Drug Administration (FDA), and the UPC comes from the Uniform Code Council (UCC), an organization of commercial businesses all seeking the objective of standardized codes.

When content is standard, an accepted standards body has to approve new values or additions to the base code. In the case of UPCs, the Uniform Code Council (UCC) issues the code instances but typically reserves the first digit of the code as a means of indicating whose code it is (e.g., vendor or local identification). In this way, a retailer is still able to use internally generated codes, but would require all interfacing vendors to conform to the internal numbering scheme or else eventually translate external or standard codes to its own scenario. From an outsider's perspective, this defeats the purpose of the code to some extent. Use of nonstandard codes or formats risks the inability of others (software, firms, etc.) to interpret your product's identification. But who is responsible for setting standards in confusing situations, such as the sale of an OTC drug? A consultant would say, "It depends" on what the *standard content* covers.

What Is Standard Processing?

To complete our discussion of information exchange, we have to put the "standards" that we have discussed into the exchange perspective. If the identification of an item follows a standard format (perhaps within an industry only) with values or content associated with its identification that would indicate, for example, the manufacturing company, the product, and the size, then the standard would be doing its job—as long as everyone followed it. If only that were true! There is one additional aspect to all of this, and that involves what is done with this standard data, and *how* it is accomplished.

Usually, standards that address data identification do not address its processing in any way. The access and creation of this data are usually believed to reside at a "lower level," that of the application or operating system code. In the more technical arenas, the processing of the contents of a floppy disk or CD-ROM varies depending on the purpose of its creation (e.g., Read Only, Read/Write). But without splitting hairs, *a true standard has a boundary around the standard that addresses the processing of the standard's contents.* Usually, operating systems address this nicely, and of course, our standard file system metamodel (see Figure 3-1) is a perfect example. Consider the file system standard in terms of the three components of a true standard:

1. *Standard format:* All files have a name and a type; the name precedes the type and does not exceed 32 characters; the type follows a period and is 3 characters long.

2. *Standard content:* Common file types have values defined within the operating system's main registry, all of which have been created and approved by software vendors participating in operating system development and standardization efforts.

3. *Standard processing:* Once a file type is registered, any file of that type will be processed identically within the boundaries of its definition.

Are the standards of today's data exchange broad enough? Do they encompass most instances of data and information? For the most part, their intents were well targeted. However, because their creation was based on some degree of tunnel vision, they all seem to address one specific industry, one specific type of data within that industry, or even worse, one particular purpose of that data within the industry. The time has come to move our standards into a more generic role—that of universal exchange, regardless of the type of data, its source, or its target.

So, despite the fact that the information in organizations has its problems, the information outside organizations is not necessarily any better in terms of consistency. This realization alone is a major step forward in continuing the quest for the ultimate metadata solution.

Chapter 4

Integrating Our Data
Where the Repairs of the 1990s Broke Down

At this point we have reviewed the state of our information—that which we nurture and that which we acquire and try to nurture. We have addressed the realities of our attempts to control and manage our information. We discussed the differences between data and information. All the discussions so far have been based on information's existence within a predefined tunnel or processing scope.

Many of us have been aware of these tunnels and have been trying to "integrate" our information. That is, we have been trying to combine our existing tunnels, at least logically, so that they could be analyzed as if they are a uniform whole.

This chapter discusses attempts in the 1990s to integrate information, including the various means with which we started and continue to integrate data.

Data Modeling: Does Anyone Remember What It Is?

Data modeling has been around for a long time—since the advent of Codd's Relational Model in the 1970s. (Additional readings about data modeling are listed in the Readings section of this book.) Many application developers and database administrators continue to provide part-time logical data modeling services for specific projects. Does anyone remember any more why it all began?

Note: Portions of this chapter were contributed by Patricia Cupoli, Database Design Solutions, Inc., Bernardsville, New Jersey.

In the beginning, data models were created to reflect business data requirements in a graphic way. Data modeling standards (there are many) dictate the format of these diagrams, but they generally depict things (entities) about which we need to collect data, the interrelationships of the entities, and of course, the actual data items (attributes) that we need to collect. These models were created for brand-new applications (projects) and typically resulted in a new database for every project.

What occurs when there are many project-oriented, standalone logical data models? If analysis is done across the project-specific models, one may find that data item names lack consistency; some data items may appear redundantly; and the data may not be defined or, if definitions are available, they are sketchy.

Data Model Types

Any database development effort could involve three types of models: the enterprise data model, the application data model, and the physical data model. This section discusses the enterprise and application data models with their variations, but not the physical data model because it is closely tied to database technology.

Enterprise Data Model

The enterprise data model is a high-level data model organized by subject area. Each subject area has the entities (usually nouns) and relationships (i.e., associations between these nouns or things). This model can include the attributes of the entity (i.e., descriptive characteristics, which eventually become physical data elements). The enterprise data model provides the "big picture" as the starting point for both operational application and data warehousing models. Consider the flow of data illustrated in Figure 4-1.

Standard Subject Area

The model organized according to standard, corporate or master, subject area is the highest level of the enterprise data model. It categorizes the enterprise or corporate data by subjects that have been standardized in an organization.

A subject area model can be used as a starting point for a data access model. Data access models, as illustrated in Figure 4-2, organize data so that it is retrievable by topic. They are typically set up for data access by end users, which could include Web interfaces.

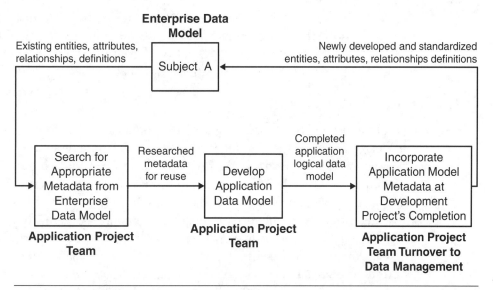

Figure 4-1 **Synergy between the enterprise data model and application data or warehousing models**

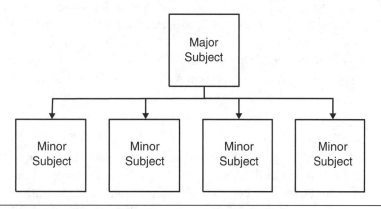

Figure 4-2 A sample data access model

Application Data Model

This model, the most common, is the intermediary between the enterprise data model and all resulting physical data models. The application-specific data specifications drive the development of this logical data model. Application project-specific entities, attributes, and relationships must be identified, named, and defined according to the organization's data standards. The last step in the creation of this type of model is the application of the process known as normalization, through which all attributes are evaluated in terms of their relationships to their associated entity's keys, or identifiers. The result is a relational model geared toward flexibility and business-specific access.

Penetration

One of the biggest issues with logical data modeling of the 1990s was its obvious lack of penetration. Data management organizations would try their best to convince the world that logical data models were required in application development, but as they lost more and more control over data management itself, many applications seemed to "just happen" without data modelers even knowing about them. All sorts of data management reorganizations tried to keep the modeling effort alive. At best, however, only new applications were modeled, once, at the beginning, and few models were maintained over time. Not until databases became such an unmanageable part of the corporate information picture did the model itself start to have renewed credibility.

Logical data models provide the organization with sharable, reusable, standardized data and objects that can be communicated across business groups. However, simply developing a standalone, logical data model does not guarantee the existence of standard shared data. Unless data modeling efforts are related, ideally at an enterprise data model level, the best organizations have is documented data requirements, on an application basis. True, many organizations do not have even this, but there could be so much more.

Tool Usage

In general, data modeling tools provide various levels of support for both logical and physical data modeling. Unfortunately, a logical data modeling term in one tool may be a physical data modeling term in another. And of course, because there is no such thing as a standard data model representation, the way in which tools are deployed in each organization is usually left to the individual modeler. The result is often a series of models, many excellent in terms of their business representation, many quite physical, and some in between. Connecting and integrating the data that is represented by the various model renditions often becomes quite a nightmare.

Because there has been no consistency in the development and subsequent use of data models in organizations, many have used data modeling tools for their reverse engineering capabilities. With this feature, the tool reads the physical database catalog and obtains the physical design by reading the database definition. It then generates a diagram, representing tables as boxes (physical entities) and connecting them by generating relationships based on defined keys. Existing columns are used as attributes, and all names in the resulting model are equivalent to their actual physical renditions. Once the reverse engineering has been accomplished, the project often moves forward by enhancing this design to become more "logical" and then translating it into a physical database design for a revised target relational database.

Advantages and Disadvantages

Logical data modeling for the relational environment has benefits. It provides a business perspective of the data before its translation into a physical application database. The logical models (enterprise data and application data models) give project teams a place to start leveraging previously developed data and metadata without the constraints of physical technology. The project teams can avoid "reinventing the wheel" by reusing the documented data and metadata.

Standardized definitions for entities, attributes, and relationships can be very beneficial. However, the process of standardization involves conflict resolution between standardized models and the logical model under review. This process is often quite political. Compromises have to be reached so that, for example, an entity can be called "retail customer" or "wholesale customer"— something more descriptive than "customer" with twenty definitions.

Logical data modeling does not occur magically. To have an organized approach to logical modeling, dedicated personnel are required in a data management organization. The data management organization has the broad mission to analyze and develop the enterprise data model as a blueprint for future database development. The enterprise data model requires constant maintenance as new business decisions are made that affect the corporate data. Application-level data models require maintenance and management as data changes are made to the applications based on changing business requirements.

Despite the possible benefits of logical data modeling, many organizations did not obtain them during the 1990s. One problem is clearly that the development of a proper logical data model adds time and cost to the project application development's life cycle, especially when a project's time frame is very short. There is definitely a learning curve involved focusing on both the modeling tool that supports the data modeling method and the data/metadata that is involved from a business perspective.

A greater disadvantage, however, is the unwillingness of many organizations to realize that the development of standalone models without planned connectivity and accessibility to beneficiaries outside the modeling organization can prove to be more detrimental than beneficial. What good are excellent models (as excellent data) if no one knows they exist? What good is accessing a data model if the consumer does not know what to do with it? It takes a long-term perspective to support this function. Eventually, the time and cost decrease as more data and metadata are developed for reuse.

The Data Management Organization

The data management organization was in and out of vogue throughout the 1990s. When organizations can't get to their data, they clearly see the need for such a dedicated data management function. But when the function's accomplishments do not result in standardized, integrated data, the data managers are the first to be blamed. Data management is not a standalone function; it should be part of an organization's approach to application development.

Data Management's Benefits and Shortcomings

The successful data management organization does not focus solely on data modeling or the maintenance of a corporate metadata repository or dictionary.[1] It does not work on an enterprise data model for years without applying it to the application development process. If the data management organization operates this way, its "tunnel vision" will limit its future.

Benefits

The successful data management organization expands its vision to value-added data management activities at all levels of the enterprise. It must support the process of achieving stated goals for the management of data and metadata. The process is often a cultural shock for an organization accustomed to focusing on application-specific data. This process must center on identified data management customers that will drive the development and maintenance of the policies, standardized practices, and standards and procedures that comprise the enterprise data/information framework. Without consideration for the effects of data management on the average developer and business user, the deliverables of most data management organizations are often self-serving. Managing

---

1. Metadata repositories are discussed in Part III.

data must result in satisfied customers—if it is more work to adhere to data management policies than to recreate data, something needs to be reevaluated. Successful data management results in the following:

- *Standardized corporate data* for major sharable subject areas
- *Common data access* that allows anyone to get to corporate data using standard access routines
- *Elimination of data conflict* via the slow and steady infiltration of common data
- *Shorter reporting cycles* through encouraged common data access
- *Clearer understanding of business data* via the access of common data definitions

CASE STUDY: A Data Management Reintroduction

IMS Health, a large information-intensive vendor of pharmaceutical and healthcare data, decided to develop a North American logical data model. One purpose of this logical model was to provide the basis for a physical dimensional model of a data warehouse. Another purpose of this modeling effort was to provide an architectural framework for future application development. In the past, logical data models had not been part of the application development process.

The primary sources for this logical model were physical application models developed in Computer Associates (CA) Erwin, a data modeling tool, and stored in CA ModelMart, a repository of completed models. Other sources included existing databases, existing pharmaceutical data classification schemes, new user interviews, and existing models from IMS subsidiaries including Canadian operations. Seven major subject areas were developed at the enterprise level, then approximately one hundred and fifty entities were developed and associated with each subject area in CA Erwin. The entities were fully attributed with robust definitions.

Subject matter experts at IMS Health then reviewed and validated this logical data model. When completed, appropriate sections of the logical data models were used by the data administration (DA) and database administration (DBA) staff as a basis for developing application and data warehouse models in Erwin.

Interest in the expansion of this model grew as various global groups realized that it made sense to identify and model common data across the globe for reuse in systems development projects. A project was started to develop this common data model with global cooperation. The project began with the standardization of the entities that had already been associated with the enterprise model's subject areas. Attributes were then defined and standardized internationally. Through this effort IMS was able to validate the concept that common data from different countries could be combined.

Concurrent with the global logical modeling effort was the reestablishment of a data administration group with dedicated headcount. In the past, "data management" at IMS Health had stressed database administration, and most of the responsibilities focused on tuning physical databases in reaction to performance issues. The new DA group was responsible for logical data modeling, focusing at the outset on large application projects that involved multiple data sources. As a way to keep the data administration group's responsibilities practical, the application developers and DBAs continued to perform the logical data modeling on smaller application projects. However, all data modeling efforts were now being reviewed by the DA team.

This group soon found that it needed to provide additional services, such as expanded logical data modeling support. Because the legacy data was not modeled or documented properly, new application integration efforts required the mapping of newly modeled logical attributes to their source physical legacy data elements. This new documentation was placed initially in an interim metadata repository accessible via the intranet. As of this writing, a purchased metadata repository package is being installed with the objective of releasing it for enterprise-wide access.

In its first year the data administration group showed progress toward its stated corporate goal of data and metadata integration. The demand for logical modeling services on projects already has outstripped the resources of the DA group. This successful group looks forward to proactively expanding its services and its customers.

The group is training the application developers and end users on logical data-modeling techniques as a way of standardizing the reuse of enterprise model entities and the associated data definitions. Data stewards are being identified and processes have been defined to review all developed models for consistency. The new data standards, policies, and procedures being rolled out have had DBA and developers' input.

The revitalized data management organization is the result of learned shortcomings. It now focuses on the management of data and metadata at its creation, and its expanded "management" includes the full purpose of data—identification, definition, location, sourcing, and access (The 5 Questions[2]). In addition, the DA organization has been called on to provide professional services to client companies and is helping to cement relationships.

Note: This case study was submitted by Ray McGlew, Manager Data Administration, IMS Health Inc., Plymouth Meeting, PA. Used with permission.

---

2. The 5 Questions is a trademark of and the questions and method are copyrighted by Database Solutions, Inc., Bernardsville, New Jersey.

Data Warehousing

Data warehousing was one of the biggest trends to hit information technology (IT) organizations in the 1990s. Ideally, it is an organized way to provide end users with timely, accurate, value-added, integrated, and maintained data in a desired format. This process enables organizations to provide more than just a data extract or an extract of an extract in a "spider web" fashion. Data warehousing allows the end users to query and report on maintained data when they need to, not when the IT organization gives them the access via customized extracts.

Definition of Data Warehousing

In data warehousing, the database contains summarized and aggregated data in terms of facts (e.g., a sales transaction) and dimensions (e.g., product, region, time) under which the facts are usually analyzed. These facts and dimensions are typically combined in a star schema design, as illustrated in Figure 4-3. A data warehouse differs from a typical database in that a data warehouse contains information about one aspect of an organization's business instead of its ongoing operations. The data in a data warehouse is typically more data oriented in that it represents the captured result of a process already executed (e.g., an order). Standard relationships among data entities are not usually captured in this type of design.

Typically, the data warehouse is initially scoped and modeled in terms of data sources and its target design. Data for warehouses comes from multiple

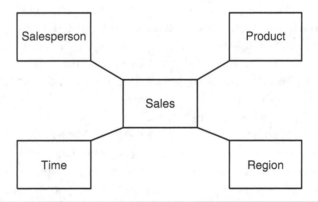

Figure 4-3   *A sample star schema design*

sources and, therefore, an intense data analysis is usually required at the beginning of every data warehouse requirements phase. Extract, translation, and load (ETL) processes are designed and a full data warehouse architecture is defined in terms of interfacing tools and their parts in these processes.

The data warehousing life cycle is iterative, which means it is continuously being maintained while evolving. The warehouse development life cycle repeats itself in an enhancement pattern as changing business conditions affect the demands for decision supportive data.

Approaches to Data Warehousing

Organizations perform the data warehousing process in different ways. Some organizations follow the classic approach of data warehousing (defined earlier). Some organizations simply dump data from the source data systems to the target databases with little regard to whether the source contains quality, properly aggregated, or summarized data. Other organizations develop operational data stores (ODS), which represent cleansed data retrieved from various operational systems and stored by major subject area in a "staging area" that feeds numerous data warehouses.

Data Warehousing's Benefits and Shortcomings

The result of well-planned data warehousing is integrated, quality data that has been properly formatted and defined for queries and retrievals by end users. There should be enough confidence that the data is accurate to base corporate decisions on it. The realities have often been quite different, however, and as a result *metadata* is now a popular topic.

Data that is not accurate does not become accurate simply by being loaded into a data warehouse. More important, if the data's accuracy and integrity are clearly relative—that is, applications have different definitions and formulas associated with the creation of the data—the process of integrating multiple sources may not be straightforward. It is best to have the initial project scope cover a highly visible, low-risk area.

The success of data warehousing depends on source data that is "clean"; that is, it contains no errors. The data fields should contain the data they are supposed to contain and nothing else. The data should be defined as the "true" source of the data so that it can be reused in other data warehousing efforts. These requirements should have convinced you that not all data is meant to be integrated.

Introducing "Objects"

As the 1990s saw many failed data management efforts, many organizations considered tying processes and data together as a means of standardizing and sharing. They began to adopt "object-oriented (OO) modeling" as an attempt to standardize the processes associated with corporate data. An object represents both data values (the object's state) and the set of operations (process or behavior) that acts on that data. Each object has its own identity that distinguishes it from other objects. Both the data and the operations are combined or encapsulated so that the data and some operations are hidden. As with the other integration attempts of the 1990s, to be successful the initial and continued deployment of OO techniques needed to address shareability and remain focused on anticipated multiple applications.

Object-Oriented Models

Object-oriented methodologies include modeling as a way to provide a framework to analyze, design, and build a prototype of a system (see Figure 4-4). They are not silver bullets that construct systems without analysis or design, or replace the traditional approaches. Some of the OO methodologies actually have a strong

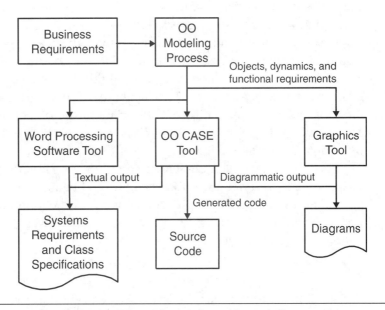

Figure 4-4 **The object-oriented modeling process**

data modeling origin. The object-oriented modeling process requires business requirements inputs, the actual development of OO models, and the generation of model "outputs." To develop these deliverables, organizations use software such as OO CASE tools, word processing packages, and desktop graphics tools.

Object-oriented models comprise three major types of deliverables. The first type of deliverable is textual and includes the system requirements, class specifications, data dictionaries, event lists, and messages (interaction scenarios). The second type of deliverable is diagrammatic. There are many models or diagrams to be created including the use case diagram (business view), activity diagram (temporal sequencing of use cases), class diagram (object class modeling and design), state transition diagram (dynamic behavior of an object), and object interaction diagram (collaboration and sequence). Other possible diagrams include the component diagram and the deployment diagram. The third type of deliverable is the generated source code from an OO CASE tool for prototyping. This code can be new or modified from existing object classes to fit the application requirements.

Class Libraries

Objects are organized into classes. A class defines the operations and data for a set of common objects. The operations source code can be modified so that a class inherits properties of an existing object, yet is defined appropriately for a new application. A new object is known as an instance.

A class can be organized into a hierarchy with superclasses and subclasses. Through inheritance, classes can be added to the class hierarchy by expanding the inherited class definition with the addition of instance variables and new methods (what the object does). The ability of the same method to result in different behaviors, depending on the class of the object receiving the message, is called polymorphism. A subclass shares or changes the data values or operations from a superclass.

The object classes are implemented with a class library that contains hierarchies of superclasses and subclasses. At the beginning of OO development an organization may not have a class library and will purchase a third-party library. Then that library is developed and refined over time and during the course of several projects.

Reusability

A class library provides for the availability of reusable, previously developed objects. Object classes are more reusable than components. The feature of inheritance makes it possible to change the source code of an object for a new task.

If planned properly, the reusability procedures can result in dramatically improved productivity during OO development. Ideally, developers are expected to spend effort up front planning and designing for reuse in current and subsequent projects. The dependencies and interactions of the reusable object have been tracked and documented. Guidelines are then in place as to how to create class hierarchies and how to define the relationships with existing classes. There is less code to test once reusable modular code has been tested and found to be free of defects.

Is Our Information Integrated?

During the 1990s information increased exponentially. In organizations with application development foresight, some planning and prevention minimized the conflict and redundancy that can result from lack of data management. But many organizations are still looking for that silver bullet that will stop the information chaos. The technologies identified in this chapter were all potential integrators. But in each example, it was clear that without an organizational focus that included the information lifecycle, the resulting improvement was better than nothing, but often not nearly adequate.

Chapter 5

Identifying Information
The Directories of the 1990s

What good is the current information overload if we don't know where the various components are or how to get to them? This basic but simple question is often ignored, even by people responsible for establishing the *information directory*. The location of data and information was never considered an issue. Why should it have been? We only looked for the data *we* created. If someone else needed to get ahold of it, they simply came to us and we showed them our bag of tricks.

As corporate IT environments expanded, technical newcomers came into the information space. These "outsiders" were often already bred to be self-sufficient, not expecting to rely on others to get their work done. In addition, desktop workstations and personal computers (PCs) made self-reliance an instant byproduct as long as each individual could figure out where to go for the desired information . . . and, of course, how to get to it. But when *directories* came to be, their original emphasis was not access to data. Instead, the primary concern was data's characteristics, that is, the name, meaning, and related qualities of the data itself.

Off-the-Shelf Repositories

As the need for directory functionality spread beyond the people responsible for creating and maintaining the data, repository tools entered the picture. They were an "off-the-shelf" software product, purchased as a full set of data management tools with an associated database. Considering the fact that data was now being documented in more ways than one, and that a data administration/data management organization became primarily responsible for this function, it wasn't long before commercial repositories were offered as the place for this documentation. Originally sold as data dictionaries in the 1970s, additional functionality converted these fixed designs into so-called repositories in the late 1980s.[1] Their original market niche was the identification, storage, maintenance, and retrieval of all of data's characteristics, as defined by their targeted customer, the data management organization.

In the beginning, IT professionals couldn't have been happier. There was the "master" file, clearly characterized within this single repository and functioning as the *one* source of data documentation. But it wasn't too much longer before that master file fed an exponential number of downward data stores, which became "master files" in their own realms. And the documentation of these voluminous data occurrences was also propagated. The off-the-shelf repository started to feed other off-the-shelf repositories (or other simple databases). Even with the best intentions, the contents of the off-the-shelf repository quickly became outdated and the "metadata web," as illustrated in Figure 5-1, began.

It is a bit too soon to decide if these early repositories *actually* contained metadata—we start that discussion in the next chapter. Off-the-shelf repositories represented the vendors' best attempt at making their contents accessible to those who wanted them. The products came with a predetermined design, covering the types of data characteristics to be tracked and the way to track them. More important, the ways to access and update the documentation were also predesigned. Few data administrators had the skills or desire to change or customize these purchased repository products. Because they were often happy to have a place of their own in which they could control corporate definitions and data standards, the marketplace off-the-shelf options were taken as they came, with few requests for customization or integration with the existing sources or receivers of the documentation stored in these repositories.

Because of this lack of integration, it wasn't very long before the accuracy of these implemented repositories became questionable. Without a direct tie to the processes that created and updated either the data or its documentation, the data management group became responsible for the repository's maintenance, and often this was a manual process. Even worse, in very large organizations, it was highly likely for new data instances, data stores, and appli-

---

[1]Repositories and their physical characteristics are introduced and described in Chapter 14.

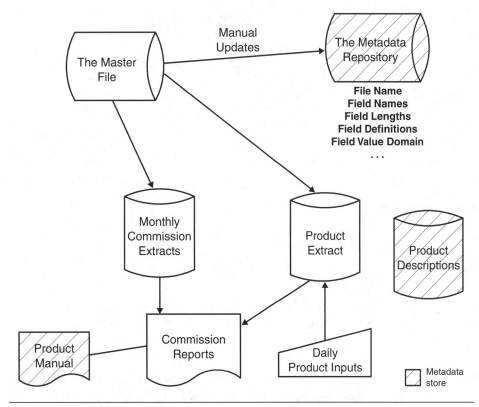

Figure 5-1 **The beginnings of the metadata web**

cations to be created without the data administration group's knowledge, and the repository's contents quickly represented a documented subset of the corporate data world. Once the contents of the repository were proved to be inaccurate, the repository died a slow death. More significantly, the repository was never again trusted as a source of accurate metadata in most organizations, and the credibility of those responsible for maintaining it was often reduced significantly.

In the early days of data dictionaries/repositories, most IT shops, in an effort to keep their hands on data and its unrestricted propagation, established processes that required some type of logical, business-related definition of data before a new database was implemented (see Figure 5-2). An internal data management organization would approve basic designs created by members of project teams, looking primarily at names and relationships. In most organizations, though, the data management team had little override power when it

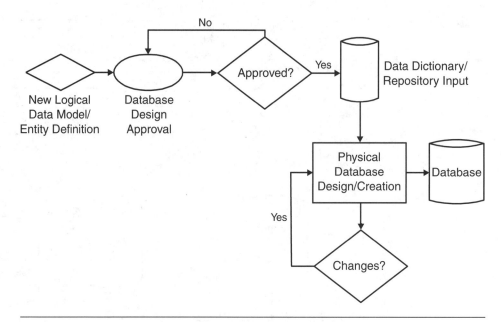

Figure 5-2   **Early data documentation process**

came to stopping data redundancy. Once the dictionary's design was approved, a (usually) manual process would input the names, definitions, and other required documentation into a corporate data dictionary. However, after the database was in operation, these small data management organizations had little time to review post-production changes and/or enhancements, and the data dictionary entries became out-of-date fairly quickly.

The success stories centered on full repository-based development architectures, which took into account the development process from the point of view of documentation creation, maintenance, and access. (See Figure 5-3.)

What Data Do We Have?

In the best managed data worlds, however, the populated repository of the 1990s rarely grew to represent the full world of data as it existed in the corporate data environment. At best, it contained the logical data models of not yet implemented databases, many of which, once implemented, seemed to live their own unrestricted lives. At worst, it had a one-time inventory of legacy data, put together for some type of impact analysis (e.g., determination of the occurrences of "date" for a year 2000 impact assessment), which was not kept

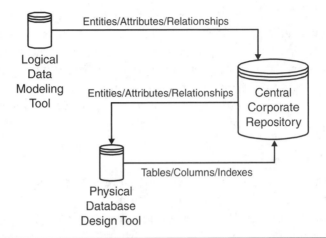

Figure 5-3   **The beginnings of repository architectures**

up to date or revisited after the impact analysis had been completed. In neither of these scenarios was it possible to determine "what data do we have (in the corporation)?" The ultimate result, more common than exceptional, was that off-the-shelf repositories were repackaged, remarketed, and renamed by the vendors.

Standalone Metadata Stores

By now, most people were talking about metadata and were mandated to start tracking it. Because off-the-shelf repositories didn't seem to provide that full, enterprise world of data documentation, many organizations in need of accurate documentation delivery and maintenance began to focus on pieces of the enterprise. As discussed in the preceding chapter, many of these needs were magnified with the advent of the data warehouse. Irrespective of the motivation, however, it became substantially easier to create a standalone simple metadata database, often designed by the documenters themselves, rather than to plan and implement a full-fledged enterprise-affecting metadata maintenance system.

In the best of situations, the requirements were determined during the application/database definition stage. These requirements were generally obtained from the same user community that helped shape the application and/or database itself. So, because the requirement suppliers were not familiar with the deep implications of metadata, the stated requirements rarely went beyond the attributes of a data dictionary. In rare cases, knowledgeable or frustrated users made a point of asking for a few characteristics beyond the norm, such as data source, formula, and domain/code set. Although some of these frustrated data analysts improved the system a bit, even their requirements often took a single-user perspective—that of the data analyst. Is this bad? Not for standalone metadata stores.

The Custom-Built Process

Once the metadata requirements were obtained, some semblance of order had to be placed on them. The resulting standalone metadata store was typically a small client database, often implemented in the DBMS of convenience, if the responsible party was familiar with one. Many requirements gatherers had to take full reign over this responsibility—gathering the requirements, coordinating them, designing a metadata store, and defining the database. This explains why so many self-implemented standalone metadata stores are small MS Access databases. It also explains why so many of them are MS Excel spreadsheets or MS Word documents. Nevertheless, in all situations, the data's documentation has a place to reside, and the person who put the documentation there knows exactly how to find and retrieve it.

Once the standalone metadata data store was designed, its population was typically a one-time effort, focused primarily on information gathered once the documented application was in place, or at least being tested. Most of these metadata stores were populated manually, despite the fact that most of the desired metadata was not being created for the first time.

When these customized standalone metadata stores were in operation, the maintenance was quite variable and depended almost exclusively on the responsibilities of their creators. In many scenarios, data management teams were responsible for support as needed. More often, the responsibility fell by the wayside when the original development team, including the individual responsible for data documentation support, moved on to other projects and responsibilities. In general, because the result was created based on the requirements gathered and analyzed by one individual, a member of a specific project team, it was project-specific and representative of that individual's design experience. The standalone product was never intended to outlive the usefulness of the particular application and, in many cases, the values populated within it were never expected to change. Finally, the role of the metadata in all of these initial standalone solutions was to provide dictionary-type information about the data that resided in a particular application, database, or data warehouse. Documentation of "what data we have" was provided as long as the data resided in the described data store. But because the documentation was generally developed apart from the data store and its associated application, the metadata store was restricted in terms of both its perspective and its value.

Enter the Vendors

After distinct sets of metadata requirements exponentially reproduced, it became apparent that solutions of limited focus were in demand. At this point, vendors began to offer packaged solutions, with various perspectives on the metadata's purpose and scope. More important, they offered a generic solution, targeted to a specific functional need, but taking away the need for detailed requirements analysis. In many situations, because of the fact that documentation was a dreaded topic, task, and responsibility, it was easier to opt for an off-the-shelf storage solution than to go through the tedious task of gathering and documenting metadata requirements. Purchase of a vendor tool eliminated the need to gather requirements, categorize data, and do all the other things this book discusses.

Initial vendor solutions were also standalone in that many of them did not integrate even with tools supplied by the same vendor. In recognition of an after-the-fact need for the capability, initially extra components were retrofitted into disparate tool suites. Over time, consumer demand increased the level of integration of these metadata stores with vendors' other offerings. Eventually, the vendor-supplied standalone metadata store was nothing more than a means of accessing the metadata that was either already being captured by the vendor's tool or was being captured through manual inputs that supplemented the vendor's metadata stores of other products.

Standalone became a relative term with the advent of limited-focus vendor metadata stores. In many scenarios, they provided an integrated storage ground for sharing the documentation among the various tool components (see Figure 5-4). Often, however, even the vendor's offering added no benefit to the collection and reusability of the stored documentation within the same vendor's product offerings (see Figure 5-5). At best, vendors were providing a new architectural component (the "metadata repository"); at worst, it was a mere case of tunnel vision. The new component now simply supported a new and specific client base (the "metadata people") and was led by a separate and distinct product manager within the vendor organization.

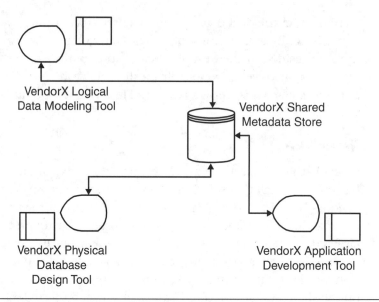

**Figure 5-4   Metadata storage in an integrated,
standalone toolset**

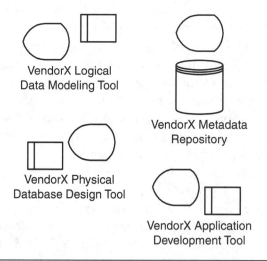

**Figure 5-5   Metadata storage as a standalone add-on
to a software development toolset**

Within each scenario, however, progress was being made in that the identification of and access to the stored contents now became a part of the solution. It may have been unfortunate that the limited scope of these vendor products kept those who did not use this vendor's product from knowing about the stored documentation, but at least progress was being made.

Internal Directories

It was still common during the 1990s for stored data documentation to have a narrow scope and to become obsolete. Furthermore, even when they were functional, the early repositories were a combination of massive functionality in areas that were not necessarily in demand (e.g., generation of physical Database Definition Language, or DDL) and minimal to no functionality in areas of basic needs and wants (e.g., allowing reuse and tracking of specific pieces of data). The need for a data directory in most organizations was so simple that it was often dismissed and complicated by those in the data management areas. Both end users and technical developers were very simply looking for a *data inventory*, one that answered the question, "What data do we have?"

This simple need was probably one of the most complicated to satisfy because most of the data that was being searched for was not necessarily structured. That is, it was not fixed, numeric, or textual data, stored in a defined database; but rather, for example, unstructured information in documents and program code, as well as structured information for which we did and did not know the underlying designs. By this point, vendors began to offer packages that allowed the indexing and retrieval of unstructured data, and corporate libraries were the first to deploy them. Thus, the need for a directory became exponentially more complicated, because we were, in a sense, looking to create a directory of directories.

The data-intensive corporation was now at a crossroads. Simple directories could be implemented manually by logging everything one could identify in a standard way, but it was clear that this would always be a catch-up process. How could a data management organization, or an internal librarian, come close to keeping up with the identification of relevant corporate information? Who would determine what was relevant? Would there be a process that actively involved directory maintenance as new information was created, updated, and deleted? Early internal *information directories* were created with grandiose intentions, but in the end, many of them became yet another stand-alone metadata store.

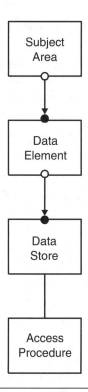

Figure 5-6 The simple information directory

During the 1990s successful information directories were centralized and controlled by software. They typically were not implemented with market repository tools, but were either custom developed or deployed with market-available *directory* tools. In either scenario, the underlying database design concerned itself with the type of data store that needed to be indexed, the characteristics of the data in that data store, and last, how to open the data store to get to the stored information.

For the model in Figure 5-6 to be successful and long lasting, all *data elements* would need to be categorized into standard *subject areas*. Likewise, *data stores* would have *standard types*, and each store of that type would be accessible with the same, reusable *access procedure*. In many scenarios, this operating system–like approach required a "comply or be excluded" philosophy. Success would therefore be determined by what was easier for the target population—compliance or exclusion. If it was easier to "do your own thing," then the directory failed. But if complying with standards made life easier, then it was surely not a hindrance but a help, and the directory lived on.

Some vendor offerings made compliance amazingly easy; others made it not worth the price of the software. The implementations of these directories varied: some required a singular, centralized picture of the world being described; others were distributed with weekly reconciliation recommended to keep all directories accurate and in sync. In either scenario, the secret to success rested with the following characteristics:

- The ability to make data easily retrievable through meaningful categories, no matter where the data resided
- An active connection to the world of data that was being created and accessed
- Security capabilities that prevented people from creating their own *subject areas* and *access procedures*

With success, the directories remained internal to the implementing enterprises, or on a smaller scale, to the implementing organizations.

CASE STUDY: Internal Directory Implementation in an Insurance Company

The Guardian Life Insurance Company of America, the fourth largest mutual insurance company in the United States, originally sought to establish an information directory that supported a new data warehouse, developed to support Group Insurance Year 2000 requirements. The original directory was implemented with a commercially available "data dictionary" product, already installed at Guardian. The product came complete with its own user interface and internal database structure, which gave Guardian little work in the directory development arena.

However, Guardian needed bulk input or output without being constrained to a product's specific file format requirements. The need for another solution became a major objective, and the Meta Data Administration function was pressed to use the already installed Guardian software.

Various best practices within Guardian were evaluated before selecting Lotus Notes. Guardian was already fully functional with Lotus Notes and used the software as the main means of sharing information across the firm. As such, because most directory users were already fluent in Lotus Notes, it seemed like the appropriate alternative. A new directory was created, providing the necessary internal database schema.

The revised directory was used to support the data warehouse by providing the following:

- Business definitions of all warehouse resident data
- Mappings of logical element names to physical element names
- Source-to-target data element mappings

The directory's users were able to access this information via a front-end "search." Searches could be conducted by business description (logical element name). See Figure 5-7 for sample of Guardian's directory output. Various standard reports, delivered in the form of Excel spreadsheets would result, including information on how the information could be obtained as well as its COBOL source record identity. Information is also available on the entire ETL process: extraction, transformation, and load. Most noted in Figure 5-8 is the use of the data replication tool, IBM Data Propagator. The record shows how these replication control columns provide specific information on the sequence of events taking place when information is loaded onto the data warehouse.

Usage of the directory was not what was anticipated. In fact, monitoring showed approximately 12 developers (all involved with the specific data warehouse) and 13 additional developers (from other projects) as the sole users of the directory. There originally was little to no business user usage, despite what was intended. Business users considered the directory to be "too technical" at first. However, once the data warehouse became more of a data analysis source, business users became more and more interested in overcoming the technical obstacles. In fact, the directory was literally the only place that gave the users the eventual capability to validate warehouse data, by showing the specific source of all warehouse elements.

Shortly users became the prime customers of this directory. Many consider it to be "very useful" and "very informative." This increased interest has led the Meta Data Administrator to pursue a redesign. The current structure, not relational, and fixed based on the original directory product, does not allow the addition of relationships and therefore requires users to pursue several queries to get to the desired information. The entire directory is in the process of being moved to a relational database, and new schemas are now being evaluated and considered by the Meta Data Administrator. In addition, other data marts are now being documented in this directory, as its scope expands.

Note: This case study was submitted by Christina Tom, Technical Specialist, Guardian, August 2000. Copyright © 2001 by The Guardian Life Insurance Company of America. All rights reserved. Text and Figures 5-7 and 5-8 used with permission.

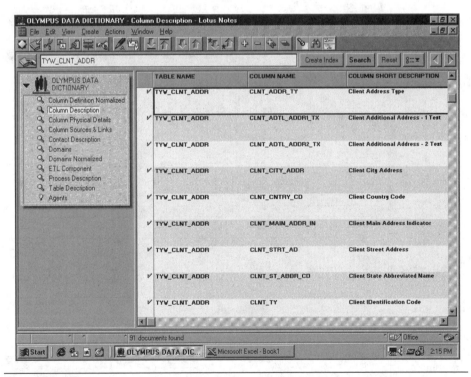

Figure 5-7   **A request for information from the Olympus Data Dictionary**

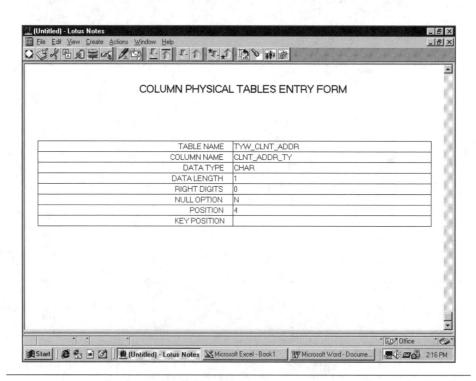

Figure 5-7 A request for information from the Olympus
Data Dictionary *continued*

Figure 5-8 Sample Olympus Data Dictionary report output

Table Name	Column Name	Column Short Description	Column Long Description
TYW_CLNT_ADDR	CLNT_ADDR_TY	Client Address Type	The function this site serves for the client. For example, the site could represent a residence, a place of work, or a mail drop.
TYW_CLNT_ADDR	CLNT_ADTL_ADDR1_TX	Client Additional Address—1 Text	The additional line of client's address information to be used for instructional purposes (i.e., c/o, attention to, forwarding address).
TYW_CLNT_ADDR	CLNT_ADTL_ADDR2_TX	Client Additional Address—2 Text	The additional line of client's address information to be used for instructional purposes (i.e., c/o, attention to, forwarding address).
TYW_CLNT_ADDR	CLNT_CITY_ADDR	Client City Address	The client's city of residence.
TYW_CLNT_ADDR	CLNT_CNTRY_CD	Client Country Code	The client's home address country code.
TYW_CLNT_ADDR	CLNT_MAIN_ADDR_IN	Client Main Address Indicator	An indication that this site represents the main address for this type of address. Y is the main address (e.g., the main residential address).
TYW_CLNT_ADDR	CLNT_STRT_AD	Client Street Address	The client's street address.
TYW_CLNT_ADDR	CLNT_ST_ABBR_CD	Client State Abbreviated Name	The client's state of residence.
TYW_CLNT_ADDR	CLNT_TY	Client IDentification Code	Code to indicate clients belonging to Guardian Plans. This code is used as a security device to restrict access to records of specific clients, in particular Guardian Employees.
TYW_CLNT_ADDR	CLNT_ZIP4_CD	Client Zip4 Code	The client's four-digit zip code.
TYW_CLNT_ADDR	CLNT_ZIP5_CD	Client Zip5 Code	The client's five-digit zip code.
TYW_CLNT_ADDR	DW_BTCH_CNTRL_NR	Data Warehouse Batch Control IDentifier	Generated identification number used to identify the session in which a given object's data were refreshed.
TYW_CLNT_ADDR	DW_CLNT_NR	Data Warehouse Client IDentifier	The identifier generated for a client by the data warehouse. Each client is uniquely identified when information about the client is initially loaded into the warehouse. *continued*

Figure 5-8 Sample Olympus Data Dictionary report output *continued*

Table Name	Column Name	Column Short Description	Column Long Description
TYW_CLNT_ADDR	DW_DPROPR_STAT_CD	Warehouse Data Propagation Status Code	Indication of the state of update processes during the data replication processes. Three states are recognized: Initialized, In Process, Complete.
TYW_CLNT_ADDR	IBMSNAP_COMMITSEQ	Replication Commit Sequence	Replication control columns used by DataPropagator. Unique identifier for this change; it describes the sequence of a change within a transaction.
TYW_CLNT_ADDR	IBMSNAP_INTENTSEQ	Replication Capture Sequence	Replication control columns used by DataPropagator.
TYW_CLNT_ADDR	IBMSNAP_LOGMARKER	Replication Capture Date And Time	Replication control columns used by DataPropagator. The transaction commit sequencing value.
TYW_CLNT_ADDR	IBMSNAP_OPERATION	Replication Sql Command	Replication control columns used by DataPropagator. The approximate commit time at the source server.
TYW_CLNT_ADDR	PLN_NR	Plan Number	The ID number assigned by Guardian to a group planholder. The plan number is automatically assigned based on the next available sequential number and case type.
TYW_CLNT_ADDR	SRCE_LST_UPDT_DT	Source Last Update Date	The date of the last transaction.
TYW_CLNT_ADDR	VERSION_END_DT	Version End Date	The final date on which this version of the entity was thought to be valid. Terminate the visibility interval.
TYW_CLNT_ADDR	VERSION_STRT_DT	Version Start Date	The date on which the version of this entity was created. Defines the beginning of the visibility interval for the entity.
TYW_CLNT_ADDR	VERSION_STRT_TS	Version Start Timestamp	The timestamping denoting the time and date when this entity was refreshed by external data. Used to establish the precise beginning of the visibility interval.

Internal Web-Based Data Management

When the Internet and associated Web-based searches became a functional part of corporate data management during the latter part of the decade, many efforts that had been attributed to the customized development of internal information directories were now paralleled by a readily available search-and-retrieve mechanism. Based on the power of generic searches with Web browsers, many data management organizations began experimenting with intranet-based solutions, that is, internal Web implementations. With internal intranets as primary locations for data documentation, the available power of the Internet search engines eliminated some of the need to categorize corporate data into standard subject areas, as discussed earlier with internal directories.

Of course, the targets of Web-based searches must *exist* on or be able to be referenced from the Web. As such, many data management organizations began creating data management pages on their internal Web sites, accessible internally throughout the organization. In most cases, these pages introduced data management principles, explained the role of the organization, and presented the growing directory-based inventory of major corporate data. The directory usually pointed the page's visitors to areas in the corporate data world, but did not always give access to the data.

Typical intranet implementations began with a high-level enterprise data model[2] as a means of identifying corporate data categories. Then, depending on the scope of the directory, it ended by displaying a list of the major corporate data stores associated with a selected subject area on the enterprise data model. As data management organizations began experimenting with the strength and power of Internet searches, a whole new type of directory structure unfolded. Populating areas of the Web with corporate data, assigning standard HTML tags, and using XML, made many types of data accessible with the click of a mouse. However, this was a new way of thinking for corporate data management, and new Web-based development methodologies would call for new IT standards.

The Web was never anticipated as a data management vehicle. In fact, many data management specialists criticized the Internet as a technology that could kill an organization's internal data standards by making it easy to obtain data and populate intermittent data stores throughout an end user organization. Yet,

---

[2]Enterprise data models are covered in Chapter 4.

its ease and availability had to be acknowledged, by both the data management organizations and the repository vendors.

At the close of the twentieth century, data management was beginning to avail itself of Web technology. Directories were sporadically and incompletely implemented on corporate intranets. Most considered the initial plunge into Web-based data management searches experimental; many awaited the completion of fully functional Web-based communication standards such as XML; still others simply sat back and watched. But the fact remained that it was innately easy to determine:

- What data do I have (on our intranet)?
- Where is it (what URL)?
- Go get it!

With the click of a mouse and virtually no planning and development (i.e., assigning a Uniform Resource Locator, or URL, to the database application), an organization had an instant directory. It was clear that the Web was bringing the issues of metadata, data standards and reuse, and data accessibility to a new level.

CASE STUDY: Using the Intranet to Provide Metadata Access at a Pharmaceutical Company

In an attempt to make the benefits of data modeling more widely known, the Information Management Services organization at Merck and Company, a major international pharmaceutical firm headquartered in Whitehouse, New Jersey, considered distributing logical data models in such a way that anyone would be able to view them, even without the installed modeling tool. The intranet was becoming more and more suited to this task.

The basis for this effort was a new enterprise data model. This model, viewable as a .pdf file from all workstations in the firm by using the internal web (intranet), served as the initial master directory for accessing any and all models that were registered via a newly created model publication procedure. Eventually, by drilling down from this master directory, a metadirectory of common business terms (approximately 250) became accessible to refine the data model search.

As data models became viewable, the focus of this effort became the distribution of accurate and accessible metadata, with data models as the first focus. Eventually, the same directory was used to make pharmaceutical reference data (or vocabularies) accessible. Most of the interest stemmed from the IT development community.

Design and development of this prototype took approximately three months. Most time after that was spent determining the best model publication process, to make sure that the directory always reflected the most recent rendition of a particular model. All models are accessed through links, in real time. Change control is accomplished via one dedicated individual, responsible for completing model registration and adding each model to the directory by associating new models with the relevant business terms in the directory.

With implementation of this prototype, an enterprise data environment was expected to fall out. However, it has been a very slow process. The implementation was successful, and the directory still gets new customers! Although the usage of this directory is not estimable, the prototype has been well accepted.

Note: This case study was provided by Cynthia Wiggins who works for Merck in Whitehouse Station, NJ. Used with permission from Merck & Co., Inc., Rahway, NJ.

Chapter 6

A Disaster Crying for Solutions

*Our technological powers increase,
but the side effects and potential
hazards also escalate.*
—Alvin Toffler

By the 1990s information was an available asset to anyone with a computer. Unfortunately, information does not always result in the knowledge that someone has been seeking. In many cases, people may be worse off with this information than without it.

Attempts at managing this information have been less than ideal. One area's success is usually contradicted by another area's major mistakes. In the end, we are slightly better off, at best.

Anarchical Data Management

Often, when a resource is considered valuable, organizations create suborganizations responsible for its management. For example, many large corporations have departmental human resource areas, where all aspects of an individual's career (other than salary and benefits) are tracked and managed. The ease with which individuals can get training through such a suborganization, as opposed to a centralized human resource function, is dramatic and often encourages the existence of subareas. On the other hand, attempts to integrate information about an individual's career at the corporation, across many departments, do not always reveal the same amount of detail in the same style and format

---

Note: Quote from Alvin Toffler, *Future Shock* (New York: Bantam Doubleday Dell, 1971).

when all the subcorporate information is gathered in one place. Hence, the perpetuation of anarchical data management.

When data first became valuable, it was clearly an IT resource. The data that was tracked and organized outside of IT was not considered to be of "corporate" value in most situations. Aside from the fact that non-IT data was often tracked manually, it was generally designed, created, and maintained by the benefiting organization. Over time, the people responsible for data management have changed, evolving eventually to IT, and that has had a big impact on how data has been managed by large organizations.

Standard Data Resource Management

In the beginning, data in most organizations was clearly managed via naming standards and data dictionaries. The use of the data was not of concern, nor were the copying and extraction. As data propagated, it was clear that the existing data management standards were not sufficient (see Figure 6-1). Data management then moved into its next historical phase—reactive data management.

Reactive Data Management

As data propagated, the standard management practices could not keep up. Data management organizations saw the need not only to manage data at its inception but also to ensure its integrity and value throughout development and well into the maintenance of post-production applications. The advent of client/server applications made it much easier to bring applications to fruition in their own limited world, and this often included the creation and definition of *new* data. In many cases what was perceived to be new data was just a new version of existing data, or a simple set of derived *information*.

Data reproduced; information was created, Data Management reacted. New policies and procedures were created; the infiltration results were assessed. Abstainers from procedures were eventually discovered and Data Management began introducing new techniques: Enterprise Data Models, Data Stewards, and Corporate Data Definitions. In many cases, data issues were believed to be restricted via the purchase of packaged software at the Enterprise level (ERP Solutions). With standard software, most felt the software's internal data would become "standard." Little did they realize that the term *extract* is as familiar to business users as it is to a dentist.

Data warehousing became a popular means of providing integrated data views to those who needed them most. Metadata became popular, but only from the viewpoint of those using the data warehouse. Eventually data man-

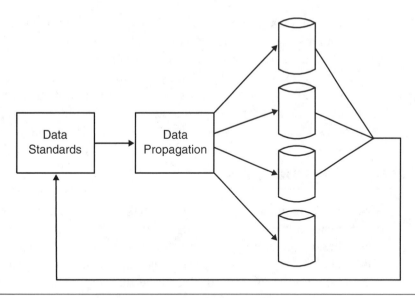

Figure 6-1 Cyclical data management

agement got tired of not being able to catch up—of not being able to manage the data that was fueling warehouses and not being able to control the quality of the "metadata" that was going along with all of this data.

Proactive Data Management

Once data became out of control, two major events occurred in the data management community:

1. Creation of proactive data management practices that would prevent data chaos
2. Entry of newcomers into the data management world, who had never heard of data management but were now unconsciously suffering the repercussions

With *proactive* data management, policies and procedures *affect* the life of data, rather than vice versa. In theory, data is then defined from the point of view of the organization rather than that of a single application, with the intention of having it standardized for the purpose of reuse as opposed to redefinition. Many organizations have embraced this philosophy, yet its implementation has not quite penetrated to the depths for which it was intended.

Today data management exists not only in scattered parts of most IT organizations, but also, because of data's newfound value, outside the IT organization. Each suborganization may or may not have its rules, and the rules may or may not have their impact. Despite all the variations in implementation, data management is still not an exact science as we begin the twenty-first century. Methodologies abound, interpretations of the methodologies abound, and software supporting the methodologies abounds—what better definition of anarchy!

The Data Warehouse Web

Anarchical data management does not make it easy for people who need data or information the most to access and interpret it. So data warehouses began populating the corporate coastline, focusing first on the integration of transaction data (i.e., invoicing and sales transactions) geared toward the analysis of corporate market penetration. Corporate decision makers wanted answers to these questions:

- Who is buying our products?
- Who is not buying our products?
- When are they buying our products?
- Which products are popular?
- Is product popularity based on region? Time of year?

Actual data has more value than market projections do, especially when the data is accurate. Multiple sources, multiple interpretations, multiple definitions . . . and each organization has its own analysis requirements and its own reasons for performing the analysis, perhaps with the same data, perhaps not. Data warehouses became the source of instant gratification, the place to get quick bar and pie charts. Once they were created for one part of an organization, it wasn't long before smaller variations began rampaging the overall organization, many created by the end-user organizations with minimal IT assistance. In fact, many have been renamed "data marts" based on their simplicity and single source.

Multiple data marts and warehouses resulted in an unplanned data warehouse web. These data warehousing webs caused problems not only from the previously discussed data management point of view, but also from the data integration and interpretation angles as well. The exponential increase of "integrated multidimensional data stores" caused a reevaluation of data warehouses:

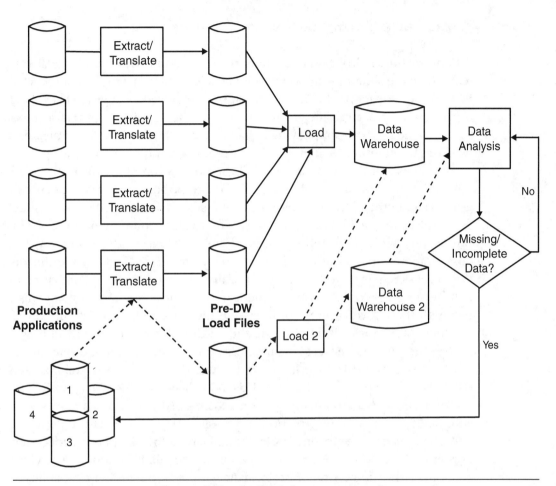

Figure 6-2   **Cyclical data warehousing**

What are they really? Are they the best quick fix for every data-reporting situation? Data managers were forced to revisit their philosophies, which resulted in new concepts. Corporate data staging areas that represented extracted, cleansed, and translated data from many production systems were to be placed in a single location for use and further extraction by those who needed them.

It doesn't take long, as illustrated in Figure 6-2, for a data warehouse web to take hold as more and more sources are combined, resulting in more and more data warehouses, data marts, operational data stores (ODSs), or general reporting databases. But because these data stores are designed for "decision support," they are never as stringently controlled as production data is.

Tools, Tools, and More Tools

Whenever the IT process is not quite what it should be, vendors are always ready with the solution—another tool. The acquisition of a myriad of tools has had a global impact on the data, information, and metadata in virtually every IT organization, both large and small. Seldom was the decision to purchase a tool based on the tool's accompanying metadata. As such, the growth of a metadata web was unintentionally fueled to its current state, and it is still growing!

It makes sense to evaluate a tool based on its functionality. In the early 1980s the "best of breed" philosophy became popular, whereby specific IT groups had permission to acquire their own set of tricks, specifically a distinct set of software development tools, from a particular vendor in most cases. This philosophy actually started the repository bandwagon.[1] Unfortunately, vendors would not be in business if their tools were not distinct . . . and this distinctiveness requires an associated set of distinct information . . . or is it really that distinct? In most cases, one vendor tool's information shares many qualities with the information used, accessed, and created by their competitors' products. What varies is usually *how* the information is processed and how it is correlated with other resident and nonresident vendor tool information.

An easy example is the portrayal of the world of the database administrator (DBA) and the tools he or she uses. This individual is distinctly responsible for the performance of an organization's databases, many of which are very large and vital to corporate information processing. Depending on the deployed DBMS and platform/operating system combination, specific performance monitoring tools are available, in many cases from the DBMS vendors themselves. Aside from the monitoring of performance, there is tool-resident capability to modify the underlying database structure. In even the best of scenarios, these modifications are typically not shared with anything other than the DBA tool itself. So, in the best of worlds, a logical data model may have originated from a modeling or CASE tool, and the connections between these business-level definitions may have been created when the physical database was created. But that is usually the extent of business-implementation connection. Once the database becomes part of a production world, DBA organizations are typically responsible for its fine tuning. If that means the definition of new keys, new

---

1. IBM began the early repository movement with AD/Cycle in an attempt to integrate information from major CASE tool vendors.

indices, new database structures, or even entirely new databases, those actions are well within their responsibilities; vendor tools that also monitor the associated performance typically also perform associated changes.

In most organizations, these changes are not "backtracked" to any other tool or repository. So the best organization's intentions are squashed once the DBA, or any other group, acquires its own set of vendor software with its own database documentation.

Likewise, the frustration of the business user community has led vendors to pursue the largest area of growth in recent years—that of decision support tools. Most of this growth is based on the recent ability of users to obtain, decipher, and store data for the purposes of marketing-based analysis with or without a data warehouse. Now people outside of IT can obtain data (downloading, extracting, consolidating, or creating for perhaps the *n*th time) and create more information. And as more information gets created, the data and information web propagates, without organization or overview, often to the point of no return.

Tools are perhaps an immediate solution to immediate problems, yet they have a profound tendency to create more of the problems that they were originally marketed to solve, such as the following:

Can't get to your data? Don't worry, Tool X can download it at the click of a mouse, and Tool Y can extract it from virtually any type of database. All you need to do is make sure you have permission to read it (which most users do).

Can't organize your data into a decent database structure? Don't worry; you don't have to do that anymore. Decision support tools assume a standard STAR Schema design, and most can load the data for you into a predefined set of facts and dimensions. All you have to do is tell the tool where to go to get the stuff.

Don't understand the difference between your new data and its original source? Don't worry; every one of these tools has a metadata repository, a place for you to store the definitions that you finally decipher, so that from now on no one will ever question the reports that result from this new tool.

Maybe metadata is the solution to these problems. *Metadata* has become the buzzword since the year 2000, and it with all its supporting functions has become a specialty with a required role on most data warehousing teams.

Metadata: The Silver Bullet

We can understand why virtually every reporting tool comes with a disclaimer that relates to the vendors' lack of liability due to improper analysis and data-based conclusions. IT people usually "plead the fifth" and blame improper conclusions on the "lack of proper metadata." Whose job is it to create this stuff to begin with? What exactly is it?

Metadata is often defined as the "data about the data" and most organizations perceive it to represent descriptive information (element names, definitions, lengths, etc.) about the populated data fields. In fact, metadata is much more, and the choice of items actually described and detailed is up to the responsible metadata specialist. True metadata involves not only the descriptive information pertinent to the *users* of the items in question, but also the generation, maintenance, and display of the items by tools, applications, other repositories, and the users. Unfortunately, very few of today's metadata deliverables consider this bigger picture. And the bigger picture must permit each tool, application, piece of software, and individual who touches a piece of data to answer the 5 Questions:[2]

1. What data do I have?
2. What does it mean?
3. Where is it?
4. How did it get there?
5. How do I get it?

Remember that *data is useless without metadata*. Most members of the user community are well aware of this fact, but are not aware that their *individual metadata solutions are now making metadata just as useless as the described data*.

The Metadata Web

Metadata, metadata everywhere, and not a drop has meaning. Narrowly focused solutions have caused major organizations to have so much metadata that much of it has to be scrapped and redefined. In a typical data warehouse

---

2. The 5 Questions is a trademark of and the questions and method are copyrighted by Database Solutions, Inc., Bernardsville, New Jersey.

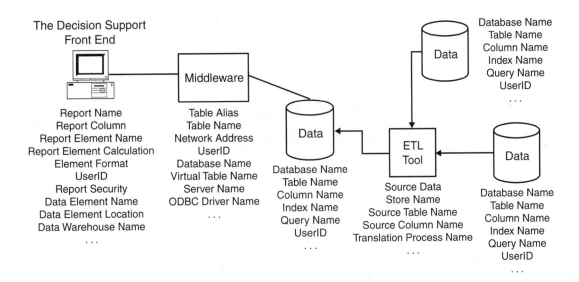

The Decision Support
Front End

Middleware

Report Name
Report Column
Report Element Name
Report Element Calculation
Element Format
UserID
Report Security
Data Element Name
Data Element Location
Data Warehouse Name
. . .

Table Alias
Table Name
Network Address
UserID
Database Name
Virtual Table Name
Server Name
ODBC Driver Name
. . .

Data

Database Name
Table Name
Column Name
Index Name
Query Name
UserID
. . .

Data

ETL
Tool

Source Data
Store Name
Source Table Name
Source Column Name
Translation Process Name
. . .

Data

Database Name
Table Name
Column Name
Index Name
Query Name
UserID
. . .

Data

Database Name
Table Name
Column Name
Index Name
Query Name
UserID
. . .

Figure 6-3   **A sample metadata web**

architecture, for example, virtually all architectural components contain their own processing-specific metadata (see Figure 6-3), and few of the individual instances can be related generically to the metadata in the other warehouse components. The result is a complicated metadata web, with virtually no official starting point.

To avoid the disasters described in this chapter, the best approach to data management is to consider the current state of your data and metadata environments. Would it be better to add strings to an existing metadata web, or to plan, design, and implement a true *metadata solution*? The difference between isolated metadata stores and a true metadata solution rests with an understanding that there is a difference.

Regardless of the planned scope of your metadata solution, it is crucial that you view each possible solution in its larger corporate environment. Continue to discover what metadata really is, why metadata is created, and how you can leverage that which you already have.

Part II

Metadata as Part of the Solution

We should realize how most organizations got into a state of metadata madness. It is great that so many managers realize the importance of metadata, but it is unfortunate that almost as many are forced to implement metadata solutions without realizing the repercussions of improper approaches.

This part begins the in-depth discussion of metadata—what it is, where it comes from, and why it is important to approach it with the same philosophy that we use to approach data integration. In other words, metadata itself is not only a part of the data management solution but also of the metadata solution, for that matter.

We begin Part II by discussing metadata's relationship to data and information and the ultimate transition to knowledge. We then discuss the process of analyzing metadata requirements and ways to organize metadata into distinct *metamodels*. Finally, this part ends by briefly introducing the rest of the metadata solution—how all the tools and metadata storage areas must fit into the architecture of a metadata solution. Of course, this architecture will unfold throughout the book's subsequent parts.

Chapter 7

Moving from Information to Metadata

Regardless of one's profession, the ability to thrive is based on the ability to access, interpret, conclude, and generate information. In some cases, human lives depend on our information-generation capabilities; in others, split-second business decisions rest upon the world of information.

In Part I we clarified the differences between data and information. Because metadata has so many perspectives, it is essential to clarify where metadata comes from and what its general role is expected to be. To do that, we have to take our information discussion one step further and relate it to *knowledge*.

Much ado has surrounded the question of the differences between information and knowledge. In the world of IT, the "knowledge factor" has become a subprofession. There are specialties surrounding:

- *Expert systems*—applications that capture rules, both preceding and concluding, to arrive at results based on a set of conditions.
- *Business rules*—the practice of capturing and relating the above rules, so that from a newcomer's viewpoint, all undocumented facts surrounding a business or business process are accessible and help explain the processing within an existing application
- *Object oriented and management*—the methodology of combining processes and associated data categories to ensure standard and reusable action/result combinations.

Why is each of these areas considered a specialty? Each specialty has affected the IT profession in its own positive way, but the fact that they remain specialties is a bit disconcerting. Consider the fact that the documentation requirements vary, then consider the fact that when we evaluate the effect of each of these specialties on the businesses at hand, many of us may have seen little to no embracing impact outside the IT area. Yet because knowledge and information are so often confused, the first prerequisite to moving forward with metadata is a detailed understanding of information as it compares to knowledge.

Comparing Information to Knowledge

Ironically, most definitions of information, outside the IT world, contain the word *knowledge*. As far back as the early Greek and Roman classics, definitions such as the following were common:

❖ **Information** Something told; knowledge, items of knowledge; news.[1]

As information technology (IT) was born and began to evolve, it became common to separate the terms *knowledge* and *information*. Those little ones and zeroes that we process were clearly only *data*, applications processed them into *information*, and the business users converted the information into *knowledge*. But the ingredients that get us from data to knowledge are not always readily identifiable and usually serve as second fiddle to the knowledge itself.

There is an evolving hierarchy to the definition of knowledge. Within IT, most of this evolution, as Figure 7-1 depicts, as well as the differences between each succeeding phase, plays a major role in the practicality of most metadata solutions. Outside IT, many people have forgotten how they got where they are and when they crossed the line from information to knowledge. Remember the various phases as distinct eras in our general accumulation of information:

1. *The creation of characters without context.* Initially characters were created manually, using typewriters and eventually computers. Individual num-

---

1. *The Oxford Dictionary and Thesaurus* (New York: Oxford University Press, 1996), p. 765.

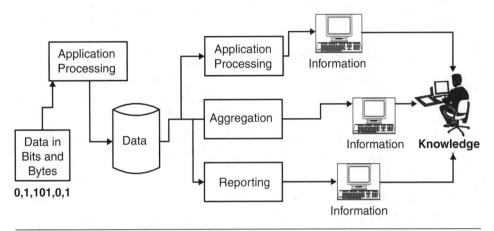

Figure 7-1 From data to knowledge

bers and letters, regardless of language or penmanship style, had no meaning of their own.

2. *The identification of character context.* Before characters take on meaning, a contextual framework is created for the purpose of communication and interpretation. *Context* determines how these characters should be grouped and for what reasons. Initially, usage formed various languages, with continual evolution creating contextual requirements and rules. Using the English language as an example, *context* created words and sentences. Upon formalization of language specifics, areas of study and research, both technical and nontechnical, then created specialty areas (e.g., science and mathematics), each specialty with its own contextual words and framework, typically in support of, but in many cases in addition to, the base language context.

3. *Specialty contexts permeate across languages.* As specialties and areas of study became formalized, the concept of *translation* allowed people to share specialties across cultures, countries, and other context-specific distinctions.

4. *Context becomes information.* Specialties continue, each with a basic backbone of facts and discoveries. Languages all have underlying grammar, rules, and syntax. We assimilate these facets of our context, and the result is *information*.

This evolution provides an important perspective when considering information and its role within the world in which we function.

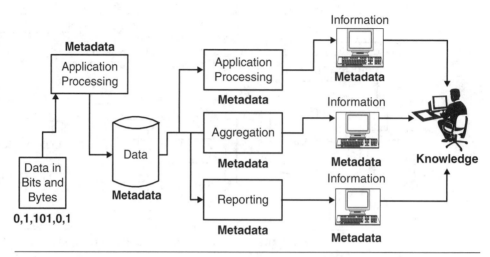

Figure 7-2   **The addition of metadata to the evolution of knowledge**

It is important to realize that named specialties determine the context of information. These specialties were originally scientific and mathematical, but in the IT world have almost become application- and database-specific. To re-evaluate the definition of *information* based on today's web of contextual specialties, a practical viewpoint puts the following boundaries on a definition:

❖ **Information**   A combined set of character group instances, typically collected into a predefined context that when processed in a specific specialty creates a fact and/or statement of discovery.

If we separate information from knowledge we are assuming the specialty processing to be inaccurate or inaccessible at first glance. In other words, we don't trust the specialties or the way they define the information, or we at least question them, based on our resident *knowledge*. This is exactly where we begin to see the value of *metadata*. But metadata's role and content depend on its location on the "knowledge timeline." (See Figure 7-2.)

Defining *Metadata*

What a mess! In many cases, people cannot agree on the value of information (as a literal instance or within a figurative context), and now we are fighting and misinterpreting *metadata*. One definition that is never questioned or doubted, however, is the following:

> ❖ **Misinterpreted metadata** Data about data.

The Greek term *meta*, literally translated to mean "about," is an easy stop-gap to any misunderstanding or misuse of the term *metadata*. But even this definition has flaws, because "about" is defined in several contexts, most of them subject to the interpretation of the audience that is questioning the data. So because metadata appears everywhere on the data-to-knowledge time line, the clarification of what is being described requires a reclarification of *data*.

Redefining *Instance Data*

Most people think of data as pure numbers, that is, the values displayed on a report, application screen, or other type of generated, calculated result. To most people, "data" can be used to generate other "data," hence the terms *inputs* and *outputs*. But even the most flexible interpretation considers data a raw element in need of processing, either via application programs or applied knowledge. This need to be processed is a crucial aspect of metadata's role, and one that is usually forgotten when most metadata is established. Considering the fact that the ultimate objective is not metadata, but a metadata solution, it is important to widen our perspectives.

Preprocessed data is almost guaranteed pure. In fact, the same data could result in several different outputs depending on the type of processing and whether other data was used or referenced *during* the processing. *Data* is really too generic a term; it should be renamed *instance data*, defined as follows:

> ❖ **Instance data** That which is input into a receiving tool, application, database, or simple processing engine.

The accuracy of metadata depends on an accurate definition of instance data. Notice in its definition that *instance data* no longer includes just the numbers printed on a report, or stored in a database. The intermediate processes also use and define, create, or generate this instance data, or the stepping-stones to seeing the instance data. Hence, *what is data to some is metadata to others*.

Employee SS#: 187-33-0595
Employee Name: Mark Merriman
Employee Start Date: 03-09-62
Department Code: 411
Payroll Code: 14B

Data or
Metadata?

Table Name: EMPLOYEE

EMPLOYEE_SSNO,	X(9)	**Primary Key**
EMPLOYEE_LAST_NAME,	X(20)	**Index**
EMPLOYEE_FIRST_NAME,	X(15)	
EMPLOYEE_DEPT_CODE,	X(3)	**Foreign Key**
EMPLOYEE_PAY_CODE,	X(3)	**Foreign Key**

Table Name: DEPARTMENT

DEPT_CODE,	X(3)	**Primary Key**
DEPT_NAME,	X(15)	
PAYROLL_CODE,	X(3)	**Foreign Key**

Figure 7-3   *The confusion of data and metadata*

The type of instance data being evaluated and/or described determines the value and types of the associated metadata and the remaining perspectives. For example, as Figure 7-3 illustrates, most would question whether items such as *Table Names* and *Primary Keys* indices are data or metadata. Most people think of the data as the values that are underlined. But database administrators are more inclined to disregard the underlined values, and focus on the labels of those items, as defined in the respective database management system and/or application. The DBA's metadata would be the information *about* those labels.

Some of us may already be aware of the confusion between data and metadata. Our metadata solutions reflect an integration of the various perspectives that must be satisfied. In most situations, there is no clear distinction between data and metadata. Therefore, the people responsible for maintaining these solutions are responsible for understanding the means in which all metadata instances relate to the simple instance data, which is often processes apart.

Clarifying Metadata

The value of metadata depends on a wholly accurate perspective of instance data in the context of the already presented 5 Questions:[2]

---

2. The 5 Questions is a trademark of and the questions and method are copyrighted by Database Design Solutions, Inc., Bernardsville, New Jersey.

1. What data do we have?
2. What does it mean?
3. Where is it?
4. How did it get there?
5. How do I get it?

These questions are the best eye openers to the reasons that most of yesterday's and today's metadata was and is too narrowly focused . . . because the instance data that was being described was representative of one specific scope in a larger world, *irrespective of the fact that the metadata in combination was not!*

So, if we adopt the philosophy that instance data is that which is input into a variety of receiving buckets, many of them used almost exclusively by application developers or by end-user data analysts, a flexible definition of metadata is:

❖ **Metadata**   The detailed description of the instance data; the format and characteristics of populated instance data; instances and values dependent on the role of the metadata recipient.

Metadata solutions of yesterday attempted to put all perspectives in one bucket, describe them from a point of view that could be handled by a sole individual, and relate them to whatever the main focus of the particular metadata store was, which in many cases was the end-user analysis of warehoused data.

Today's metadata solutions recognize various perspectives as well as the need to address their requirements differently. But more important, they also recognize that today's as well as yesterday's instance data is already described with the metadata terms of all of these perspectives. The missing piece is the logical connection between perspectives via organized metadata solutions. The process begins with the first and simplest relationship.

Relating Information to Metadata

What keeps information from fulfilling its potential as a resource? According to our 5 Questions, instance data needs to be

1. identified,
2. defined,

3. located,

4. sourced, and

5. accessed.

With metadata hype expanding daily, most metadata emphasizes the second and fourth listed items—definition and sourcing. Ignoring the others assumes prerequisite knowledge. Consider this simple example.

> A data warehouse is built and as part of the overall delivery a set of metadata is defined and made available. An initial set of users worked hand-in-hand with the data warehouse developers to identify reporting requirements and to help interpret much of the source data, many years' of which was undocumented. Finally, the warehouse was ready, and a solid set of metadata accompanied its production release.
>
> The IT people were enthusiastic about this new way of developing applications, and decided to require metadata with all new application deliveries. The data warehouse metadata set was used as a basis for development and enhancement of other applications. It seemed that, with this new philosophy and metadata system, requests for specific reports could only lessen.
>
> Metadata was populated and included the following key instances, all focusing on the warehouse elements:
>
> - Data Element Name
> - Data Element Definition
> - Data Element Source (application name)
> - Data Element Translation Rules

Usage of the data warehouse never expanded beyond its initial beneficiaries, even with the defined metadata and its maintained accuracy. The data warehouse team went on a public relations mission and was surprised to learn that most of the end-user community had no idea that the warehouse existed, and was in fact maintaining standalone databases with almost identical data.

What was the basic quality that was missing from the simple set of metadata in the example's data warehouse? *Identification*. But, isn't Data Element Name supposed to take care of that? Of course, but how does a potential data warehouse user know that this metadata exists? *How is the metadata identified?* If identified via word of mouth, then take the question one more step and ask, How does a potential data warehouse user know how to access the warehoused metadata and relate it to the warehoused instance data? As we will see throughout this book, the 5 Questions also relate to metadata. But the connection depends on the information being described.

Unless metadata is tied directly to its defined information, chances are great that you are creating yet another metadata store, for yet another isolated purpose. Remember the five roles that all metadata must play, and remember that it must be an almost invisible effort to obtain the metadata that describes the instance data of interest. In other words, not only must we be able to use metadata to identify and locate the *instance data*, but we must also be able to have our *metadata* easily identified and located!

You can now see why centralized metadata stores started becoming obsolete with the popularity of the Internet. Search and you will find! *Where can I find customer data? Where can I find data warehouses in my firm?* The possibilities are endless as long as the infrastructure and metadata (all five types!) are in place.

Metadata Perspectives and Beneficiaries

The type of instance data is a direct indication of a specific perspective. Likewise, perspectives are associated with metadata customers, or types of *beneficiaries*. It is important to realize that metadata beneficiaries are not always people. Most metadata solution architects, in the past, did not consider this fact and created metadata solutions that did not account for metadata suppliers, users, and recipients that were not direct user interfaces.

Consider the fact that a metadata beneficiary *uses* metadata. Although we will clarify the types of usage in the next chapter as we delve deeper into the identification of these beneficiaries, it is important to realize that metadata is used by:

- People
- Tools (all types!)
- Applications (custom developed as well as purchased packages)
- Metadata stores (often called repositories)

The number of beneficiary types is a factor that is trimmed or expanded by scoping an entire solution,[3] and a very important aspect of every metadata

---

3. Solution scoping is discussed in Chapter 11.

solution. It is important at this early stage of metadata definition to keep metadata perspectives related to the various types of instance data that beneficiaries might deal with:

- Raw numeric data
- Raw textual data
- Documents
- Reports
- Program code
- Application definition
- Database contents
- Database definition
- Data models
- Process models
- Object models
- HTML
- XML tags
- Business rules
- And so on (yes, the list is almost endless!)

Why Metadata?

Is there a need to justify the cost of a metadata solution? If so, it is clear that the organization's metadata beneficiaries misunderstand the significance and role that good metadata plays in daily decision making. The role includes:

- *Locating information.* How much time is spent looking for things? How often are the things not found? What poor decisions have been made based on incomplete information? How much money was lost (or not earned) as a result?

- *Interpreting information.* How many times have businesses needed to rework or recall products? What impact does this have on the bottom line? How many of these mistakes were due to the misinterpretation of existing documentation? How much of this information interpretation is based on incomplete or inaccurate metadata? How much interpretation results from too much metadata? How much time is spent trying to determine if any of the metadata is accurate?

■ *Integrating data.* When we put data together for new analysis objectives, we often have no clear indication as to how the various data perspectives connect. How much time do we spend trying to figure that out? Do we make the results available for other data integrators? How much do this inefficiency and the lack of metadata affect project time lines?

Data without metadata results in blind decision making. Arbitrary creation of metadata results in too much metadata, none of which represents the actual detailed story.

As we conclude this chapter, realize again that metadata's roles *do not* vary from perspective to perspective. Realize again that the *definition* of instance data *does not* vary from perspective to perspective. It should be obvious at this point then that the *values* of both instance data and the associated metadata can and do vary across beneficiary categories. Everyone in an organization has a need for metadata, and everyone in an organization uses instance data daily. How well these two are connected in support of each individual's role and requirements determines whether you are pursuing a solid metadata solution, or just an isolated metadata database.

This chapter should have opened your eyes to the variations in *metadata requirements,* which depend on where in the data-to-knowledge evolution the metadata will be used. Requirement similarities could also result in differences in *metadata values*, for the same reason.

Metadata beneficiaries represent the solution's customers. Not all beneficiaries want or need the metadata that you are targeting. In today's IT world we are surrounded by metadata webs galore. It is not essential that all metadata be in one place, but it is essential that each metadata perspective be solidified and organized. Metadata beneficiaries are the identified result. The process of getting from one to the other is called identifying metadata requirements, which is described next.

Chapter 8

Identifying Metadata Requirements

Perhaps one of the biggest shortfalls to metadata implementations has been the lack of good planning. The planning process consists of many stages, beginning with requirements gathering. Many of you may be familiar with this process from an application or database perspective. If so, you may have interviewed users, developed flowcharts, documented data and process requirements, and delivered initial models.

The world of metadata differs from the application world in many respects. Probably the first and most important difference is the end-user base. Traditional application and database development is geared to serve the individual. Individuals may be categorized and grouped, often by job function, but their needs share commonality, specifically in terms of how and where application inputs and outputs are delivered. Next, as we mentioned in the preceding chapter, metadata for the most part already exists; that is, the inputs and outputs are created and delivered to nonhuman intermediaries in most cases, many of which eventually provide or receive metadata to and from a metadata repository of sorts. These two reasons alone justify the need for a metadata-specific approach to requirements.

In this chapter we begin the formal metadata requirements process. The methodical process involves several steps, each of which is covered in detail beginning in this chapter. Note that this requirements process is required for implementation of virtually all metadata solutions, whether they be standalone metadata stores or full-fledged enterprise implementations. As the upcoming book sections will uncover, requirements can usually be fulfilled by more than one type of metadata solution. Typically, issues beyond the metadata requirements are weighed to select the appropriate implementation.

The Overall Metadata Requirements Process

Determining the appropriate metadata solution begins with a methodical requirements process. The general steps are as follows:

1. *Identify metadata beneficiaries.* In this step, all potential users and/or suppliers of metadata are identified. Remember, of course, that beneficiaries can be individuals (users), tools, applications, or metadata repositories.

2. *List metadata requirements by beneficiary.* Here we begin true requirements analysis because the metadata instances are organized by identified beneficiary or beneficiary category.

3. *Determine the source of metadata.* By determining the source of each identified metadata requirement, the "metadata of record" can often be named. More requirements issues are typically identified during this step, and they are typically finalized during the scoping and clarification of the metadata solution technical environment.

4. *Plan preliminary architecture and scope of metadata.* Based on the results of preceding steps, a box is drawn around the metadata to be included in the initial metadata solution. The preliminary "box" will be finalized during clarification of the technical environment.

5. *Recategorize metadata.* Refining metadata requirements to include usage categories based on demand by beneficiary category helps to categorize all identified metadata as *specific, unique*, or *common*. This categorization begins the *metamodeling* process.

6. *Build a metamodel.* Organizing the identified and categorized metadata forms the basis for the underlying metadata stores. This process, similar to data modeling, will relate to the full metadata solution architecture and help determine where the metadata should be stored.

7. *Consider access and display of metadata.* Based on confirmed metadata and beneficiary categories, as well as the identified architectural components in the overall metadata solution, this phase determines how metadata will be accessed (CRUD = Create, Read, Update, Delete), how it will stay in sync (if distributed or multiple metadata stores are planned), and what custom interfaces/display mechanisms will be necessary.

8. *Anticipate metadata processing.* At this point in the process, the type of solution determines the remaining requirements diversions. (A *requirements diversion* is my term for anything that was not thought of or considered at the beginning, but now becomes important because of nonhuman metadata processing.) Metadata-specific processing is evaluated and architectural customization at the meta-meta[1] level is specified as needed. If a repository is planned, meta-metamodels are evaluated for extensibility. If Web-based solutions are planned, standardized tags and exchange requirements are unraveled in this phase. If customized solutions are planned, process flows and requirements are finalized. If packaged solutions are being considered, their available metamodel component–based processing is evaluated against specific requirements.

9. *Consider nonmetadata requirements.* Finally, the other features, none of which plays second fiddle to metadata, are evaluated and specified. At this point the solution is officially scoped. Tools in the environment are evaluated in terms of their roles, if any. The full architecture is confirmed and all display, access, and processing of metadata is revisited. Repository administration, technical support, and the role of the new metadata solution in the development and end-user environments are finalized.

This chapter discusses the first three steps in the process.

Identifying Metadata Beneficiaries

You must know who your customers are. The problem, however, is the usual assumption that customers are human beings. With metadata, we have to consider the software side of the world as a customer. In fact, most human customers see and deal with metadata through some sort of software interface—an existing development or reporting tool, one developed as part of the metadata solution, or one of many Internet browsers. *Very rarely does an individual look directly at the metadata as it is known to (i.e., stored and labeled in) the metadata solution.*

---

1. Meta-meta processing is discussed in Part III.

People

We always begin with the source of our requirements—*people*. Getting started can be both the hardest and the simplest part of the overall metadata requirements process. Many failed metadata solutions began with a selected implementation (e.g., a particular repository product) and then tried to retrofit metadata requirements based on the capabilities of the selected solution. This is similar to being talked into needing a sunroof on an automobile you are about to purchase, no offense to our car dealers. Likewise, with off-the-shelf metadata solutions, people often change their "requirements" to meet the capabilities of the purchased tool, in most cases, settling for a tool that is not exactly what was wanted.

Begin by asking what metadata issue is in dire need of resolution. The answer to this very simple question gives a good indication of where we are on the metadata maturity scale. In fact, because our to-be-labeled beneficiaries are not sure what true metadata is (because of the commercial hype that has surrounded its definition), it is often easier to answer the question if it is posed in terms of a data issue (if data is the problem) or an issue surrounding another named element. For example:

- What is the biggest problem surrounding your customer data inaccuracy? (Do not put words in people's mouths. This should have been identified or presented as a problem; you are asking for expansion or clarification of it.)
- What area do you feel would benefit most from the use of standardized development processes?
- Why are sales reports not receiving the appropriate seal of credibility?
- Why do you feel Y2K was such an eye-opener in this IT department?
- Why have so many attempts to incorporate standardized development methodologies failed at this company?
- What is the biggest issue that new employees face when it comes to locating corporate data?
- Do your data models ever get referenced?
- Why are there so many "employee databases" in this organization?

The list could be endless, but these kinds of questions will begin discussions of *metadata*. A well-trained analyst, JAD (Joint Application Development) session leader, or experienced metamodeler[2] is able to target questions and to elicit answers that lead the group to discussing true *metadata requirements*. At this stage in the process, it is not so important to capture these requirements exactly, but instead to obtain an accurate perception of where requirements come from (e.g., Does everyone in Sales have the same set of requirements?), and why these requirements exist.

For example, suppose that your initial set of potential metadata beneficiaries was asked this question:

Why are your product introduction dates always criticized for being too late?

In an actual meeting, the audience—marketing professionals, IT developers and project managers in support of marketing, product research, and select sales professionals—answered with some of these responses:

SALES   By the time we find out that a product is due to be introduced, our competitors already have it on a "special offer."

IT DEVELOPERS   We don't even get the new product codes and descriptions from Marketing until the product has already been sold and ordered for an entire month. How do you expect us to develop Web-based B-to-B transaction processing?

IT PROJECT MANAGER   It's the same problem we always have—our systems don't talk to each other.

PRODUCT RESEARCH   We aren't the ones who come up with the new product codes—that is done in Marketing.

MARKETING   We have our own internal processes for naming and standardizing new products. Right now, we cannot release these new codes and descriptions until they have been approved by Legal . . . and we all know how slowly they operate. I suspect all of this is going to change once our e-commerce strategy gets finalized.

Do any of these responses identify metadata requirements? Not really. But a quick response from the analyst might be something like this:

ANALYST   So are you all saying that the problem is the lack of an **accessible** product code master? Don't we already have one of those? Whose **responsibility** is it to keep it **up to date** and guarantee its accessibility?

---

2. Metamodels, metamodelers, and the entire process are discussed in Chapter 11.

The bold words begin a sway toward metadata. Note that we have not even brought the word *metadata* into the discussion yet, but we are already looking at the beginnings of our 5 Questions[3] and their associated metadata components. Let's continue with answers to this metadata-targeted question:

MARKETING   The problem is we have too many of those product masters, at least in Marketing!

IT DEVELOPERS   Yes, the Product Master is at least four months behind Product Research. If we could at least get a code while the product name was being reviewed by Legal, our systems would be right on board!

IT PROJECT MANAGER   The DBMS that we have now selected as a standard is not what the Product Master is implemented in.

MARKETING   So what?

IT PROJECT MANAGER   We are the ones who have to implement new systems using the standard DBMS, but no one ever wants to convert the old but very important files, like the Product Master.

At this point, and not before, metadata can be introduced. The standard question is:

ANALYST   Is this a data issue or a metadata issue?

And the standard answer is:

EVERYONE   Both!

In the illustrated example, there are issues with product data itself as well as the availability, definition, and release of this data. During this simple meeting, the following metadata beneficiaries were identified:

- *Developers* interested in the accessibility of new codes and a way to know when they are official.

- *IT project managers* interested in the new codes also, and in the "conversion" specifics that relate to the standard DBMS, most likely "access metadata."

- *End users*—From a metadata perspective, at this point Marketing, Sales, and Product Research may have the same requirements. It is unclear how the various Product Masters fit together, if at all, or whether their

---

3. The 5 Questions is a trademark of and the questions and method are copyrighted by Database Design Solutions, Inc., Bernardsville, New Jersey.

separate existence is a necessary fact to be noted. These issues will come up during the formal metadata requirements gathering sessions.

Tools

There are probably other beneficiary categories to be determined, most of which are software packages, tools, or other users of the metadata that was alluded to. To determine these metadata beneficiary categories, the analyst's questions would have to continue, as follows:

- Does Marketing use any applications to track the status of product codes and the rollout of the official descriptions? Who developed them? Why do you have so many Product Masters?
- Is a DBA (Database Administrator) working with IT project managers to convert existing data to the new DBMS? Has the Product Master been considered? Why or why not? Whom should I follow up with?
- Isn't Marketing working on an E-business strategy that will allow us to take direct orders on the Web for products that are not actually developed here?
- Are there applications, packages, or tools in use in Product Research or Sales that affect the accessibility of product information to other organizations?

Follow-up meetings with the following groups are justified:

- Product Research, Sales, Marketing to discuss tools and applications, focusing on product codes
- Database Administration to discuss DBMS standards and legacy conversions

The results of these meetings will begin the process of identifying metadata beneficiaries. Note that this is only a start. Before the identification of the beneficiaries can be final, we must confirm the actual metadata requirements; the full metadata solution architecture in terms of tools, applications, and packages that will contain, supply, or access metadata; and the role fulfilled by each type of metadata in the specific architectural component. Continuing with our example, a likely list of metadata beneficiaries is:

- Developers
- IT project managers
- End users
- DBMS catalog

Don't worry at this point if you are unclear as to how certain beneficiaries ended up on the list. The list assumes knowledge of database definition and the use of physical database metadata (table names, column names, characteristics, etc.) by database accessing tools. More of this will unravel as we get into a detailed definition of requirements in the metadata technical environment.

Metadata by Beneficiary

Once a preliminary list of beneficiary categories compiles, it is essential to identify metadata requirements, typically at the metadata element level, for each category. Usually at this stage the specifics of metadata are introduced in order to put all players at the same level of understanding.

Most identified user groups will consider metadata simply at the level of defining and naming data elements. Because data warehousing has put redundant and inconsistent metadata into a wider corporate audience, data-warehousing metadata is the most demanded and the most valuable. In most situations, if initially the user communities are asked a simple question such as, What type of metadata do you need? you can be assured that their responses will focus on:

- Data Element Business Name (as opposed to physical implemented name)
- Data Element Definition
- Data Element Source/Calculation

A brief (15-minute) overview of metadata, its value, and its source(s) in the organization will put everyone on the same page and open eyes up to metadata requirements that go beyond data definition. Focus on the fact that effective metadata ensures that data can be located, identified, sourced, defined, and accessed. Explain that depending on the various perspectives of the individuals in each group, the means by which we accomplish these five tasks can and do vary. Explain that tools almost always play a part in these processes, but that for now we are set on identifying their particular needs and requirements in terms of metadata. Based on this expanded focus, metadata requirements are guaranteed to expand. It may be necessary for an experienced Metadata Requirements Analyst to focus discussions, as shown in the following example.

If you were able to have instant access to the metadata that you identified (i.e., data warehouse metadata), would that solve all your current
information interpretation problems? What would happen if you came
across more than one piece of information (data element) with the same
business name? How would you distinguish one from the other? Would
the name of the *source* be enough? What values should be used in
naming sources? Should there be a standard set?

From *where* would you need to be able to access this metadata?
How should the metadata be *identified?*

What if the *calculation references* fields or elements that you do not
have *definitions* for?

Is it ever important to know *where* else these business elements are
used or *referenced?*

Do you need a *point of contact* for each data element? What would
you use this person for?

Are there *process-related definitions* or characteristics that might also
help? When would you need them? Can you give me an example? Is it
valuable to know what *programs create* this business element and
under what *condition?* Do you need to know *when* the business element was *initially created and if it has been copied?*

Questions can vary by audience. The preceding set of questions assumes
an end-user base, and it should not be considered all encompassing. A quick
rule of thumb would be to consider the individual's function as it relates to the
particular information used to accomplish the desired results:

- How is the information located?

- How is the information named? When? Does the name make business
  sense?

- How was that information created? When? Why?

- How will the individual access the information? Will accessing the
  information require technical skills and/or know-how? Will a tool be
  involved? Sometimes or always?

Depending on the type of information, its availability and accuracy in the
organization, and the security that surrounds its distribution and accessibility,
different user groups could be addressed initially or referenced eventually.

Continuing our example, we are simply listing metadata requirements by beneficiary category at this point. Remember our initially defined beneficiary categories:

- Developers
- IT project managers
- End users
- DBMS catalog

Consider the initial stabs, from each group, at their metadata requirements, based on the identified problems surrounding the timely distribution of new product codes. More important, consider the fact that virtually no one addressed metadata requirements for Internet-based transactions, a near-future technology switchover in this firm. This is just food for thought at this point, but important to consider in the overall scoping of the result.

Based on the information obtained from initial and follow-up discussions, evaluations of tools used on a routine basis in each beneficiary category, and an initial assessment of what is planned, metadata requirements were identified by beneficiary category (see Table 8-1). The metadata elements are listed according to the nomenclature used by each beneficiary category. Where appropriate, additional names based on the terminology deployed by that beneficiary category are included in parentheses.

Notice that the metadata requirements in Table 8-1 seem to focus primarily on data and its characteristics. Remember that we are still in preliminary stages of requirements definition, and in the next stage another dimension of metadata will unfold.

Metadata Sourcing

After preliminary metadata requirements have been identified by beneficiary category, it is time to figure out where this metadata is coming from. Consider the impact existing metadata webs can have on this effort. During this phase of metadata requirements definition, I cannot stress enough how damaging tunnel vision can be.

The source of metadata elements can be as near-sighted as the individual beneficiary category or as far-sighted as the metadata creating application's data definition components. In most situations, the actual source is somewhere in the middle of this metadata flow. Very rarely is there only *one* potential source,

Table 8-1 Metadata Requirements by Beneficiary Category

Developers	IT Project Managers	End Users	DBMS Catalog
Data Element Business Name	Data Element Business Name	Data Element Business Name	Data Element Business Name
Data Element Physical Name	Data Element Physical Name		Data Element Physical Name (Column Name)
Table Name		(Data Element Location)	Table Name
Database Name	Database Name		Database Name
Data Element Definition	Data Element Definition	Data Element Definition	Data Element Definition
Data Element Type			Data Element Type
Data Element Domain		Data Element Value Set	
			DBMS Version
DBMS API Name			DBMS API Name
Source Data Element Name	Source Data Element Name	Source Data Element Name	Source Data Element Name
Source File Name	Source File Name		Source File Name
Source File Type			Source File Type
Source Application Name	Source Application Name	Source Application Name	Source Application Name
Data Element Derivation Rules	Data Element Derivation Rules	Data Element Derivation Rules	
			Table Primary Key
			Table Alternate Index

hence the need to identify a "metadata of record" for each metadata requirement that has multiple source possibilities. In fact, we are now answering the third of the five questions that form the 5 Questions' methodology—Where is it?

Consider where the most accurate metadata source exists, if at all, and consider what perspective is represented by its instances. This often cannot be determined without looking at the metadata instances themselves. It is often necessary to draw a metadata flow of sorts, like the simple example in

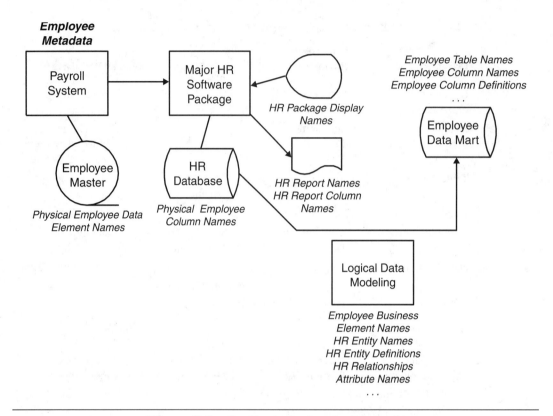

Figure 8-1 An illustrated metadata web

Figure 8-1. This example is quite elementary; only data stores and applications are involved. In today's more complex world, the Web and an increasing number of reporting tools are usually in the picture.

If we revisit our initial metadata categorization table (Table 8-1), we now need to add a column for metadata source, as in Table 8-2.

As we begin to source the metadata elements, we run into conflicting or redundant sources in the first row of our table: Data Element Business Name. This piece of metadata is crucial to all the identified beneficiary categories, yet an evaluation of where each category obtains instances of this metadata element adds some potential beneficiary categories:

- *Data Modeling Tool X*—the place where data elements are initially defined, usually as part of a logical data model

Table 8-2   Sources of Metadata for Beneficiary Categories

Developers	IT Project Managers	End Users	DBMS Catalog	Metadata Source
Data Element Business Name	Data Element Business Name	Data Element Business Name	Data Element Business Name	
Data Element Physical Name	Data Element Physical Name		Data Element Physical Name (Column Name)	
Table Name		(Data Element Location)	Table Name	
Database Name	Database Name		Database Name	
Data Element Definition	Data Element Definition	Data Element Definition	Data Element Definition	
Data Element Type			Data Element Type	
Data Element Domain		Data Element Value Set		
			DBMS Version	
DBMS API Name			DBMS API Name	
Source Data Element Name	Source Data Element Name	Source Data Element Name	Source Data Element Name	
Source File Name	Source File Name		Source File Name	
Source File Type			Source File Type	
Source Application Name	Source Application Name	Source Application Name	Source Application Name	
Data Element Derivation Rules	Data Element Derivation Rules	Data Element Derivation Rules		
			Table Primary Key	
			Table Alternate Index	

■ *Corporate Data Dictionary Y*—the only organized list of data elements that exists at this firm, despite the fact that it is not complete and not maintained

So how do we determine which, if any, should be deemed the official metadata source? Here, as illustrated in Figure 8-2, is where the metadata flow becomes crucial. It is necessary to evaluate the development process, as it applies to the metadata solution's objective, from the point of view of the metadata that is created and accessed throughout. Often, this involves an assessment of additional individuals and additional tools, some of which may not have been mentioned during the initial metadata requirements analysis.

In the perfect world, everyone agrees on the place where metadata originates, and this place consistently serves as the metadata source throughout the application development processes, including data warehousing, legacy application engineering, and the deployment of new Web-based technologies. Of course, none of us lives in a perfect world, and unfortunately, exceptions exist everywhere and will probably continue to be created until well beyond our retirement years.

As we briefly alluded to earlier, redundant metadata sources are a way of life. Hence the need exists to identify a metadata of record (this process is discussed in the next chapter). For now, however, consider diagramming the way metadata flows in our illustrated example.

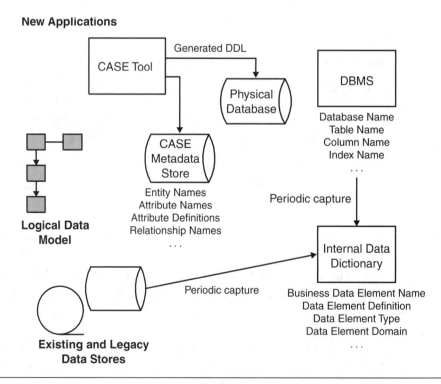

Figure 8-2 **The metadata flow of the metadata web in Figure 8-1**

As depicted in Figure 8-2, there are different places to go for metadata, depending on whether the application was developed in the guise of a new application, and whether a logical data model had been created as the basis for the application data store. There also exists a data dictionary in this example that could have much of the same information as these original data models. The accuracy of the logical data models compared to the organization's current production environment cannot be gleaned from this metadata flow, however. Likewise, it is not possible to tell how accurate or encompassing the data dictionary is compared to the production environment.

In the best of situations, some manual comparisons would be suggested. For now, we can fill in our anticipated metadata source values based on whether the metadata element was created in a logical data model or captured via data dictionary procedures. See Table 8-3.

Where more than one possible source exists, identifying a metadata of record is crucial. It is also obvious that some metadata sources were not ascertainable from the metadata flow analysis in Figure 8-2. It is possible that other aspects of the development environment (copylibs, program libraries, etc.) need to be investigated to obtain the information that relates more to the programs than to the data, or more to the relationships between programs and applications than to the characteristics in an individual application. Much of this will unfold as we consider the architectural requirements of a metadata solution and its interaction with the beneficiaries.

As a final note, most metadata sources should also be evaluated as potential beneficiary categories. In most cases, they become part of the overall metadata solution architecture, minimally as metadata suppliers, but potentially as links or "foreign keys" to additional metadata. But how and when special metadata sources (that could become beneficiary categories) supply metadata, and what additional information these suppliers need to perform their jobs as metadata suppliers give these sources specific rights in the metadata framework. For the purposes of our illustrated case study, those of expediting and standardizing the development and access of new product codes and descriptions, these two metadata suppliers do not appear to have requirements of their own. However, a mental note should be made at this point, since these two metadata sources are bound to resurface during architectural planning and metadata solution scoping.

Metadata requirements analysis thus far has covered:

- The preliminary identification of metadata beneficiaries
- Their subsequent collection of initial metadata requirements

- Metadata beneficiary categorization
- Metadata sourcing

In the next chapter we begin to organize our metadata requirements.

Table 8-3   **Chosen Sources for Beneficiary Metadata Requirements**

Developers	IT Project Managers	End Users	DBMS Catalog	Metadata Source
Data Element Business Name	Data Element Business Name	Data Element Business Name	Data Element Business Name	CASE Tool
Data Element Physical Name	Data Element Physical Name		Data Element Physical Name (Column Name)	Internal Data Dictionary, DBMS
Table Name		(Data Element Location)	Table Name	DBMS
Database Name	Database Name		Database Name	DBMS
Data Element Definition	Data Element Definition	Data Element Definition	Data Element Definition	Internal Data Dictionary
Data Element Type			Data Element Type	Internal Data Dictionary
Data Element Domain		Data Element Value Set		Internal Data Dictionary
			DBMS Version	DBMS
DBMS API Name			DBMS API Name	DBMS
Source Data Element Name	Source Data Element Name	Source Data Element Name	Source Data Element Name	Internal Data Dictionary
Source File Name	Source File Name		Source File Name	Internal Data Dictionary
Source File Type			Source File Type	??
Source Application Name	Source Application Name	Source Application Name	Source Application Name	??
Data Element Derivation Rules	Data Element Derivation Rules	Data Element Derivation Rules		Internal Data Dictionary
			Table Primary Key	DBMS
			Table Alternate Index	DBMS

Chapter 9

Organizing Metadata Requirements

We've gathered our requirements and identified our metadata beneficiaries. Many metadata beneficiaries not only receive and use metadata but also supply it. As such, it is time to start organizing these requirements. This chapter describes the process of organizing these metadata bundles.

Because metadata, data, and information in general have been distributed for quite some time, the way to survive in this scenario is via an organized and planned view of the distributed environment. Metadata solutions are no different. I have always emphasized the need to "get an organized grip" on what is; today it is finally possible to use an organized metadata-based approach to view and access the components of our distributed worlds. A distributed world is based on one simple philosophy: Keep things where they are most needed and used. There are correct and incorrect ways of adhering to this philosophy.

In the incorrect (and easiest) scenario, things are simply recreated (over and over again in many cases) so that they can be stored where they are needed most (even though *everyone* thinks *he or she* needs these things the most). This wouldn't be so bad if there were some sort of master/copy relationship in all situations, guaranteeing synchronization across the various creations. But many people simply "do their own thing," which results in a metadata web. In the correct use of the philosophy, there is a more time-consuming distribution plan and an architecture is developed *before* the metadata is stored anywhere. This architecture describes the source and access characteristics of all metadata within the solution scope. We continue to answer our 5 Questions,[1] focusing now on the questions, How did it get there? and How do I get it?

Beginning the Architectural Planning Process

After we identified our metadata requirements, we began our metadata sourcing exercise in the previous chapter (answering the question, Where is it?). This task opened up the world of requirements to other potential architectural components based on their role, current or previous, as metadata suppliers. In most situations, this can be like "opening a can of worms" in the sense that metadata webs are now the norm, as opposed to the exception in most IT organizations. Determining a preliminary architecture at this point in the requirements process ensures that the following elements are not overlooked:

- *Tools, applications, metadata repositories, or other software packages* that could have an impact on instances of identified metadata requirements
- *Processes* that rely on the existence of instances of the identified metadata requirements
- *Metadata beneficiaries,* as discussed in the previous chapter, that need to access metadata instances

A *metadata solution architecture* depicts the metadata from the perspectives of *all* metadata beneficiaries. That is, it reflects the tool/application/package/repository interfaces that are necessary to maintain an accurate set of metadata throughout the continuing execution of the metadata-reliant processes. In a properly defined and scoped architecture, all metadata requirements are only once from the point of view of instance creation, update, and access. Each beneficiary category may intersect various components of the architecture in totally different ways and for different purposes, but as a whole the entire architecture provides a unified metadata solution that relies on the interaction of all architectural components.

---

1. The 5 Questions is a trademark of and the questions and method are copyrighted by Database Design Solutions, Inc., Bernardsville, New Jersey.

The beginnings of metadata solution architectures are the results of the following types of analysis:

- *Process flows.* Relevant processes are depicted, focusing on metadata identified as required and on its travel between processes. (What metadata do I need? What metadata do I have? Where is it?)

- *Metadata flows.* A metadata perspective depicts where required metadata would originate in the fully architected scenario as well as where it currently originates. (How did it get there?)

- *Metadata of record determination.* Determining, as necessary, a metadata or record reduces metadata redundancy in a well-planned metadata solution architecture.

- *Metadata categorization.* Grouping metadata by category enhances the efficiency of a distributed metadata architecture. This step is the beginning of metamodeling, which is discussed in the following chapters.

Process Flows

Remembering that all requirements identified thus far should support a metadata solution objective, we now look at the "way things are" and perhaps think about a process reengineering of sorts. In most situations that require a metadata solution, existing problems create processing backlogs or inefficiencies due to the inaccessibility of accurate metadata. It is not essential that the solution be determined at this point; but, to confirm that the solution's objective is on target, it is necessary to be aware of how the availability of accurate metadata would change particular events in the beneficiary community.

From the previous chapter, recall the example concerning new product introduction. Despite the fact that "new application development" may not have been mentioned during metadata requirements analysis, a high-level analysis of this process is a prerequisite to architectural planning. Likewise, a high-level review of the database development process, using the newly "blessed" DBMS, is also worthy of an assessment.

The process flows depicted in Figures 9-1 and 9-2 do not necessarily concur with the process flows that may have been derived from our metadata requirements analysis. Also it is quite obvious that each flow, despite its high-level representation, was presented from a different perspective. Figure 9-1 represents application development, yet it was clearly put together by an analyst because the actual requirements gathering process is represented. However,

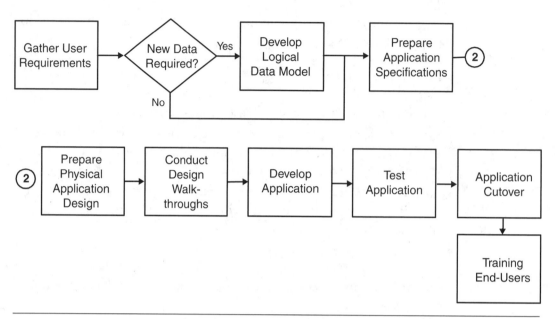

Figure 9-1   A sample flow of a new application development process

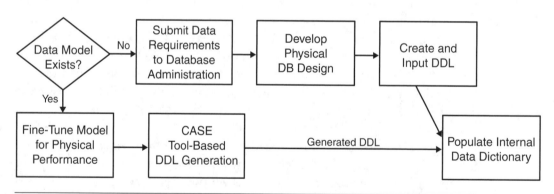

Figure 9-2   A sample flow of the database development process

there appear to be no discrimination or decision points in the string of development processes that differentiate client/server, mainframe, Web-based, or software package implementations. Perhaps in this organization everything is done the same way, despite its technology target, or perhaps the process flow is not comprehensive enough. Figure 9-2 clearly represents the perspective of a database administrator. It is interesting that the process begins with the search for a logical data model.

Consider the fact that application developers, for example, had identified the following metadata requirements:

- Data Element Business Name
- Data Element Definition
- Data Element Type
- Data Element Domain
- Data Element Physical Name
- Table Name
- Database Name
- DBMS API Name
- Source Data Element Name
- Source File Name
- Source File Type
- Source Application Name
- Data Element Derivation Rules

It is likely, based on the way application and database development processes are depicted, that much of the previously identified source information may require a revisit. The same is going to be true of the metadata requirements of other beneficiary categories insomuch as the same types of metadata are necessary. At this point in our metadata requirements analysis process, it is important to assess how source information could be obtained based on the current system. The following are possibilities:

- Based on the name of a source data store, the internal data dictionary could be accessed to obtain a list of all physical data elements in that data store.
- The source information could be input (manually) for the first time into either a current metadata store (modifications may be necessary) or into a to-be-created part of the overall metadata solution architecture.

With these deficiencies identified, a metadata flow depicting the metadata that supports current processes should be created to support our initial theory that all metadata requirements cannot be fully met. Our initial metadata solution architecture will propose a solution to this problem, and an illustrated metadata flow will substantiate new processes that may now be required.

Metadata Flows Revisited

Information Overload! I am sure we have all been victims of "analysis paralysis." This point in our metadata requirements analysis is exactly where many organizations give up and decide to take the easy way out—the creation of yet another isolated place for metadata. I have had excellent success convincing people to stay with this metadata analysis—based on a very simple argument, as shown in the example below.

Having evaluated two specific processes (see Figures 9-1 and 9-2), it is now necessary to take a different perspective and look at the metadata that flows from and to these processes, and compare them to the identified metadata requirements.

Remember that our metadata flow, in Figure 9-3, is presented from the point of view of a potential metadata solution. That is, we are very concerned with the places that *already have metadata*. In other words, the inputting of the metadata into the CASE tool, for example, may be out of scope at this point in the analysis. If, however, the same metadata that exists in the CASE tool is input into another tool for the same project, we need to address the metadata redundancy across tools. In many cases, taking a "metadata perspective" can

Do you remember all of those meetings that you were invited to attend based on your reputation as the company expert on XXXX (e.g., an application, a type of data, an internal process, or the knowledge of external data suppliers and/or recipients)? At the beginning, it felt great! You definitely controlled the meeting; everyone looked to you for the answers and never questioned anything you said.

After a while, you dreaded this role. It interfered with your daily responsibilities, and in many organizations, it actually kept your career on a stand-by peak. If you stopped attending these meetings or answering these questions, your reputation immediately suffered. If you tried to get someone else to become the expert, the other individual never seemed to share the interest that you tried to inspire. You found yourself at a dead end.

What did you do to salvage your role? What did anyone else in the firm do to prevent this situation from constantly recurring with other projects (YYYY or ZZZZ)? How much time was added to development or analysis efforts when you weren't around? How many incorrect conclusions were drawn before you were contacted? The solution to all of these problems is the same—a well-architected metadata solution.

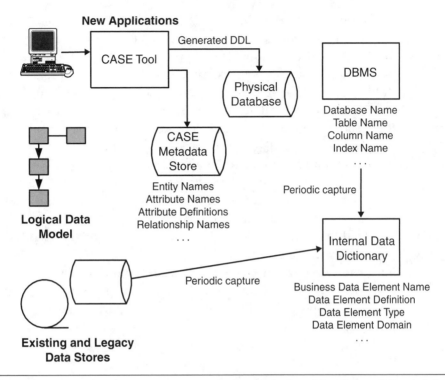

Figure 9-3 **The original metadata flow as depicted in Figure 8-2, revisited**

help identify additional processes. More important, analysts have a tendency to take many of these processes for granted, because they often involve the metadata flows that are internal to tools used in support of certain processes in the process flow.

This comparison of process flows to metadata flows is the last step in the gathering of metadata requirements. From this point onward, architectural issues as well as categorization, organization, and scoping will be refining these requirements.

Comparing the Flows of Processes

Perhaps the first contradiction among our various process perspectives is the starting point. Our existing metadata flow (see Figure 9-3) starts with a data model in a CASE tool, yet the new application development process (see Figure 9-1) shows that logical data models are only created if *new* data is required; that is, when only existing data is to be used in a new application, the entire logical data modeling process is bypassed. Furthermore, the existing database development process (Figure 9-2) checks for the existence of a data model, and if one does not exist, physical database design continues without the model. Only when a model exists is it fine-tuned and used to generate the database definition. Finally, our existing metadata flow (Figure 9-3) begins with a CASE tool. Should we assume that all user requirements are documented in this CASE tool? What fields in the CASE tool's metadata store are populated? Is there additional metadata that is tracked elsewhere? Is the same metadata that is input into the CASE tool also tracked in other places?

These questions need to be addressed one last time. Typically, as they are being reanalyzed, some preliminary scoping decisions may be considered. The metadata solution's functionality and contents are really not ready to be finalized at this point in the process.[2]

Readdressing these questions involves analyzing the full development process one more time both from a metadata point of view and by considering processes for both new application/database development as well as existing application/database enhancement/maintenance. This analysis revealed the following additional metadata requirements and their associated metadata beneficiaries:

- *CASE Tool Name*—Developers
- *CASE Tool Version*—Developers
- *Data Model Name*—Developers
- *Data Model Creation Date*—Developers
- *Data Model Creator*—Developers
- *DBMS Type*—DBMS Catalog, Developers
- *DBMS Version Number*—DBMS Catalog, Developers
- *Legacy Application Name*—Developers, IT Project Managers
- *Legacy Application Project Manager*—IT Project Managers
- *Data Dictionary Input Date*—IT Project Managers, Developers
- *Data Dictionary Last Update Date*—IT Project Managers, Developers

These metadata elements must be included in the list of elements (see Table 8-3) and sourced, which yields Table 9-1.

---

2. Metadata solution scoping is addressed in Chapter 17.

Table 9-1 Adding Metadata Requirements to the Original Set

Developers	IT Project Managers	End Users	DBMS Catalog	Metadata Source
Data Element Business Name	Data Element Business Name	Data Element Business Name	Data Element Business Name	**CASE Tool Metadata Store**
Data Element Physical Name	Data Element Physical Name		Data Element Physical Name (Column Name)	**Internal Data Dictionary, DBMS**
Table Name		(Data Element Location)	Table Name	**DBMS**
Database Name	Database Name		Database Name	**DBMS**
Data Element Definition	Data Element Definition	Data Element Definition	Data Element Definition	**Internal Data Dictionary**
Data Element Type			Data Element Type	**Internal Data Dictionary**
Data Element Domain		Data Element Value Set		**Internal Data Dictionary**
			DBMS Version	**DBMS**
DBMS API Name			DBMS API Name	**DBMS**
Source Data Element Name	Source Data Element Name	Source Data Element Name	Source Data Element Name	**Internal Data Dictionary**
Source File Name	Source File Name		Source File Name	**Internal Data Dictionary, Corporate Program Library**
Source File Type			Source File Type	**Internal Data Dictionary, Corporate Program Library**
Source Application Name	Source Application Name	Source Application Name	Source Application Name	**Internal Data Dictionary, Corporate Program Library**
Data Element Derivation Rules	Data Element Derivation Rules	Data Element Derivation Rules		**Internal Data Dictionary**
			Table Primary Key	**DBMS Catalog**
			Table Alternate Index	**DBMS Catalog**
CASE Tool Name				**CASE Metadata Store** *continued*

Table 9-1 Adding Metadata Requirements to the Original Set continued

Developers	IT Project Managers	End Users	DBMS Catalog	Metadata Source
CASE Tool Version				**CASE Metadata Store**
Data Model Name				**CASE Metadata Store**
Data Model Creation Date				**CASE Metadata Store**
Data Model Creator				**CASE Metadata Store**
DBMS Type			DBMS Type	**DBMS Catalog**
DBMS Version Number			DBMS Version Number	**DBMS Catalog**
Legacy Application Name	Legacy Application Name			**Internal Data Dictionary, Corporate Program Library**
	Legacy Application Project Manager			**Internal Data Dictionary**
Data Dictionary Input Date	Data Dictionary Input Date			**Internal Data Dictionary**
Data Dictionary Last Update Date	Data Dictionary Last Update Date			**Internal Data Dictionary**

Next, we need to revise the metadata flow by taking into account the new metadata requirements and the recently identified metadata sources. A revised and virtually final metadata flow appears in Figure 9-4.

When revisiting the flow, sometimes it becomes apparent that some metadata elements exist in more than one place, and perhaps any or all of them are equivalent. The flow is crucial in these situations as a means of identifying the *metadata of record*.

Identifying the Metadata of Record

When metadata webs perpetuate themselves, an overall strategy is essential to prevent continuous uncontrolled replication of the same metadata. It is dis-

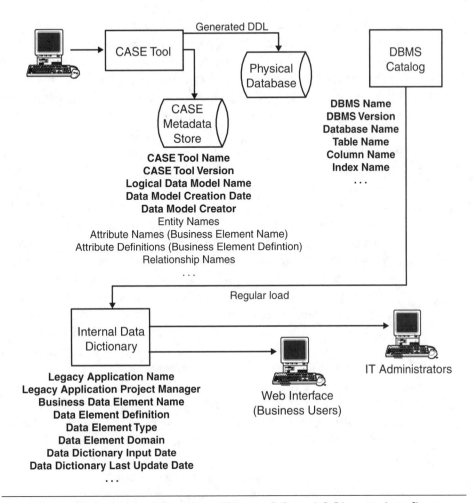

Figure 9-4 The original (see Figures 8-2 and 9-3) metadata flow
revised to accommodate other processes

heartening to see organizations implementing their 65th metadata solution
with no consideration or relationship to the metadata solutions that already
exist and no plans for replacement or integration. It is not necessary for one
and only one enterprise-wide metadata solution to be installed in order to minimize the growth of existing metadata webs. In fact, this is often an impractical
solution, as we will see in Chapter 20. Furthermore, it is essential that new
metadata solutions be implemented in the context of the existing metadata
environment. The analysis must consider where the metadata should originate, both currently and eventually.

The metadata of record serves as the official version of a piece of metadata. Similar to the data of record, it should be standardized and controlled to the largest extent possible. More important, it should serve as the primary source for all variations that show up farther along in the metadata flow.

Evaluation of the organization's processes is necessary if our revised metadata flow (Figure 9-4) shows some potential problems. As we discussed earlier, and as illustrated in the process flows, there is no standard way to do things in this organization. It appears that there is an attempt to model data, but everyone in the development area agrees that this is done only for first-time, new data stores. If the data needed for a new application already exists, there is no attempt to model its business or logical relationships. Instead, the modeling effort is bypassed and specifications are prepared in an unstructured, nonstandardized way, typically with desktop word-processing tools. In addition, it is not clear whether the internal data dictionary can be relied on as a supplier of "metadata of record" values, since the updates and loads appear to be periodic. It may be premature to assume the readiness of the corporate data dictionary for access by direct business users. Finally, we can only assume that the corporate program library contains all production application sources; however, it is not clear when the library is populated, or whether applications under development or being tested reside in the library.

To determine the best choice for metadata of record, it is essential that the supporting processes be understood. In fact, once the source for each metadata requirement is identified, a process flow should be finalized that shows these sources in sequence, as either inputs or outputs (or both) to these supporting processes.

Often during this analysis step, organizations decide to change the way they perform the supporting processes by optimizing the metadata flow in a standardized way. For example, using our illustration, it is extremely likely that further analysis will result in a formalized standard development process that will guarantee population in an internal data dictionary or the corporate program library, or perhaps a to-be-implemented metadata solution to ensure consistent values for the metadata of record.

Our revised metadata flow (Figure 9-4) shows the planned metadata of record selections in bold. Note that a regular load has been established to track the physical nature of new databases. This metadata flow does not include the corporate program library. It is essential that the information in the Internal Data Dictionary be validated manually to ensure that all legacy applications are represented. Of course, when we do eventually scope this metadata solution, the possibility of revision still exists.

At this point in our metadata requirements process, we have identified all metadata requirements, including those that resulted from a process analysis. We have analyzed metadata redundancy and determined the metadata elements that will become the official metadata of record values. We are now ready to organize these requirements. If you are familiar with data modeling, this is similar to the way we organize data.

Categorizing Metadata

With metadata, just as with data, success depends on a set of organized metadata groupings. We have already organized our requirements by metadata beneficiary. As we will see throughout this approach, beneficiary perspectives affect not only the metadata itself, but also the location and presentation of the metadata. Now, an additional categorization is required, one that bypasses individual beneficiaries temporarily and considers them as a group, across the overall architecture. This effort begins an organized view of the metadata requirements, from the perspective of the metadata solution and its surrounding architecture.

This last categorization depends on the relationship of each metadata requirement to not only its source, but also its desiring beneficiary group. In fact, the demand and availability of metadata requirements both contribute directly to the architecture of the eventual metadata solution. Individual categories confirm the placement and role of metadata instances in the architectural result.

To perform this categorization exercise, all metadata requirements must be grouped by beneficiary category (see Table 9-1). Comparisons across beneficiary categories must be performed.

Specific Metadata

Specific metadata is a term that can be misunderstood easily. To be clear, let's use the following definition.

❖ **Specific metadata**   Any metadata that is preferred and required by only one beneficiary category, and is so precise that it originates from a source equivalent to the beneficiary category itself; all metadata that is functionally separate from both an architectural and a usage perspective.

Generally, metadata in this category is preferred by one beneficiary category based on its role in a specific function restricted to this group. I always call it specialist metadata.

Examples of specific metadata range from configuration management (production program and application configuration) metadata to object-oriented modeling metadata to decision support reporting metadata. The categorization depends on (1) where the metadata *originates* and (2) who (person, tool, application, repository) *uses* the metadata. All specific metadata is organized by source, into its own metadata groups.

Revisiting our example, the only metadata elements that are requested by a single group *and* originate from a single source are the following:

- *Table Primary Key*—sourced and needed by the DBMS catalog
- *Table Alternate Index*—sourced and needed by the DBMS catalog
- *CASE Tool Name*—sourced and needed by the CASE tool metadata store
- *CASE Tool Version*—sourced and needed by the CASE tool metadata store
- *Data Model Name*—sourced and needed by the CASE tool metadata store
- *Data Model Creation Date*—sourced and needed by the CASE tool metadata store
- *Data Model Creator*—sourced and needed by the CASE tool metadata store

From these groups of specific metadata, we will create two more exact groups of specific metadata—one for the CASE tool metadata store and one for the DBMS catalog. We will use this information later in the metadata requirements process.

Unique Metadata

Moving up the ladder of metadata categorization, we need to differentiate the specialist metadata that can originate from a source other than the beneficiary category. We are looking for metadata that is still wanted, needed, and used by one beneficiary category (as with specific metadata), but that does *not* originate from the same architectural component. This new category is called unique metadata and can originate from multiple sources or an unknown source, but always from a *different* source. Note the distinction from specialist metadata. We are still differentiating a niche, but the *unique niche* is not quite as isolated as that of the specific niche.

Why make this distinction? In most metadata solution architectures, the delineation has major implications as to where metadata should be stored and managed. We will revisit these issues when we solidify our metadata solution architecture in subsequent chapters.

In our example, only one instance of unique metadata has been uncovered:

- *Legacy Application Project Manager,* which is wanted and needed by only IT project managers, and sourced from the Internal Data Dictionary

In situations such as this, a "double check" of each beneficiary category is recommended to confirm why individual pieces of metadata are needed. There may be no other reason than "It would be nice to have." Most likely, though, the metadata that is really needed is information about legacy applications (e.g., the beneficiary knows that currently the only way to get to that information is to know the legacy application name). Such situations require a reassessment of the metadata requirements. The result would be a set of either specific or unique metadata, requested, needed, and used by only project managers, for example. The assessment as to whether or not the metadata is unique or specific would depend on where the metadata originates.

Common Metadata

At last, we have to deal with all of the remaining metadata, which purports to be *common*; that is, metadata that is *wanted, needed, and used by all beneficiary categories.* But is it really all common? In my metadata solution work, I have never seen a scenario in which all metadata that was listed as a requirement was wanted, needed, and used *by all beneficiary categories.* This is a very relevant statement, and perhaps one of the most crucial factors in determining whether your fully implemented metadata solution will remain productive and successful over the years.

In the quick and easy metadata solution, all metadata that is identified by anyone as a requirement gets put into a standalone database. The database is maintained (manually) for a period of time, usually until the repository administrator gets transferred, promoted, or resigns. During the gap between administrators, the repository becomes slightly outdated. Perhaps another metadata requirement gets identified, or more commonly, the metadata instances are not relevant as new data gets added or loaded into that which is being described by the metadata.

In gathering metadata requirements, it is essential to differentiate common metadata from the rest of the metadata. Common metadata is typically the only metadata that requires centralization or standardization with some amount of corporate control. Of course, requirements change over time, and we will address the fact that what is not common today can become common tomorrow (and vice versa).

Let's revisit our example. What metadata is common?

- Data Element Business Name
- Data Element Definition
- Source Data Element Name
- Source Application Name

That's it! So our original table of metadata requirements, with its identified sources, now has an additional column—Metadata Category, as Table 9-2 shows.

Note the amount of metadata that has not been categorized in Table 9-2. This is quite normal; many of these requirements will be refined as we go through the metadata solution rollout.

At this point our metadata requirements have been sliced and diced into the following subgroups:

- *Beneficiary category,* as in Tables 9-1 and 9-2
- *Metadata source,* as in the fifth column of Tables 9-1 and 9-2
- *Metadata category,* as in the last column of Table 9-2

These categorizations, the metadata flows, and the identification of the metadata of record where necessary are all part of a practical metadata requirements methodology. (See Table 9-3.)

Table 9-2 Adding the Metadata Category

Developers	IT Project Managers	End Users	DBMS Catalog	Metadata Source	Metadata Category
Data Element Business Name	Data Element Business Name	Data Element Business Name	Data Element Business Name	CASE Tool Metadata Store	Common
Data Element Physical Name	Data Element Physical Name		Data Element Physical Name (Column Name)	Data Dictionary, DBMS	
Table Name		(Data Element Location)	Table Name	DBMS	
Database Name	Database Name		Database Name	DBMS	
Data Element Definition	Data Element Definition	Data Element Definition	Data Element Definition	Internal Data Dictionary	Common
Data Element Type			Data Element Type	Internal Data Dictionary	
Data Element Domain		Data Element Value Set		Internal Data Dictionary	
DBMS API Name			DBMS Version	DBMS	Specific
			DBMS API Name	DBMS	
Source Data Element Name	Source Data Element Name	Source Data Element Name	Source Data Element Name	Data Dictionary	Common
Source File Name	Source File Name		Source File Name	Internal Data Dictionary, Corporate Program Library	
Source File Type			Source File Type	Internal Data Dictionary, Corporate Program Library	
Source Application Name	Source Application Name	Source Application Name	Source Application Name	Internal Data Dictionary, Corporate Program Library	Common

continued

Table 9-2 Adding the Metadata Category continued

Developers	IT Project Managers	End Users	DBMS Catalog	Metadata Source	Metadata Category
Data Element Derivation Rules	Data Element Derivation Rules	Data Element Derivation Rules		Internal Data Dictionary	
			Table Primary Key	DBMS Catalog	Specific
			Table Alternate Index	DBMS Catalog	Specific
CASE Tool Name				CASE Metadata Store	Specific
CASE Tool Version				CASE Metadata Store	Specific
Data Model Name				CASE Metadata Store	Specific
Data Model Creation Date				CASE Metadata Store	Specific
Data Model Creator				CASE Metadata Store	Specific
DBMS Type			DBMS Type	DBMS Catalog	
DBMS Version Number			DBMS Version Number	DBMS Catalog	
Legacy Application Name	Legacy Application Name			Internal Data Dictionary, Corporate Program Library	
	Legacy Application Project Manager			Internal Data Dictionary	Unique
Data Dictionary Input Date	Data Dictionary Input Date			Internal Data Dictionary	
Data Dictionary Last Update Date	Data Dictionary Last Update Date			Internal Data Dictionary	

Table 9-3 A Regrouping of Metadata Requirements

Beneficiary Categories			
Developers	**IT Project Managers**	**End Users**	**DBMS Catalog**
Data Element Business Name	Data Element Business Name	Data Element Business Name	Data Element Business Name
Data Element Physical Name	Data Element Physical Name	Data Element Location	Data Element Physical Name
Table Name	Database Name	Data Element Definition	Table Name
Database Name	Data Element Definition	Data Element Value Set	Database Name
Data Element Definition	Source Data Element Name	Source Data Element Name	Data Element Definition
Data Element Type	Source File Name	Source Application Name	Data Element Type
Data Element Domain	Source Application Name	Data Element Derivation Rules	DBMS Version
DBMS API Name	Data Element Derivation Rules		DBMS API Name
Source Data Element Name	Legacy Application Name		Source Data Element Name
Source File Name	Legacy Application Project Manager		Source File Name
Source File Type	Data Dictionary Input Date		Source File Type
Source Application Name	Data Dictionary Last Update Date		Source Application Name
Data Element Derivation Rules			Table Primary Key
CASE Tool Name			Table Alternate Index
CASE Tool Version			DBMS Type
Data Model Name			DBMS Version Number
Data Model Creation Date			
Data Model Creator			
DBMS Type			
DBMS Version Number			
Legacy Application Name			
Data Dictionary Input Date			
Data Dictionary Last Update Date			

Metadata Categories			
Specific (to DBMS)	**Specific (to CASE Metadata Store)**	**Unique (IT Project Managers/Internal Data Dictionary)**	**Common**
DBMS Version	CASE Tool Name	Legacy Application Project Manager	Data Element Business Name
Table Primary Key	CASE Tool Version		Data Element Definition
Table Alternate Index	Data Model Name		Source Data Element Name
DBMS Type	Data Model Creation Date		Source Application Name
	Data Model Creator		

Looking toward Metamodels

At last! Consider all of the analysis and categorization that has occurred up to this point. These metadata groups are moving us toward the metamodeling task, which is discussed in detail in the next chapter.

Metamodels are models of metadata, and they always represent a particular perspective. In fact, there are so many perspectives to metadata (beneficiaries, sources, metadata category, function support) that metamodels always overlap. Many commercial metamodels try to cover everybody's needs in one big metamodel. Is this the way to go? Should we have separate metamodels? Do they ever come together? How does a metadata solution manage all of these models? Have I piqued your interest? Keep reading!

Chapter 10

Introducing Metamodels

So far we have sliced and diced our metadata requirements from many per-spectives: those who originally wanted and needed the metadata, others who wanted and needed it, and also where the metadata came from. As we reorganized our metadata, many of us probably could not resist beginning to model it. But at the same time, those of us who are dying to draw our pictures are still noticing that we don't quite have all that we need to put these models together.

Moving from Metadata to Metamodels

Our metadata classifications serve many roles. First, they provide a basis for organized metadata perspectives. These perspectives result not only in potential designs for physical metadata storage, but also in the design and implementation of metadata display and exchange mechanisms. As we move from lists to models, additional criteria will come into play, all of which will be uncovered and discussed in this chapter.

Dealing with Unclassified Metadata

Table 10-1 gives the metadata classifications of the previous chapter. It is important to note that a decent portion of our metadata requirements remain un-classified—not common, unique, or specific. How do we handle unclassified metadata? Which metamodel will it ultimately join? Will it remain isolated throughout our metadata solution architecture?

To illustrate our dilemma, let's review Table 10-1. All of the metadata that has not been categorized as common, unique, or specific appears in bold in Table 10-2.

Table 10-1   Reviewing the Metadata Classifications

Beneficiary Categories			
Developers	**IT Project Managers**	**End Users**	**DBMS Catalog**
Data Element Business Name	Data Element Business Name	Data Element Business Name	Data Element Business Name
Data Element Physical Name	Data Element Physical Name	Data Element Location	Data Element Physical Name
Table Name	Database Name	Data Element Definition	Table Name
Database Name	Data Element Definition	Data Element Value Set	Database Name
Data Element Definition	Source Data Element Name	Source Data Element Name	Data Element Definition
Data Element Type	Source File Name	Source Application Name	Data Element Type
Data Element Domain	Source Application Name	Data Element Derivation Rules	DBMS Version
DBMS API Name	Data Element Derivation Rules		DBMS API Name
Source Data Element Name	Legacy Application Name		Source Data Element Name
Source File Name	Legacy Application Project Manager		Source File Name
Source File Type	Data Dictionary Input Date		Source File Type
Source Application Name	Data Dictionary Last Update Date		Source Application Name
Data Element Derivation Rules			Table Primary Key
CASE Tool Name			Table Alternate Index
CASE Tool Version			DBMS Type
Data Model Name			DBMS Version Number
Data Model Creation Date			

Table 10-1 *continued*

Beneficiary Categories			
Developers	**IT Project Managers**	**End Users**	**DBMS Catalog**
Data Model Creator			
DBMS Type			
DBMS Version Number			
Legacy Application Name			
Data Dictionary Input Date			
Data Dictionary Last Update Date			

Metadata Categories			
Specific (DBMS Catalog)	**Specific (Developers/CASE Metadata Store**	**Specific (IT Project Managers/Internal Data Dictionary)**	**Common**
DBMS Version	CASE Tool Name	Legacy Application Project Manager	Data Element Business Name
Table Primary Key	CASE Tool Version		Data Element Definition
Table Alternate Index	Data Model Name		Source Data Element Name
DBMS Type	Data Model Creation Date		Source Application Name
	Data Model Creator		

Table 10-2   Unclassified Metadata

Metadata by Beneficiary Category			
Developers	**IT Project Managers**	**End Users**	**DBMS Catalog**
Data Element Business Name	Data Element Business Name	Data Element Business Name	Data Element Business Name
Data Element Physical Name	**Data Element Physical Name**	**Data Element Location**	**Data Element Physical Name**
Table Name	**Database Name**	Data Element Definition	**Table Name**
Database Name	Data Element Definition	Data Element Value Set	**Database Name**
Data Element Definition	Source Data Element Name	Source Data Element Name	Data Element Definition
Data Element Type	**Source File Name**	Source Application Name	**Data Element Type**
Data Element Domain	Source Application Name	**Data Element Derivation Rules**	DBMS Version
DBMS API Name	**Data Element Derivation Rules**		**DBMS API Name**
Source Data Element Name	**Legacy Application Name**		Source Data Element Name
Source File Name	Legacy Application Project Manager		**Source File Name**
Source File Type	Data Dictionary Input Date		**Source File Type**
Source Application Name	**Data Dictionary Last Update Date**		Source Application Name
Data Element Derivation Rules			Table Primary Key
CASE Tool Name			Table Alternate Index
CASE Tool Version			DBMS Type
Data Model Name			DBMS Version Number
Data Model Creation Date			
Data Model Creator			
DBMS Type			
DBMS Version Number			
Legacy Application Name			
Data Dictionary Input Date			
Data Dictionary Last Update Date			

Note: **Bold metadata** is not classified by usage/source.

Table 10-2 *continued*

Metadata Categories			
Specific (DBMS Catalog)	Specific (Developers/CASE Metadata Store	Specific (IT Project Managers/Internal Data Dictionary)	Common
DBMS Version Table Primary Key Table Alternate Index DBMS Type	CASE Tool Name CASE Tool Version Data Model Name Data Model Creation Date Data Model Creator	Legacy Application Project Manager	Data Element Business Name Data Element Definition Source Data Element Name Source Application Name

Unclassified metadata forms its own category to some degree. Here, we have metadata that is in demand (it is wanted by at least one beneficiary category), but with issues with respect to its sourcing or lack of commonality. In general, the following conditions typically cause unclassified metadata:

- *Metadata variations*—In almost every situation, our beneficiaries use their own terminology. In fact, what one beneficiary category calls a Data Element another may call a Field. These variations are often hard to pinpoint, but detailed metadata analysis by an experienced analyst usually eliminates about 20 percent of metadata requirements for this reason alone.

- *Multiple metadata sources*—When the same metadata requirement can be sourced from more than one place, these are almost always metadata variations (each source may call the same piece of metadata by a different name). More important, it is often unclear which one should be used.

- *Multiple beneficiary categories*—If more than one group wants a piece of metadata, but the metadata instance itself is not universally required (that is, it is not common), this piece of metadata is usually left unclassified.

Dealing with each of these situations brings us closer and closer to organized models.

Metadata Variations

When different perspectives result in different ways of identifying something, it is often unclear whether the name variations truly identify the same instance of metadata. To identify similarities, a metadata flow is often helpful. In Chapter 9, metadata flows helped us determine the metadata of record. An analysis of each metadata supplier's contents in terms of metadata element names also identifies metadata variations as they occur. Even more important, however, is the ultimate confirmation that variations really exist by manual examination of the actual metadata instances.

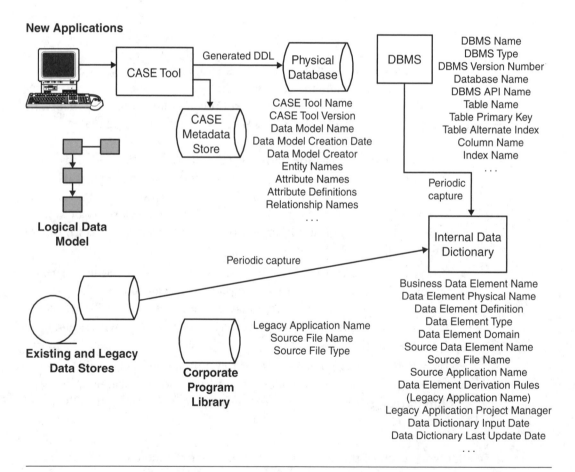

New Applications

CASE Tool → Generated DDL → Physical Database

DBMS

CASE Metadata Store

CASE Tool Name
CASE Tool Version
Data Model Name
Data Model Creation Date
Data Model Creator
Entity Names
Attribute Names
Attribute Definitions
Relationship Names
. . .

DBMS Name
DBMS Type
DBMS Version Number
Database Name
DBMS API Name
Table Name
Table Primary Key
Table Alternate Index
Column Name
Index Name
. . .

Periodic capture

Logical Data Model

Periodic capture

Internal Data Dictionary

Existing and Legacy Data Stores

Corporate Program Library

Legacy Application Name
Source File Name
Source File Type

Business Data Element Name
Data Element Physical Name
Data Element Definition
Data Element Type
Data Element Domain
Source Data Element Name
Source File Name
Source Application Name
Data Element Derivation Rules
(Legacy Application Name)
Legacy Application Project Manager
Data Dictionary Input Date
Data Dictionary Last Update Date
. . .

Figure 10-1 Determining metadata variations

According to Figure 10-1, many metadata variations look possible:

- Attribute Name, Business Data Element Name
- Attribute Definition, Data Element Definition
- Legacy Application Name, Source Application Name
- Source File Name, Database Name
- Source File Type, DBMS Type

As we evaluate each of these for similarities, actual values must be reviewed instance by instance. For example, our Unclassified Metadata (Table 10-2) depicts *Data Element Location* as one piece of unclassified metadata. Further analysis will probably show that Data Element Location is equivalent to Database Name, the validity of which would remove it from our unclassified list; then we would add Database Name to the Common Metadata set. Likewise, Legacy Application Name would most likely prove to be the same as Source Application Name; we would remove it because Source Application Name is already represented.

The other potential variations will be ironed out by a chronological evaluation of their sources.

Multiple Metadata Sources

Metadata also remains unclassified when its official source cannot be ascertained. Again, a metadata flow is helpful because it puts a chronological twist onto metadata requirements analysis. Which metadata instance is created first? Does it contain the exact value as its variations down the road? Does one instance feed the next? Should one instance be the official metadata of record? These decisions are based on knowledge of the metadata creation processes as well as evaluation of sample instances. The first accurate value in the metadata supply chain should be deemed the metadata of record. Its ability to replace variations that are part of the identified metadata requirements depends on:

- Whether the source of the metadata of record is also the source of other metadata requirements. Ideally, it is.
- Whether the values required to identify the metadata of record (e.g., key or indexing metadata elements) are also part of the identified metadata requirements. As we will see later on, *identifiers* are often added to metadata requirements, regardless of whether they were specified as needed.

Multiple Metadata Beneficiary Categories

The ultimate reason for being unable to classify metadata rests with its potential demand. In general, metadata targeted for an architected metadata solution is either specialized or common. There are intermediate exceptions, most notably unique metadata, as discussed in the previous chapter. However, metadata classifications begin simply by focusing on the distinct, thus making it easy to organize and model.

When multiple categories are involved as beneficiaries, the metadata requirement is clearly important. The issue, therefore, is not whether a piece of metadata is a variation, but whether or how it should be modeled and which model it would join.

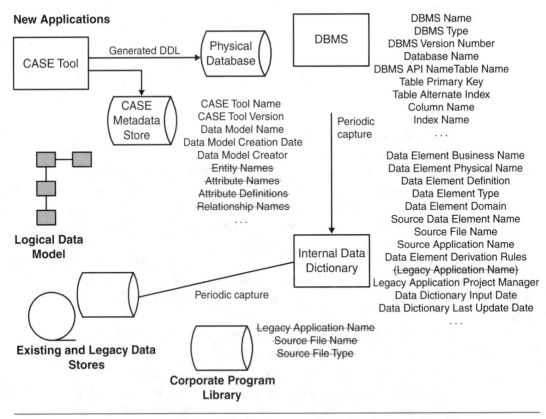

Figure 10-2 An updated flow, with variations considered

Note the removal of some metadata requirements, as shown in Figure 10-2:

- Legacy Application Name was determined to be a variation of Source Application Name.
- Source File Name was determined to be a variation of Database Name.
- Source File Type was determined to be a variation of DBMS Type.
- Attribute Name and Attribute Definition turned out to be unreliable based on discoveries in the previous chapter with respect to the creation of data models. As such they were replaced with Business Element Name and Business Element Definition, which became the metadata of records.
- Entity Name and Relationship Name, although present in the CASE metadata store, were actually not requested by any metadata beneficiaries (as of now).

Once variations have been cleared up, we can begin to move from metadata to metamodels. Sources as well as each required metadata of record should be confirmed at this point. As the final premodeling perspective, unclassified metadata requirements should be organized by source, as shown in Table 10-3.

Making Sources into Metamodel Perspectives

As we evaluate Table 10-3, it is important to notice the additional perspectives that each metadata source brings to the overall requirements process. The architecture has been finalized, and the illustrated sources depict where each metadata requirement will originate. In addition, the original metadata categories are confirmed. In many scenarios, this final metadata slicing shows the experienced modeler what is missing.

To determine whether the metadata requirements are comprehensive enough to begin metamodeling, you must become aware of how each metadata element is referenced within its source data store. For now, be prepared to answer the following questions with respect to each source's required metadata element:

How is each instance of the particular metadata element identified? Is it required to know the value of another metadata element in order to get to the one you want? For example, in many CASE metadata stores, you must know a model name in order to get to *any* information that is tracked within that

Table 10-3   **Organizing Unclassified Metadata**

Metadata by Official Source		
Case Metadata Store	**DBMS Catalog**	**Internal Data Dictionary**
CASE Tool Name	DBMS Name	Data Element Business Name
CASE Tool Version	DBMS Type	Data Element Physical Name
Data Model Name	DBMS Version Number	Data Element Definition
Data Model Creation Date	Database Name	Data Element Type
Data Model Creator	Table Name	Data Element Domain
DBMS Type	Table Primary Key	Source Data Element Name
	Table Alternate Index	Source File Name
	Column Name	Source Application Name
	Index Name	Data Element Derivation Rules
	DBMS API Name	Legacy Application Project Manager
		Data Dictionary Input Date
		Data Dictionary Last Update Date

Metadata Categories			
Specific (DBMS Catalog)	**Specific (Developers/ CASE Metadata Store)**	**Specific (IT Project Managers/Internal Data Dictionary)**	**Common**
DBMS Version	CASE Tool Name	Legacy Application Project Manager	Data Element Business Name
Table Primary Key	CASE Tool Version		Data Element Definition
Table Alternate Index	Data Model Name		Source Data Element Name
DBMS Type	Data Model Creation Date		Source Application Name
	Data Model Creator		

model (e.g., entities, attributes, etc.). If Model Name was not specified as a metadata requirement, in this example, it would have to be added.

Is it necessary to access other metadata elements before you can get to the required metadata element? In some tools, tool-specific security prevents outside access to anything that was not created by the accessor.

What does the metadata element actually describe in its source? Despite the fact that a metadata beneficiary may be interested in a Source Data Element Name, it may not be considered in that context in its home location. Typically, it is a Data Element associated with a Data Store. Depending on whether the Data Store was considered part of the metadata requirements set, it may be difficult to isolate a Data Element without knowing its associated Data Store.

Can the metadata element be retrieved independently of its related metadata? As noted, elements typically describe something else, and the something else typically has an associated identifier. Much of this may be considered extra baggage, but to a metadata solution, it could be *required* extra baggage.

Responding to these answers after categorizing your metadata requirements by beneficiary category, metadata category, and official source will leave enough information to begin the metamodeling process.

Table 10-4 finalizes our premetamodel requirements. Metadata elements were re-named to eliminate variations as appropriate. All perspectives are presented, and we are now ready to begin metamodeling.

Defining the Metamodel

To create a metamodel requires knowledge of data modeling. This book is not a data modeling reference text, but excellent texts can be found in the Additional Readings section at the end of this book. Suffice it to say that for the purposes of this section, *models* are pictorial representations of a set of requirements. As in most disciplines, a model shows the way things relate and gives a broad yet precise view of implementation of the requirements once development begins.

Much like an architectural drawing, a *metamodel* graphically depicts metadata requirements.

❖ **Metamodel**   A tool's view of its underlying metadata; the details behind the metadata. Also, the graphic representation of an organized set of metadata requirements, typically organized by any of the following perspectives:

■ The metadata's source (a tool, application, repository, etc.)

■ The metadata's classification (common, unique, or specific) and associated beneficiary category

■ The metadata's usage (e.g., a particular development methodology)

Metamodels are depicted based on an underlying modeling methodology (e.g., object-oriented versus entity-relationship)

Table 10-4   **Fully Categorized Metadata**

Metadata by Beneficiary Category			
Developers	**IT Project Managers**	**End Users**	**DBMS Catalog**
Data Element Business Name	Data Element Business Name	Data Element Business Name	Data Element Business Name
Data Element Physical Name	Data Element Physical Name	Data Element Physical Name	Data Element Physical Name
Table Name	Database Name	Data Element Domain	Table Name
Database Name	Data Element Definition	Database Name	Data Element Type
Data Element Definition	Source Data Element Name	Data Element Definition	DBMS Version
Data Element Type	Source File Name	Source Application Name	DBMS API Name
Data Element Domain	Source Application Name		Source Data Element Name
DBMS API Name	Data Element Derivation Rules		Source File Name
Source Data Element Name	Source Application Project Manager		Source File Type
Source File Name	Data Dictionary Input Date		Table Primary Key
Source File Type	Data Dictionary Last Update Date		Table Alternate Index
Source Application Name			DBMS Type
Data Element Derivation Rules			Database Name
CASE Tool Name			Data Element Definition
CASE Tool Version			Source Application Name
Data Model Name			
Data Model Creator			
DBMS Type			
DBMS Version Number			
Data Dictionary Input Date			
Data Dictionary Last Update Date			

Table 10-4 *continued*

Metadata by Official Source		
Case Metadata Store	**DBMS Catalog**	**Internal Data Dictionary**
CASE Tool Name	DBMS Name	Data Element Business Name
CASE Tool Version	DBMS Type	Data Element Physical Name
Data Model Name	DBMS Version Number	Data Element Definition
Data Model Creation Date	Database Name	Data Element Type
Data Model Creator	Table Name	Data Element Domain
	Table Primary Key	Source Data Element Name
	Table Alternate Index	Source File Name
	Column Name	Source Application Name
	Index Name	Data Element Derivation Rules
	DBMS API Name	Legacy Application Project Manager
		Data Dictionary Input Date
		Data Dictionary Last Update Date

Metadata Categories			
Specific (DBMS Catalog)	**Specific (Developers/ CASE Metadata Store)**	**Specific (IT Project Managers/Internal Data Dictionary)**	**Common**
DBMS Version	CASE Tool Name	Legacy Application Project Manager	Data Element Business Name
Table Primary Key	CASE Tool Version		Data Element Definition
Table Alternate Index	Data Model Name		Source Data Element Name
DBMS Type	Data Model Creation Date		Source Application Name
	Data Model Creator		

Regardless of the modeling method, to create a metamodel we must have the following sets of information about the metadata:

- A full list of *metadata requirements*—All requirements representative of a particular perspective, as discussed, or belonging to the common metadata set. Note that metadata that belongs to each perspective should be modeled separately.

- *Entity or Object Names*—Within each set of metadata requirements, metadata elements should be listed by their main subjects.[1]

  - *Identifiers*—The pieces of metadata (or, in some cases, data) that are necessary to obtain the specific metadata values from the respective metadata source.

  - *Dependencies*—Any prerequisite metadata that determines the value or existence of each metadata requirement.

  - *Relationships*—If a dependency of sorts is assumed, it is often possible that metadata requirements are related. Relationships usually occur at the entity or object level, however, and are either optional or mandatory.[2]

As we begin the process of metamodeling, readers should be aware that *most* metadata requirements are actually *attributes,* or characteristics of a described entity or object. Therefore, combining these requirements into a metamodel usually involves more analysis of *how* and *where* the requirement describes the *what*.

Specific metadata is the easiest metadata to put together, based on its isolated perspective in terms of both source and usage. Considering that fact, let's begin preparing a metamodel of the specific metadata that developers use and that originates from the CASE metadata store:

- CASE Tool Name
- CASE Tool Version
- Data Model Name
- Data Model Creation Date
- Data Model Creator

It is interesting to note that "extra" information appears in this metamodel, as depicted in Figure 10-3. Most of this reflects the way models and creators are related in the metadata source, as well as an attempt to generically repre-

---

1. Subjects are called entities or objects, depending on the modeling method. They are the "things" about which we are collecting metadata, usually based on the way the information is tracked in the metadata source.

2. For more information on relationships, see the data modeling references in the Additional Readings section at the end of this book.

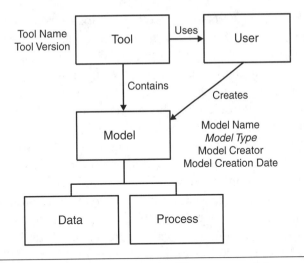

Figure 10-3 A specific metamodel

sent items such as "tool" so that other types of tools (aside from CASE tools) can participate in the metadata solution architecture. As previously mentioned, tunnel vision is the primary reason that metadata solutions fail.

Continuing the metamodeling process, we move to the next set of specific metadata, that of the DBMS Catalog. All of the following metadata requirements are used by DBAs and originate from the DBMS Catalog:

- DBMS Version
- DBMS Type
- Table Primary Key
- Table Primary Index

As we evaluate each of these metadata requirements, we can see that something seems to be missing. When we group each requirement by the subject/entity that is being identified, we get the results shown in Table 10-5.

Table 10-5 Metadata Requirements Organized by Their Described Subjects

Subject/Entity	Metadata Requirement	
DBMS	DBMS Version	DBMS Type
Table	Table Primary Key	Table Alternate Index

Further analysis into the relationships between DBMS and Table indicate a missing entity—Database. It is not always obvious based on supplied metadata requirements that the relationships will not pan out. This is why the metadata requirement analysis is crucial. If you are not familiar with data modeling, it might appear that a direct relationship can be drawn between DBMS and Table. However, the problem will be evident when the internals of a DBMS catalog are evaluated. All tables are associated with databases.

As we evaluate the model in Figure 10-4, we see that keys and indices are special types of columns, which are typically associated with tables. Again, without the connections, or relationships, it would be virtually impossible to maintain architectural integrity in the metadata solution.

Another way to arrive at the same conclusions with respect to our DBMS Catalog metamodel is to evaluate the catalog's underlying database structure. Most database administrators are aware of this, and DBMS software and associ-

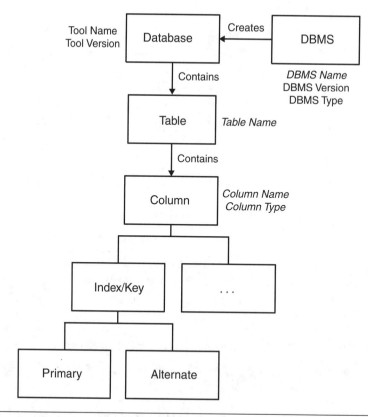

Figure 10-4 **A specific DBMS metamodel**

ated documentation make it possible. By searching for the metadata requirements specifically, we would see clearly where they fit in the database design hierarchy and what additional metadata elements would be necessary to access those specific to our metadata situation.

Continuing the evaluation of the DBMS Catalog requires us to revisit the metadata requirements, as identified by source (see Table 10-4). The addition of *DBMS API Name* as a metadata requirement becomes part of the metadata list supplied by the DBMS Catalog. Likewise, the additional connecting metadata, even though it was not specifically required by DBAs, is referenced. Figure 10-5 shows a revised DBMS Catalog metamodel that accounts for all metadata requirements sourced from this area.

Again, notice that API Name has been modified to reflect the fact that an API is a specific type of database access procedure. This flexibility prevents tunnel vision and its effects on the metadata solution.

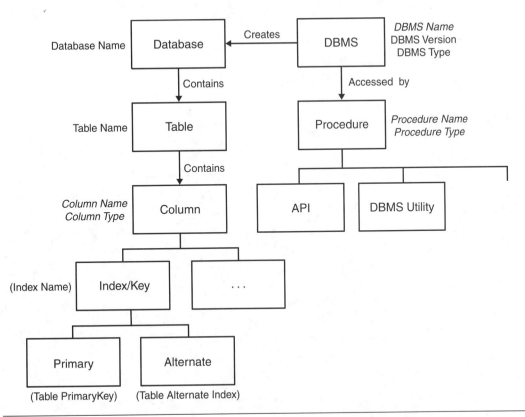

Figure 10-5 Revised DBMS Catalog metamodel

It is essential that the metamodeling process address all specific metadata and all common metadata, as well as an organized view of each metadata source, emphasizing the pieces of metadata required by beneficiaries. Therefore, for the purposes of our continued case study, in addition to the metamodels we have already completed, we need to model metadata requirements for the Internal Data Dictionary and the identified common metadata. Those metamodels appear in Figures 10-6 and 10-7.

There are obvious similarities among the metamodels we have developed. These similarities form the basis of the metadata solution that will be implemented. In addition, the more generic a metamodel becomes, the more likely metadata will be reusable across the various perspectives.

To summarize our metamodeling focus, review the various perspectives that we have arranged:

- *Common metamodel*—an organized view of the common metadata, typically geared toward implementation in a neutral metadata solution

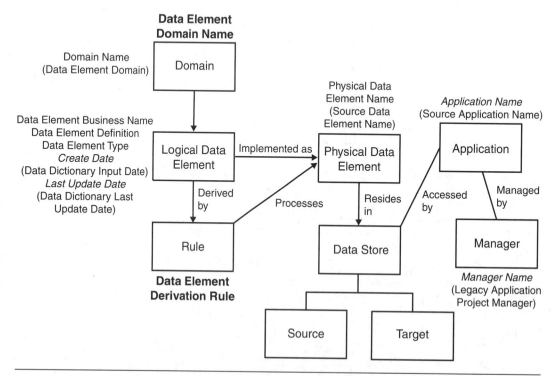

Figure 10-6   **The data dictionary metamodel**

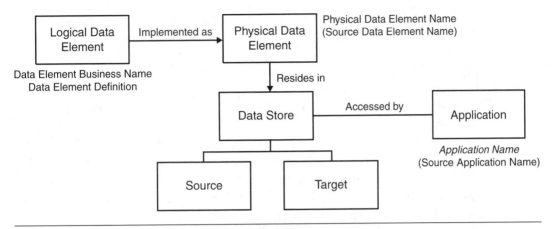

Figure 10-7 **The common metamodel**

- *Specific metamodel*—an organized view of distinct metadata perspectives, architecturally remaining in most cases with the metadata source as part of an overall metadata solution architecture. More details about the metadata solution architecture are presented in the next chapter.

- *Source metamodel*—organized based on where metadata originates, and usually used as the primary means of addressing unique metadata requirements

- *Beneficiary metamodels*—organized based on requirement perspectives, but not typically implemented directly in a metadata solution. Beneficiary perspectives are used not only to ensure that all metadata requirements can be addressed in developed metamodels but also as a means of designing beneficiary-specific interfaces and front-ends. More details will unfold as we finalize metadata solution architecture.

After metamodels have been completed, all metadata requirements should be addressed in at least one metamodel.

Vendor versus Custom Metamodels

So far our efforts have focused on custom metamodels developed to meet our specific requirements. Standard metamodels are also available, many from the vendors of metadata solutions, some from standards organizations.[3]

---

3. Metadata standards are discussed in Chapter 16.

Vendors' metamodels can meet the metadata requirements in many situations. Many excellent metamodels are available and often their scope is well beyond that of the average set of metadata requirements. Is it worth the increased perspective and associated functionality to adapt a vendor's metamodel, or should the metadata solution reflect only customized requirements?

Despite the metamodel's origin, it must satisfy the gathered metadata requirements from all relevant perspectives. All metadata requirements should be gathered *before* any vendor or standard metamodels are evaluated. In other words, if work is to be saved, it is only in the organization of these requirements. Once the requirements have been grouped by the various relevant perspectives (as in Table 10-4), each perspective should be compared against any preexisting metamodel under consideration.

- Does the metamodel address all metadata requirements?

- Is it necessary to add metadata requirements (e.g., as identifiers) to obtain the specifics of your situation?

- How much of the preexisting metamodel is not of immediate interest? Will it be of long-term interest?

- Can the metamodel be implemented in a variety of software options? Is the vendor open to customizing the metamodel and/or the metadata solution? What ramifications will transpire if the metamodel is changed?

Off-the-shelf metamodel solutions are becoming more popular. Many address specific data-related functions (e.g., data warehousing), and others address specific vendor packages, development tools, or retail metadata solutions. By comparison, through efforts to allow intertool communication, standard metamodels are becoming an option as standard-setting bodies work toward a united objective.

The Object-Oriented Metamodel

In addition to the off-the-shelf solution, object orientation has had an impact on the metadata solution area, particularly in the design of basic metamodels. With an object-oriented solution, not only is the metadata organized, but so are the processes that should be associated with various types of metadata. Although most of the object-oriented metamodels are more popular at the meta-meta level,[4] they are available as off-the-shelf solutions as a means of uncovering metadata

---

4. Meta-metamodels are discussed in Part III.

stored within application development tools. Again, off-the-shelf solutions should be compared against metadata requirements, particularly if they reflect heavy developer emphasis.

Object-oriented metamodels preclude most tunnel vision. Consider whether the metadata will require an associated standard process, irrespective of the beneficiary category. If so, the requirements are most likely targeted for a higher level of abstraction, usually known as the meta-meta, or solution level. We will revisit the object-oriented metamodel in Part III.

Metamodel Extensibility

When considering vendor or standard metamodels, support of your requirements usually requires a change or extension to the ready-made metamodel. In the early days of repositories and tool-specific metamodels, this was not always possible, and changes to a vendor metamodel always required vendor intervention. Eventually, these product consumers were permitted to revise metamodels, but the revisions (extensions) were not always treated with the same power as the base metamodel constructs.

In all of my metadata solution experience, I have yet to find a standard or vendor-supplied metamodel that met client requirements without extensions. This fact is important. It tells us that vendors typically try to meet generically the metadata requirements that we so carefully analyze and group. As a result, we always get more for our money, but there are usually just a few minor things missing. These minor inconsistencies can be as simple as the following:

- Missing metadata elements
- Missing metamodel constructs (entities, objects)
- Missing relationships
- Incorrect relationships
- Extra metamodel constructs
- Extra metadata elements

Extensibility is a necessary feature of any off-the-shelf solution. The results of our extensions should be treated as if they were vendor-supplied. Metadata solutions have been rearchitected at the meta-meta level to handle extensions better and avoid consumer nightmares. The old saying "The problem with extensions is that they are too easy to make" should go the way of the hierarchical data store as object orientation becomes established as a base metadata solution design.

Extending the metamodel should not affect the processing associated with the populated metadata. Metadata solution architectures should reflect not only the customized metamodel (or extended off-the-shelf metamodel) but also the associated metadata solution processing. This processing makes the metadata the useful commodity it was meant to be—the power of this statement cannot be understated. As we will soon see, the metamodel is only a piece of the pie, and metadata solutions all vary in how the metamodel affects the power of the full metadata solution in terms of processing, tool exchange, and ease of access.

All these metadata solution specifics and their relationships to a metamodel's structure and specifics are part of the meta-meta framework. Before we discuss the metadata solution's internals (Part III), we will complete Part II by considering the potential power metadata can have in your organization if it is

1. identifiable (What metadata do we have?),
2. understandable (What does it mean?),
3. locatable (Where is it?),
4. traceable (How did it get there?), and
5. accessible (How do I get it?).

Full metadata solutions address these five characteristics. The metamodel is an important aspect of the overall solution, but it is also just the beginning. Chapter 11 discusses the other components of our metadata solution.

Chapter 11

Metamodels as a Piece of the Pie

If you think you can, you can. And if
you think you can't, you're right.
—Mary Kay Ash

The four previous chapters focused on the customization of metadata requirements. As a result, we have created several metamodels—organized views of metadata boundaries. Many metadata solution efforts seem focused entirely on this aspect of the solution, that is, the "what" of the problem. I cannot overemphasize the potential harm that tunnel vision can play—and this tunnel vision also applies to the incompleteness of a metadata solution design. This chapter defines *metadata solution*. We will briefly revisit its remaining objectives as a reminder that metamodels are indeed only one piece of the pie, and then focus the rest of the chapter on the metamodels themselves. The remaining aspects of the metadata solution are addressed in more detail in Part IV.

Defining the Metadata Solution

When we look at an organized set of metadata, we realize now that the metadata itself exists in many places. It is the *metadata solution* that puts some semblance of purpose and order around this disparate metadata. It is obvious, therefore, that the metadata solution encompasses many additional components, which may or may not be a part of the component that stores or generates the integrated metadata view.

Note: Ash quote (in *The New York Times,* October 20, 1985) from *The New York Public Library Book of Twentieth-Century American Quotations.* Copyright © 1992 by The Stonesong Press, Inc., and The New York Public Library. Used with permission.

> ❖ **Metadata solution**   An organized and integrated set of related metadata, logically connected but physically separate, with common access points and methods. The solution can embrace one or more metadata stores with distinct or common metamodels and must be accessible to metadata suppliers and beneficiaries who may or may not reside in the metadata solution's architecture.

Interpreting the definition confirms that metamodels are indeed just one piece of the pie.

Remembering the Objective

Why *are* we designing and implementing a metadata solution? Often, participants forget the main objective. Despite this seemingly myopic vision, "solutions" do result, but they are not always geared to original purpose. A continued naïveté almost always reflects in the metadata requirements themselves. It is essential to realize that a standalone metamodel will not serve metadata objectives if it becomes the only implemented component of a metadata solution.

How will the metamodels be populated? Will they be populated at all? How will the metamodels serve as access points for the metadata beneficiaries? How will metadata remain up to date? What relationship will the metadata suppliers, often tools, have with the metamodel contents?

Reviewing the 5 Questions

Although the 5 Questions[1] focus on data and its qualities, they are transferred easily to the metadata arena. When we review them, it is clear that the metamodel in and of itself will not handle the objectives of *any* metadata solution.

1. What metadata do we have? Although a metamodel depicts the scope of metadata coverage, the traversal of the model is often quite clumsy and inefficient for most metadata beneficiaries. Therefore, to answer the question, a directory or high-level categorization of the metamodel contents is often an additional requirement.

---

1. The 5 Questions is a trademark of and the questions and method are copyrighted by Database Design Solutions, Inc., Bernardsville, New Jersey.

2. What does it mean? How did we come up with the instance values of metadata? What does "Data Element Definition" really mean? Is it the definition according to one set of users, or is it a definition that has been sanctified as corporate? Where can we find out how this value was obtained? Do we define metadata, or just metadata instances?

3. Where is it? The location of the metamodel contents has not been discussed yet. This is a crucial component of all metadata solutions and depends on many architectural factors.

4. How did it get there? How and when was the metadata created? Why was it created and stored in its current location? This information is always of great significance to the metadata beneficiaries and often implies levels of credibility that are not necessarily documented.

5. How do I get it (Go get it for me!)? Last, but certainly not least, access to the validated and organized metadata must not be forgotten. If all this work goes into designing and creating a metadata solution, it should be available to all metadata beneficiaries—they are tools, users, applications, or repositories.

We address each of these questions in this chapter and validate our definition of *metadata solution.*

Storing Metadata

Perhaps the most common metadata storage mechanism is the centralized, custom-developed metadata database. This option seems to be the easiest to implement; most beneficiaries appear to get what they want immediately. In fact, the population of this storage solution is also quite simple; many implementers manually reinput metadata that already exists throughout the organization. There are many options to the storage scenario, including not storing the metadata directly in the repository solution. The pros and cons of each option vary with the timing and planned duration of the metadata solution.

Options

Once the metamodels are defined and the metadata instances have been officially sourced, it is important to decide how the metadata instances will be a part of the metadata solution. Simply speaking, this means deciding how and where to store the metadata. There are various options, none of which is necessarily better or worse than the others, but they depend on many architectural issues at hand, all of which need to be revisited. In addition, the storage option could address not only Question 1 (What metadata do I have?), but also Questions 3 (Where is it?) and 5 (How do I get it?).

The metamodel and its associated storage capabilities are related directly to the type of storage option(s) selected. Specifically, choices include one or any combination of the following:

Centralized custom database designed to reflect an integrated, all-encompassing metamodel perspective.

Metadata storage at the source with a main database functioning as the metadata directory or gateway by interpreting each metamodel's addressing and location-specific information.

Distributed metadata storage with separate metamodels and associated metadata instances residing in distinct locations. A master metamodel or search engine would be available to track and locate specific metadata instances (similar to the enterprise portal, which is discussed in Chapter 15).

Centralized repository tool with vendor-supplied metamodels populated either manually or via vendor-supplied interfaces and APIs.

Distributed repository tools, also with vendor-supplied metamodels, but populated in a distributed scenario such that coexistence is planned and integrated.

Let's discuss each option from the perspective of advantages and disadvantages.

Centralized Custom Database

Based on the ease of setup, this solution directly mirrors the results of the metadata requirements analysis. All metamodels are combined, typically at junction points, and each metamodel component represents a table in a relational database implementation. Instances are loaded either via bulk one-time load, with periodic updates, or manually, depending primarily on volume and the frequency of update. Front-ends can be simple client (e.g., VB) access, or in many cases, intranet search engines are placed "on top of" the custom database to allow subject-based queries and access.

In the best of worlds, this custom database is monitored and quality is controlled by an individual assigned to metadata administration. His or her responsibilities include the validation of metadata instances as well as the guarantee of the database's availability. Database design and enhancement also fall within this individual's job description, and the position remains filled even after this

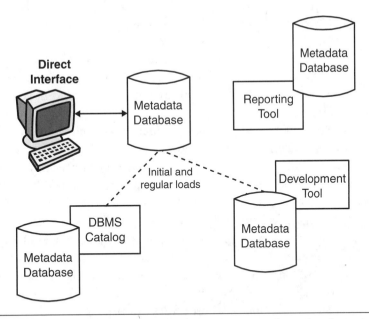

Figure 11-1 A centralized custom metadata database

individual moves on. The metadata database remains an active part of its beneficiaries' metadata analyses. Figure 11-1 illustrates this scenario.

In the worst of worlds, this database is soon out of date. In most cases it is established to meet a narrowly scoped initial objective (e.g., one data warehouse, definitions of one OTS package's data) and is typically requested by one specific user community. Despite the fact that the metadata probably exists elsewhere, it is recreated yet again so that the beneficiaries have easy access based on its new, integrated single location. In a short time, typically one year, the metadata database is no longer in demand because of its inaccuracy, and metadata beneficiaries seldom use it. The number of active users dwindles, and those responsible for its initial design and creation move on to newer endeavors.

In the most likely scenario, the metadata database's content and scope are too restrictive. Designed to meet a specific metadata beneficiary's set of requirements, they are usually not flexible enough to expand beyond that initial focus. Because the metamodel is one part of the metadata solution, a direct implementation without the other architectural features is incomplete. As metadata requirements and/or the number and types of metadata beneficiaries expand, the initial implementation loses its leverage and a more flexible, better planned metadata solution typically replaces this custom database within two years. The result is yet another node on the corporate metadata web.

Metadata Storage at the Source

In response to the trend of reducing unnecessary redundancy in both the data as well as the metadata worlds, most metadata solutions are adopting the philosophy of leaving metadata where it is used. In many cases, this metadata is created, updated, and maintained within a specific development or reporting tool, or in some cases, as part of a custom or purchased application package. Here, the metamodels and metadata requirements analysis consider the location of the metadata of record, as previously discussed. In other words, whether an official value exists to correct conflicting metadata instances is usually the key to whether metadata can remain solely where it is.[2] In situations where metadata instances conflict based on *instance value* but not intent or meaning, the metadata solution design *must* have assigned metadata of records and active maintenance plans tied to the overall architecture. Without such a strategy, the various metadata values and conflicts will eventually sever the overall architecture. Metadata maintenance strategies must coexist with the overall architectural plans.[3]

By keeping metadata in diverse locations, as illustrated in Figure 11-2, the metadata solution database becomes a metadata directory or gateway. Instead of tracking metadata instances, the database contains the metamodel, depicting metadata interrelationships as well as location specifics (answers to Questions 1, 2, and 5) for unique and specific metamodels. As anticipated, the specifics of the addressing schemes depend on the deployed technology and architecture of each metadata source. In addition, the ability of the deployed metadata database technology to interface with each of the metadata sources puts a major emphasis on the feasibility of the solution.

From a benefit perspective, this type of implementation obviously targets the reduction and eventual elimination of metadata conflict. As metadata instances are requested, typically they are retrieved from their actual source, with the metadata repository functioning as a gateway. As metadata is updated, the latest instances are accessed. There is no need for synchronization among separate metadata stores, because they are all connected via the gateway's common metamodel.

On the downside, technology certainly plays a major role in the feasibility of this solution. Metadata standards are moving toward universal metamodels with associated access routines. Our patience is worth its weight in this sce-

---

2. For a full discussion of the treatment of the metadata of record, see Chapter 9.

3. Maintenance plans are discussed in Chapter 30.

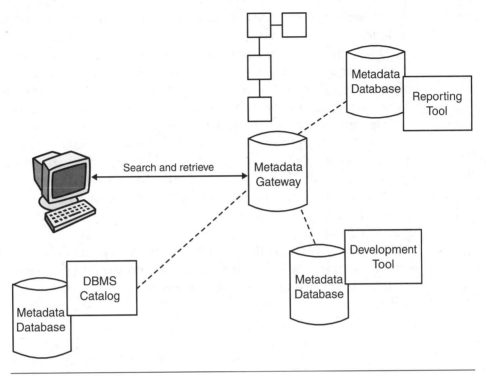

Figure 11-2 Metadata storage at the source

nario. Until standards become universal and easy to plug in, interface capabilities depend on the compatibility of the underlying metadata stores as well as the completeness of API (application programming interface) sets or the maturity of standard intertool exchange mechanisms such as XML.[4]

Distributed Metadata Storage

In the distributed scenario illustrated in Figure 11-3, metamodels and their metadata instances reside at distinct locations. There is no master metamodel or repository, as there is with the previous option, because the search engines have the ability to scan the contents of each metadata store directly, typically by accessing individual metamodels in order to retrieve the metadata of choice. There is no need to organize or integrate the various metadata stores, but the practicality of this solution depends substantially on the deployed

---

4. XML is discussed in Part III.

search engine and the existence of the particular engine's required contents in each distinct metadata area.

Distributed metadata storage is becoming more popularly known as an enterprise portal. Although most portals are used to retrieve data, the same concepts apply with metadata retrieval. In this implementation, the search targets remain unchanged, except for some standard portal-wary identification. The search engines become the power behind the practicality of this solution. Despite this apparent ease of implementation, the efficiency of such a setup depends substantially on how well organized each metadata store is in relationship to the others. For example, having the same information in more than one place without forethought as to a logical separation concept guarantees only that the same information, with perhaps different intentions, is retrieved over and over again.

Properly implemented portals require both architectural and metadata instance planning. Without such advanced design, the portal can end up returning lots of unrelated metadata and the user would be stuck with making sense of it all.

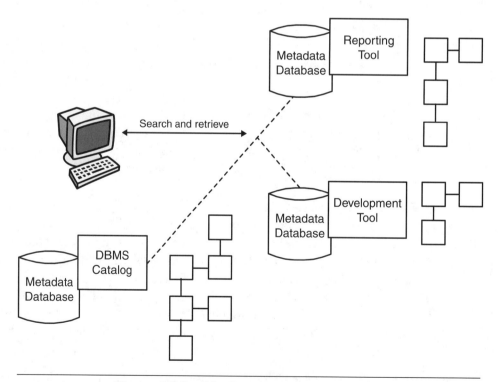

Figure 11-3   **Distributed metadata storage**

Centralized Repository Tool

Repository tools, vendor supplied, offer much more than metadata databases. Their architecture assumes interfaces, and in many cases, full sets of APIs are included as part of the base repository offering. Although their full design and functionality is covered in a later chapter,[5] it is necessary to introduce them here as an option in the storage of metadata. Most initial metadata solutions during the 1990s involved repository technology. The amount of functionality that was part of the standard tools varied substantially by vendor, and the latter part of the 1990s involved many vendor acquisitions and mergers so that today's offerings represent distinct architectural variations.

With a centralized repository tool, most installations use the repository's metadata store as the sole integrated metadata area. Initially, other sources of metadata are loaded into the repository, usually through a vendor-supplied batch interface. The means of metadata maintenance varies from installation to installation, but in general, a repository administrator oversees the integrity of the repository's contents. Likewise, some aspect of metadata creation usually involves automated repository update.

Purchased repository tools are often called a "repository in a box" because the vendor provides metamodels along with standard interfaces to and from the populated repository. The supplied functionality comes with a price tag, however, and therefore purchased repository tools are not usually considered for small-scope metadata solutions. Finally, as discussed in Chapter 14, each repository product is typically focused on a specific type of metadata functionality (e.g., data management, application development, or data warehouse support) and therefore is architecturally designed to interface only with products that are targeted to support the same functional market space.

Distributed Repository Tools

When vendor-supplied repository tools are designed to coexist, metadata storage takes on another option. In this scenario, the tools are deployed throughout an organization, typically with each metadata repository representing a subset of the overall enterprise's metadata. The synchronization of these tool instances as well as their participation in the full metadata indexing schema is quite vendor dependent. Again, as with distributed metadata storage, an overall metadata distribution plan is a prerequisite to success in this scenario.

---

5. Repository tools are discussed in Chapter 14.

Distributed repository tool implementations are not the same as distributed database implementations. Repository software provides a key part of the metadata-based functionality and must also be functionally distributed.

Accessing Metadata

Once metadata is stored, it must be accessed. Metadata beneficiaries have different access requirements, and a beneficiary-specific analysis process, covered in Part IV, is a prerequisite to finalizing the overall metadata solution interfaces. The following metadata access possibilities exist:

Direct query—Either via a front-end interface or a DBMS query language, the metadata store is queried directly based on its underlying schema.

Tool-driven access—An interfacing tool (development tool, reporting tool, etc.) presents metadata to the beneficiary. The metadata exists in the tool's metadata store.

API-driven access—Tools, applications, or other software use metadata solution-specific APIs to get to the stored metadata.

Remote procedure calls (RPCs)—From a reverse point of view, the metadata solution uses procedures inherent to the "keepers of the metadata," so to speak, as a means of retrieving metadata from its resting place. Typically, metamodels in this scenario need to accommodate the location and access procedures associated with each metadata source that falls within the scope of the served beneficiaries.

Batch export—Creation of a simple extract, download, or file brings a set of metadata from the metadata solution to the requesting beneficiary.

Standards-based metadata exchange—As exchange standards become finalized, more metadata solution implementations leave the access of the metadata to exchange mechanisms that are not vendor specific. XML is a popular example.

Portal/directory-based access—Based on specific search engines, metadata is retrieved and displayed to the requestor by matching metadata instances to search requirements.

The type of access that is best for a beneficiary is selected based on the analysis of architectural requirements.

Revisiting the Metadata Architecture

Metadata everywhere, beneficiaries everywhere, and the relationships among them never seem to be planned or logical. The *metadata architecture* organizes the metamodel components based on a logical spread of metadata sources. Specifically, metadata of record assignments are validated based on the availability of a specific metadata store, whether it is part of a tool, application, or other metadata solution. Consider Figure 11-4 and the patterned relationships among metamodels. In a well-planned metadata architecture, the integrated metamodel represents a uniform conglomeration of the specific and unique metamodels that reside across the architecture. Common metadata

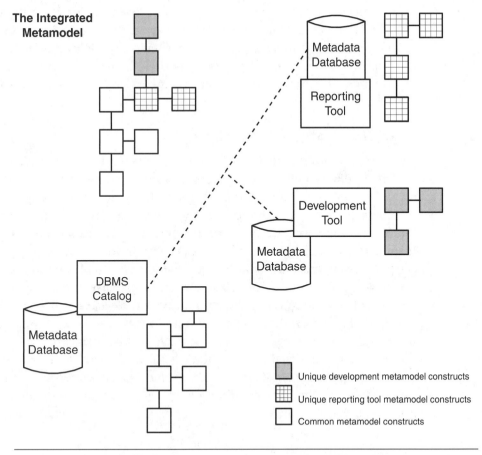

Figure 11-4   A sample metadata architecture

is represented in a common metamodel. It is then supplemented with the interface points that may be necessary to connect the common metadata to the metamodels of each architectural component.

Where the Tools Fit In

As we evaluate metadata access, one questions always is, How do various metadata suppliers and recipients fit into the overall plan? The most common metadata forces in the architecture are those tools we all know and love. We use them to create data, analyze data, and process data. We use them to develop source code, configure applications, and maintain hardware/software assignments. We use them to tune our databases and monitor system performance. A day without tools is like a day without sunshine. As we use all these tools, we create and use metadata over and over again. Now that we have not only strategically identified which metadata is of importance to our beneficiaries, but also sourced all of it, the tools are crucial components of the overall metadata solution inasmuch as they buy and sell metadata. The metadata solution architecture relates all components into an organized and accessible set of logical metadata.

Determining the Scope of Coverage

As we evolve our metadata architecture, focusing on the participating tools and their ability to either access metadata or be accessed, the scope of metadata coverage begins to tighten. Although there are formal ways to scope a metadata solution,[6] it is important to note that sometimes technical issues force the elimination or redirection of some metadata aspects of the solution. If some tools are full of valuable metadata, but have no clear-cut way of being accessed, many metadata solution designers may rethink the immediate solution to account for this lack of clear interface capability. Other ways of scoping the metadata solution relate the amount of beneficiaries to be covered in the first implementation to the specific functions that will be addressed by the metadata solution, or even to what metadata will be included.

Metadata solutions that try to address all needs with the first implementation are destined to fail. When metadata solutions are scoped so that increased functionality, metadata accessibility, and beneficiary service are added over time, the metadata solution becomes exponentially more successful.

---

6. Scoping is covered in Chapter 17.

Consider the fact that metadata is just one part of the overall metadata solution. Consider also that metadata is typically addressed by a full metadata solution as part of an overall metamodel or series of metamodels.

Metamodel and Metadata Relationships

Remember that our focus on metadata and its associated beneficiaries will now take a step up to a higher level of sorts, that of the metamodel. As discussed in the previous chapter, metamodels depict metadata relationships graphically, at the entity or object level. By grouping various metadata elements according to "what is being described," we create a series of entities. Each entity must have a primary key or identifier; relationships happen at the level of the primary key. For example, in relating customers to stores, we know that every customer visits one or more stores, and all stores are visited by one or more customers. Without getting into too much jargon, we can consider this a many-to-many relationship. The importance, however, rests with the fact that we identify stores, perhaps, by store numbers, and we identify customers, perhaps, by customer name and credit card number combined (a compound key). For simplicity, we assume no cash transactions.

Taking this analogy back to the world of metadata, remember that Data Element Business Name and Data Element Description were two pieces of metadata that were common throughout our examples. Where in the metamodel would they fit? It is often hard for newcomers to the world of metadata to realize that *Data Element* is a major topic or, in fact, what is being *described by* many of the other metadata elements, including Data Element Description. Hence, in a metamodel, Data Element would be an entity unto itself, and participate in many relationships, including relationships with specific types of data stores (files, databases, tables), entities within logical data models, reports, and applications, to name a few.

So as we evaluate any metamodel, we have to realize the level of our evaluation. Metamodels reflect a specific perspective on the way entities can connect. Each entity consists of a series of attributes, most typically our metadata elements; but sometimes, as previously discussed, other information needs to be tracked in order to maintain the stability of the metadata.

If we look again at the metamodel for our common metadata, illustrated in Figure 11-5, note that the two metadata elements that we are discussing (Data Element Business Name and Data Element Definition) are attributes of the *Logical Data Element* entity. This entity relates to *Physical Data Element* from the

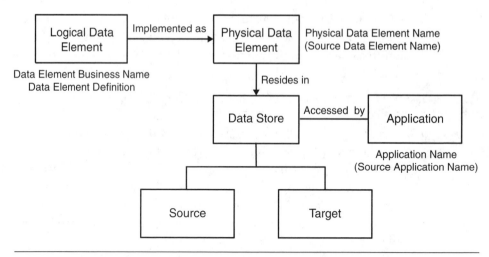

Figure 11-5   **Revisiting a metamodel**

common perspective of all beneficiaries. The perspective is an important one to keep in our back pockets as we look at some of today's competing models.

Sample Metamodels

Metamodels can be purchased, downloaded, copied, or custom developed. Sometimes, metamodels are an inherent part of a metadata solution, and implementers simply adopt them. It is always valuable to look at what is out there as a means of justifying your specific metadata approach or to help you decide whether to buy or build (more on that topic in Chapter 20).

Metamodel Types

Perspectives are represented via distinct metamodels. The types of perspective include the following:

Tool-specific—The metamodel reflects the way a tool uses its own metadata. In many cases, this metamodel is a logical or physical data model of the tool's underlying database.

Methodology-specific—The metamodel's representation is based on a particular modeling methodology, most typically object-oriented versus entity-relationship modeling. Current efforts are trying to adopt the Unified Modeling Language (UML) as a standard means of structure (content) as

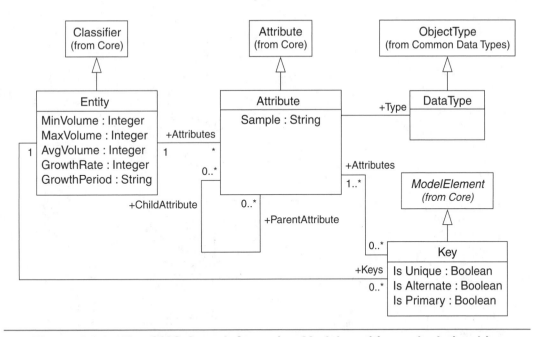

Figure 11-6 **The OMG Open Information Model, entities and relationships**

Source: Used with permission from the Object Management Group, Needham, Mass. Copyright © OMG, 1993–2001.

well as syntax. Models that appear later in this chapter are illustrated with UML.

Function-supporting—Metamodel constructs represent those used to support a particular task, set of tasks, or function. For example, there are configuration management metamodels, application testing metamodels, and data management metamodels.

Generic—Usually used for integration, these metamodels represent the components that are common to all renditions of the metadata-described information. Generic metamodels are intended to be compatible with this information irrespective of where it exists.

The sample metamodel in Figure 11-6 depicts the entities and relationships aspect of the Object Management Group's Open Information Model, part of their efforts to set standards.[7] This model, diagrammed in UML, reflects the

7. Metadata standards are discussed in Chapter 16.

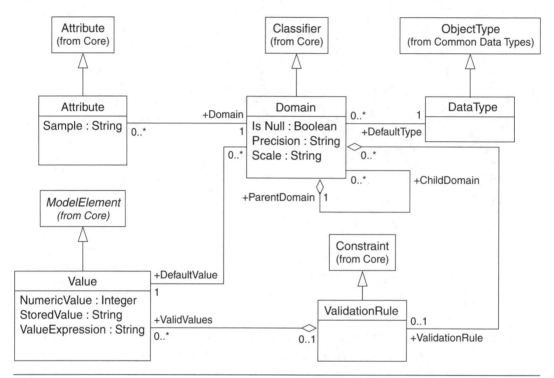

Figure 11-7   **The OMG Open Information Model, attributes**

Source: Used with permission from the Object Management Group, Needham, Mass. Copyright © OMG, 1993–2001.

metadata relationships to be used by all compliant tools, thus guaranteeing metadata interaction and shareability. Compare this model to your data modeling thinking. If connections or entities seem to be missing, it is easy to assume that the standard will not address your needs. In addition, it may be too easy for vendor tools to comply with a model that is not detailed enough to address the full usage of entities and relationships. Finally, it is safe to assume that parts of compliant tools will be shareable, while the nonaddressed items will remain in the vendor's control.

The *Attributes* and *Model Packaging* submodels of the Open Information Model (Figures 11-7 and 11-8) show us more of the OMG's metamodel perspectives. Notice some differences with our requirements. In Figure 11-7, *Domain*, for example, although directly tied to an *Attribute*, can consist of parent and child domains, all of which are named and tied to a specific *Classifier*. This approach encourages the reusability of domains in a model, across many, if not all, attributes. However, when this model is compared with Figure 11-8,

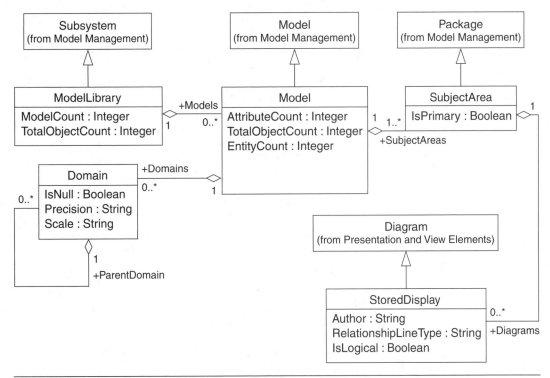

Figure 11-8 **The OMG Open Information Model, model packaging**

Source: Used with permission from the Object Management Group, Needham, Mass. Copyright © OMG, 1993–2001.

which represents *Model Packaging*, it is clear that Domain is intended to be reusable *across* models; there is a relationship *between Domain and Model*, irrespective of Attribute.

As we evaluate existing metamodels and compare them to our requirements, we need to consider whether their way is better than our way, or whether our way is an absolute requirement. If the latter is the case, we must consider *extending* a purchased or noncustomized metamodel.

Extensions are any changes made to a marketplace model. They are easy to make, but not always so easy to maintain. The benefits and disadvantages should be weighed.

As we conclude Part II, you should have a firm feeling for the characteristics and power of metadata. Part III takes us into the heart of metadata solutions by describing how metadata comes together across the metamodels *within* an implemented metadata solution.

Part III
Entering
Meta-Meta Land

We have explored data, information, knowledge, and metadata. We organized metadata into metamodels. We also defined the metadata solution, and realized that the metamodel in and of itself is only a component, although a major component. To understand fully and relate the other components of a metadata solution, it is necessary to enter *meta-meta* land. Many people get uncomfortable in meta-meta land. Meta-meta land is the only place where all metadata is treated equally, irrespective of its origin or destination. In fact, it is in meta-meta land where we have to begin thinking like a tool.

Part III discusses our metadata solution from a higher level, the one that is uncomfortably theoretical yet universally practical. In this part of the book, we begin by changing our mindsets to conform to those of today's tools—metadata suppliers and recipients. We start by discussing what metadata means to a tool in Chapter 12. We then move to the meta-metamodel in Chapter 13, or the "chapter for glazed-over eyes." This chapter, clearly only for those who have to go through metadata and multitool integration, introduces a new way of thinking. In this chapter, things we think of as attributes, or characteristics, become entities, or subjects. Things that we had never concerned ourselves with, such as how tools store metadata, are now of major importance. Although the chapter is labeled technical, it is a clear prerequisite for those who intend to build their own metadata solutions or customize an off-the-shelf product. Chapter 14 introduces repositories, that is, *metadata repositories*, an example of a true metadata solution.

The remainder of Part III discusses other metadata-based technologies such as the Web, including XML, file systems, and database management systems, to name a few. Finally, Part III closes with a brief discussion of the impact of standards, today's and tomorrow's.

Chapter 12

Meta-Metadata
What Metadata Means to a Tool

*Scientists, like game players, prefer
to devise their own strategies,
even though these depend on an
assimilated, shared body of knowledge.*
—S. E. Luria

The full metadata solution includes substantial metadata processing power. In fact, much of this power is becoming inherent to *standardized* metadata solutions. Until standardization matures, metadata solution processing will reign, however. How does a metadata solution process metadata? The answer lies in meta-meta land.

The Tool's View of Metadata

So far, to keep it simple, the depiction of metadata requirements as well as their subsequent categorization has been from the outsider's point of view. As long as *we* receive what we need, we consider our metadata requirements gathering sufficient. Ironically, we used to complain often about this naïveté in our ultimate IT customers, those business users whom we always aimed to please. They typically did not concern themselves with how the inner workings of our developed applications supplied information. Nowadays, however, that is often a different story. In fact, our business users are often quite annoyed when they are not given those hidden business rules so that they can intelligently analyze the very information products of which we are so proud. The same fact is now true with respect to metadata.

Note: Luria quote (in *A Slot Machine, A Broken Test Tube: An Autobiography*, 1985) from *The New York Public Library Book of Twentieth-Century American Quotations.* Copyright © 1992 by The Stonesong Press, Inc., and The New York Public Library. Used with permission.

The inner workings of not only metadata suppliers but also the metadata solutions are of paramount importance. When we organized the metadata requirements into distinct metamodels, we represented only the outward perspectives. Within each tool, other metadata exists, and a substantial portion of it may appear to have nothing to do with beneficiary requirements. To a tool, however, all metadata is processed equally, and carries the same weight in the overall scheme of things.

As Figure 12-1 illustrates, the meta-meta design (called the meta-meta-model) relates our metadata instances to other metadata instances, irrespective of the metamodel in which each instance resides. In addition, other solution-specific metadata is tracked and resides in the metamodel, which determines what happens to metadata as it becomes a part of the overall metadata solution.

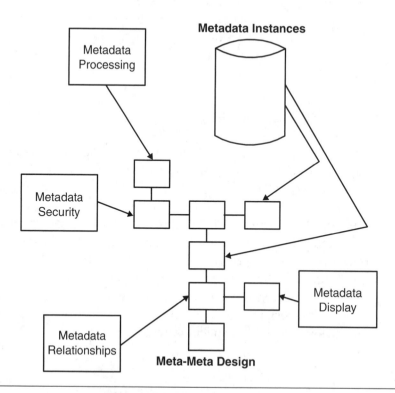

Figure 12-1   Meta-meta land

Meta-Metadata

Once we get to the design of the metadata solution, our perspective moves up one notch to the multitool, or meta-meta, perspective. With the perspective of the metadata solution, each tool's metadata is now an instance in an overall set of multiple metadata perspectives. The meta-metadata now describes the metadata, and instead of thinking of our metadata as describing data (which it does), we widen our perspective and consider the fact that metadata is also being described—by *meta-metadata*.

What Is Meta-Metadata?

Considering that the Greek term *meta* represents things that "occur later than or in succession to,"[1] meta-metadata typically occurs later on the time line than metadata does. Following this reasoning, literal interpretation would put meta-data *after* data. Because we are in the process of integrating various metadata occurrences, however, and have already organized them based on their values as organized requirements, we know that *meta* is not interpreted literally in our world. However, as we will see, the hierarchy of descriptive levels does mirror the time line order to some degree.

> ❖ **Meta-metadata**   The descriptive details of metadata; metadata qualities and locations that allow tool-based processing and access; the basic attributes of metadata solutions.

In order to specifically relate meta-metadata to the world of metadata and the ultimate world of data, an example is usually beneficial. Table 12-1 shows that perspectives change as we get closer to the meta-meta level. Read the table from right to left.

Once metadata solutions get concerned with the meta-meta level, entire perspectives as to what constitutes data and metadata begin to change. Boundaries become fuzzy, and solutions become confused and mixed. Here the saying "One person's data is another person's metadata" starts to make more

---

1. *Merriam Webster's New Collegiate Dictionary,* 10th ed. (Springfield, Mass.: Merriam-Webster, Inc., 1993), p. 730.

Table 12-1 Taking Instance Data to the Meta-Meta Level

Meta-Metamodel Construct	Metadata	Data	Instance Data
MetaEntity (MetaObject)	Data Element	Zip Code	07979
MetaEntity (MetaObject)	Data Element	Employee Last Name	Johnson

sense. In fact, "one tool's data is another tool's metadata" is a more accurate restatement. *In meta-meta land, all tools' metadata are described by meta-metadata.*

Remembering the definitions in Chapter 7, *instance data* is "that which is input into a receiving tool, application, database, or simple processing engine." Table 12-1 shows a new distinction, *data,* for the purpose of illustrating how different perspectives can come together at the meta-meta level. Because what is instance data to an application (illustrated in the last column of the table) may not even be part of a development tool (e.g., a modeling tool), Table 12-1 needs an intermediary column. The time line that is most likely involved in relating all of the perspectives, from instance data to meta-metadata, appears in Figure 12-2.

Remember that starting perspectives determine remaining perspectives. The meta-meta level that brings all perspectives together by relating them at the appropriate place in the meta-meta schema is otherwise known as meta-meta land.

Probably the most confusing aspect of meta-meta land is the fact that, as illustrated, a *Column* and a *Data Element* eventually become *MetaEntity* instances in meta-meta land. Most of us think of entities as a person, place, thing, or event about which we collect data. Well, if we were tools, we would be collecting data about Columns and Data Elements. So to a tool, these are in fact entities, but at the meta-meta level, the common term is *MetaEntity*.

Meta-Metadata's Purpose

Meta-metadata adds consistency to the various metadata perspectives by giving each type of metadata a distinct spot in the meta-metamodel. Many metadata solution novices find the concept of meta-metadata difficult to grasp at first. If you have mastered the art of metadata by mastering the ability to think like a tool, you are more than halfway there. To grasp the purpose of meta-metadata, it is now necessary to think like a *metadata solution*, that is, a tool that integrates other tools, or minimally allows multiple tools to access metadata that is not part of that particular tool's world.

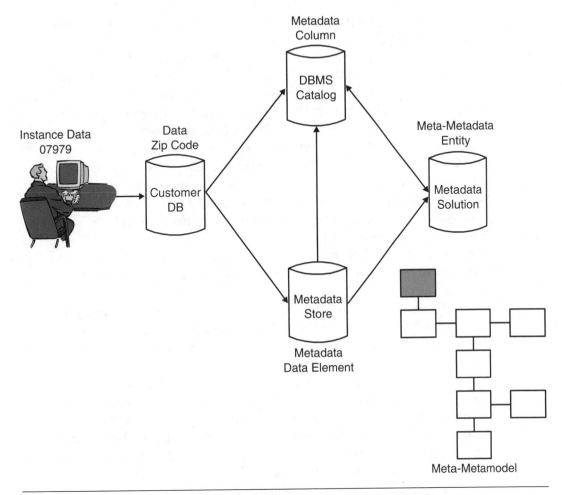

Figure 12-2   From instance data to meta-metadata

Regardless of the type of metadata construct represented by each piece of metadata (Data Element, Data Store, Program, Application, Tool, etc.), each piece of metadata must have a name, a definition, a length, a type (numeric, alphabetic, free-form, etc.), and other standard qualities. This fact is a significant statement in meta-meta land. Because of these similarities, *all* the aforementioned metadata constructs are occurrences of the same "box" in the meta-metamodel. In other words, each metadata construct is an instance of *the same* model *component*. As noted earlier, in an entity-relationship (ER) world, this component is called a *meta-entity*. In an object-oriented (OO) world, this component is a *meta-object*. The meta-metamodel groups all meta-metadata according to the perspective of one metadata solution. (Meta-metamodels are discussed in detail in Chapter 13.)

To bring the meta-meta concept to reality, I always use the public library analogy. In a library each book, or library item, contains both data and metadata. The library borrower is interested in the data (the pages in the book), but needs to know the metadata (title, author, chapter number) in order to get to the data. The librarian *organizes* all this metadata into distinct metamodels, depending on the role of the metadata and its immediate beneficiaries. Each metamodel is represented in a particular metadata store—examples include the card catalog, interlibrary borrowing system, and *Readers' Guide to Periodical Literature*. Each metamodel contains metadata, sometimes the same metadata as other metamodels, but also some distinct metadata. Think of the library itself as a *metadata solution*, the place where all these metamodels and metadata stores come together. The way in which a particular item is represented in *all* metadata stores requires a meta-meta perspective. Librarians work with meta-metadata daily.

In Figure 12-3, the library is represented very simply. Every library indexing method (microfiche, *Readers' Guide*, card catalog, etc.) is treated in the same way, and represents a conglomerate of library items. Consider the fact that each library indexing method is a metamodel in and of itself. Note also that in this high-level meta-metamodel, *library items* are categorized by more than one *library indexing method*. Likewise, each *library indexing method* categorizes more than one *library item*. More important, consider the fact that whenever a new indexing method is contemplated, the library cares more about how the new method will relate to existing indexing methods and how each existing library item will be indexed in the contemplated method. If only corporate America did that with metadata solutions!

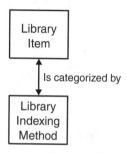

Figure 12-3   The library as a meta-metamodel

Types of Meta-Metadata

At the meta-meta level, there are various types of meta-metadata, including the following:

Generic meta-metadata is used to integrate discrete levels of metadata based on instances in the meta-metamodel.

Processing meta-metadata is used to standardize the processes associated with generic metadata.

Access meta-metadata is used to standardize the interface and retrieval of generic types of metadata.

Security meta-metadata is used to restrict and/or permit the access and processing of generic types of metadata.

Generic meta-metadata is the type of meta-metadata most common to all metadata solutions because it rarely varies based on the type of solution. At this meta-meta level the solutions are geared toward standardizing metadata instances despite their origin. In fact, at the meta-meta level, constructs tend to be representative of the modeling method used to depict them. Examples include Object, Feature, and Service.

Processing meta-metadata determines the level of impact of particular metadata solutions based on the use, distribution, and maintenance of specific metadata instances. The types of processing meta-metadata as well as their inherent impact vary by metadata solution since the location in the meta-model where the processes relate to the metadata is typically reflected by the meta-metamodel design and resident relationships among meta-metadata constructs. Examples include Operation, Policy, and Method.

Access meta-metadata is typically combined with security meta-metadata; it describes the "packaging" of the metadata that is being retrieved or supplied to the metadata solution by those (tools) that are allowed to do so. The most common examples of access meta-metadata are Procedures, particularly when the procedures refer to standard APIs (application program interfaces).

Meta-metadata that deals with the security of the metadata solution is also a part of the overall meta-metamodel. Security-specific meta-metadata is typically invisible to all but metadata solution administrators, and it affects the availability of most of the metadata solution and its contents to all targeted beneficiaries and suppliers. Specifically, this meta-metadata reflects userids and associated permissions in terms of which metadata should be part of each beneficiary world. Examples include Template and Userid.

Table 12-2   Metadata as Instances of Meta-Metadata

Meta-Meta Construct	Sample Metadata Instances		
MetaObject	Model	Relationship	Program
MetaRelationship	Is associated with	Resides in	Implemented as
MetaAttribute	Object name	Definition	Creation date

Meta-Metadata's Relationship to Metadata

Metadata is characterized and described at the meta-meta level. Consider the fact that metadata has to be stored and qualified somewhere. Typically, metadata resides in a *metadata store* of some type. To depict the relationship between the meta-metadata and its described metadata, a tabular representation is usually best (see Table 12-1).

Metadata should be considered an *instance* of a particular meta-meta construct.

In Table 12-2, the metadata instances are occurrences of the meta-meta constructs identified in the first column. This may represent a new way of thinking for some people, since we don't often think of things like Definition as being instances. Instead, we think of "a unique means of identifying an occurrence of an employee" as an instance. Remember, what is data to some is metadata to others. Now, we also know that *what is metadata to some is meta-metadata to others, the others typically being metadata solutions*. For example, Table 12-1 shows a progression from data to metadata to meta-metadata. Table 12-2 begins with metadata and goes to meta-metadata. The "meta-meta construct" is the place in meta-meta land, or the "box" in the meta-metamodel, where this meta-metadata will reside as an instance. All of these connections are depicted in the meta-metamodel.

Storing Meta-Metadata

In the simplest of worlds, meta-metadata describes one set of metadata, and both the meta-metadata and all its associated metadata reside in the same database. This philosophy works best in terms of its ease of implementation, but not in terms of practicality. The storage location of metadata is a direct contributor to the overall architecture and usefulness of every metadata solution.

In today's world of metadata webs galore, metadata is already everywhere, and to some degree, so is meta-metadata.

Since meta-metadata is the ultimate stop in the data/metadata chain of description, its location must be accessible from all metadata suppliers and recipients within a particular metadata solution. Likewise, the flexibility of the meta-metadata storage design must reflect the needs and wants of similar suppliers and recipients. With today's distributed and disconnected metadata storage, it is likely that multiple meta-metadata stores are part of the solution. What varies from solution to solution, however, is the depth of each meta-metadata store's functionality and coverage. Finally, in order to integrate these sporadic but potentially connected meta-metadata stores, a meta-repository, or enterprise portal, is often a required part of the solution.

The Tool's Repository

It is obvious that tools form a part of our information processing lives. It should now also be obvious that each of these tools has its own metadata. All this metadata is stored in the tool's database, which some vendors call a repository.

At its simplest, most people think of a repository as a "box, room, etc., in which things may be placed for safekeeping."[2] In this simple world, virtually every software product on the market has a repository, and most, if not all, contain some types of metadata.[3] Because of this perspective, it is safe to say that repositories abound. However, if the intent of the tool has nothing to do with the role of the metadata, then the actual role and subsequent storage of the meta-metadata may not be of significance in meta-meta land. Tools and their associated repositories, therefore, should be categorized based on their metadata intentions.

Also-Ran Metadata Storage

If, in fact, the purpose of the particular software product does not in any way, shape, or form contain a metadata aspect, then metadata was not part of the tool's original focus or underlying design. The metadata is an inherent part of the tool, not intended to be shared or exported. No consideration as to whether the tool-specific metadata already exists or existed elsewhere was or typically ever will become the groundwork for a feature of the tool itself. At

---

2. *Webster's New World Dictionary and Thesaurus* (New York: Simon & Schuster, 1996), p. 527.

3. Repositories are discussed in full in Chapter 14.

best, based on customer demands, some of the metadata will be exported along with the data itself. Examples of tools in this category include accounting systems, purchased application packages, word processors, and desktop publishing tools. All are part of what is called "also-ran metadata storage."

Metadata Generators and Recipients

Once a tool becomes part of the development world, it is usually geared toward one or more aspects of the overall development lifecycle. For instance, the design of an application inherently creates metadata that is intended to be used by downstream recipients of certain aspects of the application's design. Database Management Systems (DBMSs) have a catalog with massive metadata that describes the physical databases. This Database Definition Language (DDL) can often be received from modeling tools, and so on. Tools in this category not only contain meta-metadata describing their own tool's metadata, but are capable of receiving metadata from other places and integrating it with their own. Finally, many tools are capable of generating metadata in a form that is usable by other tools. Examples of metadata generators and recipients include modeling tools, application development aids, programming languages, and object class libraries.

Metadata Storage and Retrieval Tools

Moving into the *metadata solution* arena puts a different emphasis on meta-metadata. Tools established not only for the purpose of integrating various metadata stores but also for allowing external metadata access are typically very concerned with the design and location of the involved meta-metadata. Only this tool category is truly a potential *metadata solution*, based on the existence of a well-designed meta-meta component.

This third example is a true repository, as we will see in Chapter 14. Others are simply databases, many containing both data and metadata in an inseparable design. However, the actual architectures of each tool could imply some metadata import/export/access capability, particularly in the second category, metadata generators and recipients.

The Meta-Repository

When multiple repositories or even multiple metadata stores become part of a metadata solution, a meta-repository is the only way to find out what is where. In this scenario, a meta-metamodel now contains an additional box, representing *repository* instances. Enterprise portals are in fact meta-repositories. They

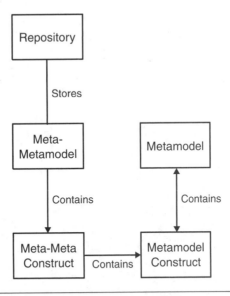

Figure 12-4 A meta-repository/enterprise portal metamodel

locate each repository based on a supplied description. They may then process the contents of the located repository based on meta-meta instances that qualify security and access characteristics.

As Figure 12-4 illustrates, the Repository is now a named and characterized component. Standardization will ensure consistent descriptors and access (more on that later!). Note that each repository has an associated meta-metamodel. That meta-metamodel contains meta-meta constructs (e.g., MetaEntities), which are populated by metamodel constructs (e.g., Database, Table), which populate particular metamodels (e.g., DBMS). Metadata components (or metamodel constructs), associated with metamodels, are stored in various repositories. Chapter 13 discusses the meta-metamodel in more detail.

Processing Meta-Metadata

Every metadata solution varies in terms of the impact meta-metadata has on the tool's functionality. The meta-metamodel determines where processes affect meta-metadata occurrences. Metadata solution architectures determine which processing options are solution specific and which are user tunable. As standardization becomes more widely focused and accepted, fewer and fewer variations in meta-metadata processing will be required.

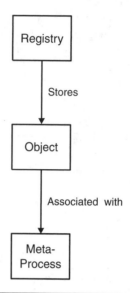

Figure 12-5   **The Microsoft Explorer meta-metamodel perspective**

Consider the all-encompassing Microsoft Explorer® example. Meta-meta-data reflects the fact that various types of files must be integrated for similar processing, irrespective of where the metadata was created or where it (file contents) resides. In fact, each installation of Explorer® should be viewed as a repository, with a meta-metamodel similar to the model in Figure 12-5.

When we expand our metadata solution world to include repositories (registries) that exist outside our immediate computer, we usually go to the Network Neighborhood. How does the Explorer implementation know where other metadata exists? How does it process the meta-metadata that tells us how to access and decipher the other meta-metadata? Portals are one step ahead of us as right now . . . and standardization will make the access and processing of meta-metadata invisible, like Network Neighborhood.

Chapter 13

The Meta-Metamodel

Metadata solution success depends not only on a rational subdivision of all of the metadata that lies within, but also on the existence of logical relationships *among* the various subdivisions. Most metadata solution practitioners cringe at the thought of meta-metamodels. In fact, glazed eyes are quite common. But the fact remains—*if you want to make separate, messy piles come together, you have to understand what they have in common*. Even if the separate piles have been organized logically, they still need to come together as one. If you have no intention of analyzing these separate worlds from perhaps the first-time *integrated* perspective, then you may want to skip this chapter. I assure you, however, that without this type of analysis, you will always be jumping from one pile of metadata to the other . . . and you may not be able to go back to your originating position without major headaches.

Outside IT, much of this philosophy can be illustrated by any country's highway system. We are all very familiar with the routes that get us from our houses to many of our common destinations—the office, our favorite ski slopes, our favorite beach, a set of shopping malls. When we need to trek to an uncommon destination, we pull out a map (or in today's Web-enabled age, we download a map). The map, in a relatively standardized fashion, shows us what routes connect us to other parts of the country. Whether all possible routes appear on the map depends on the level of detail on the map. In the United States, interstate maps usually show only the interstate highway system. State maps show most county roads and their connections to the interstate highway system. But when we need to visit "Small Town, USA," we usually have to pull

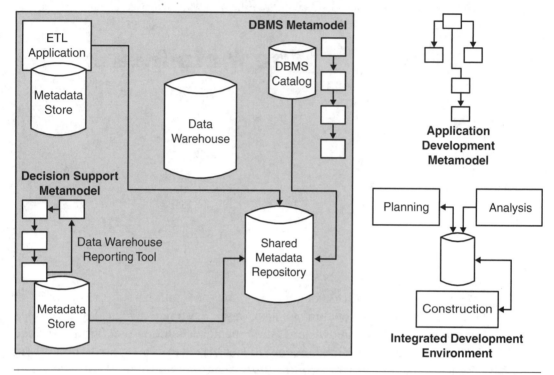

Figure 13-1 Today's metamodel web

out the county map, which shows all the little local streets and roads. What if we are traveling from one country to another, by automobile? Getting an atlas for each country is usually our first option. Again, the details in each country get further refined as the scope of the particular map lessens. But even with these adjustments, virtually all maps use common symbols to represent roads, cities, lakes, mountains, and oceans. This meta-meta perspective is what ties one map to another.

In the metadata world, some of this common connection is reflected in the meta-metamodel, which we discuss in this chapter.

Organizing Metamodels

I remember when I first started working in the metadata/repository space in the early 1990s. Vendors misinterpreted the terms *metadata, metamodel,* and *meta-metamodel.* What was considered a meta-metamodel in one tool was a metamodel in another. What was data in one tool was metadata in another. No

wonder the concept of organizing metamodels, especially those that originated from different vendors, was foreign. In fact, early repository vendors did
not even discuss their meta-meta perspectives with their consumers. Only
when the concept of tying things together despite their origins became important (late 1990s) did meta-meta concerns arise . . . and for the most part the
only interested consumers were the software vendors themselves.

When we are organizing metamodels as opposed to metadata, we enter
meta-meta land. We start by looking at meta-metadata, and the organization of
meta-metadata is not something that metadata solution planners and implementers typically can control. Depending on the scope and breadth of the
meta-metadata instances, otherwise known as metadata, the meta-meta perspective embraces one of the following:

A vendor's integration strategy, targeted at providing a single-vendor solution that embraces distinct functions. These functions are typically presented in terms of application development or data analysis, which are
carried out using other products from the same vendor. The boxed data
warehouse environment illustrated in Figure 13-1 represents such a
single-vendor solution.

One metadata repository, offered by one vendor for the purposes of allowing
metadata creation, definition, and limited sharing among members of a
predefined toolset. The metamodels represent distinct views or underlying tool designs within the overall repository architecture. The Integrated
Development Environment illustrated in Figure 13-1 represents single-
vendor integration. Each component can be purchased separately as a distinct tool, or with other components as part of an integrated environment.

A metadata solution, geared toward integrating any combination of the
above as well as outside metadata. In this scenario, virtually anything can
become part of the metadata solution, as long as the metadata is categorized and labeled with predefined meta-metadata. This meta-metadata
(instances of particular meta-meta constructs) resides in a meta-metamodel of sorts.

It is helpful to evaluate each of these categories in terms of how it can be
organized at the meta-metamodel level. Consider Figure 13-2 as we evaluate
what it takes to put separate worlds together. Note that the metamodels contain
metamodel constructs, whose instances are otherwise known as metadata. In
this illustrated representation, the metamodel constructs themselves are associated with one or more metadata stores, each accessible by a repository

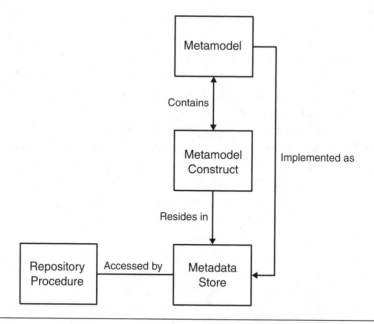

Figure 13-2   Metamodels as part of a bigger picture

procedure. In other scenarios, an entire metamodel may reside in one meta-data store. Implementations vary.

Vendor Integration Strategies

When a metadata solution is designed and built by a vendor of disparate tools, whether these tools are used for end-user analysis or IT development, the integration of these tools is the main focus at the meta-metadata level. Rarely does the metadata solution have the flexibility required to incorporate outside vendors' products and their associated metadata. As such, the meta-metadata and its associated meta-metamodels are not only part of the integrating product, but are also already populated with the metadata inherent in the individual vendor's product metamodels. As we mentioned, much of this philosophy is "old school" philosophy; today's metadata standards (discussed in Chapter 16) are slowly replacing the need for individual vendors to build an underlying meta-metamodel–based platform intended to integrate their own products.

Although Figure 13-3 is shown for illustration purposes only, it is realistic because it depicts the fact that each product is represented in terms of the metadata that its database tracks. Hence, at the meta-meta level, there really is no organized integration. In other words, each product's database is in fact a

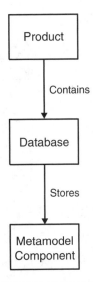

Figure 13-3   A meta-metamodel of a single-vendor solution

physical representation of the product's metamodel. Tying the various meta-models together at the meta-meta level is not possible without a top-down perspective, which answers these questions:

- What metadata does each product track?
- Where in the product's database does the metadata reside?

This meta-meta approach, if we can indeed call it one, is a product-specific database approach.

One Metadata Repository

When one separate vendor-developed metadata repository is the target, the meta-metamodel represents a metadata-based integration approach. The vendors of the original products of this genre were typically proud of their metamodels as opposed to their meta-metamodels. The metamodels showed the distinct categories of metadata in an organized format, as discussed in Part II. At the meta-meta level, the *vendor* organized the underlying structure of these metamodels. In fact, each metamodel's constructs were instances of a grander meta-meta schema. Creating a new database, for example, populated another database instance in a specific area of the DBMS metamodel. At the

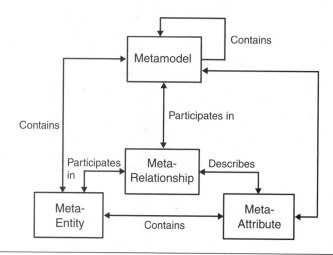

Figure 13-4   **The standalone meta-metamodel**

meta-metamodel level, the new database was related as an instance of a meta-entity, in most relational setups. Which instance in the meta-metamodel is populated depended on the underlying design of the metadata repository itself.

Figure 13-4 depicts the original meta-metamodel following an entity-relationship modeling method. Note that meta-entities are associated with metamodels and, quite obviously, are reused and reassociated depending on which perspective or metamodel they are associated with. Likewise, the meta-attributes are commonly reused according to their associated metamodels and/or meta-entities. For example, everything has a Name, and this meta-attribute would be an example of a consistently reused metadata instance in meta-meta land. Remember that metadata describes not only data, but also itself. The only difference, of course, is that when metadata describes metadata, it becomes meta-metadata. If you are headed toward the implementation of a metadata solution, you must understand this statement fully.

A Metadata Solution

When both a standalone meta-metamodel and a single-vendor metadata solution become part of a scoped metadata environment, the meta-meta framework needs to include additional meta-meta information. Most commonly, this information is now at the meta-repository level where it must not only integrate metadata across repository and tool implementations (i.e., at the individual metamodel level), but it must also track which metamodel is associated with which meta-metamodel (repository) and what the implications will be for

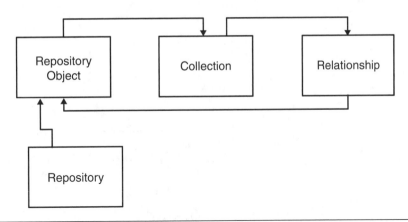

Figure 13-5   **The Microsoft Repository Engine object model**

metadata access. The meta-metadata characteristics of multiple metadata solutions reflect portal tendencies, and meta-metamodels now contain access and addressing information in addition to the standard "what exists where" metadata. The number of vendors involved in the metadata solution as well as the role of standards adherence influence not only the type of addressing metadata that has to be tracked but also the level at which that addressing takes place.

For example, Figure 13-5 depicts the original Microsoft repository engine object model. Interestingly, a meta-meta construct, Repository, relates meta-metamodel constructs based on which repository they are associated with.

In this illustration of Microsoft's Repository Engine, Repository Objects are associated with Collections (as opposed to, for example, Metamodels), and the Repository Objects, irrespective of the Collection they belong to, can be tracked at the Repository level. This setup reflects a metadata solution approach, one that does not rely on the existence of one and only one integrated repository. The model's depiction is based on object-oriented modeling.

Inside Meta-Meta Land

The insides of a meta-metamodel typically function similarly, irrespective of the type of tool or solution with which an instance is associated. Each component of a meta-metamodel relates to a separate physical metadata storage vehicle. In the relational world, this is often a DBMS table. The meta-metamodel is arranged and overseen by one main indexing, or meta-meta, construct. It is in this physical meta-meta table that the metadata solution, tool, or repository

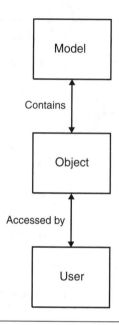

Figure 13-6   Inside a meta-metamodel

determines where to find metamodels, their instances, and associated processes. We can begin this illustration by looking at Figure 13-6 and then evaluating how the internals of this meta-metamodel, otherwise known as our meta-metadata, are represented in a sample metadata solution. Commonly, each box in Figure 13-6 is referred to as a type of meta-entity, also known as a meta-metamodel construct.

In the simple example in Table 13-1, a meta-metamodel's underpinnings show the main meta-entity table that lists every type of meta-entity common in our meta-metamodel. Each one has an associated Table ID, Process Name, and many other meta-characteristics that apply to *all occurrences of that meta-entity type*. It should be clarified that the process depicted here is an *internal process*, that is, it is inherent in the metadata solution software. This meta-entity table instructs the metadata solution software, by meta-entity type, as to which internal processes are allowed to be executed with this meta-meta construct, in this example.

Taking a look at "Table 43" (note the Table ID of the second table), our Object Table, we see which objects reside in this metadata solution's world, and with which metamodels each is associated. In many cases the metadata

Table 13-1 Viewing the "Insides" of a Meta-Entity Table

Meta-Entity Type	Table ID	Process Name	. . .
Object	43	Create	
User	33	Create	
Model	24	Create	

Table 13-2 The "Object" Table

Table ID	Object Name	Metamodel ID	Object Class	. . .
43	Program	56	Implementation	
43	Database	46	Data	
43	Entity	65	Business	
43	Relationship	65	Business	

solution administrator can define other qualities, such as Object Class.[1] In fact, it should now be clear that when we extend a metamodel, we are creating new instances in the meta-metamodel . . . not new constructs, but *new instances of an existing construct*.

Meta-Metamodels

At the meta-meta level the objective is integration and standardized processing. This statement is quite significant because it shows the validity of meta-metamodels in terms of their original intents. It is important to discuss how the original development of particular metadata solutions so closely correlates with their core meta-metamodel and its resultant impact.

Tool versus Repository

An easy way to determine where a particular meta-metamodel fits in meta-meta land is to look at its role within the total package. Is the meta-metamodel representative of the design of a tool's database or an intermediate point of tool integration, such as a repository? Does the meta-metamodel include standard processing? Are the answers to these questions ascertainable from a meta-

---

1. Extensibility, or the ability to customize metadata solutions, is covered in Chapter 10.

metamodel evaluation? Will the associated vendor share this information and perspective?

A simple way to determine whether something is a tool or a repository is by looking at the resident constructs. Meta-metamodels are extremely simple. Because they represent all that is common among metamodels, they typically describe the metamodels in terms of their components (e.g., metamodel constructs). If a vendor's metamodel includes a substantial number of constructs (database, data warehouse, translation procedure, report, etc.), in all likelihood, it represents a metamodel, or a subset of a multitool perspective. Although it is true that multiple tools can be integrated by adhering to a common metamodel (the Common Warehouse Model is an example of a standard that is headed in this direction), they must all follow the model *exactly* in order to do so. At the meta-meta level, different metamodels come together since they are all instances of the same meta-meta construct.

Many marketplace metadata solutions are really nothing more than tools or products geared toward the storage and treatment of metadata that originates in that product's defined architecture. As Figure 13-3 illustrates, the database of that particular product is designed to track specific metadata components. Hence, the organized view of the metadata aspects of this particular solution would be depicted in a metamodel. The term *meta-meta* is often used inaccurately in this scenario. There is only one view of the metadata's interrelationships, and in fact, data and metadata are often mingled in the tool's framework and underlying architecture. The underlying view of one tool's *metadata* world is a *metamodel*, as opposed to a meta-metamodel.

Tools should not be eliminated, however, from the world of metadata solutions. Understanding how their associated metadata is stored and related is crucial to determining whether they can participate as metadata suppliers or recipients in a total metadata solution.

Common examples of tool-based metadata solutions exist in the data warehousing[2] space. Here, tools created to handle one or more aspects of the data warehousing creation and/or reporting processes may or may not offer metadata tracking and access as a side benefit. If they do, the key indicators as to whether the tool has a higher-level metadata objective usually rest in the architecture of the tool. For example, if the tool is a data warehouse reporting tool, period, with no optional add-ons, the metadata support is usually part of the

---

2. Reference books about data warehousing are listed in the Additional Readings section at the end of this book.

tool's underlying design, and not targeted for integration or standard processing as defined at the meta-meta level. If, however, the same vendor offers other tools (or tool components), the shareability and standardization of metadata would generally require either a meta-metamodel or a standard, common metamodel. In fact, this objective has been a priority with the data warehouse space for quite some time, and a Common Warehouse Model (CWM) is now in existence (see Figure 13-7), as noted earlier. (Chapter 16 discusses this standard, but it is

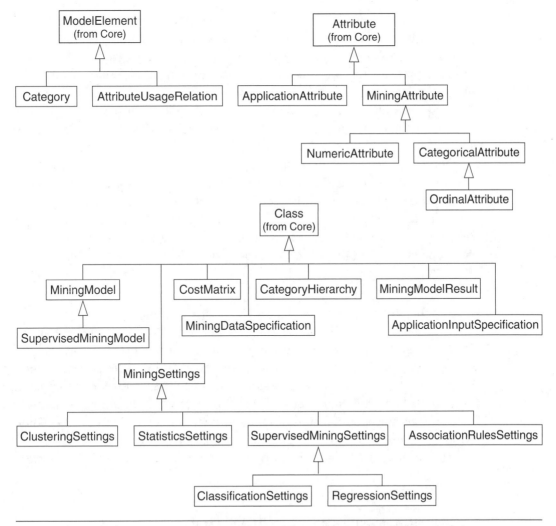

Figure 13-7 Aspects of the CWM data mining metamodel

Source: Used with permission from the Object Management Group, Needham, Mass. Copyright © OMG, 1993–2001.

important to note CWM's intent.) Any vendor who represents his or her tool's metadata in CWM terms is attempting to incorporate meta-meta characteristics. For example, by considering each setting in a Data Mining Tool to be an instance of a Class, the likelihood of standardized settings exponentially increases. However, if a vendor has a unique setting, he or she can simply create another instance and claim adherence to the CWM standard. Similarly, category hierarchies could share standardization as yet another type of Class. Vendors' compliance with this model is still being carried out, as of this writing.

For true repositories, however, integration and standardization are the main objectives in life. Hence, the meta-meta level is depicted strategically and accurately by a meta-metamodel. The meta-metamodel not only represents the common constructs contained in the separate metadata views, but also shows what the repository product *does* with them, how this processing occurs, and when. These meta-meta specifics vary by repository tool; however, as metadata standards become more unified and finalized, the mere existence of a particular meta-meta construct in a vendor's metadata solution will guarantee, and to some degree require, certain types of construct-specific processing.

One major standards body, the Object Management Group (OMG)[3] has a Meta-Object Facility (MOF), which serves several purposes, including the standardization of metadata and its associated processes and formats based on where it fits in the MOF model, which is in fact a meta-metamodel. Figure 13-8 shows the way model elements are represented at the meta-meta level. The Meta Object Facility (MOF) is described in more detail in Chapter 16.

Common Constructs

Despite the source of a meta-metamodel, it shares common constructs with other meta-metamodels. Again, as standards become finalized, meta-metamodels will be quite standard not only in their associated constructs but also the way they are handled across meta-meta implementations. The more common the constructs and associated processes are at the meta-meta level compared to the outside world, the easier it will be for metadata solution implementers to exchange and share common metadata. How do we define the outside world? In many scenarios, the outside world consists of any and all software products designed to send, access, or receive metadata. Practicality, however,

---

3. Metadata standards are discussed in detail in Chapter 16.

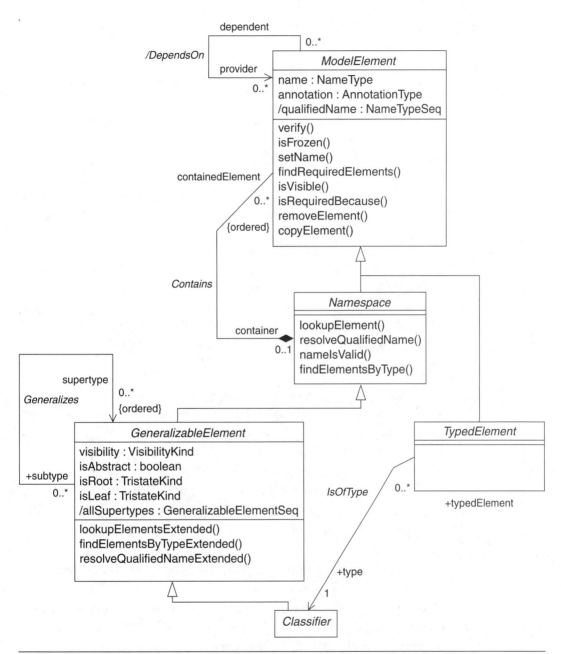

Figure 13-8 **Base abstractions within the MOF model package**

has given rise to categories of the outside world based on distinct divisions according to the following:

- *Industry*—the world in which the user of the metadata solution does business.
- *Software tool category*—the specific software development process that a set of tools is geared toward (e.g., modeling, testing, database management software, etc.).
- *Exchange format/location*—how the metadata needs to look in order to be part of an interface, as well as where the interface operates from/to. Internet access and categorization requirements, such as XML, form a big part of this category.

Each of these categories may also share constructs, or in the broader world now being addressed by metadata standards, they may share constructs across the subdivisions.

Regardless of the scope of a metadata solution's outside world, the meta-metamodel includes most of these common constructs. This list is not all-inclusive, but does represent a functional overview:

- *Meta-Object, Object, Meta-Entity, Entity*—the ultimate "thing" that is being described at the meta-meta level. *Everything* is eventually instantiated in this space!
- *Meta-Attribute, Attribute, Meta-Characteristic, Characteristic*—qualities that are permanently associated with *all* instances of one of the above constructs. Examples include Name and Create Date.
- *Metamodel, Model, Collection*—named groups of things, each representing a specific function, metadata solution, or user category.
- *Meta-Association, Association, Meta-Relationship, Relationship*—named connections that link things depending on a particular event, characteristic, or purpose.
- *Meta-Operation, Operation, Meta-Process, Process, Meta-Function, Function, Service*—named executable procedure that occurs, is initiated, or results from the population or access of all instances of a construct.

The list is basic in that virtually all meta-metamodels need to contain one of each of the bulleted items. Other meta-metamodel components, varying of course by objective and associated metadata solution implementation, relate to metadata display, metadata solution security, and metadata solution users, to name a few.

The Information Connection

The various addressed perspectives come together in meta-meta land. But unless these perspectives relate directly to the purpose of a metadata solution, many people would consider meta-meta land to be more theory and philosophy than anything else. How do we get from meta-meta connections to the need to integrate disparate sources of data? How do we connect the meta-metamodel to the metadata that exists in unconnected yet similar metadata stores across an organization? Do business users even need to be concerned with meta-meta land?

We connected metadata to data. We related our experiences with the various perspectives to the fact that the terms *data* and *metadata* can be quite variable. The connection with our ultimate objective can also be quite variable, depending on the world or worlds that we define within our target metadata solution. Regardless, it is always a good idea to connect the meta-metadata to the metamodels to the metadata in the models to the actual information being represented.

Inside IT

Making the connections in the realm of Information Technology requires us to adjust the starting points, as we have been discussing all along. Figure 13-9 shows the connections that are paramount to IT success. In this simple example, the meta-metamodel relates existing metamodels by standardizing the constructs that are populated in each of them. This metamodel could be a data warehousing metamodel; as we move vertically down the diagram, we stop at the names of some data warehouse tables, to illustrate examples of our information and how it connects via relationships and perspectives.

Outside IT

When the business world becomes a part of these connected perspectives, data or information are not the table names, as illustrated in Figure 13-10. Instead, *data* and *information* begin with the *values that are stored in these tables*, thereby affecting the relationships all the way up the ladder to meta-meta land.

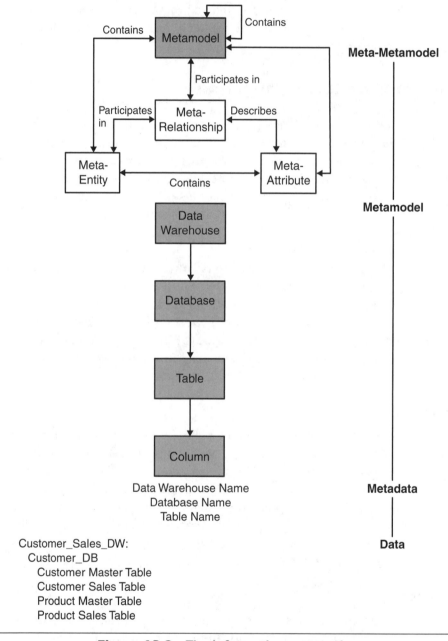

Figure 13-9 **The information connection**

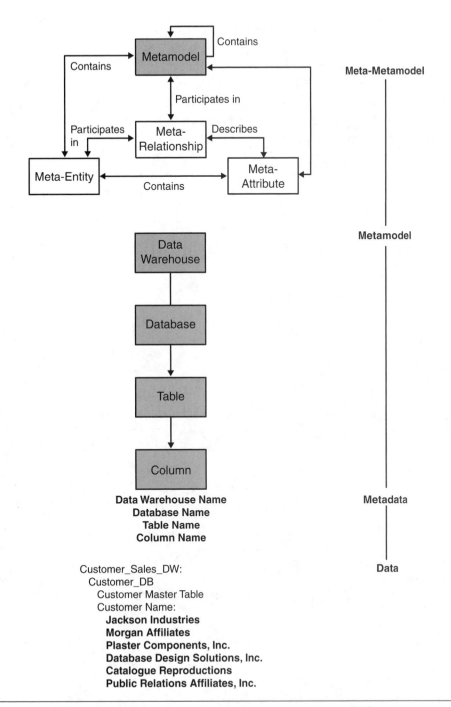

Figure 13-10 The information connection, revisited

The similarities between the two perspectives rest with the fact that at the lowest level, much of the metadata becomes *both* data and metadata. In other words, the name of the tables and of the column of interest is part of the business users' information space—the value "Jackson Industries" is not significant or even the slightest bit meaningful without the context to which it is associated. This context is so embedded that because the word *industries* is part of the value set, we assume it is a commercial enterprise. We have no way of knowing, from the value alone, that it is a customer.

Integrating the information connections that exist outside IT with those that exist inside IT requires *common metadata*. Our metadata requirements analysis returns once again!

Chapter 14

Introducing Repositories

Where there is the necessary technical skill to move mountains, there is no need for the faith that moves mountains.
—Eric Hoffer

Most readers associate metadata with repositories. In fact, the software community has adopted the term in so many ways that many now distinguish a special type of repository as a *metadata repository*. Based on the apparent demand to put metadata *somewhere*, special repository software was developed during the 1980s, and it has changed both in terms of its design as well as its function. Most of today's metadata solutions include a repository of sorts, and this chapter explains how the technology has evolved.

Repositories Defined

The term *repository* is not a new one. In fact, from a dictionary perspective, it refers to "a box, room, etc., in which things may be placed for safekeeping."[1] When this definition is transferred to the world of information, it is easy to see why any type of database can be called a repository without confusion. In fact, many data warehouses have been called corporate repositories.[2]

Note: Hoffer quote (in *The Passionate State of Mind,* 1954) from *The New York Public Library Book of Twentieth-Century American Quotations.* Copyright © 1992 by The Stonesong Press, Inc., and The New York Public Library. Used with permission.

1. *Webster's New World Dictionary and Thesaurus* (New York: Simon & Schuster, 1996), p. 527.

2. My first book, *Implementing a Corporate Repository* (New York: Wiley, 1994), addresses corporate metadata repository implementation, but the title has been misinterpreted by many!

Based on the lack of consistency in the software marketplace, many vendors have been advertising the existence of a repository in their product lines. It is time to set the record straight. If a standard definition were to exist in the information technology arena, products would strive to conform to a set of capabilities. We begin by formally defining the term *repository,* discussing the expected features that go along with the standard definition set, and then relating these capabilities to today's metadata solutions.

> ❖ **Repository**   An integrated, "virtual" holding area with vendor-independent input, access, and structure; used to directly store metadata and/or the metadata-based gateways to external metadata.

To clarify this definition, it is important to evaluate the meaning of each major component:

- *Integrated*—What comes from one metadata source can be accessed from another metadata source. More important, what is in one metadata source can be *related* to another metadata source. True repositories allow the multisource connections based on relationships that exist among and within metamodels.

- *Virtual holding area*—Not all metadata has to be resident or stored in the repository in order for it to be accessed. In fact, the "holding area" becomes virtual in that true repositories need only the addressing information and associated executable processes in order to get to the metadata. Many have renamed "virtual holding areas" as *enterprise portals*. Portals use metadata to get to other metadata or to externally stored information.

- *Vendor independent*—It should not be necessary for all repository-resident or accessible information to exist or be supplied by tools that are created by the same vendor that created the repository.

True repositories store metadata or give the impression that they store metadata. A defined repository is the place for access to defined metadata in the truest sense. The definition is based on several factors, none of which should be determined by vendors of repositories and their marketing communications.

The Generic Repository Architecture

In standard repository software products, distinct components exist, regardless of the developing vendor or target metadata market. The design of each component may vary, giving products market distinction. Regardless of the vendor, however, as illustrated in Figure 14-1, each repository product consists of:

1. An underlying database
2. A repository metamodel (meta-metamodel) and various subordinate metamodels
3. Repository software, representing the functionality necessary to bridge the components and present them as an integrated metadata solution

Let's discuss each component in detail.

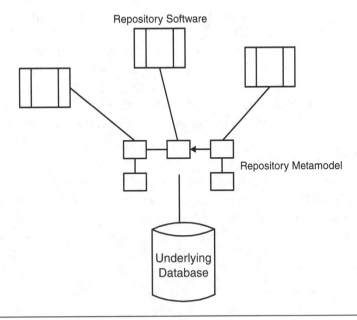

Figure 14-1 **The generic repository architecture**

The Repository Database

The database stores not only repository metadata contents, but also the addressing and execution data that the repository needs in order to get external information. The structure of the repository can be open, that is, developed in a commercially standard Database Management System (DBMS) that is accessible via commercial query languages such as SQL, or closed, in that the only way to access the information within is via vendor-supplied access routines. Neither one is fundamentally better than the other; the usefulness depends, of course, on how comprehensive and easily executable vendor routines are, as well as the complexity of the underlying database structure.

The Repository Metamodel

As we discussed in Chapters 12 and 13, every repository has a meta-meta-model, otherwise known as the *repository metamodel.* This model correlates directly to the underlying repository database, and tracks the relationships among all resident metadata, associated metamodels, and the software required to create, access, and display database contents. The repository metamodel (the meta-metamodel) also handles and addresses other specifics such as repository and metadata security; for this reason, it can be thought of as the repository's blueprint.

The repository metamodel relates all the various metadata views (represented in distinct metamodels) by coordinating common metamodel components. Understanding this level of abstraction requires a tool-focused mindset, and many people are satisfied dealing with repository tools at the metadata level, or within the perspective of one specific metamodel.

Repository Software

Most repository consumers minimize the importance of repository software. This product component is inevitably the place to evaluate what you are getting for your money, and how easily the repository product can become integrated with an organization's existing metadata sources. Although software is a grandiose category, *repository* software typically falls into these major categories:

- *Go-get-it routines*—The application program interfaces (APIs), remote procedure calls (RPCs), and external interfaces that allow the outside world to access repository contents

- *Repository policies*—Repository program code that is implemented, controlled, and executed by the repository; used to *control* repository access and repository update as well as other repository functionality. These policies define "What functions can be performed by whom?"

- *Repository templates*—Views that control and format the display of repository contents
- *Repository utilities*—Vendor-supplied functions that perform standard repository functions (back up, load, etc.)

The breadth of functionality clearly depends on the compatibility and completeness of supplied repository software. We illustrate in Part V (Sample Metadata Solutions) how to add to vendor-supplied functionality.

Essential Repository Characteristics

The components of the generic repository architecture must act together as a metadata solution, as opposed to a metadata storage area. Essentially, true repository tools are capable of the following (according to my six rules for a true repository product):

1. Integration of repository content
2. Vendor-independent input, access, and structure
3. Metamodel extensibility
4. Template-driven access to the repository's contents
5. Versioning of the repository's contents
6. Defining security

Integration of Repository Content

In the truest repository products, all aspects of a repository's contents can be related not only to other content instances in the repository, but also to contents outside the specific repository. Metamodel relationships handle the implementation of this capability.

Vendor Independence

It should not be necessary for the repository's defined world to reside in one set of vendor's tools in order to be accounted for. True repositories have the capability of accessing metadata that resides in another vendor's product. Likewise, they have the ability to be accessed from another vendor's product.

Metamodel Extensibility

The boxes and lines of metamodels are not fixed in the world of true repository products. Because (as discussed in Chapter 13) metamodel components are instances of the repository metamodel, extensibility, or the ability to change a metamodel, simply adds or subtracts instances of the meta-metamodel. In other words, to change a metamodel in a repository product, you add rows to or subtract rows from one or more underlying database tables.

True repository products allow these changes to be made without an impact on the functionality of the repository software. If a "box" is added to a metamodel and the instances of that box do not get backed up by the repository backup utility, then maybe the product is only partially extensible.

Template-Driven Accessibility

No one wants to look at the entire repository in order to get to the few pieces of metadata that are of interest to him or her. Likewise, tools are interested only in their own metadata world, and should be allowed to update only things that reside in their own metamodel.[3]

Versioning

What do we do when some repository users want to treat the same metadata differently? Perhaps they are using different versions of the same data warehouse reporting tool or other repository-interfacing product. It is essential that repository products allow the ability to version metamodels, keeping track of which versions are used by which repository customers.[4]

Definable Security

In a true metadata solution, "who does what with which pieces of metadata" is of paramount concern. For this reason, repository products must allow security at the lowest level of the metamodel, the metamodel construct, or in some situations, the metadata instance. This capability is reflected in the meta-metamodel, as discussed in Chapter 13.

---

3. We talk more about templates in Chapter 18.

4. More details on repository/tools architectures appear in Chapter 18.

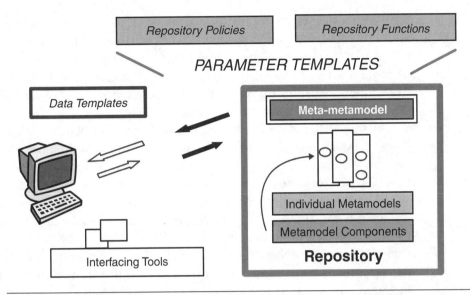

Figure 14-2   **How repository components fit together**

Source: Adapted from Tannenbaum, A. *Implementing a Corporate Repository,* copyright © 1994 by John Wiley & Sons, New York. This material is used by permission of John Wiley & Sons, Inc.

How the Pieces Fit Together

The pieces of a true repository product are intermingled and heavily dependent on each other. As illustrated in Figure 14-2, the typical repository user, often a tool, sees and processes repository contents based on template-driven policy and function execution. Although these internals may represent a bit more than metadata repository users care to know, they are an important aspect of the full metadata solution's potential. When we revisit our metadata requirements from a technical perspective in Part V, it will become clear that connectivity is a significant aspect of a metadata solution's architecture.

Old versus New Repository Technology

As the groups espousing repository interest have evolved, so too has the technology as a means of accommodating these perspectives. Originally, repository technology was developed to support data administration and management. For the most part, metadata was manually input into a centralized (or perhaps the only) metadata database. Data administrators preferred the "repository in a box" setup, and vendors accommodated by providing, for the most part, a full set of metamodels and relatively functional front-ends and reporting features. The "old" technology always seemed to fall short, however, in its ability to interface with other tools and products on terms besides those of the repository vendor.

As metadata became more prominent in the typical corporate installation, so too did the need to bring these pieces together, at least logically. Irrespective of metadata source, every repository product, despite its developing vendor, needed to become part of an overall metadata solution. When many vendors need to address the same requirements, it becomes apparent that a single vendor's repository software is unlikely to fulfill the need for a generic integration function. Hence, the movement toward standards for vendor-neutral repository and metadata exchange.

From the repository architectural perspective, however, these external exchange mechanisms are affecting the generic repository architecture as well as the way in which nonrepository software can be tied in with an overall metadata solution. We are now entering the standards-driven metadata world, using the Internet as a major aspect of metadata-based search and retrieval. Today, metadata and its associated repositories are being looked at not only for data explanation, but also as the key to data sharing and exchange. Ultimately, metadata has grown to represent not only traditional data, but also application development components, and noncorporate values including graphics, music, animation, and all kinds of electronic signals—all of which need to be related, exchanged, and shared. It is a natural result that repository technology is growing to adapt to this new metadata-driven world, and vendors are realizing that combined multivendor efforts are far more productive and effective than the old single-vendor standalone repositories. This new philosophy has influenced each component of the generic repository architecture and has moved certain standards efforts to the forefront in terms of both capabilities and expectations.

The New Repository Architecture

New repository technology has affected each generic architectural component. Each has been made more flexible, yet more standardized, to accommodate the need for interoperability with other repository and metadata storage tools.

The New Repository Database

Today most underlying repository databases are object-oriented, as opposed to relational. The object-oriented DBMS (OODBMS) allows specific types of metadata to imply the execution of standard processes more easily than other DBMSs did. In fact, it is the DBMS that now offers this relationship, as opposed to constructs within the repository metamodel.

The New Repository Metamodel

Models are also becoming object-oriented. This restructuring is requiring standard object types and associated standard behaviors. Within these standard object types are standard classes, with typically one default class that can be defined either by the vendor or by a standards effort. For example, consider some standard objects that we deal with on a regular basis:

- File
- Program

Each object has some standard object types:

- File
  - Sequential
  - Manual
- Program
  - COBOL
  - C
  - JAVA

As these objects and types become standardized (across metamodels, across repository vendors), the *processes* associated with them will become standardized. (Is there only one way to open a sequential file?) It won't be long before the metamodels become so standard that vendors would be crazy *not* to follow them![5]

The New Repository Software

Finally, an obvious fallout of the new repository architecture is that the vendor-specific software now included with repository tools will become less vendor-dependent. Hence, the opening up of repositories, metadata solutions, and general metadata exchange. The next chapter (Chapter 15) discusses many of these readily available features from a Web perspective by including XML and enterprise portal examples.

---

5. Chapter 16 discusses standards and their impact.

The Quasi Repository

The repository features discussed in this chapter categorize as true repositories a small subset of marketplace options. Over the years, fewer and fewer repository products have been distinguishing themselves as true repository tools, and have been focusing on one subset of the repository space in terms of functionality and capabilities. Despite this fact, they are marketed as repository products. Many of these other repository products are not quite full repositories, but are certainly much more than standalone databases. For this reason, I call them *quasi repositories*.

In general, a quasi repository offers *some* repository features. In most scenarios they have a semi-extensible metamodel, in that they allow some customization via the naming of reserved additional fields to suit your specific metadata requirements. This is common in the data warehouse metadata support area where a set of predefined metadata fields is included with a base tool. In addition to these predefined fields, many user-definable fields are provided. The quasi repository administrator has the option of renaming these user-definable fields. However, the ability to relate them to other fields, or to add an amount that exceeds the number of available user-defined fields, is usually nonexistent. Hence, the term *semi-extensible* quasi repository.

Typically, the renaming of these fields affects any quasi repository front-ends in that input screens, for example, reflect the new names. As Figure 14-3 illustrates, however, users of this quasi repository would not be able to add four attributes to the Subject Area list, nor would they be able to relate anything other than Data Element to Subject Area. For many limited-scope directory-like applications, this may be sufficient, however.

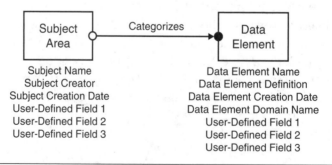

Figure 14-3   *Semi-extensible quasi repository metamodel*

Custom-Built Repositories

Traditionally, custom-built repositories focused more on a single metamodel than anything else. In an attempt to gather everyone's metadata requirements and organize them logically, a new database was created and organized in the most efficient way possible. Front-ends, many of them Web-based, allowed the repository users to retrieve and/or maintain the database-resident metadata.

While many organizations awaited the ultimate standard repository technology, custom-built repositories were seen as a temporary solution. Likewise, when repository/metadata scopes were limited to the support of one data warehouse, end-user metadata was often stored in a standalone database, accessible via a customized reporting tool or other data warehouse front-end. Many of these temporary solutions have been in existence for several years, however, and now they should be considered legitimate parts of an overall metadata solution architecture. In fact, their contents may turn out to be solid metadata sources for a wider scale solution.

Aside from these standalone databases, many repository-building toolboxes exist. These products offer the basic components of a repository solution, with the repository implementer being responsible for:

- Defining the metamodel
- Designing the repository templates and front-ends
- Combining supplied repository software functions into executable repository functions

Despite the fact that a commercial product is the backbone in this example, the final repository does represent a custom-built solution.

Repository Examples

At the close of this chapter, after discussing what separates the true repository from the repository wanna-be and the quasi repository, examples are required. The world of repository technology is currently divided into old and new technology.

Most vendors who offer old repository technology are either revamping their products to accommodate the new metadata solution philosophy—one that allows metadata to exist in several places and be accessible with a metamodel-like set of relationships—or restricting their functionality to integrate only their own product lines. Examples of old repository technology include:

- Standalone, passive data dictionaries
- Modeling tool encyclopedias, which are used to version and share multiple models created with one particular tool
- Centralized standalone vendor-neutral repository products that offer various metamodel and interface options, all developed by the repository's vendor

The new generation of repository technology is moving toward a metadata solution architecture, one in which the repository itself is only a piece of the overall metadata management and exchange environment. This environment is typically geared toward:

- Application component reuse
- Metadata standardization and exchange
- Multiple coexistent repositories

When a repository product is being evaluated, it is important to understand the vendor's approach to multiple metadata sources. True repositories are able to handle the fact that metadata exists outside of their own world. If not, other metadata-based techniques, like those discussed in the next chapter, must be part of the plan.

Whether a standalone repository is suited to your requirements depends on the determined scope of your metadata world. The power of the Internet and its browsers are widening the scope as the Web becomes more of a backbone. Again, *planned metadata solutions* widen the impact and benefit of metadata in an organization.

Chapter 15

Other Metadata-Based Technologies

Our consideration of meta-meta land would not be complete without mentioning its impact on additional metadata-centric technologies. These technologies may not have grown up in the metadata solution space, yet they clearly rely on metadata and its connections at the meta-meta level in order to function. This chapter provides an overview of several of these core metadata-based technologies. They have already affected the perceptions of metadata. They will likely have a growing effect on organizational use of metadata as a strategic asset. On the other hand, each technology also represents a specific challenge to the metadata solution architect—many clearly originated from different beneficiary perspectives, yet they each have the potential to coexist in a metadata solution strategy. The next four sections describe the role and origins of metadata as they concern:

- The Web
- File managers and file systems
- Database management systems
- Object-oriented class libraries

Note: This chapter was co-authored by Peter Aiken, Institute for Data Research/VCU.

Each technology should be analyzed from the point of view of the 5 Questions:[1]

1. How easy is it to locate your target? (What data do we have?)
2. How easy is it to assess whether the result is what you really want? (What does it mean?)
3. How easy is it to determine where it is? (Where is it?)
4. How easy is to determine the source? (How did it get there?)
5. How easy is it to access? (How do I get it?)

The metadata in each technology is here and is staying. Becoming familiar with their similarities and differences at the meta-meta level will give us a good foundation to begin the metadata solution process in Part IV.

The Web

Collectively we understand the Web as a place. Originally, it was a "place" where scientists and technical researchers shared ideas. In fact, during my early days as a UNIX developer, whenever the need to consider an alternative technology or methodology arose, the standard comment was, "I'll check the Web." The lack of secrecy, security, cost, and restriction as well as the ease of search were probably the Web's key assets as a place to get "stuff." Over time, the only asset that has really changed is the variety of stuff available. Many people say that the Web is "more accessible than ever," but the reality is that virtually all organizations now have a Web site, and the qualities that it always had make the Web a low-cost advertising medium. Place a message there and potential customers are sure to come across it.

Although the Web is searched by all kinds of users with all kinds of objectives, it is generally a place to perform *search and retrieval operations*. The objects of the search and the source of requests have varied over time. Regardless of these variables, metadata is clearly at the heart of the Web's performance. To consider the Web as part of a metadata solution, it is necessary to evaluate the search and retrieval operations not only from the point of view of "what is being looked for and retrieved," but also from the points of view that

---

1. The 5 Questions is a trademark of and the questions and method are copyrighted by Database Design Solutions, Inc., Bernardsville, New Jersey.

allow a successful result. These points of view are controlled only by the quality and stability of the underlying metadata.

Search and Retrieve

As more of the world becomes wired with direct Internet connections, is it any wonder that so many people reach for their browsers first when they want to locate something? Be it a phone number, an organization's Web site, directions to a colleague's place of business, or a newly published report—increasingly we (especially those of us continually wired) turn to our browsers for the information. Unfortunately, few people care *how* the results show up, until they can't find what they are looking for.

The Markup World

The first requirement of a Web search is that we identify something to look for. In general, we use various browser options to identify text strings, and then wait for the "matches" to return. The means by which matches are determined is based on two qualities: (1) how text is *marked up,* and (2) the inbred processing powers associated with the *deployed search engine.*

Initial search engines looked for specific types of "markup," which is metadata. The means by which markup is deployed and related to that which is being marked up is not really standardized. So, more powerful search engines are arriving on a regular basis, and these engines search the actual contents of a page, as opposed to *tags,* or markup values.

Web searchers used to complain about the lack of standardized markup, but more powerful search engines arrived more quickly than standardized markup values (which we are still waiting for), so the complaints in this arena are no longer so loud. Instead, many people are realizing the *potential* that standardized markup values have, and these voices are attempting to establish markup standards.[2]

In fact, SGML (Standard Generalized Markup Language) has really been around for more than 20 years, but it is more of a specification than an actual language in the sense that it shows organizations how they can label their text consistently so that it can be located easily. The markup is a *tag* that an organization applies to documents in its control. The purpose of SGML was to separate content from formatting, thus beginning the era of *markup*. Hypertext

---

2. Metadata standards are addressed in Chapter 16.

Markup Language (HTML) was the first implementation of SGML that seemed relatively simple. But the initial versions lacked great formatting capabilities, so even though it was possible to mark up documents with HTML, it wasn't possible to make them look pretty. As a result, subsequent HTML versions emphasized formatting capabilities rather than markup capabilities, and the values of the tags that supported markup (e.g., <ADDRESS>, <CLIENT NAME>, etc.) were used less frequently than the tag values that supported *format* (e.g., <B> for bold). In fact, the only reliable meta-tags (tags that implied information about the *content* of the document rather than the format of the document) were those that fell within the <HEAD> or <TITLE> tags of a document.

```
<HTML>
<HEAD><TITLE>Meta-Tags</TITLE>
<BODY>
<H1>Useless Information</H1>
<P>This is an illustration of how important the metadata
can be in discovering the contents of a Web site or any
other Web-based document.</P>
<P>While we might retrieve this particular set of text
based on the title of meta-tags, it really tells us nothing
about meta-tags. In fact, I never mention the term again
except for in the heading.</P>
</BODY></HTML>
```

As a result, as the preceding code illustrates, markup was not really markup, and metadata was not really metadata, in the truest sense. Most tags could indicate what something would look like, but had a very low probability of predicting *what the something was*. So the markup languages could not be counted on to match requests with received information. Initial search engines matched on the values of tags that were most inclined to relay content. But since HTML did not require use of tags, they often were not there. As a result, most Web searchers began to rely on multiple search engines, and still never seemed to hit the majority of the true matches. As mentioned earlier, newer search engines began checking the contents of the Web site or page in addition to the values of the content-describing tags. But as we all know, if we look for information on *cats*, we could receive matches to sites from veterinarians to museums to lost pets to pet stores. So even with the benefit of receiving multiple results, the results must be deciphered.

What Does It Mean?   Once located, the search target is associated with the target's Web address—its Uniform Resource Locator (URL). Manual and programmatic examination of potential target URLs can reveal much about the "meaning" of a Web-based data object. For example, a data object located on a student's home page might not carry the same worth as one located at the Library of Congress. When scanning the results queries, people must take into account the actual URLs of the query of results because they tell so much about the object's source. This manual scanning has been incorporated, to some extent, into filters that try to separate junk and nonjunk e-mail messages based in part on the originating domain name. Despite all the technology incorporated into Web-based metadata, we understand received data and information and we make conclusions as individuals, and they are typically neither shareable nor retrievable.

Continuing the 5 Questions Analysis   Because URLs are standardized in terms of structure, much of the remaining analysis in terms of our 5 Questions is based on the existence of *intelligent metadata*. Like *intelligent data*, the values imply something about the meaning. The domain, or last part of the URL (before country codes, where applicable), has standardized values that indicate certain facts about the credibility of the returned information. Table 15-1 lists the common domain names.

Because so much "intelligent metadata" exists on the Web to compensate for the lack of standard tags and values, Web sites have been categorized based on their content:

Type I Web sites provide a single, public, authoritative source of information. They are designed to provide a single user with the current response to a specific question.

Type II Web sites have the same objective as Type I sites, but the data is accumulated privately, hence the .com domain. Usually these sites

Table 15-1   *Sample Intelligent Domains*

Domain Value	Definition
com	Commercial enterprise
gov	Government agency
org	Organization, nonprofit
net	Network management firm
edu	Educational institution
mil	Military

collect information by surveys and will send it to you if you choose to participate.

Type III Web sites are commercial, and designed for you to purchase something.

Type IV Web sites are public interest sites, geared toward a specific subgroup of the general population. Usually, content is submitted and maintained voluntarily.

Type V Web sites are maintained by an individual or a group for the purpose of pointing others to other Web sites, and are also known as bookmark sites.

Type VI Web sites are similar to Type V sites, but with some sort of humorous or sarcastic slant. The contents could be false, but are posted as if they were true.

Even with these metadata-based categorizations, many people have invested several hours in the development of personal bookmark systems (because it took so long to find the *right* site!). These collections have become so valuable that competing browsers come with the ability to import each other's bookmarks. This situation is the result of unplanned metadata-based information retrieval. The next step for the Web was, therefore, the attempt at standard categorization.

Categorize

Extensible Markup Language, or XML, is a technology that attempts to address the areas where HTML falls short.[3] XML is the most promising technology to address the problems associated with categorizing Web content. Briefly, XML allows previously unstructured organizational data (e.g., internal reports and e-mail messages) to be categorized automatically with rudimentary, searchable metadata structures. These metadata structures are probably the first to separate style from content. In fact, the natural partner to XML is XSL (Extensible Style Language), which addresses the formatting aspects of Web documents.

True Markup

Because XML was intended to be a markup language, it was designed with meta-tags in mind. However, as with most limited metadata solutions, the meta-tag perspective was focused mainly on the ability to locate the information

---

3. See Additional Readings for recommended XML literature.

described by or surrounding XML tags. At a grander level, the proper use of XML would allow predefined XML values to result in consistent retrievals, with virtually no variation. XML was designed to be strictly standard and able to be parsed via "XML parsers" with the same results every time. It was not intended to replace HTML, but rather to enhance use of HTML. The difference rests in consistent and more valuable markups, or tags.

Who decides the values of these tags? Who decides where the tags should be placed in the overall document? Who decides which tags should be required? Now, we begin to understand the value of metadata solution design and consistent metadata usage. Despite the fact that there are no real standard tags or associated values, the ability to create your own tags with your own set of standardized values makes the Web a very powerful means of categorizing and exchanging unstructured information across your enterprise.

With true markup, we are able to categorize all our Web documents with the utmost level of granularity. XML, a language geared toward markup, with only the slightest restrictions, allows us to create as many tags as we like, and insert them wherever we want in our documents. Tags can be embedded in other tags and parsers can be used to specifically pull out the information that immediately follows named tags.

In the following code, notice that we enhanced our original HTML example. Now, instead of just a *title*, we could match on *major* or *minor topics* as well as *author* and *publication date*. In fact, this example is the simplest usage of XML; tags can be combined into Document Type Definitions (DTDs), which can then be used to represent a template of sorts. These templates represent named combinations of tags and formats that can be used to standardize information of specific types for use by the XML parsers. As a minimum, they can be used to validate the existence of required fields, and many templates have become public standards as a means of ensuring specific formats.

```
<?xml version = "1.0">
<MAJOR TOPIC="Meta-Tags">
<MINOR TOPIC="Search and Retrieval">
<TITLE>Useless meta-tags</title>
<H1>Useless information</H1>
<P>This is an illustration of how important the metadata
can be in discovering the contents of a Web site or any
other Web-based document.</P>
<P>While we might retrieve this particular set of text
based on the title of meta-tags, it really tells us nothing
about meta-tags. In fact, I never mention the term again
except for in the heading.</P>
```

```
<P>Notice that simply adding major and minor topic tags
has widened the likelihood of a match on searches
looking for the specifics that are addressed in this
document</P>
<AUTHOR="Tannenbaum, Adrienne">
<PUBLICATION DATE="June 30, 2001">
```

A simple DTD for submitting articles (named *publication.dtd*), shown in the following code, illustrates the required elements and associated formats. In this very basic DTD, all elements can be text—XML uses PCDATA as a named format for text elements that do not contain other elements. XML capabilities go well beyond the example depicted here, but the ease with which transfer of Web information can become metadata based should be obvious.

```
<?xml version = "1.0">
<!DOCTYPE ARTICLE SUBMISSION "publication.dtd">
<!ELEMENT MAJOR TOPIC (#PCDATA)>
<!ELEMENT MINOR TOPIC (#PCDATA)>
<!ELEMENT TITLE (#PCDATA)>
<!ELEMENT AUTHOR (#PCDATA)>
<!ELEMENT PUBLICATION DATE (#PCDATA)>
```

Interface and Exchange

The third category of Web use is for information **interfacing** (evolution of data from one format, location, and/or purpose to another) and **exchange** (transfer of data from one organization to another).

XML

Transfer of XML-based information can become standardized easily. With a set of standard, enterprise-focused DTDs, not only will the data that is passed around be consistent, but the resting places will be categorized and retrievable. The advanced reader should be questioning this statement; and the potential to use XML for disastrous results should not be underestimated. As with full metadata solutions, the planning and standardization of the metadata to be used as a basis for XML deployment must be agreed upon *prior to* the implementations. If each group creates its own DTDs, and several of them conflict, XML is not going to be the silver bullet that everyone expects it to be.

The XML-based ability to send descriptive metadata along with each data transfer permits much rich-content information to be understood by both browsers (automatically) and knowledge workers (manually). It significantly increases the ability to have the content and location understood programmatically in terms of which answers to the questions "How did the data get there?" and "How do I get it?" can be inferred and (in the case of the latter) implemented automatically or with minimal manual intervention.

XML-wrapped data (data transferred concurrently with its associated metadata) presents an opportunity to evolve data interfacing/exchange technology to a new generation. Until XML, it was cheaper to develop one-time solutions to data interface/exchange challenges than it was to develop programmatic solutions. Consequently, organizations developed a myriad of individual, point-to-point solutions. Although cheaper to implement, these solitary, undocumented interfaces are proving to be a major barrier to the evolution of organizational technology. XML equips organizations with the tools to develop programmatic solutions to manage their data interchange environments using the same economies of scale associated with their data management environments. Now organizations that move to XML-based metadata management will reap the benefits of economies of scale and organizational dexterity associated with "best practices" in data management.

In the following sections, the capabilities of the Web's data interface and exchange to serve as a metadata solution component are examined and the challenges for each core metadata question are articulated.

XML-Based Portal Technologies

XML-based portals are specifically delineated subsets of enterprise portal technologies that provide inherent XML-based data exchange and interface capabilities to all knowledge workers who access the technology. Disparate, unforeseen data integration queries and/or exchanges can be accomplished by having the portal interpret the query, translate it into XML, and access the data required to supply the requested information. The result is based on an understanding of XML and the associated metadata wrappers, or tags. Portals act as information distribution hubs, providing access to the XML-wrapped metadata that describes the legacy environment. Integration tasks shift. No longer is integration handled on a case-by-case, legacy system–to–legacy system basis, but instead on a portal integration basis. The single fixed target mapping onto the portal environment simplifies all aspects of this previously difficult task.

As Figure 15-1 illustrates, portals provide opportunities to manage organizational metadata programmatically in an XML-based environment. Mapping a data object known to the portal is roughly equivalent to publishing it from an object-oriented perspective. Once data objects are known to the portal, they are accessible within security partitions. Granular transaction objects can be assembled into meaningful information as object types are introduced to the

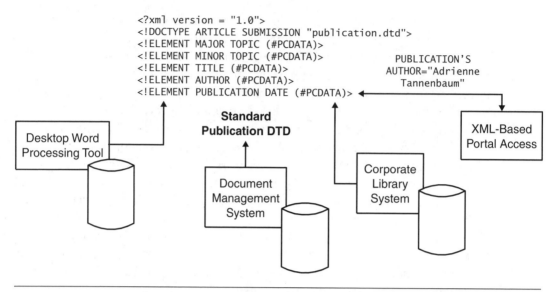

Figure 15-1 *An illustrated XML-based portal*

portal. Guided by an information architecture, these objects can be combined in numerous methods, allowing management of a relatively small amount of metadata to indirectly manage a relatively large amount of data.

The portal (understanding its XML-based descriptions of its own data) is able to "know" far more about its data, structures, and quality than just XML-wrapped data. The portal can be used to represent complex data structures that have been virtually integrated among legacy systems and infer meanings from metadata components.

The information that becomes associated with the portal information is now a *brand*. This 'brand' represents whatever the organization chooses to use as an imprint on the data produced by the portal. In Figure 15-1, our *brand* is that of the *publication*.

In summary then, the Web, XML, and portal technologies can be combined to enable organizations to introduce substantial amounts of manageable Internet-based and intranet-based metadata into a metadata solution.

File Management Systems

We have discussed file managers and file management systems throughout this book as examples of metadata-intensive applications. Many people do not realize the obvious standardization of metadata in these systems, and clearly do not take advantage of the underlying file system metamodel.

Recall that a *file type is a file type,* so reusability and standardization abound once new file types are defined. This philosophy is significant in the metadata-based technology world. Nevertheless, about the best that most modern operating systems provide is the ability to embed URLs into objects such as word processing documents, spreadsheet cells, presentation objects, and e-mails. So, as you might imagine, much of the intelligence of electronic filing systems lies dormant—untapped by modern metadata management techniques. In the following sections, an examination of file management systems yields the information in response to each core metadata question.

Locate

The objects in a file system are associated with one or more applications (applications include application program code, software packages, associated libraries, etc.; see the section Object-Oriented Component Libraries later in this chapter). While document objects are often able to invoke programs that can access them, much of a document's content is unavailable to the operating systems' file management system. We are retrieving only metadata when it exists in a file's name, in most cases. The contents of the file can be searched in many file manager add-ons, but again, we must have compatible file types and contents. (Exceptions for full-text indexing capabilities are not common.)

Process by File Type

As is illustrated in Figure 15-2, every file type has an associated *access procedure*. Accessing data (e.g., opening the file) involves using a file system to invoke a file access method on a specific file (or group of files). Data in the documents is made available to the application program that launches it. Again, metadata-controlled processing has been with us a long time.

In summary, file management systems are metadata intensive, and the optimum use of that metadata is by the file management system itself. The ability to incorporate this metadata subset into larger metadata solutions is becoming less of a challenge. Previous passive solutions such as reverse engineering the file management system and wrapping it with useful XML were stand-in solutions. However, the creation of a new file would immediately discredit the existing reengineering effort, unless new metadata was created along with the file.

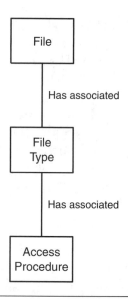

Figure 15-2 **The file system metamodel**

Database Management Systems

A DBMS has capabilities that can potentially serve as metadata solution components. All DBMS software has a catalog that contains the physical definitions of all defined databases. These definitions relate the database to its implemented components (e.g., tables, files, columns, elements) and describe the respective physical characteristics (e.g., database type, table names and sizes, column names and formats, creation dates, security settings). Most modern DBMS software allows the definition of these factors through Data Definition Language (DDL), which can often be generated by modeling tools. Reverse engineering and/or "capture," a modern name for reading the catalog file looking for the physical qualities of an existing database, has become a popular way of capturing this metadata and using it for enhancement by a larger metadata solution.

"It is in the database and should be easy to obtain" is a phrase uttered by many database administrators and developers. Unfortunately, DBMS catalog-resident metadata is physical. Often, *definitions* are not populated, and the names are established by database administrators for use by developers, not end users. Therefore, the metadata in a DBMS should not be expected to represent the needs of a business user, but might serve as a starting point for a data inventory when nothing is in existence.

The DBMS catalog describes the physical nature of stored data. It often will not show available access procedures, because they are usually associated with custom-developed software. What are the access methods supported by this database and how are they invoked? The answer will come in the form of one or more systems using one or more application and/or utility programs. Power users are often the best source of information about the best use of a DBMS's metadata.

DBMSs are primary sources of an organization's data-specific metadata. Often they represent the state-of-the-practice for organizational data management technology. Each data collection should be examined in great detail because there is a lot of potential metadata already being managed inside these systems.

Object-Oriented Component Libraries

As with DBMS-based metadata, OO component library capabilities also present some enticing opportunities to obtain source metadata. More important, their existence implies potential standardization of the way data is defined and accessed in an organization. The ability to gain access to well thought-out metadata, on which entire systems have been based, is usually not the focus when the components are defined and made accessible. It is highly probable, however, that the metadata associated with object-oriented libraries represents fundamental metadata-based descriptions of the software components used to develop the OO system. The potential metadata value increases with the number of systems developed using the components.

Each application developed with an OO development tool supports a need for information required by a business process. Understanding the data and processing associated with each component permits reuse of the organizational process and of the base-level component metadata. These represent programmatic information on the structure of the applications providing the information required by associated business processes.

At least one OO component library access must be developed for each type of OO component library system. Once developed, the access method provides a read-only copy of requested metadata directly from the component library.

Origins of OO Metadata

This metadata will have "gotten there," we hope, as a result of careful identification and integration of the organization's business requirements, followed by an architecture of a series of business systems designed to meet the requirements yet enable the organization to maintain sufficient dexterity to change.

Once business requirements are understood and the business systems are designed the organization waits until both are sufficiently mature in concept. It is only then that the specific technical information system requirements to support the business system should be developed within the OO framework.

This is typically the highest level of abstraction of the system's documentation as an OO library component. Once the system information requirements are understood, the system design activity, if standard in terms of potential impact, can provide the bulk of OO library components. Additional integrated components are added to the OO component libraries during the system's construction.

Object-Oriented Metadata Access

Unfortunately, access to the OO component library metadata is developed especially for each type of OO component library. Accumulated and actively managed OO component libraries can provide a valuable source of technical system metadata and can be integrated relatively easily with existing business process metadata. The use of OO component libraries by business processes can result in yet another place with development metadata, or a well-planned reusable set of metadata-based application components, many of which are directly related to the data being processed. Again, metadata solution design should precede the acquisition of such tools, or at least the definition of the components and their associated accessibility.

Metadata Everywhere?

The technologies described in this chapter share one characteristic—they are designed with an underlying metadata layer. In meta-meta land, this statement is significant. The integration and combination of metadata that resides in one or more isolated metadata stores requires the ability to relate that metadata to its role in that tool's functionality. The ability to "think" like a tool is paramount to the ability to use the meta-meta layer as a means of joining these metadata technologies.

Most of these metadata idiosyncrasies and similarities are the exact characteristics that have fueled the metadata standards movement. The next chapter explores the impact of these standards and what might lie in store in both the near and distant futures.

Chapter 16

The Impact of Standards

We clearly understand the impact that metadata can have on an organization's information. But metadata can be just as disheveled as the data it describes. Typically, data management or data administration organizations are given the responsibility of ironing out data discrepancies[1]... but how do these efforts roll over to the treatment of metadata discrepancies? At a larger level, how is metadata standardized outside the organization? Does one set of standards contradict the other? How can we assure synchronization?

This chapter discusses standards, those dull and dreary efforts geared toward making our jobs more miserable at first (or so it seems), but much easier eventually.

Internal Standards

Metadata is not the first consideration in the internal standards arena. Most efforts, if any exist, focus first on the standardization of *data*. For example, defining standard values for a company's products, resulting in a shared or standard product master, is usually initiated at the same time as application or data integration, or in forward thinking organizations, when development of an enterprise data-driven application begins. The emphasis during the initial go-around is on the data itself, not the metadata.

---

1. Data management organizations are discussed in Chapter 19.

Table 16-1   The 5 Questions and Affected Metadata

Question	Affected Metadata
1. What data do we have?	Data Element Name
2. What does it mean?	Data Element Definition
3. Where is it?	Data Element Location (e.g., Data Store Name), Data Element Identifier
4. How did it get there?	Data Element Source, Data Element Transition Procedure(s), Data Element Translation Rule(s)
5. How do we get it? (Go get it for us.)	Data Element Access Procedure Name, Data Element Access Procedure Execution Step(s)

As these data standards evolve, the first type of metadata-driven standard usually focuses on names for data identification—program names, data element names, field names, and job names. These initial naming standards always include standard abbreviations, primarily because early programming languages had physical constraints (e.g., the need to fit a name into 16 characters or fewer). The enforcement of these abbreviations was almost always performed manually, and left to the "data police" in these data administration organizations. As the "last stop" in many organizations, these people ensured that names were changed to what they should be, and developers often resented the necessary after-the-fact changes.

Based on developers' resentment as well as the advent of application development tools, naming standards in many organizations slipped through the cracks. In addition, modern database management software no longer imposes length restrictions that require abbreviations. As such, most developers (regardless of whether they are part of an IT organization) use full words based on their perceptions of data element meanings, and the "standard" names are often no longer standard.

Internal standards have now evolved to include and affect metadata beyond names. In fact, true internal metadata standards should include all metadata associated with the ability to respond to our 5 Questions,[2] which are listed in Table 16-1.

---

2. The 5 Questions is a trademark of and the questions and method are copyrighted by Database Design Solutions, Inc., Bernardsville, New Jersey.

Table 16-2 The 5 Questions and Affected Process-Specific Metadata

Question	Affected Metadata
1. What processes (programs) do we have?	Application Name, Program Name, Process Model Name
2. What functions do they perform?	Function Name, Process/Program/Function Matrix/Relationship
3. Where are they?	Program Location (e.g., Program Library Name)
4. How did they get there?	Developer/Analyst Name, Program State (Development/Test/Production)
5. How do we get them? (Go get them for us.)	Application/Program Library Access Procedure Name, Access Procedure Execution Step(s)

In Table 16-1, the minimum internal metadata standards are represented. In fact, it is essential that as data is created, the associated metadata also be created. It is obvious that as this metadata is created, it is populating distinct parts of an organization's metamodel. These metadata standards are data-driven, certainly, but they are *essential to supply information on demand*. If process-specific metadata is also of importance and concern, other metadata elements likely to become standard requirements will reflect a different angle on the 5 Questions, as Table 16-2 shows.

Most organizations already require a substantial amount of the metadata in Table 16-2 as applications are developed. However, the accessibility of the metadata varies, depending on where the actual programs are stored and the accessibility of the "place(s)" to those who are looking. Finally, the tunnel vision mentioned in connection with implementation projects applies to metadata also in that the "process" metadata is usually treated separately from the "data" metadata, and it is therefore virtually impossible to figure out what data is processed by what applications. As with data-focused metadata standards, the process side of metadata should be required when the process is created.

When internal metadata standards are created, it is important to consider the role of the metadata instances. Will the metadata *identify* the occurrences of the described objects? Will the metadata be used to *locate* these occurrences? Will the metadata be used to *format* these occurrences? Depending on the situation, metadata requirements could expand beyond those previously identified.

Last, internal standards must not ignore *external* standards, or those created by external organizations for the purposes of intercompany and intertool exchange. Although many of these metadata standards seem always to be in the process of being rolled out and not quite final, it is a fair statement that many have reached the point where they should be considered influential. These standards efforts involve input from various sectors, including software vendors primarily, industry-specific representatives, national and international government committees, and last, targeted users.

External Standards

Many years ago after the publication of my first book (Tannenbaum, 1994), I was speaking at an industry conference and made the following statement:

Because there is an s at the end of standards, we obviously don't have any.

To some degree, a standard implies the only way to do things. For example, there is only one way to draw a map, indicating levels of altitude and direction. However, maps can vary in the colors used to indicate county, state, and interstate highways. They can also vary in the symbols used to represent town and city populations. In fact, there are many other variables in map depiction, which is why a map's legend is important. But which parts of map development are standard, and which parts are not? How do we integrate maps that have been developed by different companies?

Standards variation is a fact of life. Throughout standards-driven industries, the idiosyncrasies have been around for such a long time that they are almost as standard as the standards themselves. Why, then, is the lack of a universal metadata standard killing us all?

A Brief History

The world of metadata, accompanying metamodels, and metadata solutions has been with us formally since the early 1990s. At that time, major vendors tried to use a set of "standard metamodels" as a means of exchanging application-focused models from their best modeling tools. Before the 1990s, designers of standalone data dictionaries were not concerned with the standardization of metamodels for the purposes of connectivity to other products' instances. Many of you may remember IBM's AD/Cycle, and the fact that it never came to be. Based on this blatant failure, individual CASE (Computer Aided System Engineering) tools agreed on a standard exchange format, known as CDIF (CASE Data Interexchange Format), which allowed *some* models and components to go back and forth between tools, as long as they were CDIF compliant and shared common modeling constructs. This standard, overseen by the Electronic Industries Association (EIA), was the first to emphasize similarity and exchange at the metadata level. Although the CDIF standard is not really around anymore (it has merged into other more influential standards), its design and execution are, in fact, still common.

In original metadata exchange standards, as illustrated in Figure 16-1, a batch file was formatted with a standard header, metamodel definition, and model definition. As a result, model instances, for example, were exported, and the header of the export file would indicate which metamodel occurrences were represented by the model instances. The header contained information relating to the physical characteristics of the remainder of the file. This standard did not require a specific type of processing or treatment of the export file's contents by the receiving tool. It merely made the transfer process slightly easier for vendors by providing a format that they could follow in their own product's import and export functions.

A standard as simple as this one lacked the following major components:

- Standardized metamodels
- Standardized processing of metamodel instances
- Standardized metamodel components that would encourage sharing of specific types of metadata across tools

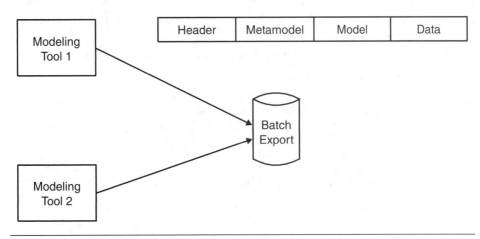

Figure 16-1 **The original metadata exchange standard**

- Standard metamodel component instances that could encourage sharing of metadata within industries, irrespective of the deployed tool or application

Metadata standardization focused initially on interexchange, emphasizing the format of batch export files. As the demand for metadata-based initiatives has grown, standards are beginning to become influential. Approximately 10 years have elapsed since the initial metadata exchange standard. Throughout this period, many conflicting standards efforts have joined hands or become eliminated, and today a small group of influential efforts remains. Each has its turf and its philosophy, yet the political vendor emphasis is becoming more consumer oriented. In fact, each standards body is now represented by individuals from the following camps:

- Software vendors (so what else is new?)
- Consumer industry representatives, focusing on the need to share and exchange data and metadata within their own set of organizations
- International standards supporters, primarily from research organizations, all advocating the need for a vendor-neutral, interindustry standardized metadata-based transfer mechanism

In addition to the makeup of standards organizations, they are also different now in that they all focus on achieving true *external* integration. The results of these significant efforts will allow software consumers to share data between products that originate from different vendors, based on the use of standardized metadata.

Today's major metadata players are focusing on three major aspects of the metadata world:

1. *Metamodels,* as a means of standardizing the types of metadata used and tracked by distinct IT functions and their supporting products both within and across consumer industries

2. *Metadata exchange,* focusing on the transfer of the instances of these metamodels (standard metadata) between software implementations

3. *Metadata architectures and frameworks,* as a means of creating a standard metadata packaging that not only includes the metamodel and exchange formats, but also the associated processes and tool compo-

nents that can be used to ensure the adherence to a defined metadata standard

Distinct standards efforts exist that originally emphasized one of the listed areas. However, each has widened its defined influence to encompass the other two required aspects of a metadata standard. In recent years, separate standards efforts have begun to share ideas and proposals. In fact, unlike in the past, many substandards are now being proposed and reviewed by what used to be conflicting standards efforts. The result is sure to become a universal standard set, compatible with each group's differentiating factors, as illustrated in Figure 16-2.

   As illustrated by the various differences in shading in Figure 16-2, the Universal Base Metamodel would allow an "area" for individual vendors to implement their product's metadata distinctiveness. This area would represent a standardized relationship to a base metamodel (the "checkered" box). Each vendor would maintain its product's uniqueness (note the horizontal and diagonal stripes) by maintaining a standard metamodel construct that connects to the universal base metamodel (note that each metamodel contains that checkered box). As a result,

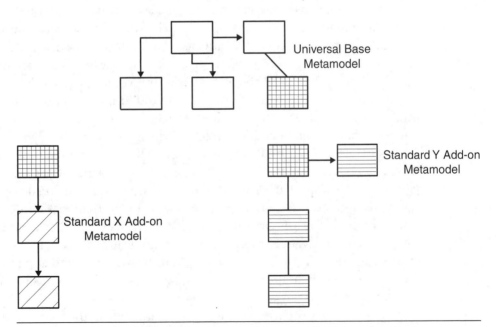

Figure 16-2 *Where metadata standards are headed*

it would be easy to have products share metadata. The connectivity would be similar to a standard relational connection in terms of the way individual product metamodels would tie together via the base metamodel construct.

In fact, emphasis of late has been focused on the data warehouse world. I remember mentioning to a major standards body that data warehouses would be the place where metadata would gain its deserved prestige. Over the years, those who typically focused on the insides of tools now consider how and why *their* tools would fit into a mixed-vendor arena. Multiple vendors are now emphasizing similar objectives, and these objectives will result in data warehouse–tuned standard metamodels, metadata exchange formats and mechanisms, and overall architectures.

As specific subfunctions (e.g., data warehousing) become finalized in the standards community, they will reflect a portion of the eventual total metadata standard. As illustrated in Figure 16-2, standards will be complete when they can be interlocked without damage to existing products.

Major standards efforts have been combined for the most part into the Object Management Group (OMG). The OMG recently embraced the MDC (Meta Data Coalition) in an exciting "metadata standard merger" and is now a major force in all three aspects of the required metadata standards components.

Other extraneous forces are still plugging away, however. For one, there used to be three repository "super" vendors, each with its own metadata solution–oriented product. However, the advent of the Internet has restricted the impact that these super vendors have had over the last few years. Many people feel that unless they give up their secrets, the vendors are likely to find the demand for their repository products dwindling. In addition, the original American National Standards Institute (ANSI) is still in existence, and has also offered a standard metamodel, geared at sharing metadata. Finally, the Institute for Electrical and Electronics Engineers (IEEE) has been known for building on this metamodel to support specific engineering-based industries. Last, but certainly not least, XML (Extensible Markup Language) is also the result of an ANSI standards body (W3C) that joined forces with an international standards body (International Standards Organization, or ISO). However, XML falls into its own category, since it has been adopted by all major standards committees. In fact, each standards body is now proposing XML standards, geared at tying XML to the exchange of their already defined standard metadata. Confusing? You bet! Overlapping? Definitely.

The best way to analyze the impact of standards on the world of metadata is to evaluate some of the significant prospects, in terms of their metamodels, exchange standards, and overall architectures.

Metamodels

Most standards efforts do not seem to focus initially on metamodels, yet this is always the area that the standards consumer tends to zero in on during a standards assessment. When metamodels are standardized, the intent is a uniform organization of metadata and its interrelationships. This uniformity is typically centered on a particular function, architectural collection, physical IT requirement (e.g., DBMS, programming language, software package or tool), or methodology-focused purpose. Unfortunately, when the development of a standard metamodel is not based on a clear-cut set of existing metadata, the definition of *standard* is often used only by the people responsible for its definition.

Standard metamodels strive toward seamless integration of metadata, despite its originating tool, application, or physical software residence. When the model is uniform, it is not necessarily required that all metadata suppliers adhere to it in total, but rather that each metadata supplier be aware of the standard metamodel in order to populate resident interface and transition points. As Figure 16-2 illustrates, the intent is for all distinct metamodels to be connectable. It will be more important, however, that common metadata become shareable, based on the fact that it would be deployed uniformly in common metamodels across the industry.

There have been several efforts over time to standardize metamodels. Beginning, as mentioned, with AD/Cycle, early metamodels focused on distinct aspects of the IT world, as opposed to the business world. The original AD/Cycle Information Model consisted of a wide variety of submodels, including an enterprise submodel that identified and organized the corporate enterprise in terms of its information, goals, resources, business models, and logical application models. Other submodels then detailed these aspects of the enterprise, and were classified as technology or application configuration submodels. The common constructs were modeled separately into a global submodel. With AD/Cycle's lack of acceptance, a pause fell over the metamodeling standards world for approximately 5 years, at which time development of the Open Information Model (OIM) began as a joint effort by Microsoft and Texas Instruments.

The Open Information Model

The OIM reflected a slightly different philosophy from AD/Cycle's. Rather than take metadata from an enterprise perspective on downward, the OIM started at the bottom and worked its way up. In addition, for perhaps the first time in metamodel development, the OIM began to address not only specific IT functions (e.g., analysis and design), but also began to establish generic elements as a means of standardizing the types of metadata that should be tracked throughout these functions, regardless of the tools being deployed as metamodel implementations. This tool-independent approach was the first of its kind, and began shortly after the initial models were released. At that time, incorporation of the Unified Modeling Language (UML) approach, originating from another standards effort (the Object Management Group, or OMG), standardized the standards, so to speak. At this point in OIM's history, many vendors joined the effort and were responsible for providing the "many-vendor, tool-neutral" approach. Figures 16-3 and 16-4 illustrate OIM's attempt to standardize the correlation of models, model components (model elements), and packages, as well as the identification of the contact information for any type of element, *regardless of the implementing tool.*

The objective of these models is to represent a specification for all vendors of tools that support IT analysis and design. Adherence to this specification would not only ease the exchange of metadata associated with analysis and design, but also allow the storage of this metadata in a metadata store other than that of the tool itself, thus encouraging a metadata solution approach to shared metadata exchange. The OIM eventually included models that represented virtually all aspects of software development and their associated implementations. Major model categories were:

- Analysis and Design
- Objects and Components
- Databases and Warehousing
- Business Engineering
- Knowledge Management

All models in these categories were to be represented with UML, the new Unified Modeling Language.

As the development of the OIM continued (to this date some models are not yet complete), yet another standards effort began, this time focusing exclusively on metadata for data warehousing. This effort, the Meta Data Coalition (MDC), was spearheaded by a vendor of a specific data warehousing tool, with the objective of standardizing the metadata required to support data warehousing, from the inception of development through the end-user analysis and decision support that ultimately resulted. The MDC had minimal impact at first, especially as a result of its public statement of the need for private consumers' support and contributions. In addition, its standard focused on a batch exchange of metadata (MDIS) similar to that of CDIF (CASE Data Interexchange Format) without any required metamodel compliance. As data ware-

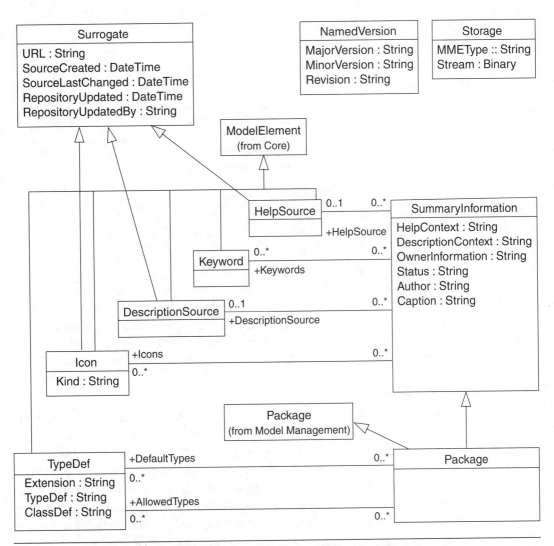

Figure 16-3 OIM analysis and generic design elements

Source: Used with permission from the Object Management Group, Needham, Mass. Copyright © OMG, 1993–2001.

housing became more popular, the OIM was extended in various areas to support data warehousing. More than 200 vendors participated in this effort, including those who were part of the initial MDC, and the conflicting yet complementary efforts were unified at the end of 1998. The OIM, at this point initially supportive of data warehousing, was turned over to the MDC.

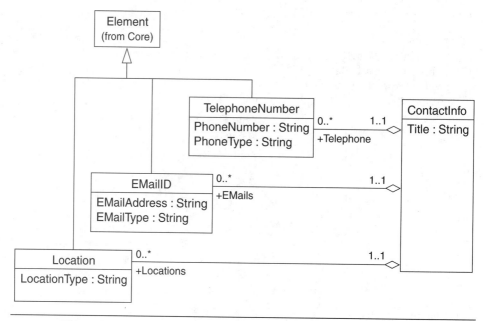

Figure 16-4   **OIM analysis and design contact information**

Source: Used with permission from the Object Management Group, Needham, Mass. Copyright © OMG, 1993–2001.

In conjunction with the MDC, another major effort began moving into the data warehousing space. The OMG (Object Management Group), the originator of UML, which was adopted during OIM development, created the Common Warehouse Model (CWM). This was an after-the-fact effort by the OMG, since their original work centered on the meta-metamodel level and the need for standardized metadata exchange, as opposed to its instances and relationships. Many traditional IT consumers did not identify with OMG's efforts at their inception, and instead saw it as a haven for software vendors, who had a tendency to discuss indefinitely the "right" way to define and exchange metadata in the context of software.

The Common Warehouse Model

When data warehousing became the first true cost/benefit application for metadata exchange, many theoretical standards efforts began to touch ground and offer the first seemingly practical and deployable means of justifying this common metadata interexchange, or metadata solutions approach to data warehousing. The OMG, in existence since 1989, has always strived to develop vendor-independent specifications for the software industry. In addition, its approach to data warehousing introduced yet another philosophical approach. Unlike the Open Information Model, whose primary objective was metadata relationship and interexchange, the OMG has always focused on standardization for the purpose of reuse. In fact, it has always strived to ease component-based software development via the definition of standard, tool-independent components. The Common Warehouse Model is an example of this philosophy—it is built exclusively using the OMG's Unified Modeling Language. Why create more model components for data warehousing than already exist? Why redefine interexchange requirements when industry resources, such as XML, and/or other already defined APIs (such as the Meta Object Facility, or MOF) have already been developed?

Based on the OMG's component-based philosophy, the CWM, although named and considered within the scope of data warehousing, reflects the fact that data warehousing is a reorganization of existing enterprise resources. These resources include data (obviously) as well as processes which, when applied to the data, result in a restructured data store with data-based analysis-driven conclusions. Following this approach, the CWM consists of several packages, each containing a set of other packages (we can consider them metamodels). Many of the packages that form the Common Warehouse Model are not specific to data warehousing. Model elements are definitely common and reusable to support the OMG's component-based approach.

The CWM consists of four major packages:

1. The *Foundation* Package identifies common metadata elements (e.g., Business Information, Data Types, Expressions, Keys and Indexes, Software Deployment, Type Mapping) as defined in the Unified Modeling Language and reusable throughout the CWM.

2. The *Resource* Package organizes the metadata related to data stores as well as the tagging of these stores with XML (e.g., Relational, Record, Multidimensional, XML).

3. An *Analysis* Package focuses on the metadata associated with data analysis (e.g., Transformation, OLAP, Data Mining, Information Visualization, Business Nomenclature).

4. A *Management* Package organizes the metadata surrounding the support and coordination of data warehouses (e.g., Warehouse Process, Warehouse Operation).

Figure 16-5 illustrates one such package, that of Software Deployment (part of the Foundation package). Notice that *components* relate to *software systems*

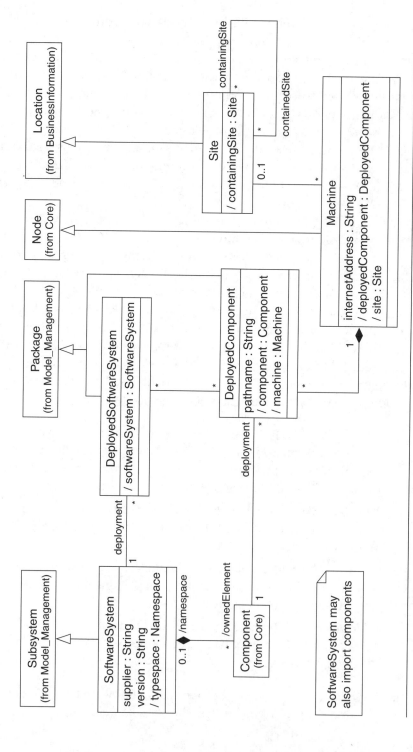

Figure 16-5 The Software Deployment Package of OMG's Common Warehouse Model

Source: Used with permission from the Object Management Group, Needham, Mass. Copyright © OMG, 1993–2001.

as well as *deployed software systems*, via a *deployment* relationship. In the world of component-based development, components can be named differently when they are deployed, yet the need to relate them to the same base component guarantees the core relationship that is necessary for reuse.

Metadata Exchange

A standard metamodel alone does not guarantee standard metadata usage and exchange. Many standards efforts have addressed the means of accessing and transporting the metamodel-populated metadata. Exchange standards vary substantially in their implementations, however. We have already discussed some batch exchange formats (CDIF, MDIS). Other means of accessing and exchanging metadata include:

- *Application program interfaces (APIs),* standard routines that can be *called* from within metadata accessing programs, remaining in that program's control

- *Remote procedure calls (RPCs),* standard routines that are *executed* by metadata accessing programs, outside of that program's control

- *Embedded processes,* which are associated with distinct components of a standard metamodel

- *Standards-based languages,* which are defined by standards organizations and available for use by metadata accessing programs. In many scenarios, these languages are combined with interfaces and required architectures.

As illustrated in Figure 16-6, the ways to identify, share, exchange, and display metadata vary with today's options. Standards efforts have embraced all categories of metadata exchange—in some situations single standards have attempted to embrace all these categories with the hopes of providing an integrated standard. In others, only a subset of these exchange options is covered. Because we will discuss standard architectures and frameworks in the final part of this section, it is important to keep in mind that metadata solutions consist of *all* of these components.

Standards efforts typically attempt to address metadata exchange in a reusable means, based usually on the type of metadata being exchanged, or in some cases, on the source of the metadata. Narrowly focused standards, as discussed, address metadata exchange formats only, without much ado about *what* gets exchanged, *how* the metadata should be processed, or *where* it

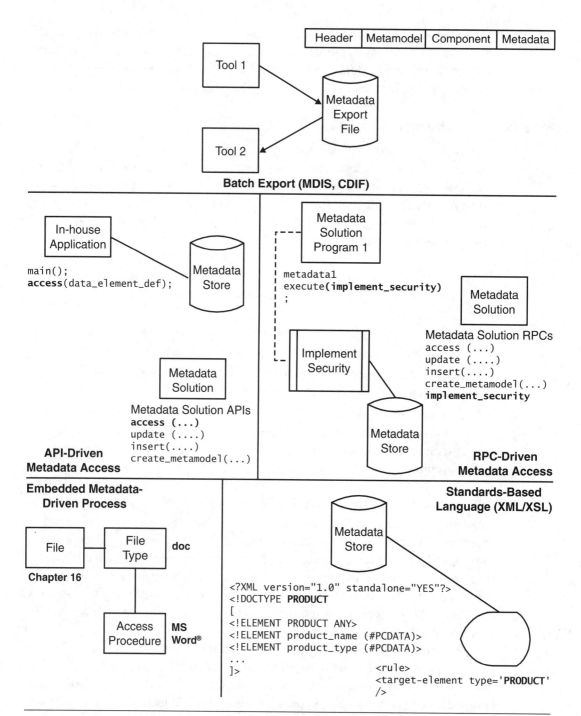

Figure 16-6   **Various metadata exchange options**

should be placed in the recipient metadata store. Recently, the issues of meta-data exchange have been considered minimally in conjunction with standard metamodels. The implementations have resulted in sets of standard APIs and/or RPCs, which are associated with types of metadata, based on their relation-ships in the meta-metamodel.

Embedded Metadata-Driven Processes

As illustrated in Figure 16-7, the OMG has an architectural approach to its metadata standards, focusing mainly on the potential reuse of most of its metamodel components. It is not surprising that the exchange of this re-usable metadata is also addressed on a reusable basis. The OMG has long advo-cated a Common Object Request Broker Architecture (CORBA), of which the Meta Object Facility (MOF) is a component. At the meta-metamodel level (the Model package is the model of the models, so to speak), it is important to note the placement of *Behavioral Features*, specifically, the *Operations*, that are indirectly associated with *Model Elements*. These Operations are typically thought of from the point of view of a metamodel instance, but are imple-mented in MOF as a type of behavior. The MOF defines specific operations, and some (e.g., findRequiredElements) are geared toward the exchange of metadata among MOF-compliant implementations. Consider the MOF an example of a set of *embedded metadata-driven processes*.

Aside from the embedded operations that we see at the meta-meta level of the MOF, each package (metamodel) has its defined interfaces, which are typi-cally geared toward instances of the metamodel itself, hence our metadata.

Standards-Based Languages

The OMG strives to standardize the language used to define new interfaces, as they are required. In fact, since all packages (metamodels) are based on the MOF, any model defined in MOF terms can be mapped into IDL, a CORBA standard Interface Definition Language. IDL is intended to be used from calling applica-tions, thus providing easy API-like interface to MOF-compliant metadata stores.

More recently, metadata standards have incorporated the Internet as a means of exchanging standard metadata. Metadata has long been a require-ment of Web-based search and retrieve, yet not until recently did metadata and metamodeling standards efforts join forces with the experienced nature of Web-based metadata usage. XML has been viewed by many as the happy con-nection between the world of standard metadata and the accessibility of the World Wide Web. For perhaps the first time, the connection could be via stan-dardized tags, each representing an aspect of a standard metamodel. For true

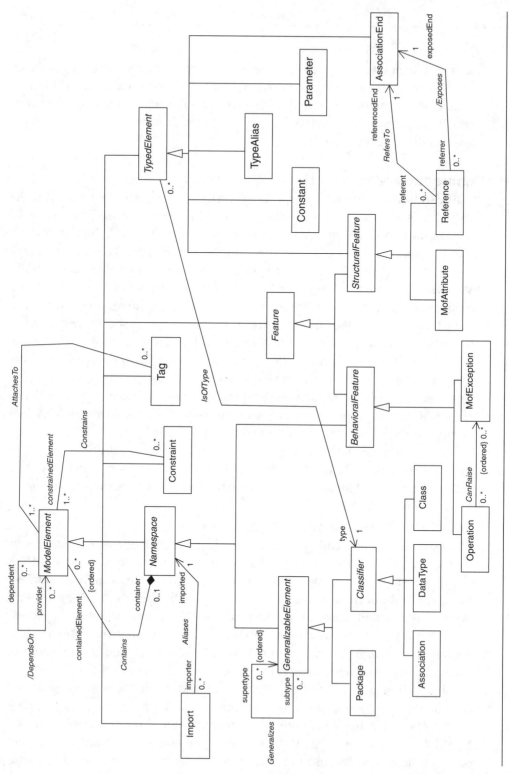

Figure 16-7 The OMG Meta Object Facility Model Metamodel (Package)

Source: Used with permission from the Object Management Group, Needham, Mass. Copyright © OMG, 1993–2001.

standardization, the values of the tags must also reflect standard instances of these standard metamodel constructs. Taking the issue of standard tags for standard exchange one step further, the W3C standards committee (developers of XML) has created the XML Metadata Interchange specification, or XMI.

XMI   The purpose of XMI is the integration of XML, UML, and MOF to result in true Internet exchange of not only UML-compliant models, but also the instances of these models, in most cases metadata. In essence, XMI supports the exchange of any kind of metadata that can be expressed using the MOF. The format of XMI's metadata streams (usually files) will be based on a standard set of XML tags. This proposed format was originally called SMIF (Stream-based Metadata Interchange Format). However, the advent of data warehousing has enhanced SMIF extensively, and it is safe to say that XMI's intent is the interchange of metadata in *any* form, as long as XML is used to represent that metadata in terms of an instance of the MOF specification. Therefore, XMI should be considered *another* common metadata interchange format, and perhaps the only translatable format. Any metadata solution or supplier that can encode and decode an XMI stream can exchange metadata. Furthermore, if these streams represent MOF metamodels or any portion thereof, the advent of standardized metadata would not be far away.

The significance of XMI's objective cannot be understated. As many readers are already aware, standards exist for one reason, but are not followed for another. Once standards are not followed, recycling standards becomes exponentially more difficult because it is now twice as hard to convince the deviators to use standards and, unless they have been unable to function, their interest in readdressing an old standard is usually nonexistent. Because XMI assumes MOF compliance, and because each model constructed as an instance of a MOF can include its own definitions and relationships in MOF terms, the standards effort is currently finalizing the ability to *generate XMI* from a MOF-compliant model. The generated result would be instances of already defined standard XML tags, thus ensuring the ability to exchange and interface. Exceptions to these standards would be permissible, as long as they *connected* to the standard at some point.

As illustrated in Figure 16-8, a common data warehouse metamodel would be represented in terms of XMI identifiers and labels, some being universal (uuid's are standard). Any metadata that is then shared or accessed from within an organization (or across organizations) would need to be represented consistently. Matching identifiers would imply equivalence at the meta-meta level (same type of metadata construct), and the processing software would immediately know that the value was, for example, a definition.

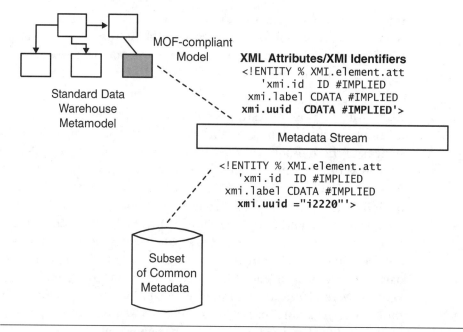

Figure 16-8   *XMI's illustrated intent*

It is important to realize that XMI is perhaps the first standard with potential practicality. It assumes compliance with OMG architectural rules (e.g., MOF-compliant model basis), but can be deployed as long as the MOF-ignorant consumer can use software that can translate individual metadata instances into MOF instances. As vendors progress, their choices will be either to emphasize making the underlying metadata of their tools compliant with a MOF model, or to translate their non-MOF–compliant metadata set into one that can be related to a standard. This is perhaps the first standards effort in history that requires this level of compromise.

Architectures and Frameworks

A final item must be addressed in the external metadata standards arena. So far, we have addressed external standards based on their primary emphasis as a metadata solution component. The Object Management Group is one of the few external standards bodies to approach each of these components as part of an overall framework. This framework, known as the Common Object Request Broker Architecture (CORBA), is the glue that seals the relationships among UML-compliant models, the MOF, and the proposed Metadata Interexchange Specification (XMI). It serves as the communication component and allows compliant components to interface, irrespective of technical platforms.

CORBA

In the CORBA architecture, a request broker sits as the basic mechanism for receiving and channeling requests. The Interface Definition Language (IDL) is the standard language required for these requests, and is independent of programming language, but contains mapping to popular programming languages so that applications can send and receive requests to CORBA facilities. The overall architecture defines the structure, interfaces, services, and objects. As such, all of the metadata solution components that form the OMG standard are defined without tunnel vision and represent one aspect of the CORBA standard.

Super Vendors

Finally, the impact of major software vendors on the standards cannot be understated. Despite the need for vendor neutrality in standards, the software economy is probably the biggest source of political effectiveness when it comes to deploying standards. Metadata solutions were originally controlled by the vendors, the major vendors being the only ones in the marketplace to benefit from metadata-based product integration. These vendors, all with distinct and unconnected products, were interested in using metadata as a seamless way to integrate *their own* product sets. It was an original theory that one such super vendor would become the first to institute a product-encompassing metamodel. As a result, the remainder of the vendors and the consumers would have no choice but to adhere to it in order to interface with the metamodel that carried the major market share.

As of this writing, no super vendor can claim the completion of this task. It is important to note, however, that all efforts to establish standards are primarily by representatives of the major metadata-interested vendors in the software community.

Is Anyone Really Following Them?

Standards are always impressive in terms of objective and potential. However, when practicality is not a major characteristic, the likelihood of adherence drops substantially. Especially in the metadata area, we know what has not worked . . . but we also know the potential of a well-implemented metadata standard.

Assess the practicality of standards from the point of view of daily information analysis. The ease of compliance is always weighed against the expected benefits. If it is easier to get to the information you need, on demand, on your own, without paying attention to standards of any sort, then it is likely that no one is *really* following the standards, whether external or internal. If, on the other hand, it is impossible to process information without following some sort of standard, or the amount of custom processing and the associated time required to process different or similar sets of information over and over again far outweighs the amount of time that it takes to conform, just once, the audience is crying for a standard.

Today versus Tomorrow

What is proposed today often becomes standard tomorrow. What is standard today often becomes defunct tomorrow. Repository standards of the 1990s are for the most part defunct, and we are now developing and expanding metadata standards. The fact that many standards groups are working on a piece of the overall metadata solution while contemplating an inevitable architecture convinces me that practicality has at long last entered the minds of the standards developers.

Yesterday, the perception was that metadata was not a business user's concern. Today, the world of metadata is not restricted to IT. Tomorrow, the term *metadata* will most likely become obsolete if the proposed metadata standards consolidate and become a requirement for information on demand. It will be there; we just won't realize how hard it was to get there . . . a true sign of standards enforcement.

Standard metamodels, modeling languages, metadata interexchange commands, and the architectures required to see all these pieces to fruition can only become a fact of life if they are so easy to implement that they are basic requirements of all software packaging. Instead of formalizing the way metadata should be shared and exchanged, the sharing and exchanging should be an automatic feature of purchased software. Similar to the way we can automatically back up and load, we should be able to locate and clarify.

To perform the metadata-centric utilities that support our 5 Questions, the supporting metadata must be standardized and available. As the Internet becomes the primary vehicle for answering the 5 Questions across organizations, the associated metadata is sure to become a built-in facet. Standards efforts are already envisioning the metadata of tomorrow. The consumers of today should begin addressing their information categorization in a similarly standard fashion.

So What Do We Do (Now)?

It is clear that we cannot sit back and wait for standards to formalize to the point where they are invisible. At the same time, we want to make sure that our metadata solution plans are not so individualized that we will never be able to conform to industry standards when they do make it to prime time. So what should we do? In general, there are two paths that the average metadata solution can take:

1. Purchase off-the-shelf vendor solutions.
2. Custom develop a metadata solution or one or more components.

When purchasing vendor products, it is essential to evaluate their compliance with standards. Require vendors to discuss their involvement with standards, and be particularly interested in how they will support metadata exchange. XML has already taken the limelight as a way of exchanging metadata, but no one has finalized the types of tags that should be required to support standardized metamodels.

Custom development leaves most decisions about adhering up to the implementing individual or organization. It would be wise to become an active participant in the W3C standards committees. It is easy to review its progress by visiting its Web site and registering as a regular participant. If you are implementing an integrated metadata solution, you will surely be exchanging metadata. Consider the need for a standard metamodel as the basis for your interexchange. Sample implementations appear in Part V, Sample Metadata Solutions.

Part IV

Beginning the Metadata Solution Process

We've defined, discussed, and organized metadata. Those with the technical prowess to do so have combined various metadata worlds into one solid meta-meta layer, and now understand how the internals of metadata solutions can access and relate bits and pieces of organized metadata. There is more to a metadata solution than metadata itself.

In Part IV we address the non-metadata factors. Beginning with our organizations and how to evaluate readiness to define and implement a metadata solution, we will look at the impact a well-defined metadata solution can have on what seems to be metadata naïveté. We then take this potential impact and continue to define our non-metadata requirements.

The technical environment consists of many aspects that surround solid metadata definition. For one, the tools are all here and will continue to participate as metadata suppliers and beneficiaries. The way each tool needs to connect is a crucial factor in all metadata solutions. The ways *we* need to connect is another, often separate, factor. This section discusses the relationships of tools and metadata solutions, as well as the ways in which metadata can be displayed.

Metadata solutions often fail if their contents are not managed and controlled. How do we ensure that metadata is shared and reused? How do we advertise our metadata? Where in the organization should this responsibility fall? This section illustrates organizational responsibilities and staffing options, and defines the new role of metadata solution administration.

Finally, how do we determine what metadata solution is right for us? Do we need one metadata store or several metadata stores? How do we distribute metadata stores? Should we purchase metamodels? How do we include the Internet? Should we custom develop a metadata solution?

All of these issues and questions are addressed in Part IV. Case studies are included as a reality check. Keep reading!

Chapter 17

The Non-Metadata Factors
Group 1: The Nontechnical Environment

Now that we have explored the history, background, definition, and preparation of metadata, it is time to begin the implementation of our metadata solution. Because a metadata solution can be as encompassing as you need it to be, it is essential to revisit our definition, focusing on both its technical and nontechnical components. This chapter discusses the nontechnical factors—issues that can sometimes be more influential than the technical specifics. In Chapter 18 we discuss the technical environment.

Redefining *Metadata Solution*

It is tempting to draw a ring around the various components of an organized group of metadata and call the result a *metadata solution*. It is now clear, however, that a successful metadata solution is a lot more than the metadata itself. In fact, the organization of this metadata into a set of metamodels represents just one component of a metadata solution. Based on the additional components that have been discussed, our definition is reiterated.

> ❖ **Metadata solution**   An organized and integrated set of related metadata, logically connected but often physically separate, with common access points and methods. The solution can embrace one or more metadata stores with distinct or common metamodels and must be accessible to metadata suppliers and beneficiaries who may reside inside or outside the metadata solution architecture.

So far, we have detailed the following aspects of a metadata solution:

- Metadata organized into metamodels
- Metamodel integration at the meta-meta level
- Metadata stores—standalone, distributed, or virtual

The architecture of a metadata solution also includes these components:

- *Metadata access functions* that are identifiable, organized, and available
- *Metadata displays* inside and outside the metadata solution
- *An overall architecture that unifies all metadata solution components*

Part IV delves into these components in order to begin preparing the full implementation of the technical metadata solution. First, however, it is important to discuss the issues that *surround* the technical environment.

Determining Readiness

It is always exciting to embark on a new technological adventure. For many people the implementation of a metadata solution is an adventure. But for most people, metadata solutions have been implemented over and over again—and none of the attempts proved to be worthwhile. In many cases, the metadata technology could be identified as the primary culprit; in far more cases, the surrounding environment was the faulty factor.

We have seen many organizations repeatedly approach the development of a metadata solution, and finally call in professional help when they *really* needed a result. Why was professional help required to make the metadata solution successful? In most cases, it was because the outsiders could be honest, impartial, and nonpolitical. In addition, many organizations acknowledge their lack of preparedness, but go ahead and implement a metadata solution anyway. The result is never a true solution, but yet another place for metadata, with no connection to all the other metadata stores already in operation. This result is not necessarily without merit, but its limited scope and purpose must be acknowledged.

Readiness is a prerequisite characteristic to every metadata solution. It needs to be assessed in terms of each metadata solution component category—its preparation, development and implementation, execution, and support.

The Metadata

People are often quick to agree that they need a metadata solution. Why do they need one? If it is because they can't get their hands on the metadata that they need, the first question organizations must honestly answer is:

Do we *have* the metadata that we need?

Many organizations do. But how good is it? Who defines *good?* How redundant is the "good" metadata, and more important, how conflicting is it? Depending on how metadata is created, its values can be quite variable and not subject to standards of any kind. It is a known fact that the more business-oriented a piece of metadata is (as opposed to being representative of, for example, a physical characteristic), the less likely it is to be standardized or consistent. Ironically, data managers and administrators are more likely to be concerned with *what* to standardize than with *how* to standardize. The result is mounds and mounds of variable metadata, some residing in tools, some in standalone metadata stores, some as part of physical implementations (DBMS catalogs, program header files, etc.). A successful readiness evaluation recognizes this ineffective approach—ineffective because the creation of a metadata solution without solution supporting procedures that determine how metadata is created is doomed from the beginning.

The format and location of metadata is often a good indicator of its accuracy. For example, metadata that resides in a tool's structure or is represented by some other fixed structure is typically targeted at addressing a specific scope based on a tool's functionality. As you organize metadata by beneficiary category (see Chapters 8 and 9), it is important to assess its completeness and accuracy. If metadata that is unique or specific to a beneficiary category does not appear to be accurate, further investigation is warranted to determine whether the metadata represents only one perspective. Ultimately, the metadata should be evaluated in terms of its:

- Accuracy
- Consistency
- Modularity
- Represented perspectives
- Ease of identification

Accuracy

Does the metadata describe its target object in such a way that there would *never* be a question as to *what* is being described? With physical metadata, a *File Name* is a *file name* is a *file_name* is an *FNAME*, but we all know what is being described. With logical metadata, "the sum of all department totals" may or may not be "the accumulation of subdepartment tallies" or "the result of adding up individual net values" . . . and all of these may or may not define *Department_revenue* or *DEPT_SALES* or *Department_total*.

If your metadata is not accurate, it should not be part of a metadata solution.

Consistency

Is the metadata compatible? Do the values represent the same principles in terms of the purpose for which they were created? Are different values equivalent? If so, according to whose terms? Once inconsistent metadata is combined, it is often impossible to realize that the data describe the same piece of information.

When metadata is consistent, different instances clearly describe the same set of information using the same constructs in the metadata hierarchy. For example, Figure 17-1 illustrates two perspectives. Perspective 1, perhaps that

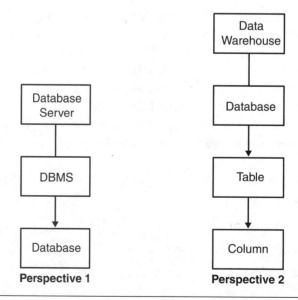

Figure 17-1 **One view of physical database metadata**

of IT operations, tracks installed DBMSs on each database server and affiliates them with database names. Perspective 2 tracks the database and its associated tables and columns by data warehouse. There are no obvious contradictions in the two metamodels, just different perspectives. To validate consistency, database names (instances) would be required for comparison—the name of the database should be the same in both models.

Consider the metadata in Figure 17-2. How do we know if the metadata in these two models is consistent? Is *Client* in Perspective 1 the same as *Customer* in Perspective 2? Where is *Product* represented in Perspective 2? Unfortunately, the only way to tell is by a detailed evaluation of the attributes associated with each, as well as a comparison of their deployed roles in relation to their surrounding data and processes.

This lack of consistency is the most common fault in well-intentioned metadata-driven organizations. Many organizations spend time and money planning, designing, and implementing a metadata solution. They also reevaluate development and data management practices to make sure that metadata creation becomes a required part of daily information processes. But does anyone ensure that standard metadata *values* are used when appropriate? Does anyone even declare a set of standard metadata values? In most cases, metadata creators are left to their own perspectives and inputs. The metadata is created on a project level, and the people on that project team are responsible for its interpretation. Why go through the effort involved in expanding standalone metadata to a full metadata solution when the metadata itself doesn't quite serve its purpose?

Because metamodels link at the meta-meta level (all of the constructs in Figures 17-1 and 17-2 are entities and relationships), this issue may not seem

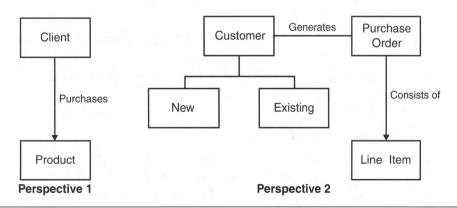

Figure 17-2 **Another view of physical database metadata**

significant at first. However, it is important to remember why a metadata solution is built—to make *good* metadata more accessible. Would you want to access inconsistent metadata more easily?

Modularity

Is the metadata represented in one long text string, or can it be broken down easily into components? Remember, if all of your metadata fits into "Project Description," it will not be easy to find the data elements associated with the project.

Represented Perspectives

We all have our own perspectives. When it comes to metadata, this fact could lead to disaster. All perspectives should be contained, yet related to a common equivalent. If one organization describes its external contacts as *Clients*, and another calls them *Patients*, the metadata that needs to be tracked, irrespective of terminology, is most likely based on the fact that both *Patients* and *Clients* are external contacts. Depending on how (or whether) you wish to combine these perspectives, you may need to rename both of them generically, to *Contact*, for example.

Ease of Identification

Beyond the metadata itself is the need for a consistent means of categorizing and identifying it. The greatest metadata in the world it isn't very helpful if no one knows about it. Worse yet, if everyone knows the metadata exists but can't seem to locate it, the metadata solution has not accomplished its goal. For these reasons, it is essential to determine how your metadata beneficiaries need to locate the metadata they seek. Most identification schemes take advantage of one or more of the following methods:

- *Straight text searches* look for the occurrence of a particular string of characters.
- *Searches by category* look for items that have been associated with one or more of a set of standard categories.
- *Searches by name* look for a known set of metadata (or data in some cases) based on how it is identified
- *Searches by metadata instance* look for a set of metadata (or data) with known characteristics, then the value of a describing characteristic (e.g., metadata instance) is used to equate that characteristic to that which is desired (Author = 'Smith, John' Creation Date = 09031995).

To use any of these identification strategies, the values used to identify the targets must be available and consistent. Many organizations neglect to establish a boundary within which these identifiers can fall. With newer Web-based technologies such as XML, it is easier to enforce and associate a set of standard "tags" or "categories" with the targets of searches. But what will these standard values be? Who will establish them? How will they become associated with the existing metadata and data?

Development Approach

Just as important as the evaluation of the metadata is the evaluation of its creation. Probably the most significant readiness factor is the *way* in which your metadata is created. If accurate metadata is not created at the same time as its described instance, the likelihood of the metadata becoming out-of-sync or obsolete is extensive. The development approach, or approaches, depending on your organization, should be evaluated not only in terms of metadata creation and maintenance, but also in terms of where they occur on the information creation time line.

As you evaluate how and when the desired metadata is created, it is important to determine the roles of standard values, standard identifiers, standard categories, and standard characteristics. Then consider the flow of this metadata throughout the lifeline of what is being described. Do the two (metadata and data) stay in sync? When the described data changes, does the metadata change along with it? Where does the synchronization fall apart? Does the development approach need reengineering? How much of the development approach falls within the domain of each Metadata Beneficiary? How many development approaches exist across Metadata Beneficiary categories? Does one approach override another?

In the truly synchronized scenario, metadata stays on par with its described target. If one set of metadata describes physical data instances, such as Data Definition Language (DDL), then it *must* change when the physical data instances do (see Figure 17-3). If this cannot be guaranteed, then neither can the metadata's accuracy.

Commitment

Everyone wants accurate and accessible metadata, but does everyone want to work for it? In order for metadata to remain accurate and stable, the current processes in most organizations require change. (We discuss the organiza-

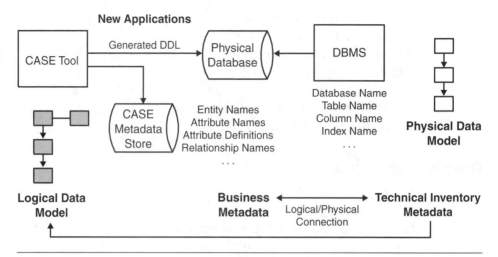

Figure 17-3   Metadata and the development approach

tional support requirements in Chapter 19.) But organizations often commit to efforts such as metadata solutions without understanding that commitment requires more than project funding. To determine readiness, consider the fact that a successful metadata solution will affect many aspects of your data and application development approaches (more specifics later in this chapter), as well as their roles in the overall business organization. A standalone metadata solution, with no ties to the metadata sources or beneficiaries, will remain just that, standalone. Standalone solutions become obsolete in a very short time.

Scoping the Metadata Solution

Deciding what to do, when to do it, and how to do it are secondary, of course, to deciding why you want to do it. Having confirmed the main objective, another common source of failure is the inability to "draw a line around" what to accomplish first. It is seems easier to plan to do everything without regard to how each component will be phased in. And it is even worse to make a plan that involves internal advertising of the plan to do everything, all at once of course—getting everyone's expectations right where you want them to be. If you don't deliver everything all at once, however, not only are everyone's expectations ruined, but so, too, is your reputation. Get the résumé updated!

There are many ways to scope a metadata solution, each relating to the ability to select a subset of the solution, phasing additional subsets into the plan over time. In general, scoping a metadata solution can be done by:

- Function
- Metadata coverage
- Architectural accessibility

Function

It is always important to remember why the metadata solution is being developed in the first place. Even more important is the ability to relate this objective to specific metadata solution functions. If there is no direct correlation, the objective is most likely too high level. A realistic initial objective will translate easily into metadata solution functions, as shown in Table 17-1.

Table 17-1 shows the detail that is necessary to finalize the objectives of a planned metadata solution. In fact, it should be clear that an objective such as "support of our data warehouse" really tells us absolutely nothing about what the metadata solution will do. As objectives are considered, their practicality should be tested by determining how the metadata solution would fulfill that objective. Looking at metadata solution functions from the perspective of the planned objective also solidifies the scope of the first rollout. Specify the type of support that the metadata solution will provide, and consider the types of metadata that will be necessary to accomplish the objective.

As the functions are detailed, the metadata solution architecture is being designed to some degree. Determining at this high level how the metadata will be exchanged, accessed, or shared among all the architectural components is at least getting initial attention. As we scope the initial metadata solution's functionality, we are defining those functions (see Table 17-1) that will be part of the initial scope. In many situations, one or more of these functions has to be postponed, due to potential architectural restrictions, or in some cases, due to the lack of immediately available metadata. Remember, one of the key readiness factors relates to the availability of accurate metadata, or minimally, the ability to create and actively maintain the needed metadata.

Continuing the functional scoping of the metadata solution requires attention to the metadata solution's role in the application development environment. Notice that some of the metadata solution functions (the first three in Table 17-1) require the metadata solution to play an active role in the data

Table 17-1 Relating Metadata Solution Functions to the Objectives of the Overall Metadata Solution

Metadata Solution Objective	Metadata Solution Functions
Support of data warehouse development	Focal point for access of metadata surrounding all source applications and their associated data
	Focal point for creation, maintenance, and access of all metadata surrounding target data warehouse design
	Tracking of ETL process results
	Provision of business metadata surrounding warehoused data and its aggregations, as reported to users
	Tracking of data warehouse access, by business user category
	Assignment of user categories and associated security profiles

warehouse development process. There are two types of "active roles" in the development environment: active in development and active in production.

Active in development implies that one aspect of the development process cannot happen without the metadata solution's presence. In other words, the metadata that is created or generated by the particular development process is guaranteed to be accurate and maintained within the confines of the metadata solution.

Active in production implies that the metadata solution is required to be up, running, and connected in order for the data warehouse (in this case) to be accessed.

Again, the metadata solution architecture and the planned metadata solution functions together form the mold for accomplishing the planned metadata solution objective.

Metadata Coverage

The scoping of the planned metadata solution is also affected by the availability of accurate metadata to support the desired metadata solution functions. After considering the metadata solution objective and how the metadata solution will fulfill it (the planned functionality), it is crucial to determine *what* metadata will be required, usually on a function-by-function basis. The initial scope requires initial metadata. Metadata requirements analysis should have identified, by beneficiary category, the required metadata. As a means of confirming the initial scope, we can tie this metadata to specific metadata solution objectives and functions, as shown in Table 17-2.

Evaluating the availability of accurate metadata, as listed in Table 17-2 by function, could narrow the scope of your planned metadata solution.

Table 17-2 Adding Required Metadata to the Objective/Function Matrix

Metadata Solution Objective	Metadata Solution Functions	Required Metadata
Support of data warehouse development	Focal point for access of metadata surrounding all source applications and their associated data	Source Application Name, Source Program Name, Source Data Element Name, Source Data Element Format, Source Data Element Definition, Aggregation and Summarization Specifications
	Focal point for creation, maintenance, and access of all metadata surrounding target data warehouse design	Target Data Model Name, Target Entity Name, Target Attribute Name, Target Relationship Name
	Tracking of ETL process results	ETL Process Name, ETL Load Statistics
	Provision of business metadata surrounding warehoused data and its aggregations, as reported to users	Data Warehouse Name, Data Warehouse Fact Name, Data Warehouse Dimension Name, Data Warehouse Element Name, Data Warehouse Element Definition, Source Data Element Name, Source Data Element Definition, Source Application Name, Source Program Name, ETL Process Name
	Tracking of data warehouse access, by business user category	Data Warehouse User Name, Data Warehouse User Access Statistics
	Assignment of user categories and associated security profiles	Data Warehouse User Category, Data Warehouse User Name, Data Warehouse Category Membership, Data Warehouse Category Permissions

Architectural Accessibility

The last aspect of a metadata solution's scope involves the affected architectural components. To achieve the desired objective, the metadata solution needs to perform specific functions with specific metadata over a specific metadata solution architecture. The determination of how each component interacts with the required metadata is necessary. Often, the result of this analysis introduces a scoped introduction of the metadata solution components.

As Figure 17-4 illustrates, the ultimate scoping decisions typically arise from the requirements of architectural interface and integration. The capture of the Extract, Translation, and Load (ETL) process statistics of this particular

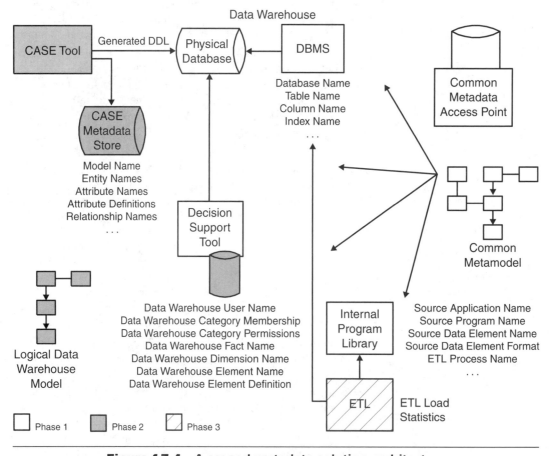

Figure 17-4 *A scoped metadata solution architecture*

data warehouse was put off until the third phase. Initial priorities and technical requirements kept most of the physical metadata available during the first phase, with the logical data model and associated business metadata being added shortly thereafter. During all phases, the common metadata access point was the interface to the metadata beneficiary community. As additional tools were added, each tool became an interface, or "front end," unto itself.

The implementation specifics depend on deployed tools and their interaction (or lack thereof) with the development processes that are actually in effect. In Figure 17-4, the direct, active connection between the CASE tool housing the logical data models and the physical DBMS catalog did not exist at the start of this data modeling effort. After a modified application development process that ensured the data model's relevance in terms of its physical implementation, the CASE component was added to the metadata solution architecture.

The Solution's Impact on the Internal Environments

Perhaps the most overlooked non-metadata factor is the world that surrounds the proposed metadata solution. This world contains people, processes, responsibilities, and methodologies. Many organizations plan, design, and deliver full metadata solutions and expect them to work magically in the confused metadata environment. Just because a metadata solution is intended to change the processes in that environment does not mean that the change will instantly occur. In fact, the impact of the solution on the environment has to be planned along with the metadata solution. To do so, the internal environments must be organized based on their desired positions in the metadata lifecycle.

Metadata typically begins when that which is being described is created. If that is not the case, it is created much later based on the fact that the item of concern has no clear relevant description. Unfortunately, metadata solutions are not always part of this sporadic recreation of metadata. It is essential that based on the rollout of a focused metadata solution, a process be put in place to ensure that metadata is created when that which it is describing is also created. Internal environments that are affected include:

- *Application development*—the planning, design, implementation, and maintenance of systems, in general, regardless of platform or function
- *Data definition*—the creation of information, with or without an associated set of processes or applications

- *Data access and reuse*—the identification of created information for the purposes of reporting or processing

Application Development

Perhaps the internal environment most affected by metadata solution implementation is application development. Because a substantial portion of metadata originates during this process, both directly and indirectly, the process as well as the involved tools must be reevaluated from the point of view of the metadata solution. Remember, from earlier in this chapter, that an organization's development approach can hinder readiness to embark on implementation of a metadata solution. At the same time, the rollout of this process, otherwise known as *application development,* has to reflect a modified metadata-based approach in order to guarantee the continued impact of the completed metadata solution.

As applications are developed, software engineering–like processes are involved. These process characteristics have changed substantially with the advent of client/server and Web-based application targets, and are even less defined now that integrated development environments have been with us for quite some time. During the application development process, each organization probably deploys a mixture of standards ranging from fully standardized processes and associated toolsets to sporadic, reactive build-as-needed application development. The impact of a metadata solution on internal environment has to be planned, not uncovered.

A symbiotic relationship between the metadata solution and the application development environment requires answers to these questions:

- How are application practices going to be affected once the metadata solution is implemented?
- Will application development practices need to change?
- What role will the metadata solution play in application development?

Each of these questions must be answered initially from the perspective of the metadata solution and its accessible contents. The metadata solution's objective must be considered in terms of how it will be fulfilled during application development. For example, if the metadata solution's primary objective is to provide business metadata for an upcoming *data warehouse,* then application development will require the collection and/or location of this metadata. If existing practices do not require this metadata and leave the whole metadata

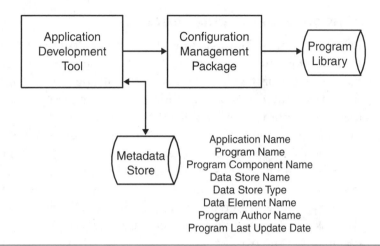

Figure 17-5 **A metadata-focused application
development environment**

creation/population processes to individual applications, the likelihood of the metadata solution being as functional as planned is downgraded substantially. If, on the other hand, the tools involved in the application development process are evaluated as potential metadata suppliers, a set of required metadata could be practically developed based on what is and is not available.[1] Processes must be in place to guarantee this on an active basis; in other words, the metadata solution has to automatically become aware of new and updated metadata as new applications are developed and updated. In addition, this metadata must be accessible as needed throughout the application development process. It should be easier for developers to get to *this* metadata than it would be to create redundant instances or variations of seemingly equivalent metadata.

In Figure 17-5, an active connection exists between a deployed application development tool and a program library. More important, a set of standard metadata is created and collected during application development based almost entirely on capabilities of this application development tool. Implied but not illustrated are restrictions on moving an application into production, thus getting it ready for export into the program library, unless the metadata requirements are met.

---

1. The impact of metadata solutions on the technical environment, specifically the metadata solution architecture, is covered in the next chapter.

Data Definition, Access, and Reuse

In conjunction with application development, data is defined. If an organization is looking to implement business-level metadata, the application development process probably had no required business metadata as part of its past practices. Physical data definition is easily handled through a standardized metadata capture during application development, but in order to extend the metadata into the business area, the standardized metadata capture has to begin in the requirements definition process. Aside from deciding whether currently deployed tools are capable of handling business-level metadata, it is essential that existing practices be changed to require the capture of metadata that is typically covered during requirements gathering. More important, metadata instances should be standardized so that they can be selected, instead of created over and over again.

The process of defining data cannot be left as the responsibility of an isolated suborganization. If data becomes defined again in order to standardize its naming and interpretation, then the metadata that supports this objective must be accessible via an organized metadata solution . . . and the metadata solution must be part of the data definition process. Finally, the resulting metadata must be accessible during application development. Although we discuss the architectural specifics of this integrated arrangement in Chapter 18, it is important to realize for now the implications of a metadata-based philosophy on data definition from the application development point of view and the business requirement and business analysis points of view. It is not practical in many organizations to centralize data definition, but it is very practical in most organizations to encourage the *reuse* of data definitions. Here, a metadata solution affects the way things are done.

Figure 17-6 shows that the identification of data requirements is followed immediately by a location process, as opposed to a definition process. This change of "philosophy" encourages an organization to look at what it has before defining more data and associated metadata. The immediate result is a trimming of the metadata web. The long-term result is encouraged metadata reuse, based of course on its completeness and accuracy.

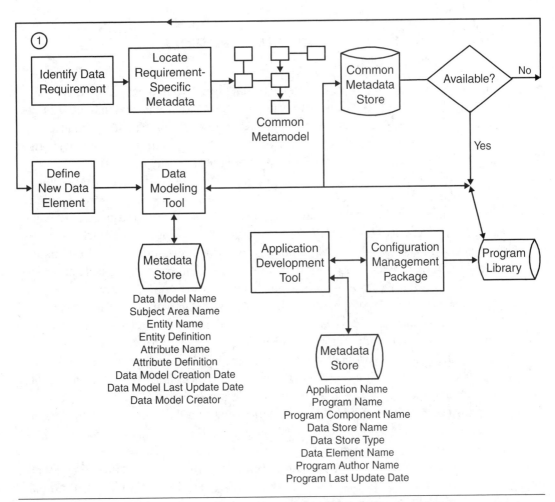

Figure 17-6 Impact of a metadata solution on data definition, access, and reuse

CASE STUDY: Non-Metadata Factors at a Chemical Company

Ciba Specialty Chemicals is an international chemical manufacturer headquartered in Switzerland. To some extent it can be considered a relatively new organization, since it separated from a merger of its original organization (Ciba-Geigy) and a major pharmaceutical company in 1996. This separation left five divisions, subsequently consolidated to three, across organizations in 70 countries.

In conjunction with a subsequent reorganization into 14 geographic regions, much attention was placed on efforts to standardize financial processing throughout Ciba Specialty Chemicals. Each region was set up with a centralized financial processing center, which included installation of a popular financial software package. In order for financial data from the processing centers to be consolidated, such data items as Account, Responsibility Center, Country, and Currency were defined with common value domains across the centers. However, within each installation, each region and each division were allowed to define other data (customers, products, etc.) to meet their own needs, and to a lesser extent, their own metadata (although most installations relied totally on the metadata that was part of the vendor's software package). Over time, not only were the common value domains becoming disparate, but also, it was becoming more and more difficult to analyze data across regions and across package installations.

An internal data management group started a Common Data Initiative, using in-house resources and the existing limited software (see Figure 17-7). Their objective was the establishment of a new metadata repository tool to enable the sharing of common data definitions and value domains. This metadata was intended to be downloaded to each region so that each financial package would continue to be able to consolidate the financial data at the divisional, regional, and headquarters levels.

Based on the reliance on manual processes in the Common Data Maintenance Process, the Information Management organization recommended the acquisition of a repository tool. This tool would be installed as a means of stopping the conversion of common data to disparate data by providing an accurate and easily accessible business resource for both common data and its associated metadata. In fact, metadata and data were to be available from the same location.

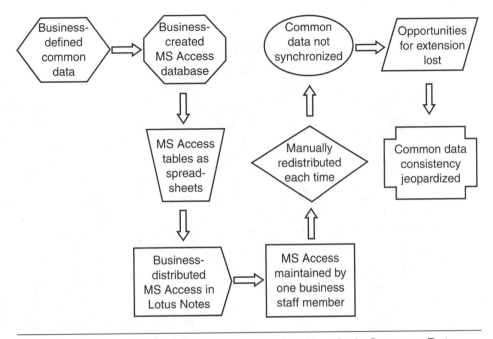

Figure 17-7 **The original Ciba Specialty Chemicals Common Data Maintenance Process**

With the assistance of a major repository vendor, a "proof of concept" metadata repository resulted. The proof-of-concept was not well received, however. Common data owners throughout the business became concerned about losing control of their "common" data to members of the Information Management organization responsible for initiating this effort. In addition, representatives from headquarters information management believed the repository was too expensive. So, without business support to justify the cost, the project was shelved.

Two years later there was no change in the financial processing architecture. Problems maintaining common data across the enterprise had not abated. The advent of e-commerce along with its need to offer Web-based business-to-business customer support was the push that strengthened the Common Data

Initiative. In addition, a business initiative to reduce supply chain costs by standardizing Common Item and Common Customer data *along with the associated metadata* were now envisioned as essential for supply chain management and e-commerce integration.

A metadata repository was once again considered. Although the business delayed development of business-driven Item and Customer data commonality, Information Management proceeded to undertake a metadata repository pilot. The pilot was designed not only to manage common data, as in the previous effort, but also to support the rationalization of various data coding schemes (metadata) in use across the regions and divisions, based on definitions of common data as well as associated business rules. Headquarters Information Management specified that the repository be implemented without purchasing software, using two inside data management professionals, and without involvement of the business staff.

A metamodel was created using the Object Role Modeling (ORM) technique available in diagramming software. The ORM was transformed into an Entity-Relationship Diagram (ERD) by the software and, subsequently, drove the creation of the metadata repository database. Currently this repository is being loaded with old and new metadata being gathered across the enterprise. The metamodel and resulting repository database provide for the linkage to the physical data to enable the automatic population of applications with the correct metadata.

Next steps involve the testing of this process with a wide range of business applications. (See Figure 17-8.) Use of the repository database to establish common value domains (metadata) for high-profile data items such as Item and Customer is also being tested.

Despite the slow progress to date and restricted resources, Ciba Specialty Chemicals envisions an increased metadata solution scope. Its existing metadata repository would be the likely choice to expand data management focus beyond common data to include common data usage (e.g., cases). In addition, the plan calls for the metadata instances to become retrievable via the company's intranet.

Note: This case study was submitted by Rachel Brownstein, Data Management Consultant, Ciba Specialty Chemicals. Used with permission from Ciba Specialty Chemicals, Tarrytown, New York.

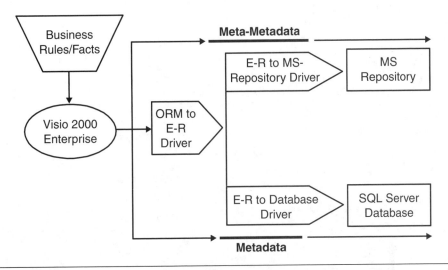

Figure 17-8 Ciba Specialty Chemicals' active metadata-based common data definition

Non-metadata factors are as important as the metadata that is derived from technical analysis. Do not begin a metadata solution unless you consider how it will fit in once it is completed, and always remember the power of phased implementation.

Chapter 18

The Non-Metadata Factors
Group II: The Technical Environment

Everybody gets so much information all day long that they lose their common sense.
—Gertrude Stein

Implementation of a metadata solution consists of two major components: the *metadata*, organized into major categories as we have done so meticulously, and the *solution*, the technical architecture that surrounds it. Clearly, this architecture includes many tools, each supplying metadata to the solution or using metadata within the solution. Without organized interaction and relationships among tools, this multitool world can become a hodgepodge of metadata stores, one contradicting the other, with no way to separate the best from the worst, the real from the imaginary.

This chapter focuses on the technical interfaces to organized metadata. Through analysis of each tool's role from a metadata perspective, the full metadata solution architecture can become well defined and ready for implementation.

Revisiting the Multitool Architecture

So far we have looked at each tool in the multitool architecture from a metadata point of view. We were concerned about which metadata elements would be created and accessed by each tool, and whether that tool was the only beneficiary of a particular set of metadata. A full metadata solution considers each

---

Note: Stein quote ("Reflection on the Atomic Bomb," in *Readings in World Politics,* ed. R. A. Goldwin, New York: Oxford University Press, 1959) from *The New York Public Library Book of Twentieth-Century American Quotations.* Copyright © 1992 by The Stonesong Press, Inc., and The New York Public Library. Used with permission.

component tool as more than a metadata beneficiary, however. In addition to "what" metadata is of interest to each tool, it is also important to determine:

- *Why* each tool needs the metadata of interest
- *When* each tool needs the metadata of interest
- *Where* the metadata of interest will reside (although much of this should have been determined by now)[1]
- *How* each tool will get to the metadata of interest

Each of these unknowns must be clarified in planning the full metadata solution architecture, and as a means of finalizing the architectural requirements. This chapter's analysis leads to the types of metadata exchange, tool interfaces, and metadata display mechanisms required. Preliminary architectures addressed the solution's components. It is now time to finalize how they will interact. Likewise, it is necessary to confirm what each architectural component will supply to which set of metadata beneficiaries.

In Figure 18-1, we revisit a metadata solution architecture. In this illustration, a metadata gateway, often called a portal, provides access to the components of the metadata solution's architecture, based on a metamodel that illustrates the location of metadata instances. Now we need to add the necessary detail. Figure 18-2 shows the ultimate objective.

As illustrated, we eventually need to know what metadata (e.g., instances) will be passed back and forth to which users, for what reasons, when, and in what way.

The Role of Each Tool

In order to define how each tool will interact with the designed metadata solution, it is necessary to consider each tool's function within that framework. One of the main secrets to success in the metadata solution space is *the ability to think like a tool*. This is why.

Once you identify which tools are going to be included in the initial scope, it is necessary to confirm the role that each will play from the perspective of a metadata solution. Specifically, not only will each tool *need* certain parts of the overall metadata picture, but it will also do something with that metadata, thus adding to the functionality of the metadata solution. For example, consider the

---

1. Part II discusses the categorization and storage decisions associated with metadata requirements.

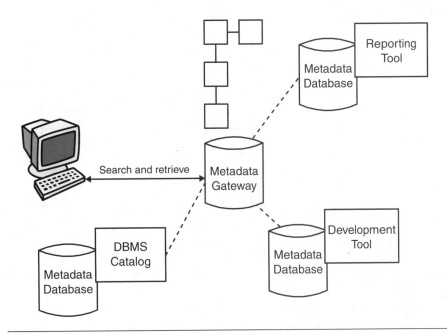

Figure 18-1   **Revisiting the multitool architecture**

metadata solution architecture in Figure 18-2. What is the role of the Reporting Tool? First, it is the only place in this architecture that supplies metadata based on the instance of data in a report. Second, it keeps track of the values of these metadata instances in case new data is added to the database that is being reported upon. Third, it ensures the validity of new metadata instances, as new reports are created. What about the not-so-obvious functions of the Reporting Tool? Will the tool be the place for establishing users' reporting capabilities? Where will security be controlled? Will there be a conflict between reporting security and database security? Who will audit transformations that may be created over time?

To distribute equitably the various functions of the metadata solution, it is essential that they be listed and assigned to the candidate "performers" of these functions, typically tools in the metadata solution architecture. Where more than one tool is capable of performing the same function, the metadata solution may need to be revised to account for the inevitable conflicts. Typically, other aspects of the metadata solution distinguish one tool's potential execution of similar functions from the other.

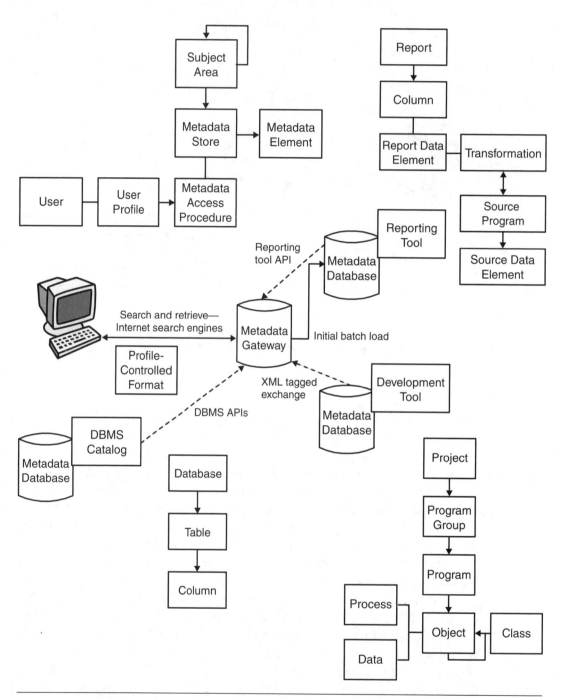

Figure 18-2 **The finalized metadata solution architecture**

For example, if we list some of the functions that can be performed by each component of the metadata solution architecture in Figure 18-2, we could come up with Table 18-1.

Notice that none of the functions listed in Table 18-1 are directly related to metadata, but to that which is being described by the metadata in the full architecture. Several of these functions can be performed by more than one component; without a clear delineation of the variations that exist across the separate component executions, metadata redundancy is bound to enter the picture over time.

When we look at retrieval of existing application designs, for example, it is clear that the designs will reside in the application development tool. But will it be necessary to use the tool itself to see the designs, or will it be possible to retrieve the designs through the to-be-developed metadata gateway? This issue needs to be resolved now, during *this* phase. A subset of the application design information should be retrievable to those not using the tool itself, with the full details retrievable only by using the tool directly. The situation, of course, could vary with user types and objectives.

Another redundant function, the definition of user security, could occur in all depicted components of this metadata solution. To prevent one tool from overriding the results created in another tool, the security function must be refined to represent the lowest level that makes a difference in component responsibility.

As the functions are listed in Table 18-2, they must correlate not only with the tool responsible for their execution, but also to the overall metadata solu-

Table 18-1 Selecting Components to Perform the Functions of a Metadata Solution

Metadata Solution Function	Candidate Component
Definition of new application designs	Development tool
Retrieval of existing application designs	Development tool, metadata gateway
Definition of new databases	Development tool, DBMS catalog, reporting tool
Creation of reports	Reporting tool
Definition of user security	DBMS catalog, development tool, reporting tool, metadata gateway
Application development	Development tool
Application versioning	Development tool

Table 18-2 Handling Redundant Functions in a Metadata Solution

Metadata Solution Function	Candidate Component
Definition of user database security	DBMS catalog
Definition of metadata security	Metadata gateway
Definition of application development security	Development tool
Definition of class library security	Development tool
Definition of reporting security	Reporting tool

tion objectives. This is a necessary task because it usually helps to refine the planned scope. In addition, in some architectures, it is necessary to list metadata solution architectures by user category as a means of determining "who" will be allowed to do "what." This is a precursor to security definition. Finally, the full intersection occurs when we relate each metadata solution component to a set of tasks and to a subset of the metadata being addressed in the metadata solution's architecture. Let's explore each of these tasks.

Determining Tool and Metadata Connections

Once the role of each tool is determined, it is essential to equate these roles to the metadata that will be associated with their fulfillment. In general, each tool's role, broken down into specific functions as shown in the previous section, will have its own metadata accessibility requirements and permissions. Once these qualities of each function/metadata connection are determined, attention is then spent on determining where the metadata should reside as a means of solidifying the full metadata solution architecture.

Metadata CRUD

For those of you not familiar with it, the acronym CRUD has been with us since the advent of organized database design as a key to determining the type of data access required by interfacing processes. Simply put, C stands for any process that *creates* data (or in our case, metadata), R for *read* access, U for *update* access, and D for *delete* access. Processes that are CRUD processes perform all types of database maintenance.

Most of us think of CRUD as specific to data, and we usually consider it a component of database access security. Some users may have read-only access (R) to a database, while others may be permitted to both read and create (CR). We have been discussing the connections between metadata and data creation

Table 18-3   A CRUD Matrix

Metadata Category	DBMS	Logical Data Modelers	Data Administrators	Database Administrators	Metadata Solution Administrators
Physical Database Definition	CRUD	R	R	CRUD	R
Logical Data Model	N/A	CRUD	RU	R	R
Subject Area Search Category	N/A	R	RU	R	CRUD

throughout this section. Focusing on the CRUD aspect of the metadata/data connection will bring in metadata beneficiaries as another variable in this maze, hence the discussion surrounding *how* each beneficiary (user categories as well as tools) will get to the metadata of interest. A CRUD matrix depicts metadata access by interfacing tools, databases, applications, and implemented software packages.

Metadata Accessibility Distribution

A CRUD matrix indicates, for each beneficiary, what is being accessed and how, as Table 18-3 shows. In general, the resulting matrix lists metadata categories along the left column and beneficiary categories as headings to the various remaining columns. Categories are listed at the smallest level that makes a difference. Note that this matrix is concerned only with the common metadata.[2] Because metadata is best kept where it is used the most, individual metadata stores that are fed and maintained only by their immediate beneficiaries (e.g., specific metadata) do not require analysis of metadata accessibility distribution, unless they are receiving metadata from other components of the metadata solution architecture. The analysis is a necessity for groups of metadata that might have access conflicts across beneficiary categories.

It is important, as noted earlier, that both the metadata and beneficiary categories be depicted at the smallest level that makes a difference. For example,

---

2. Common metadata is defined in Chapter 9.

if aspects of logical data models are off limits to one group but not to another, then this logical data model subset would need to be depicted. A completed metadata accessibility distribution would include all categories of metadata being accessed (the what), their respective types of access (a perspective on the why), and each beneficiary category (the who).

All of the matrices discussed thus far must be considered a combined set of technical requirements. This full set gives the details of the initial metadata solution's accessibility and functionality requirements. When these matrices are combined with both metadata presentation requirements (discussed later in this chapter) and beneficiary-specific security, a fully rounded set of requirements is available to confirm both the common metadata's type of metadata store and its type of interface to each metadata solution component.

Connecting to the Metadata

What good is high-quality metadata if we can't get to it when we want to? Even worse, what good is being able to get to this metadata when we want to but not being able to use it in the format and place that we need it? The metadata connection separates a good metadata solution from one that is so good that we don't realize it is there.

As we look at the objective of the technical architecture in Figure 18-2, it is important to note the various ways to connect to the metadata. It is also important to note the various types of metadata stores in the architecture. *All metadata stores must connect to either the place that contains the common metadata or a universally accessible metadata gateway*—sooner or later!

Consider the significance of this statement. Historically, most metadata stores were part of a standalone metadata solution. In fact, even today, many metadata solutions strive to become *the* metadata solution. By redundantly loading all of today's disparate metadata into an organized metadata store, some benefit does result. But the disparate metadata continues to multiply, and in many cases the organized central metadata store finds itself constantly trying to keep up. Acknowledging this fact requires the planning and design discussed in this book—and the result is an integrated metadata solution, often with a common metadata store. This "common metadata store" is not the metadata store that is common to all the metadata suppliers, but rather *the place where common metadata is stored.*[3] The difference may appear to be one of semantics, but it is in fact one of implementation architecture.

---

3. Common metadata is discussed in Chapter 9.

A common metadata store is the *bridge* to all metadata organized and recognized in the metadata solution. It differs from a metadata gateway in that it actually contains metadata *as well as* the addressing data that can get a metadata beneficiary to unique and specific metadata occurrences. Metadata gateways, on the other hand, contain *only* addressing data and associated criteria for metadata access, typically metadata categories, or subject areas. But because there are no hard and fast rules as to whether the addressing information can coexist with common metadata, the terms *categories* and *subject areas* are often used interchangeably. Regardless of definition, this "universally accessible" set of addressing information, with or without common metadata, must be part of every metadata solution.

Whether the common metadata store is physical or logical, it must represent the gateway to the various metadata stores in the architecture. Therefore, the common metadata store will be updated constantly to reflect related metadata stores, and could conceivably be accessed directly by some metadata stores.

The means to connect to metadata depends on the following factors:

- Who we are (e.g., tools, people, applications, userids, middleware)
- Where the metadata is (e.g., in a tool, in an external metadata repository)
- What we intend to do with the metadata (e.g., access it specifically or use it as a bridge to its described information)

All these factors do nothing but restrict our options. In the ideal world, which we are slowly moving toward (see Chapter 16), it won't be necessary to make these distinctions. As technology progresses, however, it is still important to determine metadata interface capabilities based on the realities of today's metadata.

Internal Tool Repositories

Most development tools have their own metadata. What varies from tool to tool is where this metadata is stored in the tool's framework. In multicomponent tools, it is fairly standard to have a central metadata store that components can share. Central metadata stores are common, however, only when the tool's various components are optional. That is, one does not have to buy the full set in order to use the product. Based on the possibilities in terms of which pieces need to coexist, the tool's repository may or may not come with one standalone component (see Figure 18-3). In that case, a separate database is available with each component. Not until the full toolset is acquired does the centralized metadata repository become part of the tool architecture.

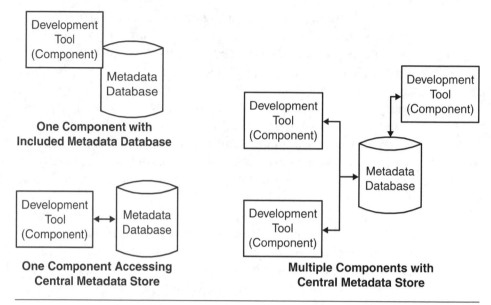

Figure 18-3 Internal tool repository options

In most situations the type of internal tool repository is directly responsible for the ease of access to metadata. Standalone tools and/or components may be packaged with the same central metadata store that is offered with the full component set. Even when they are, the included database is typically tool-centric, and not intended for access by other tools, particularly those developed by other vendors. Tool-specific utilities have been the only way to get information in and out of these products, and most of the information exchange has focused on the data that resides in the tool, rather than on the metadata. Remember that *data* is a relative term; what is data to a tool may be metadata to us. If that is the case, then the data/metadata factor is not an issue. But if we are interested in extracting or accessing what is metadata to the tool, this very well could be an issue.

For example, assume that the standalone development tool is a decision support tool, installed based on its capabilities in the database reporting area. The tool allows nontechnical users to analyze data and see results in bar and pie charts with the ability to modify the format and types of data in each report. It is clear that the tool tracks everything on either a report or a data basis. Metadata in this type of tool is of two types, the type that the user sees and the type that the user does not see but is crucial to both the tool's operation and its existence in a metadata solution framework. User-available metadata is typically input by the user (although some tools allow the importing of such metadata) and explains the values of the data that appears on the report (e.g., calculations, definitions, etc.) along with some limited information about the reports themselves (e.g., report name, creator, date of creation). It is often called business metadata. Tool-specific metadata is *not* accessible in many cases. Examples include the underlying database design, the tables and columns in which data and metadata are stored, userids, tool version, and other characteristics related to tool processes. It is often called technical metadata. If the hidden metadata is needed by beneficiaries above and beyond the reporting tool itself, metadata interface capabilities (or the lack thereof) may narrow the scope of the proposed metadata solution. The ability to access the user-defined metadata is typically limited to vendor-defined reporting and file export.

Tools that consist of identified modular components and have central metadata stores are usually geared toward the sharing and access of both types of metadata, including the metadata (technical) that the tool needs to perform its role. In fact, because a modular architecture requires each component to access a central database, database-specific load, export/import, and application programming interfaces (APIs) are almost always available. Finally, because the database now becomes a multiuser metadata store, usually an administrative role must be performed that requires the establishment of userids and associated security profiles. Depending on how generic this separate metadata store is in terms of its ability to receive metadata from other vendors' tools, it may have many of the features discussed in the next section.

Separate Generic Repositories

As discussed in Chapter 14, the true metadata repository is a separate architectural tool and intended for integration with all products, irrespective of developing vendor. As you may recall, repository administrators can implement meta-metadata–specific[4] functionality including user profiles and capabilities. In addition, because the generic repository's claim to fame is its ability to centralize shared metadata, various options exist for passing and receiving metadata to and from this type of metadata store:

Repository Utilities   These utilities export, load, download, and so on. That is, they perform the functions that come with the repository software.

---

4. Meta-meta land is discussed in Part III.

Repository Command Languages   Originating with the initial mainframe repository tools, repository command languages are tool-specific and used to interface with the repository itself. Commands cover everything from repository setup to repository load to repository access to the execution of repository utilities. Command languages are required for repository products that have proprietary metadata stores. Products that sit on top of commercial DBMS products rely on the language of the DBMS for metadata-based access.

Application Program Interfaces   Repository tools come with a set of APIs that cover the access of repository products from external software. APIs are called by interfacing programs along with a supplied set of values, typically called parameters, which are used to set specific options, if any. The functional completeness of an API set is variable from product to product and must be evaluated during this technical stage of architecture solidification.

Remote Procedure Calls   Similar to APIs in purpose, RPCs are fully packaged and do not have to be called from a controlling program. They can be invoked from the operating system and are used when they are part of a major set of procedures, which may include those of other involved tools and/or applications.

Batch Export/Import   Depending on the tool, some variability may exist in terms of deciding what is exported from the repository, or where to place what is being received via import. In most cases, the process creates a file of a predetermined format; most repository tools strive to adhere to one particular ANSI standard.[5] Issues often arise when there is no ability to determine the contents (as opposed to the format) of an import or export file. For example, if the repository export process allows the exporting only of the entire repository's contents, the target recipient would either have to read this file and selectively extract what is new or necessary, or automatically replace all resident contents that can be tied to this repository supplier. The import process does not typically address the issues that arise when a tool's constructs simply do not exist in the source repository (or vice versa). Because of these issues, many batch interfaces have been codeveloped by some vendors.

Repository/Tool Interfaces   As noted earlier, because of the inherent restrictions and complications that surround the creation and reading of export

---

5. Standards are discussed in Chapter 16.

files, many repository tools come with prebuilt interfaces to specific metadata-craving or metadata-supplying development tools. Ideally, these interfaces are built and kept up-to-date based on a permanent codevelopment relationship with the tool vendor. Consumers do not want to pay for playing catch-up with new releases when they have already paid extra for these interfaces.

A concern with tool interfaces, however, is the fact that tool interfaces do not necessarily export (or import) everything that is stored in a tool. Most interfaces will allow selective exportation (e.g., one project only) but not selective importation. Also, it is quite common that entire portions of a development tool are not covered by the interface (e.g., data models, no process models). Whether an interface can handle updates or simple replacements is also variable. It is essential, therefore, that the affected metamodel components be evaluated before a repository/tool interface is relied on for metadata exchange.

Scanners   Here we do not mean those pieces of hardware we use with our desktop computers. Repository scanners have been popular as a means of getting metadata from an organization's physical IT environment loaded into a generic repository. Often considered reverse engineering software, these software options were very popular during the Y2K repair period because they could load all data elements used in an organization's programs right into the repository for date-based impact analysis. They can be set up as batch jobs to be run apart from the repository. Depending on the product, options may be customizable to determine what to scan, from where, and when. Typically, scanners run against program libraries, DBMS catalogs, and some popular application packages. Finally, there is typically no ability to customize where the scanned results should be populated in the repository metamodels.

Manual Input   As antiquated as this metadata interface may seem, it is still available and is discussed again in the next section on metadata presentation. Most manual metadata interfaces involve the user-initiated input of metadata according to a predefined template or screen. When this method is used to exchange metadata among metadata solution components, it usually involves the manual execution of a predefined process that contains a repository template for input.

The options for sending and receiving metadata are moving toward standard interfaces and external exchange and will slowly be replaced as these interfaces mature.

Metadata Exchange

The process of getting to anything that is somewhere else has kept most consultants in business. Either there was no good way to do it and we had to reorganize and copy it to another place, or it was such a complicated task that we had to design a brand-new process to not only retrieve the little pieces that were of importance but also to ensure their relevance and accuracy. The world of metadata has been no different, hence the need to carefully plan and architect full metadata solutions.

As a means of simplifying this potentially excruciating effort, most strategies are now moving toward metadata exchange instead of metadata sharing or metadata access. The popularity of the Web and its associated markup languages has moved many of us toward the objective of simply passing metadata and its associated data back and forth, as opposed to directly accessing either of them. In fact, many standard XML interfaces are being developed for just that purpose, focusing specifically on the categorization of the data that needs to be passed back and forth in major industry areas (e.g., chemical, manufacturing, retail, etc.) using standard XML tags for uniform identification. In these scenarios, a standard metamodel would be composed for not only specific industry areas, but also for the types of data that can be passed back and forth within them. HTML tags, when combined, would equate to full metamodel instances, and would be scattered throughout the data being passed to the requestor. In XML terminology, these tags would be represented as DTDs (Document Type Definitions). Following this philosophy, many organizations are building and testing XML interfaces to and from their major data stores and applications. Likewise, software vendors of all sorts are developing these interfaces as a means of making their products easy to integrate with full-enterprise, Web-enabled solutions.

DTDs are just one part of the use of XML as a metadata exchange mechanism. Passing labeled things back and forth should be treated more like the objective than the process. In other words, most existing data is not XML tagged, and we certainly do not have uniform metadata standards that can be used as tag values when the need to exchange arises. Finally, for people who may not be sending and receiving via the Web, the immense technology catch-up that is necessary may take a while. Despite all these potential setbacks, XML and the whole area of metadata exchange should not be considered unless the sending area, or the place from which the metadata will be translated and eventually exchanged, is consistent and stable. The following basic prerequisite characteristics of the technical environment should be in place before XML or any other exchange mechanism is considered:

- Agreement as to the formats that will be followed for exchange
- Standardized conversion mechanisms to convert the existing metadata sources to the agreed-on exchange format
- Agreed-on scope or boundary for metadata exchange. If the exchanges will be sent to external (e.g., outside the company enterprise) as well as internal recipients, national and international standard formats may not be mature enough to support your own requirements.
- Last, but certainly not least, a stable set of internal information with an associated creation and maintenance process that supports the insertion of exchange-specific metadata tags

Consider the simple scenario illustrated in Figure 18-4. In this example, a development tool's metadata is being exchanged with a data warehouse reporting tool, in order to provide the warehoused data to requesting end users. As discussed earlier in the book, a multitool metadata solution requires the modeling of common metadata into a common metamodel. This model is illustrated, with simple entities, numbered instead of named, for simplicity. Each entity represents the type of metadata instances that are to be passed among components of the metadata solution. The metadata exchange process will require the insertion of these entity names as DTDs above the relevant metadata instances. The process of doing so should be generic and reusable so that all metadata exchanges involving this development tool will use the process repeatedly. Once the metadata is parsed, and the DTDs are inserted, the reformatted extract is passed to a common interpreter. Again, this interpreter should be reusable across all components of the metadata solution. The interpreted result can be passed directly to the reporting front end, or in many cases to a Web browser for immediate display. This scenario is a perfect example of foresight and the elimination of metadata redundancy. By passing development metadata to the reporting tool, the same metadata is not reinput and recreated.

Metadata exchange is probably the simplest mechanism for getting things back and forth. However, without the proper infrastructure and standardization (see Chapter 20) to support the exchange process, it is not likely to be anything more than a restricted means of talking between isolated components.

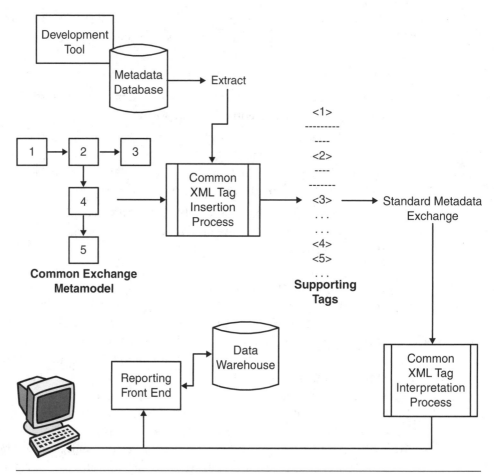

Figure 18-4 **Illustrated metadata exchange**

Presenting the Metadata

Metadata is organized and the technical architecture is planned. We have determined how each metadata solution component will communicate with not only the common metadata but also with other components of the metadata solution as applicable. Those of us who are *not* tools (and I do believe we all fit into this category) are still wondering what impact all of this has on the end user of the metadata solution. The need to plan metadata's presentation should not be overlooked.

Many of us forget that we control the way we look at things. In most scenarios, we accept a vendor's predesigned displays, reports, and front ends. In a fair amount of these accepted results, we do not see what we want, even though we know it is stored or accessible from within the metadata solution. In far more situations, we see too much metadata, lots of it irrelevant to our lives, and we have to decipher strings and strings of results before we get to what we are actually after. We often don't realize that these situations are not static—we can and should change them.

Metadata Display Methods

Once metadata is accessed or retrieved by the metadata interface, there are various ways in which it can be presented, depending on the role of the metadata solution interface. For the most part, these variations are reflected in two ways:

1. *Metadata groupings*—a named set of metadata usually associated with a particular metadata beneficiary (and remember, beneficiaries can be tools or people!)
2. *Physical presentation*—the format and characteristics of the presented metadata, focusing on position, color, size, and other physical presentation qualities

Typically, metadata presentation groups are named as *templates*, and stored within one or more components of the metadata solution, depending, of course, on the full architecture and where overall control prevails in that architecture. These templates are typically associated, at the meta-meta level[6] (i.e., in the meta-metamodel), with a particular component of the meta-metamodel, and used whenever required. Because a metadata solution is the combination of several beneficiary-specific metamodels, it is common for templates to be associated with metamodels, as illustrated in Figure 18-5.

Consider the fact that templates are usually associated with user profiles within tools. That is, administrators and typical business users see different sets of metadata. The metamodel components are associated with named metamodels as well as named templates. Figure 18-6 shows the use of templates from a deployment perspective. The importance of this type of configuration rests with the fact that each beneficiary category sees different sets of metadata. More important, these sets or templates are named and possibly assignable to other beneficiary categories as needed.

In terms of physical appearance, templates can also have associated display qualities, within the constraints of the implementation software. Typically,

---

6. The meta-meta perspective is discussed in Chapter 13.

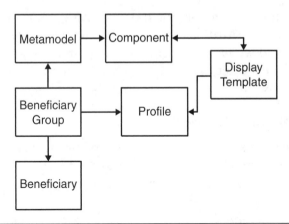

Figure 18-5   **Display templates from a meta-meta perspective**

colors, fonts, display position, and links to other templates are programmable and customizable.

Different Strokes for Different Folks

Vendor display of metadata has always had a universal flavor. Very few vendor-supplied metadata solutions have represented distinct beneficiary interests. Instead, a large set of metadata is presented to all beneficiaries in one standard display format. The technical consumers of these products rarely take the time to customize this setup by modifying display templates. As a result, much of the supplied metadata is ignored by a substantial percentage of the product's end users.

Regardless of whether an off-the-shelf or customized metadata solution is being considered,[7] it is essential that the implementation reflect customized needs, typically by beneficiary category. Database administrators should not be forced to view metadata specific to decision support reports and business users are typically not interested in primary and foreign key assignments. When end users see what they are looking for, they come back for more. When they see lots of things that are irrelevant along with a subset of what they are looking for, they go elsewhere, or worse yet, create their own metadata solutions.

---

7. Chapter 20 discusses the variables that go into selecting the right solution.

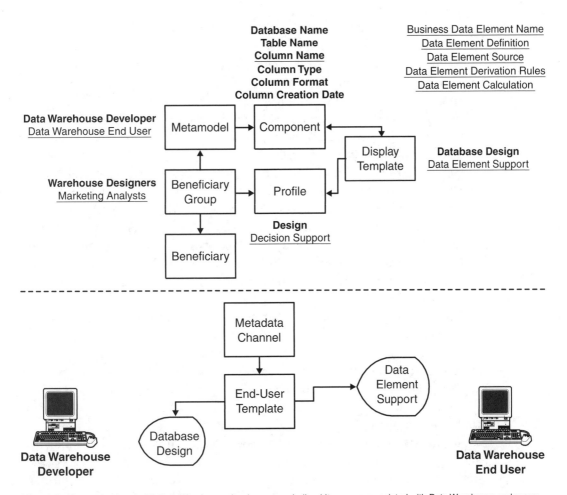

Items in **bold** are associated with Data Warehouse developers; underlined Items are associated with Data Warehouse end users; **bold underlined** items are associated with both beneficiary categories.

Figure 18-6 **Display templates from a deployed perspective**

Metadata Security

We've covered many technical specifics in this chapter. First we solidified the tools and metadata solution components and determined what metadata they all need. Next, we determined how each component tool should obtain this metadata. We also talked about the ways in which the retrieved or received metadata can be presented. How do we determine whether all this work will be abused? Should we restrict the access of metadata? How can a metadata solution prevent metadata overrides and conflicts?

Security is just as important with metadata as it is with the information that the metadata supports. As with all functions that might affect metadata being covered by a metadata solution, the potential impact of metadata security is defined at the meta-meta level. Often known as *policies*, security is implemented as a set of capabilities and/or privileges that are associated with defined *metadata solution profiles.*

Similar to the rights and privileges of professional and private lives, a metadata has rights and privileges, and the metadata solution profile defines them in the context of the metadata world. To support the ratification of these rights, policies are the pieces of software that enforce them. As with beneficiary-specific templates discussed in the previous section, beneficiary-specific policies are controlled at the meta-meta level. It is essential to note, however, that policies can also correspond to metadata components, irrespective of which beneficiary is likely to be affected.

For example, template-driven security can certainly prevent business users (a beneficiary category) from seeing developer-specific metadata (e.g., program names, program authors, etc.) if so desired. However, it is only at the policy level that business users can be prevented from populating metadata of any sort into a centralized metadata store. Such a policy would keep metadata controlled, and would be based on an association with a metadata solution *procedure* (e.g., populate).

Figure 18-7 illustrates one way policies can be implemented in a metadata solution. In this illustration (and implementations can vary) policies are associated with metamodel components. This type of scenario offers the ultimate flexibility in that a particular *portion of a metamodel* (e.g., a file, table, userid, etc.) can have a set of processes associated with instances of the particular metamodel construct, some or all of which can be protected by security policies. The ability to set up this component-based security depends on the pre-existence of this type of meta-metamodel design.

Which type of security is best for a metadata solution? Typically, a combination of any of these security levels will be required:

- The *metadata solution* level, which controls who has access (and perhaps what types of access) to the metadata solution as a whole
- The *metamodel* level, which controls who has access to a specific group of metadata (e.g., logical data models)

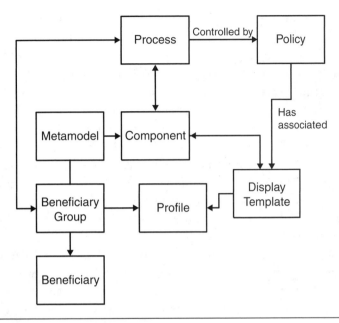

Figure 18-7 Security policies from a meta-meta perspective

- The *metamodel component* level, which controls who has access to one component of a metamodel (e.g., data elements)
- The *metadata* level, which controls who has access (and what type) to an attribute of a metamodel component (e.g., date created)
- The *metadata solution process* level, which controls who can do what (e.g., loads), typically to what groups of metadata

To determine which type of security plays best, virtually all the previously defined requirements will need to be revisited:

- The CRUD matrices to determine access at the metamodel component level
- Metadata solution function/candidate tool evaluation to show which functions will be performed by which metadata solution component
- The metadata solution architecture to depict how all metadata solution components will interact
- Metadata display templates to depict what each beneficiary category will see and access

By implementing a set of policies that tie directly to specific metadata solution processes, which in turn are associated with a set of specific metadata constructs (often grouped into distinct metamodels), the ultimate flexibility will result. Baseline security will be developed and will remain available for continuous redeployment as the metadata solution expands.

Consider the following simple example. A data warehouse is created with a supporting metadata solution. The solution is illustrated in Figure 18-8.

Note that in this particular example, not only the type of metadata but also the type of access and the source of the metadata are determined by user category. The meta-metamodel, as discussed, stores the specifics of profile/display/access process relationships as well as how they connect to specific aspects of the common metamodel. In other words, the models connect as illustrated in Figure 18-9.

For the sake of simplicity, consider the fact that each metamodel (*Logical Data Model* and *Application Configuration*) is represented as an instance of the *Metamodel* entity in the meta-metamodel. The metadata that is of concern to each user profile is scattered throughout each metamodel as attributes of specific entities.

Our meta-metamodel has also been simplified in that it does not depict the connections between *metamodel* and *tool*. This relationship is typically required in portal-like metadata front ends, which need to know where to find the metadata of interest. Our solution, however, implies that relationship's existence in the common metamodel.

Sharing the Metadata

Security is usually viewed as restrictive, and our overall metadata solution objective, as we have discussed, is to keep the metadata where it is used and *share* the metadata that is common. Unfortunately, the definition of *share* is not standardized. For many people, sharing means duplicating. For others, sharing means letting others take a peek—on paper. For most people, sharing means coming to agreement on names and definitions, but letting each do his or her own thing when it comes to storage and retrieval. To carry out our metadata solutions security means sharing via a well-defined sharing *process*.

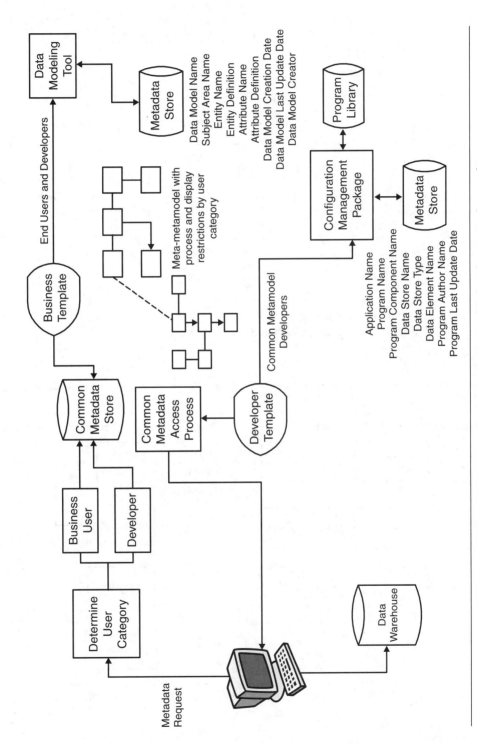

Figure 18-8   A simple metadata solution with implemented security

1. Meta-Metamodel

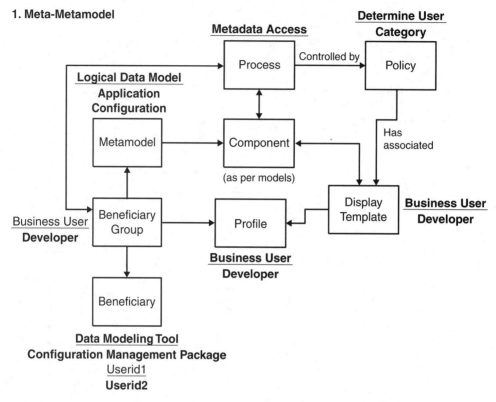

Items in **bold** are associated with Data Warehouse Developers; <u>underlined items</u> are associated with business users; **<u>bold underlined</u>** items are associated with both beneficiary categories.

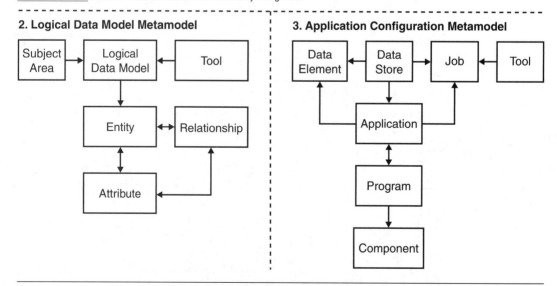

2. Logical Data Model Metamodel

3. Application Configuration Metamodel

Figure 18-9   *The metamodels behind our simple metadata solution*

A well-designed metadata solution is one that makes available the metadata that people want. Being available means that the following conditions are standard and stable:

1. Everyone (within the scope of the supported metadata beneficiaries) knows where to go to find out what metadata is available. (What metadata do I have?)

2. Everyone can easily ascertain the intent and meaning of the available metadata. (What does it mean?)

3. Everyone can easily locate the desired metadata. (Where is it?)

4. Everyone can easily ascertain how the metadata originated, as a means of determining its relevance to his or her requests. (How did it get there?)

5. Everyone can retrieve the metadata. (How do I get it?)

It is presumptuous of an organization to consider metadata sharing an objective or characteristic of the metadata solution unless the prerequisites, reiterated via our 5 Questions, are in place.[8] The first phase of a metadata solution project should strive to support these prerequisites within a predefined scope.

When the initial scope's 5 Questions are answered, metadata sharing will become a natural benefit. No longer will new metadata be created when what is required and desired is already available and accessible. But initial access to this metadata may indeed be for the purposes of replication. Replication is not necessarily a bad thing, as long as it is controlled. We never want an uncontrollable set of redundant metadata, each potentially becoming a source for other metadata solutions. We discuss the ways to ensure metadata's livelihood in Part VI.

Preventing More Metadata Webs

If the full architectural definition and planning process is completed, fewer and fewer metadata webs will result. Instead, beneficiaries will be impressed with the capabilities of initial and expanded metadata solutions in your organization and will be likely to approach those responsible for implementing these solutions with additional metadata requirements. At this time the prevention of additional metadata webs should be the ultimate objective. Consider the fact that metadata copies do not necessarily imply metadata webs. In

---

8. The 5 Questions is a trademark of and the questions and method are copyrighted by Database Design Solutions, Inc., Bernardsville, New Jersey.

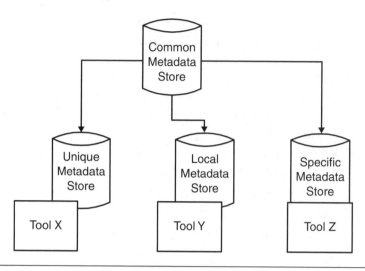

Figure 18-10 **A distributed metadata solution architecture**

Figure 18-10, a distributed metadata solution architecture illustrates one means by which this control can be implemented.

As illustrated, the heart of minimizing the extent of metadata webs rests first with the completeness and accessibility of common metadata.[9] If the common metadata rests in its own accessible metadata store, it must be available for extract to the specific, unique, and other redundant (common) metadata stores that may exist locally. Depending on the deployed tools, common metadata may in fact represent only the connection points within the local metadata stores. That is, the values represent gateways or links to the specific or unique metadata that resides in multiple locations. The integrity of a full metadata solution relies on the consistency of these links, and it is essential that their values remain in sync with local implementations. The ability to ensure this integrity rests entirely with the security capabilities of each local metadata store. If it is not possible to prevent the local creation of new common metadata instances without a reciprocal updating of the common metadata store, the integrity of the solution cannot be guaranteed. Likewise, if it is not possible to prevent these local updates entirely, minimal reliance on a common metadata store by downstream metadata recipients should be encour-

---

9. Common, unique, and specific metadata are discussed in Part II.

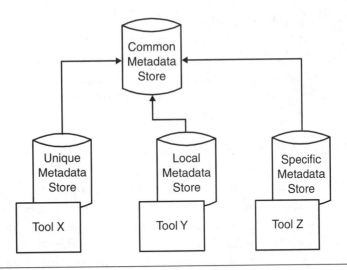

Figure 18-11   Guaranteeing the integrity of common metadata
in a distributed metadata solution architecture

aged. Without doing so, each local or distributed metadata store is likely to eventually become its own node on an uncontrolled web.

Another option for metadata integrity is the reverse of Figure 18-10, where the common metadata itself depends on its local instances. See Figure 18-11 for the specifics.

Although this option is more likely to guarantee integrity, it too depends on the capabilities of the tools and their related metadata stores. If a batch process is to be used (export/import or metadata exchange), customized processing will be required to selectively retrieve and update only the common metadata. In other words, full extract files will not be necessary. Only the linkage fields, otherwise known as the common metadata occurrences, will be required, because they are used as gateways to their related specific, unique, and local metadata.

Ultimately, neither of the preceding implementations should be necessary, however. If you use tool-supplied APIs and/or common metadata formats and associated access processes, the common metadata *will be* the actual occurrences in the tools. In other words, a common metamodel will point the metadata request to the appropriate occurrence of common metadata—the integration will be at the metamodel level, as illustrated in Figure 18-8.[10]

---

10. More discussion on how to determine the extent and type of metadata store(s) appears in Chapter 20.

Reusing the Metadata

When a metadata solution is stable, there are no webs and no controversial copies. All metadata integrity is planned and orderly. The next objective is the guaranteed reuse of the metadata via advertisement.

Advertising Your Metadata

As the saying goes, you could have the best product or service in the world, but if no one knows about it, who cares? Nothing could be more relevant in the world of metadata solutions. Because people have been so used to fending for themselves in order to decipher information and its characteristics, the instinct is to track metadata on an individual basis rather than to look and see if it already exists. This predisposition toward creating individualized metadata stores is the main force behind today's metadata webs.

Be sure to make your metadata solution at least as accessible as that which is being described. Even better, be sure that your metadata solution makes that which is being described even more accessible. And be sure this accessibility applies to all beneficiaries of both the information and its associated metadata.

Many organizations encourage the reuse of data. Others encourage the reuse of processes and application components. Still others embrace object-oriented paradigms with the objective of encouraging the reuse of the objects that will make up the newly constructed applications. Does anyone encourage the reuse of the metadata that goes along with all these components? In general, most take the metadata for granted, and accept its secondary tool-based support. Rarely does anyone consider how a reusable component needs to be identified and accessed in order for it to become reusable.

To ensure metadata's reusability, the potential consumers of this metadata must know of its existence and benefit from its values and relevance. If it is easier for a potential consumer to redefine his or her own metadata in support of an isolated data mart, then that will occur. If, on the other hand, the metadata that describes the data already exists and is tied closely to the data, potential consumers have no choice but to use the metadata along with the data. The overall architecture of a metadata solution should account for future consumers—and as with the library, new borrowers cannot take things out of the library without knowing of the metadata that goes along with them. Consider this objective from both a technical and a business perspective.

Incorporating External Beneficiaries and Suppliers

The technical metadata solution architecture must be flexible enough to consistently accommodate new players. These players can be metadata suppliers or recipients, or, in many cases, components that require a dual role. Properly designed metadata solutions provide for a set of common processes, all of which can be accessed by newcomers to the architecture.

If a comprehensive common metamodel with a direct connection to the meta-metamodel is provided, the future is just an "addition" away. Adding metadata suppliers would be the equivalent of adding a new instance if, in fact, the meta-metamodel connection determined the process that is required to get to the metadata (see Figure 18-12). These "processes" are typically associated with "tools," "metadata stores," or even "metamodels."

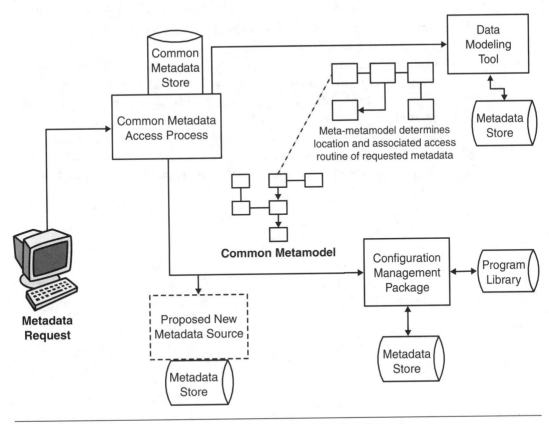

Figure 18-12 Flexibility for the future

New tools, new access routines, and new metadata stores, or metamodels, would be incorporated into a metadata solution by adding rows to the appropriate meta-meta tables. The creation of these routines is, of course, a requirement, depending on the underlying technology of the tool to be incorporated.

Likewise, additions would need to be made to the common metamodel, depending on what new metadata was being brought to the architecture by the new tool. Success in the incorporation of new metadata suppliers is directly related to how many components comprise the original metadata solution, from both design and implementation perspectives.

Adding metadata beneficiaries is sometimes as easy as adding userids and associating them with preexisting security profiles and display templates. Again, the foresight used when establishing user profiles and associated security determines whether this simplicity is feasible. At worst, metadata solutions with multiple components will require the definition of new profiles, new display templates, and perhaps new security enforcement processes . . . and the incorporation of these new functions is as easy as adding instances to preexisting meta-meta tables, as discussed.

Consider the fact that the technical architecture is the fuel required for the extended life of a metadata solution. The backbone that allows it to grow must be planned, well designed, and implemented with current requirements and future possibilities in mind. As we carefully consider the various details discussed in this chapter, it is important to realize that we are not yet finished. We still need to discuss the support aspect of our metadata solution, as well as the factors that go into determining how to pick the right overall architecture.

Chapter 19

The Non-Metadata Factors
Group III: Technical Support

The best planned and implemented metadata solutions will be very short lived unless the appropriate support is in place. With metadata solutions, technical support is a bit more complicated than a traditional Help Desk. Metadata solution support embraces the contents of the metadata solution, its usage, its troubleshooting, and its enhancement.

Administration

We mentioned earlier that metadata and its described information, called data for simplicity, should have the same lifecycles. As the data is created, so too should be the metadata. In general, various organizations seemed to have a hand in the administration of metadata (if it *was* anyone's responsibility).

Although often confused, the two types of administration associated with metadata solutions are quite different:

- *Metadata administration*, often combined with data administration, should focus on the standardization, quality, and uniform use of the metadata itself. Consider this group responsible for the "why" and the "what" of an organization's metadata.

Note: This chapter contains contributions from Patricia Cupoli, Database Design Solutions, Inc., Bernardsville, New Jersey.

■ *Metadata solution administration,* originally called repository administration, is responsible for the planning, design, implementation, and maintenance of the full metadata solution. Consider this group responsible for the "how," the "where," and the "when" of the metadata solution. This group handles technical support.

In this chapter we discuss the administrative responsibilities of each group and present staffing options.

Data and Metadata

The administration of data requires baseline metadata. As data is created, the creation of a standardized set of metadata must result. Although each organization's requirements are different, every organization should establish metadata standards. Typically, this responsibility begins in a data administration or data management organization, and eventually moves to a newly formed metadata administration organization. As a means of getting the newcomers started, the next two pages contain suggestions about the *minimum* metadata to be associated with a new or transformed piece of data or other type of information (again, traditional data has typically been the focus of most metadata efforts, but your scope can easily include nontraditional information such as graphics, sound recordings, and the tracking of physical items such as hardware and furniture).

Requiring this set of metadata encourages the use of the 5 Questions[1] (introduced in Chapter 2). Administering this process adds a new facet to your metadata solution, and puts the metadata solution's administration into a different light from the one that most people may have perceived it to be.

To point out that the metadata beneficiaries often include us, it is important to realize that the specifics of implementing the metadata administration function require a preexisting metadata solution, as well as the addition of a possibly unforeseen beneficiary category—the metadata administrator. Typically this beneficiary category has permissions that others do not. For example, metadata administrators may be the only people allowed to create corporate subject areas. They may receive proposed new subject areas from other groups and "make them official." Whatever the implementation process, they are the final stop before metadata is blessed and made accessible.

---

1. The 5 Questions is a trademark of and the questions and method are copyrighted by Database Design Solutions, Inc., Bernardsville, New Jersey.

Name—An obvious but often forgotten piece of metadata standardization. What are we going to call this thing? Two common mistakes continue to occur even in the naming space:

- *Official* or *corporate* names are sometimes created by a group of individuals (typically data management/administration professionals), some of whom may never have used the information being described. Most data management groups have updated their naming requirements to allow full names that make clear business sense.
- *Sporadic* or *limited perspective* names are sometimes created over and over again by isolated groups of business users, typically in conjunction with the creation of an isolated set of copied or reorganized data. As the data web propagates, so too does the metadata web, and anyone who attempts to navigate or relate it all cannot coordinate or connect the various names.

Viewing *name* as a standardized piece of metadata should require the following:

1. *Immediate involvement of a metadata solution.* The name should be related to major subjects initially defined by a data/metadata management organization.[2] The creation of new names, therefore, requires the existence of these subjects or categories and the ability to relate them to new name instances. There are many ways to ensure the legitimacy of these name categories, or subject areas, all of which are addressed in data management texts.
2. *Immediate accessibility of new names,* via the metadata solution. Name versioning is also required in many instances so that metadata solution beneficiaries are aware of the status of the described information.
3. *Immediate update of the common metadata model,* as appropriate. Creating new instances of metadata requires their population into the common metamodel to guarantee its accuracy.

Related subject or category—As noted, this value should be available only from the existing metadata solution.

Creation date—When was the data created.

Definition—There are many definition standards, all documented in data management texts. I like to keep definitions simple, and certainly one should avoid using the name of that which is being

---

2. Metadata management is discussed in Part VI.

defined in the definition's content. In other words, when defining "Customer Name," probably the poorest definition you could come up with would be "the name of the customer." A better choice would be the following definition:

Customer name   The term used to identify an occurrence of a party who buys products or services. Although not the only way to identify such an individual, it is the most used term throughout the organization. Standard values are reused based on their recurrence throughout the organization, and are available in the CUSTOMER_MASTER.

Although this definition may not meet everyone's needs, I hope you notice a distinct difference between the two.

Location—Where is the information going to reside? Organizational standards should exist for the identification of databases, applications, tools, and so on.

Source—Where applicable, information comes from somewhere. Again, as with location, standards should exist for depicting the values.

Accountability (responsible party)—In large organizations, this piece of metadata is often required. However, consider yourselves warned that people move around faster than the data changes! An organization's name is usually placed here so that business users will know where to go with questions. But if your metadata is good enough, there shouldn't be any questions!

Access process—How will one get to this information? Here is where the data and metadata administration functions intersect. You can describe information to death, but if the potential beneficiary wants to get to the information and has no idea how to go about it, your metadata is as good as, for example, a set of encyclopedias compared to a mouse click.

In the simple flow illustrated in Figure 19-1, two separate metadata areas are crucial to the normal operation of this metadata management process. First, there is a set of approved metadata support, which focuses primarily on the categories of metadata that can be associated with the information, as well as standard names, in this example. From time to time, there will be the need to expand this set of supporting metadata, but security will prevent anyone without authorization from updating this set of metadata. New information

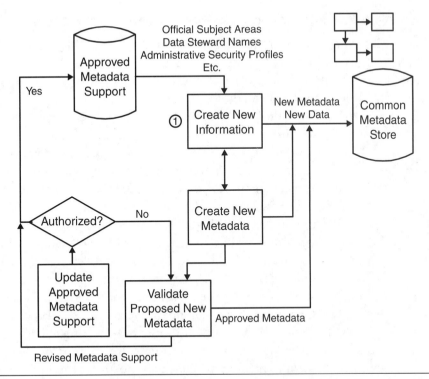

Figure 19-1 A sample metadata management flow

can be created by anyone in this scenario, and must include the associated standard metadata, typically derived via the population of a standard template. The new metadata instances are approved by the same process that validates the supporting metadata (i.e., Official Subject Areas, etc.), and approved data and metadata are then used to update the common metadata store as necessary. Success in a simple flow like this one depends on some of the previously discussed architectural components:

- Templates, which are used to require standard metadata along with new data creation
- Security enforcing processes which prevent existing metadata support databases and the common metadata store from being updated until, for example, the proper flags have been set as approved

All of this support for metadata administration is typically handled by an implementation-focused organization, as discussed next.

Metadata Solution and Repository Administration

Metadata solutions require administration whether they are custom developed or purchased as off-the-shelf metadata support tools. The setup and planning of full metadata solution architectures usually involve the people who will become the solution's administrators, at least initially. In fact, as mentioned, only those with administrative authority are able to develop and implement most of the required metadata solution component capabilities to begin with.

Many organizations have confused repository administration with data administration. Original data administrators, typically focused on the business side of data management and the logical data modeling of business relationships, often lacked the technical skills to implement a full-fledged metadata solution. For this reason, they typically accepted off-the-shelf packages, regardless of whether they fit into the organization's environment as active metadata providers. Metadata solution administrators are responsible for establishing and maintaining the metadata solution's backbone. This infrastructure includes the various metamodels, their connections to the meta-meta world, and the associated processes that ensure the relevance and stability of metadata for all beneficiaries.

Metadata solution administration grows in impact with the scope of a metadata solution. If the original scope is the support of a single data warehouse by providing meaningful business metadata, the initial responsibilities could very closely mirror that of metadata management rather than that of metadata solution administration. If, on the other hand, in order to support this metadata management a series of tools is involved, all of which form a portion of the metadata solution, the administration of the solution and its intertool symbiosis is certainly a part of the initial requirements.

Organizational Responsibilities

The metadata solution administration should be performed by a distinct organization (or suborganization), which may be tied to existing data management organizations. Individuals in this group are responsible for establishing a metadata solution architecture, developing appropriate metamodels, and rolling out the fully implemented solution. As the number and types of metadata beneficiaries increase, these responsibilities continue as phased additions to the existing architecture. Specific responsibilities of this organization include:

- Metadata requirements analysis, with follow-up metamodel development and integration

- Design and development of the full metadata solution architecture, including determination of each metadata solution component's role and relationship to the overall architecture

- Establishment of metadata solution security, specifically by defining metadata solution policies and associated processes, beneficiary and user profiles, and related metadata access/display templates

- Design and development of standard metadata solution access procedures including decisions as to technical platforms and formats for metadata exchange

- Evaluation of external industry metadata standards, in terms of both metadata exchange and metamodel compatibility

- Participation with development and data management staff in the definition of metadata-based information management policies focusing on a required role for the completed metadata solution

- Definition and maintenance of corporate, enterprise, or official support metadata in order to encourage standardization and reuse in the organization

- Continual enhancement and expansion of the metadata solution architecture in terms of functionality and increased component coverage

These responsibilities certainly do not mirror those of the traditional data administration organization. In fact, even when the purchase of a vendor solution is merited, these functions are still required. Leaving them to the vendor will ensure that you get the best the vendor product is capable of, not necessarily the best for your internal metadata objectives.

Staffing Requirements

A metadata solution administrator is involved in many aspects of the metadata solution—usually from analysis of the initial metadata requirements and evaluation of the solution to implementation and ongoing maintenance. Initially, this position requires many skills beyond those of data modeling. Skills pertinent to the following functions are required from time to time, for full metadata solution support:

- Data administration (The skill of logical data modeling, found in the data administration function, provides the basis to learn and perform metamodeling.)

- Database administration
- Systems programming
- Application programming
- Project management
- Creation and use of development tools (custom tools)
- Web development
- Network security administration

Once the metadata solution is properly implemented, the skill level required of the metadata solution staff depends on the ease of use of the metadata solution software itself. The metadata solution may offer software features that help with administrative duties. For example, easy-to-use interfaces can enable setup of user profiles, backup of metadata solution contents, lifecycle migration, and interproject data sharing.

At a minimum, two staff members are required for metadata solution administration. One administrator should have the metamodeling skills to establish and maintain the metamodel as new metadata requirements are discovered. The other administrator should have the technical skills to establish and maintain the metadata solution architecture and the tool interfaces.

The metadata solution administration organization needs to be established and maintained either as a distinct organization or as part of another organization. From a support point of view, this organization defines metadata standards and procedures for each of its identified metadata beneficiaries. These standards have to be enforced via the chosen metadata solution in an active fashion. After the metadata solution is implemented, this organization has to communicate, train, and advise the metadata solution users on how to use the metadata solution for their particular metadata needs.

Organization Charts

This section suggests options for organization charts. The options assume that metadata solution administration is a standalone organization, however, there are situations where project-specific metadata solution support is justified.

Metadata Solution Development Project and Production Support

In many project-oriented organizations, metadata solution implementation is treated as a project. A metadata solution development project, or team, with a project manager is charged with the setup of a metadata solution environment. As illustrated in Figure 19-2, this group is led by a *Metadata Solution Project Manager*, responsible for overseeing the entire effort. A *Metadata Solution Analyst* collects and consolidates requirements and designs the overall metadata solution. Template and interface design are this individual's major deliverables. This analyst also supports the design of any metadata solution utilities, particularly those needed by the metadata solution administration group. The *Metamodelers* (often one junior and one senior) translate the metadata requirements into metamodels for the metadata solution as well as for each metadata solution component. The *Programmers* implement the metadata solution architecture based on the developed metamodel and confirm the overall metadata solution architecture.

Once the metadata solution is in production, the metadata solution needs both production support and continued development support (enhancements and expanded scope). At this point, as Figure 19-2 illustrates, production support often moves to an *Operations* or *Production Support* organization. In Operations the metadata solution administration's objective is to provide support by performing such services as setting up user IDs, establishing security, monitoring performance, and conducting backups and vendor software upgrades. Some of the development team members would remain in their original groups to continue enhancing the metadata solution.

It is also quite common in project-oriented environments for a representative of the metadata solution administration group to assist projects by temporarily participating as a member of each project team. In these scenarios, the metadata solution gets the most exposure—individual project teams are shown via hands-on demonstration and observance exactly where the metadata solution fits in their daily work tasks. In Figure 19-2, the *Metadata Solution Support* role is illustrated on the *Project X* team.

Metadata Solution User Support

Another staffing option establishes a post-implementation support organization, as illustrated in Figure 19-3. This organization would be headed by a *Primary Metadata Solution Administrator.* The organization's responsibilities are to support the metadata solution users in production and to enhance the ongoing metadata solution implementation. The Primary Metadata Solution Administrator serves as the primary point of contact with the users and the Help Desk for IDs, functionality, and any problems. The *Metadata Solution Planner* is constantly evaluating the impact of enhancements and changes on the existing metamodel, and extending it as needed. The *Programmers* implement the

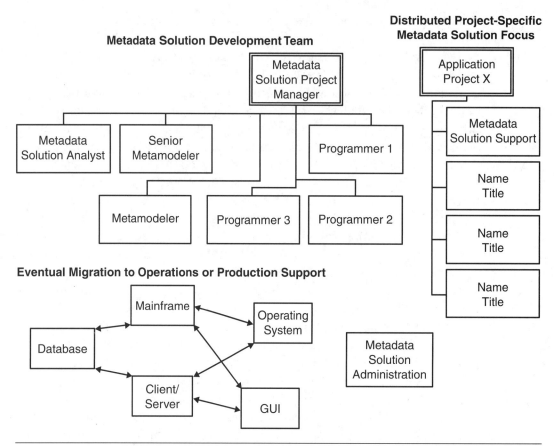

Figure 19-2 Metadata solution development team and production support

changes. This option is typically found in organizations where metadata solution administration is treated as a suborganization.

Metadata Solution Development Support and Administration

A large IT organization might have two different metadata solution groups, each with its own manager. One organization, as illustrated in Figure 19-4, is the Metadata Solution Development Support Group with a *Metadata Solution Project Manager*. This group initially designs and implements the metadata solution and all associated software. Existing and upcoming tools are integrated into the scoped environment.

The other organization, as illustrated in Figure 19-4, is Metadata Solution Administration, which handles production support with its own manager. This

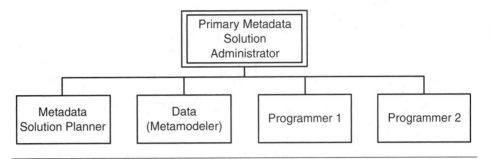

Figure 19-3 Metadata solution user support

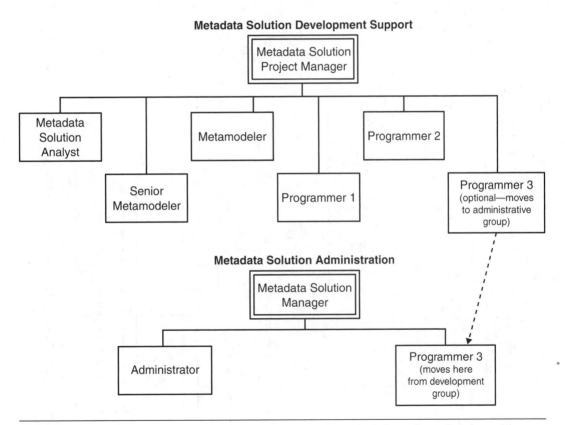

Figure 19-4 Metadata development support and administration with two groups

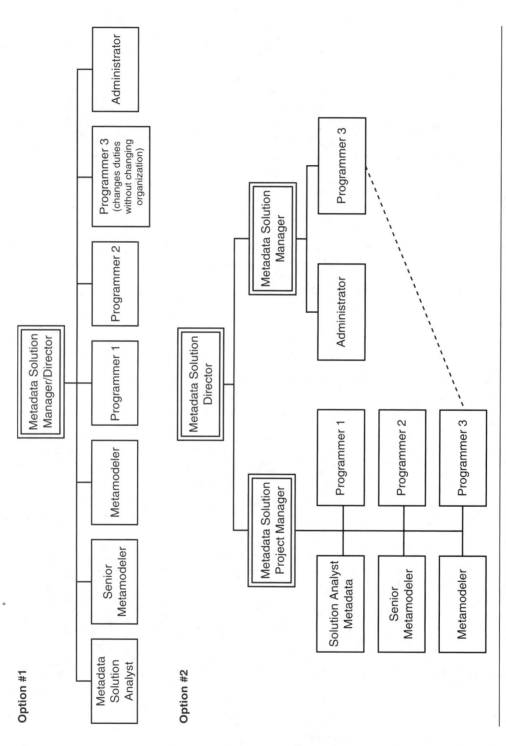

Figure 19-5 Metadata development support and administration with one group

group is established once the metadata solution moves into production. The *Programmer* that is depicted in Figure 19-4 as having moved from the development group to the production support group now handles technical queries and debugging of the metadata solution. He or she also provides input on potential enhancements. *The Metadata Solution Administrator* is responsible for establishing user IDs, establishing and changing security profiles, and monitoring the metadata solution.

As depicted in Figure 19-5, some organizations establish two groups under the same manager, or keep both development and production in the same group. This gives the staff members more opportunity to move back and forth between the two functional areas, providing more of a metadata solution-specific career path.

Staffing options depend greatly on the types of metadata beneficiaries being served by the implemented metadata solution. In areas where the beneficiaries are primarily the business user community, a Help Desk or Metadata Solution Support function is of primary concern. In situations where IT is the primary beneficiary, the metadata solution implementation is typically treated as another project in IT. In general, the more "corporate" or "enterprise focused" a metadata solution aims to be, the more individuals are required to develop and support the evolving metadata solution.

The structure of the metadata support function discussed in this chapter relies on a confirmed metadata solution architecture. The decision-making process involved in selecting the optimum architecture can be as challenging as the establishment of its supporting organization. The next chapter addresses this process.

Chapter 20

Determining the Right Solution

One man's "simple" is another
man's "huh?"
—David Stone

Enough of these requirements gathering sessions, enough design confirmation—how do we know what to do with the results? Should we buy something, build something, implement a mixture, or wait? What do we do when the world of metadata is all around us, and everyone still wants his or her own metadata solution? It's time to decide how to pick the "right" solution.

The "right" solution, as we have learned, has several components:

- Metadata
- A metamodel or series of metamodels
- A meta-metamodel or an integrated overview of the various metamodel perspectives
- Metadata stores (the places where physical metadata is kept)—unified, distributed, or standalone
- Software that controls, updates, and accesses the metadata

We have spent a great deal of time discussing each of these components as well as their architectural integration. The ramifications of looking at an isolated metadata solution should be clear at this point.

Despite familiarity with the details and complexity, many people prefer to start simply, perhaps with just one standalone metadata store, and then let that

Note: Stone quote (in *Omni Magazine,* May 1979) from *The New York Public Library Book of Twentieth-Century American Quotations.* Copyright © 1992 by The Stonesong Press, Inc., and The New York Public Library. Used with permission.

evolve into a more comprehensive solution in time. Maybe management's buy-in is not where it should be and starting small is the *only* way to start. This chapter explains how to get started. In fact, if you are beginning with a piece of the whole, the difference between success and failure rests with the ability to relate the piece to an *already defined* whole. Each of the components just listed ties directly to other components to form a well-architected metadata solution. For this reason, we have already covered requirements not only from the perspectives of the components but also from the perspective of the overall integrated metadata solution architecture. In this chapter we discuss physical implementation. The following chapters *illustrate* the various implementation options by depicting five distinct metadata solutions, each set up to solve the same problem.

No Metadata Stores, One Metadata Store, or Many?

Many people consider the physical location of the metadata to be of little importance in the architecture of a full metadata solution. Yes, most agree there is a need to analyze metadata requirements. Most also realize the need to organize these requirements into a set of metamodels. But the physical implementation? Isn't that just a question of physically implementing the organized metadata requirements? As with database design, the depth of implementation must also be considered. There are several options in today's metadata solution world, each of which has its purpose.

"Having just one" of anything is basically unheard of in corporate metadata environments. But even though there may be many metadata stores, their lack of interaction and relationship can make them each look like just one; even worse, it can make each look like a slice of the only metadata store because in order to get to what each beneficiary wants, more than one "slice" may be necessary. The differences between a distributed setup, a standalone setup, or an unconnected haphazard conglomerate rest with the metamodels, the meta-metamodel, and their relationships to the physical metadata store(s).

When an architecture is distributed (i.e., it represents a group of diverse components), it is easy to get from one piece to another, and in totality, the various pieces represent a unified whole. To be successful, implementation considerations must reflect both the single-instance and the unified perspectives.

There is a difference between distributing repositories and distributing metadata stores.[1] As discussed in Chapter 14, a metadata store is simply the

---

1. Repositories and their definition are discussed in Chapter 14.

physical database that contains the metadata, whereas a repository is a software package that *enhances* a metadata store in order to supply metadata-focused functionality.

Distributed Metadata Stores

A metadata store is a database designed to store the contents of a metamodel or set of metamodels. The existence of more than one metadata store implies several relationships among the metamodel(s) and each or all metadata store(s). The first and most common relationship is one to one. For the most part, in this scenario each metamodel represents a distinct physical metadata store. The metamodels, having been designed and integrated, are connected via common metadata, which is itself a separate metamodel. In general, each entity in a model translates to a table in a relational schema. However, there are other performance-, time-, and version-specific qualities (attributes) that can affect physical design and table relationships.

As Figure 20-1 illustrates, distributed metadata stores are not truly distributed unless you can easily get from one to the other. In the world of metadata solutions, this traversal is typically handled at the meta-meta level. As you can see in Figure 20-1(d), each metamodel, usually a separate metadata store, is related from an access point of view. In this simple example, each metamodel is logged, along with the metamodel components (objects) and types (entities, attributes, processes, etc.) in the meta-metamodel implementation. The associated metadata stores and the physical locations are related so that the main point of control or entry point of the metadata solution knows where to get specific types of metadata.

At the logical level, the various distinct metamodels are connected via a common object, which *must* reside in the common metamodel.[2] In Figure 20-1(b), *Subject Area* and *Relational System* are shaded differently to represent the connection points. Where object types are unique to one type of metamodel (relational system in the illustrated example), the shading represents a common relationship.

The example in Figure 20-1 shows the distribution of metadata stores based on the existence of separate and distinct metamodels. Their logical connection is via the common metamodel. The physical connection, as always, is via the meta-metamodel.

---

2. Metadata requirements analysis and the subsequent categorization of metadata are covered in Chapter 9.

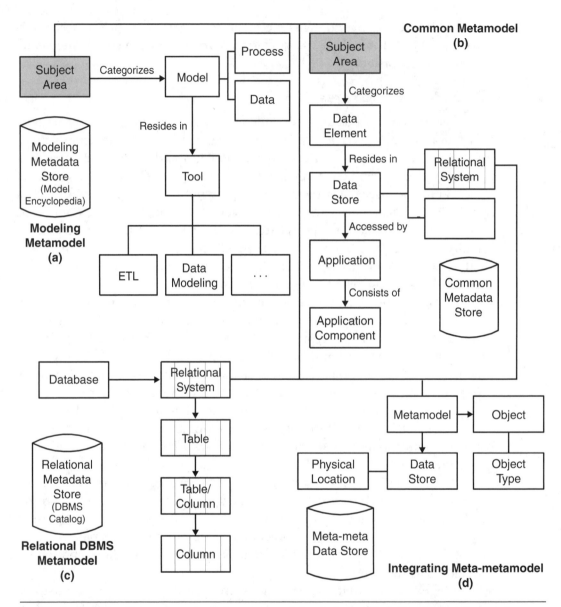

Figure 20-1 Meta-metamodel, metamodel, and physical database connections

This sample distributed metadata store is probably one of today's most complicated; however, it is also the most flexible. New metamodels and associated metadata stores can continue to be added, as long as the common metamodel contains a connection point. Likewise, as long as each new metamodel results in an instance of the meta-metamodel, the physical access requirements remain in the realm of overall metadata solution control.

There are simpler ways to establish distributed metadata stores. The most common scenario involves the use of the same metamodel at each physical location (similar to distributed databases). In this scenario, the various implementations may but need not contain the same metadata instances, and there is no need to create a separate common metamodel because each metadata store contains the same metamodel components. The meta-meta connection is still necessary, however, because it serves as the directory or point of control, as in the previous example.

Figure 20-2 shows perhaps the most common way to "start small" when building metadata solutions. Note, however, that if the initial metamodel does not contain a comprehensive enough set of constructs, it may be difficult to expand in the future. For example, what would happen to this distributed metadata store if the organization decided to track model-related or development tool–related metadata? In no uncertain terms, the existing metamodel would have to be expanded, and the connection points might not be as clean as one would hope. For this reason, most organizations that choose to implement the "standard metamodel" distributed approach must spend the time up front to plan and design a relatively robust metamodel. There are then various ways to populate each metadata store, despite the fact that they all are implementations of the same metamodel:

■ *Same constructs, different metadata instances*—Here all metamodel constructs are populated, but each metadata store represents either a different set of instances or a different perspective. For example, one metadata store could track all the metadata related to Human Resource applications and data elements while another one could track all metadata related to Finance applications and associated data. The key is the fact that the *same metamodel and the same physical database structure are used for every metadata store.*

■ *Different constructs, different metadata instances*—A twist on this type of distributed metadata store involves *not* populating the entire metamodel, and therefore, the entire physical database, at all locations. For example, the Human Resources Department may use packaged software only (in fact, they may use only one package), so that their metadata store may populate

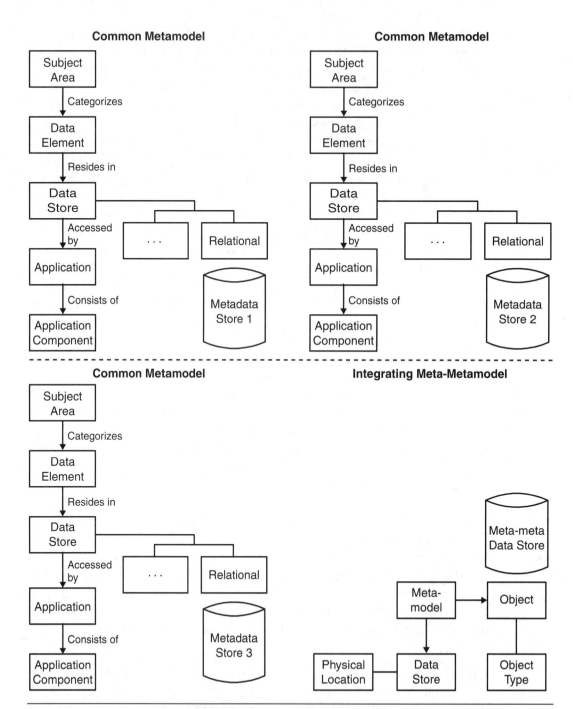

Figure 20-2   **Distributed metadata stores with a common metamodel**

only the top three constructs of the metamodel, as shown in Figure 20-3. Likewise, the Finance Department users may not be interested in Subject Area and ignore that construct in its separate metadata store. This type of scenario is very common, but could lead to the inability to cross or integrate separate physical metadata stores. In many "corporate" metadata efforts, a data administrator devises a "corporate" metamodel only to find out that it is not common and cannot be used throughout the corporation. Some user organizations may choose to ignore portions of the metamodel, as discussed. Even worse, they may actually populate those "unnecessary" metamodel components with something else . . . and only they will understand the value and meaning of the substitutions.

With an implementation equivalent to Figure 20-3, the meta-metamodel would also have to track *which objects were populated* at each metadata store location. The integrity and validity of this scenario, therefore, depends on some sort of overall control.

Distributed Repositories

Repositories are another possible implementation of metadata control. Distributing repositories is not as simple as distributing metadata stores because the repository software has inbred control functions that deal with instances of its own metamodels. In fact, distribution of repositories usually requires special considerations. Aside from the fact that the logical point of control must be able to keep track of distribution points and associated contents (as with any distributed database or metadata store scenario), the "extras" (e.g., interfaces, access routines, display templates discussed in Chapter 14) that come with repository products may not be built for distributed prime time.

It is important to realize that a repository is an application, and as such, three distinct areas surround the metadata instances:

- Application logic, or the interface between the software and the metadata store
- Presentation logic, or the display of all information that is presented to or received from the application
- Database logic, or all DBMS specific commands used to create, read, update, or delete database contents

Because the functionality illustrated in Figure 20-4 is already incorporated into relpository software as a whole, the boundaries between each category are not always as solid as we would like. In fact, some repository products have their own proprietary databases that combine the application and database functions

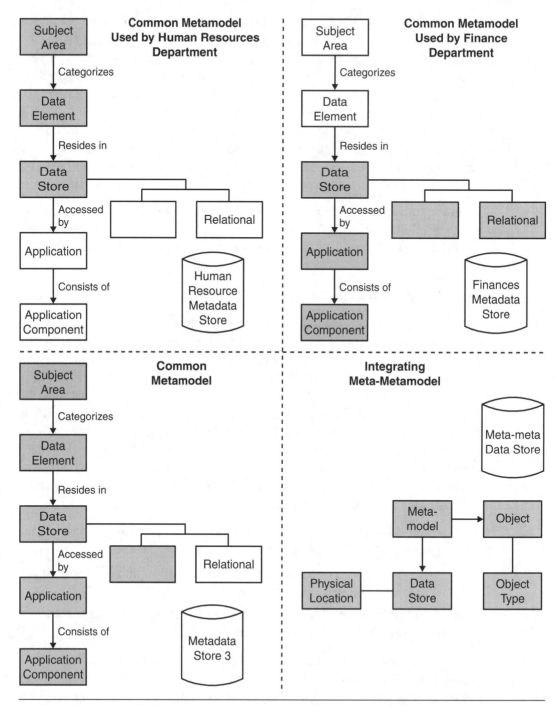

Figure 20-3   Distributed metadata stores with an almost common metamodel
—shaded constructs are populated at each site

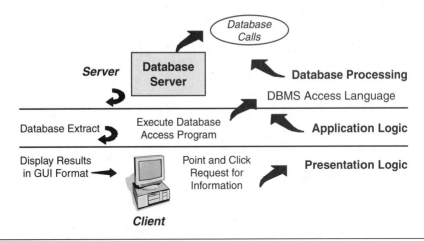

Figure 20-4 Traditional client/server processing layers

Source: Adapted from Tannenbaum, A. *Implementing a Corporate Repository,* copyright © 1994 by John Wiley & Sons, New York. This material is used by permission of John Wiley & Sons, Inc.

into a consistent set of proprietary commands. In effect, therefore, the amount of true distribution that is possible with repository products is tool dependent. Be wary of repository products that were designed and built as standalone tools and are now supposedly distributed. In most cases, unless the product's entire architecture was rebuilt, the separate installations are not able to communicate and there is no overall point of control. Each installed repository product operates separately, and the only way that they can be related or integrated is through manually invoked external processes. A true overall distributed architecture may therefore be nonexistent.

With a true distributed architecture, an overall point of control must exist (as with distributed metadata stores). But this point of control must tie the architecture to the contents of *each* distinct repository. In addition to repository access, the point of control should be involved in virtually all repository connections, including routine administrative functions (e.g., backups), user profiles and their relationship to *all* repositories, and repository consolidation (keeping contents in sync), to name a few. So distributed capabilities are clearly based on the repository software's architecture. If a repository product were designed for standalone existence and administration, an additional control layer would have to be implemented when distribution is being considered.

As Figure 20-5 illustrates, to back up all repositories, a control process must initiate the backup functions of each repository, monitor the status, and report completion when all backups are successful.

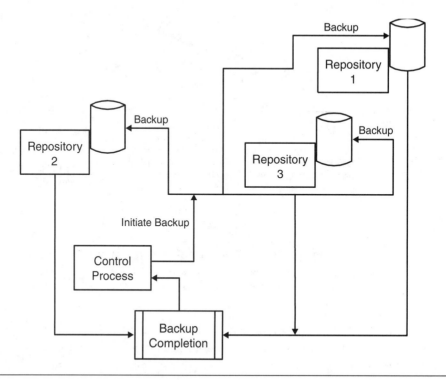

Figure 20-5   *Addition of a control layer to standalone repositories*

In general, if a vendor's product is being considered, you should decide initially whether you will be implementing multiple installations. If so, your next main concern would be whether a metadata beneficiary would *ever* need to access more than one of them. If so, an overall directory is crucial, and each product should be evaluated for its overall distribution capabilities. Specifically,

- How will each repository instance be aware of the others?
- How will contents remain in sync, so that one repository's contents do not contradict another's?
- How will security across repositories be implemented so that user profiles remain accurate and stable?
- Where will the overall point of control be implemented? How will overall repository administration occur?

Minimally, any multirepository installation can be set up with a primary/ secondary relationship, where one repository feeds all others on a regular basis. This batch update process would be implemented in conjunction with read-only access on all secondary repositories. This quasi-distributed installation would allow local access to local repositories. However, it is important to retain control over metadata distribution as well as permission to update each repository. *Without that forethought, you are guaranteed to have separate, unattached, redundant, and conflicting metadata stores.*

Generic versus Vendor-Specific Repositories

The preceding discussion applies to generic repositories, those products that are geared toward multivendor tool integration. If, in fact, you are considering acquiring a repository solution from one vendor as a means of integrating the metadata that is created and maintained *only in that vendor's toolset*, many of today's products in this category do offer distributed capabilities. Again, ask whether all the metadata is going to originate and be used by one vendor's toolset. If so, this may be the right solution, and you need not be concerned with customization and control.

Metadata User Boundaries

As you contemplate the number of metadata stores that will be required for your preliminary and subsequent implementations, be aware of the fact that your metadata solution's relationship to proposed and eventual user bases is a direct contributor to this decision. In other words, it is very likely, even recommended, that the metadata solution not aim to be everything to everyone, or supply everything to everyone. As we have been discussing throughout this book, the initial scope as well as each subsequent phase will involve a set of metadata beneficiaries. Evaluating the location of these beneficiaries and comparing each group's metadata needs will probably result in a firm physical architecture. Metadata is best kept where it is used, thus minimizing the amount of integrated access required for daily routines.

A good distributed architecture satisfies most requests locally. That is, the closest, most easily accessible metadata store or repository handles the majority of requests for metadata.

Planned Functionality

Finally, the last and most obvious determinant in metadata store assessment is the functionality of the proposed metadata solution. Metadata solution functionality should be distributed so that each function is performed as efficiently as possible. Although this objective depends completely on the technical architecture

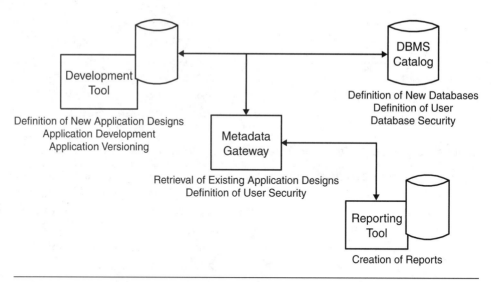

Figure 20-6 **Functional distribution across a metadata solution architecture**

of the chosen metadata solution, aspects of the overall architecture that are in the control of the designer/developer/architect should be based on the functional grids that were put together during the metadata requirements process. The functional matrix identified functions not only from a metadata perspective,[3] but also from the viewpoint of the information being described by the metadata. Finally, the matrix assigned each of these functions to a candidate component in the metadata solution architecture. It is time to revisit this functional matrix from a different point of view—to confirm *where* the functions are going to be performed.

Figure 20-6 shows that the metadata gateway is going to be used only as the place to retrieve application designs and define security from an overall metadata solution perspective, based on its knowledge of where each type of metadata is stored. All other functionality remains with the tool best suited to the performance of the specific functions. This functional distribution implies the need for only one additional metadata store, to be used as a gateway to the individual tools. If more metadata (other than that related to physical application design) becomes in demand, or more beneficiaries or tools enter the picture, it may be necessary to distribute the gateway functionality.

---

3. Functional matrices are discussed in Chapter 18.

Standard or Customized Metamodels

Another aspect of the overall metadata solution is the metamodel. As metadata solutions became more and more in demand, many vendors, particularly those offering generic repositories, began offering sets of standard metamodels either as part of the base metadata solution or as an optional add-on. Prospective consumers were never quite sure whether to buy one of the already developed metamodels or to start from scratch and develop their own.

Software vendors develop off-the-shelf metamodels as a means of documenting the types of metadata that are collected by their metadata solution products and their internal relationships. Depending on vendor policy and marketplace position, metamodels are offered as part of the base repository product. These basic metamodels are representative of the product's major functionality, as advertised. For example, during the late 1990s, many vendors of generic repositories began marketing (or remarketing) their product offerings as the best option for Y2K impact analysis, based on the fact that they could scan existing program libraries and store a copy of the physical world in the repository product's metadata store, thus resulting in a convenient place to look for all occurrences of the data element *date*. The marketing of such a product typically included a copy of the overall metamodel (often called the Scanner metamodel). Potential product consumers would be able to evaluate this model and see, for example, that regardless of the source application's physical platform or language, the repository product put all occurrences of Program and Data Element in the same metamodel.

Whether metamodels are packaged with metadata solution products is quite variable, however. At the height of Y2K anxiety, existing repository products were repackaged and bundled with reverse engineering and scanner software—and the metamodel was part of the deal. Now that Y2K is past, many vendors focus their products on the popular needs for metadata—data warehousing and data access—and bundle a repository product with an ETL tool and/or a decision support tool—thus offering a "full data warehouse solution." This supposedly complete solution includes supporting data warehouse metadata and, of course, a data warehouse metamodel. Of course, trends come and go, and they affect whether a metamodel is included in the base metadata solution product. All of this is quite amusing because, as we should all know by now, all of these nonrepository tools do, in fact, track metadata. So whether the vendors choose to disclose how they store metadata is really a marketing decision. I know of potential consumers who "capture" physical designs of these products' databases through a reverse engineering tool in order to derive a metamodel when vendors are not interested in disclosing one. Unfortunately, many of the physical names are not user-friendly and they often find themselves guessing at the meaning of the captured results.

In general, basic metamodels are only pertinent in the generic repository space. There, again depending on how the product was originally or is currently being positioned, an included metamodel typically focuses on logical/physical data connections. Supplemental metamodels are typically incorporated with additional optional software, most likely a tool/repository interface. For example, optional add-ons to a generic repository product would include the ability to load application models from an object-oriented development tool directly into the repository. The interface package would include all the software required to perform these loads and keep the models synchronized, maybe some tool-direct APIs for direct model access, and a metamodel that would illustrate where the model fits into the overall repository picture (see Figure 20-7) would also be included. Interfaces and included metamodels are usually available for an additional cost (of course!).

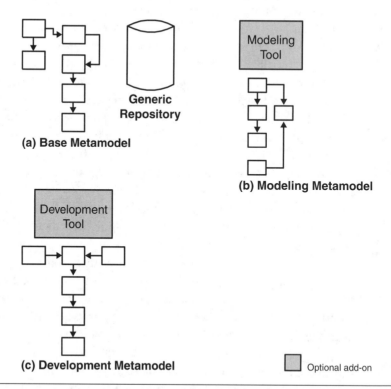

(a) Base Metamodel

Generic
Repository

(b) Modeling Metamodel

Modeling
Tool

(c) Development Metamodel

Development
Tool

Optional add-on

Figure 20-7   Base and optional metamodel packages
of a generic repository

Aside from the generic repository metamodel options, many single-vendor or "closed" development tool suites also distribute metamodels as part of their administrative or technical documentation. Again, the diagram would illustrate where the metadata is tracked within the product and how it relates to other metamodel components. For tools that allow external reporting (i.e., the metadata store is implemented in a commercial DBMS), this information can also be viewed as the physical design of the metadata store.

So how do we decide whether these offered metamodels fit the bill? First, consider the fact that they are developed by software vendors, in some cases based on vendors' perceptions of the way things are done. In more cases, the software vendors develop these metamodels based on the way *tools* (often acquired) actually track and use metadata. There is nothing wrong with either of these scenarios, but they just may not be the one that suits you. A detailed analysis of the metamodels is necessary to compare your common metamodel to the vendor's predesigned offerings. More important, however, is an evaluation of their meta-metamodel.[4] This "model of the models" shows the guts of any tool's metadata treatment, which will help you determine how a "new metadata solution process" would relate to existing metadata and decide whether an extension (change to an existing metamodel) would be worthwhile. You can see how easy it would be to customize metadata displays based on user profiles.

Vendors are seldom eager to release their meta-metamodels. They see this as a release of their inner secrets. Any discussions about customizing or changing the way their off-the-shelf product operates are usually referred to their consulting division, who may or may not be able to do things exactly as requested, depending of course on how the product is designed. At best, a vendor may release a meta-metamodel if you sign a nondisclosure agreement.

Another option, of course, is the development of your own metamodel (or set of metamodels). The process that we discuss throughout the book begins with gathering, analyzing, and subsequently categorizing metadata requirements. Obviously, a common metamodel is developed; you may also need to develop metamodels for specific and unique metadata according to beneficiaries' requirements. Custom metamodel development yields what you want; however, be prepared to assess the impact of your designs in terms of their possible interface with commercial metamodels.

---

4. Meta-metamodels are discussed in Chapter 13.

Finally, regardless of metamodel decision, the impact of standards[5] should be assessed. Standard metamodels are developed by consortium, and the consortiums are well represented by the vendor community. Therefore, the standards are biased, but they do represent an integrated perspective and the vendors' agreement to standards. To date, most required functionality, at least from a data warehousing perspective, appears to be included in metamodel standards.

Choosing the right path depends on the overall architecture of the metadata solution. If your software is for the most part purchased, with little custom development, then relying on the vendors for metamodels is probably a decent option. It is likely, however, that you have to integrate these perspectives with your own common metamodel. On the other hand, if your metadata solution architecture is intended to be internal in terms of both metadata sources and target beneficiaries, it may be better to develop your own metamodel, or purchase an off-the-shelf metadata solution that requires you to do so. (I have yet to see an off-the-shelf ready-made metamodel that meets everyone's needs—virtually all of our clients extend commercial repository packages in one way or another.) Just be sure to research the status of "impartial" vendor standards to make sure there are no major conflicts. If and when a practical metadata standard matures, we will all be following it.

Including or Excluding the Internet

Once the Web became the main vehicle for intercompany browsing and communication, it replaced many existing "lookup" tools, including phone books, business directories, and to some degree newspapers. Should anyone plan to exclude the Internet from a metadata solution? The only legitimate reason to do so is security, to keep aspects of the metadata solution private. But certainly, an organization's intranet is probably the best means to publicize and grow a metadata solution.

When Web browsers first became popular, commercial repository products started losing market share. Why would anyone use a proprietary repository browser, with restricted predefined browsing techniques, when for no additional cost, total flexibility in terms of "what is searched for" was available? Likewise, the restrictions inherent in the repository browsers forbid many potential metadata beneficiaries from "tapping in" unless they had been cleared and had access to the repository software. The immediate results of

---

5. Metadata and metamodel standards are discussed in Chapter 16.

these restrictions were limited access to metadata, limited knowledge of the metadata solution, and continued growth of the metadata web.

Consider your objective—to standardize common metadata so that it becomes practically reusable across categories of beneficiary. What other means would ensure global browser-based access than your firm's intranet? If restricted access is part of your objective, then that is perhaps the only justification for not using a Web-compatible front end.

Buy, Build, or Both?

In the perfect scenario, requirements are gathered, metadata is categorized, and a series of metamodels and a full metadata solution are developed. It is time to decide how to implement. First, determine the metadata stores—one or more, related or separate, distributed or redundant. Next, look at how the metadata should be organized and compare it against the available metamodels. Finally, evaluate the options in the surrounding software arena:

- Metadata creation, access, and update
- Metadata distribution both inside and outside the metadata solution
- Security definition and enforcement both inside and outside the metadata solution
- Metadata presentation to internal as well as external metadata beneficiaries
- Metadata solution support/administration—maintenance, tuning, and expansion
- Metadata solution customization—the ease with which existing options can be enhanced, eliminated, or changed

As we evaluate potential products from a technical point of view, we also of course need to evaluate the vendors. Vendors with longstanding terrible reputations are not preferred over new vendors with short excellent reputations (in most cases!). And of course, don't forget price as another aspect of the decision to buy or build.

In effect, each software quality must be evaluated along with the vendor's reputation to determine if an existing metadata solution will meet your needs. Never forget to look at your immediate and long-term objectives as you evaluate marketplace products. Many solutions work fine today, only to be scrapped in a year when they cannot interface with a newly acquired product or technology.

As marketplace options are evaluated, a weighted matrix is often prepared, giving higher values to qualities that are significant to your metadata solution. These numbers vary from organization to organization depending on priorities as well as organizational climate. A decision matrix should include all products being considered. Table 20-1 is an example of such a matrix. Your values will vary depending on your situation.

Each score in a matrix like Table 20-1 would be multiplied by the factor used to determine its importance (first-row value). The resulting scores would be summarized for each tool to determine which tool is more favorable, from the point of view of capabilities, customization, vendor, and price. It is important to realize that the assigned factors are subjective in that they vary based upon each organization's situation. The winner and perhaps a runner-up could be evaluated further during an in-house trial period. Most vendors allow a brief

Table 20-1   Weighing Metadata Solution Characteristics in a Decision Matrix

Factor Description	Factor Weight (0–1) [a]	Tool 1 (0–10) [b]	Tool 2 (0–10)	Tool 3 (0–10)
Completeness of existing metamodels	.7	0	4	8
Metadata access from within product	.3	6	2	7
Metadata access from outside product	.9	9	3	1
Flexibility of metadata store	.6	4	3	7
Metadata export/import	.9	7	3	9
Adherence to standards	.2	2	2	8
Security profile definition	.4	0	4	3
Security enforcement	.8	0	5	5
Metadata presentation options	.1	0	5	8
Administration of metadata solution	.3	5	3	8
Metadata solution customization options	.5	1	2	6
Vendor's reputation	.8	5	3	8
Price	.9	2	5	9
Maintenance costs	.8	5	3	8
Total Scores				

a. A weight of 0 indicates no importance, or insignificance; a weight of 1 indicates total relevance and importance. Values in between indicate variable ranges.

b. A value of 0 indicates that tool's inability to meet the factor's requirements. A value of 10 indicates full satisfaction of that factor. Values in between indicate variable abilities.

(3 months or less) evaluation period free of charge. If during that period one or more aspects of the commercial product are unacceptable, the Metadata Solution Customization Options might take on a much higher number as a decision-making factor for those products, or of course, other products could be reevaluated with perhaps a different slant.

Often, customizing a marketplace tool is the only way to satisfy the unique requirements of an organization. Developing your own metadata solution is the only other way to be sure your needs are met. The determination as to which avenue to take should be based on a cost/benefit analysis, including annual maintenance fees of purchased software.

At this point in the metadata solution process, your design is detailed enough for implementation estimates from internal development organizations as well as outside contractors. These estimates can be compared to the cost of marketplace products, additional customization, and annual maintenance. A scoped implementation plan can lessen initial costs.

CASE STUDY: Choosing XML as the Solution

PointandQuote.com provides real-time automobile quote comparisons and buying advice on a private-label basis for visitors of Web sites and members of affinity groups. Acquired by Nekema.com, Jersey City, New Jersey, in early 2001, its main business process occurs via the World Wide Web. Through its Web-based engine, visitors to Nekema.com's private-label site receive real-time quotes from multiple insurance carriers and the ability to purchase a policy online. The Web is Nekema.com's primary tool for interviewing applicants and exchanging data with trading partners. Efficiently capturing and managing the data throughout the Web-based transaction is required in order to stay in sync with competitive Web service firms.

Nekema.com had a few advantages in pursuing this objective. First and foremost, it had no existing metadata issues. As a start-up company, it had no "legacy"—every system was developed as part of its new standard metadata usage and review process. In fact, before developing any systems, it defined a set of standard metadata covering data, database, subject categorizations, industry mappings, and allowable values. This metadata would be required of all systems and associated data from the beginning.

"Mappings" were probably the biggest initial focus. Because most of its trading partners did not define things the way Nekema.com did, it was essential that its metadata cover the standard value sets by trading partner. Then it would never be an issue to code and decode when information was passed back and forth. In fact, a set of business rules covered translation issues and were also tracked and associated with the required metadata.

When members of the systems organization were charged with recording quotes and responses initiated on the Web page, along with the associated metadata, in the most timely and high-performance manner, XML looked attractive. In fact, based on the publicity surrounding XML, they were excited about the opportunity to use this state-of-the-art technology. XML seemed well suited because of its flexibility. Also, using a state-of-the-art technology was an excellent marketing feature. Nekema.com employees began an evaluation of XML and other possible solutions, including a Business Rules Engine. The original data flow is illustrated in Figure 20-8.

Nekema.com knew that a relational database would be necessary to contain all the captured data and its associated metadata so that it could be queried in all the ways, shapes, and formats that most of its trading partners would need. But at the same time, going directly from a Web page into a relational database was sure to present some problems. First, the possibility of broken information existed—people often leave Web sites arbitrarily or simply time-out while they are waiting. Next, Nekema.com did not want its Web page visitors to notice any performance delays, which are especially common with immediate database updates. Finally, more memory and resident data storage would be required to support this design option. For these reasons, its data

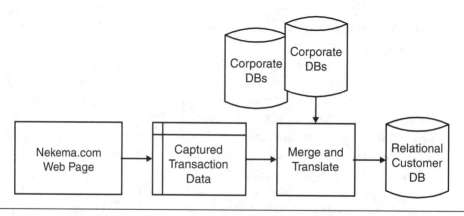

Figure 20-8 The original database design

managers considered using XML as the application's repository. In essence, the metadata would be passed along with the requested data as part of an XML document.

Requests entered by Web page visitors would become "tagged" documents (the tag values would be based on predefined metadata sets). These tagged documents would stay in place until a later process extracted the data, accessed other corporate data stores, and stored the resulting record in a newly created relational database. An existing marketplace tool would be purchased to handle the XML-to-database conversion. The application was designed with this target scenario in mind, and a tool was located that on the surface appeared to have the desired features.

During further evaluation of the XML database tool, Nekema.com had second thoughts. The tool was very new to the marketplace and the vendor could provide no solid references. In fact, Nekema.com, planning on relying on this tool for queries and XML-to-database interface, made a business decision to change the original design.

As Figure 20-9 illustrates, Nekema.com now puts the Web page transactions right into a relational data store. It is working on building XML documents in memory as a replacement for the expensive relational database processes required to rebuild the interview context. However, they learned throughout this project that XML is nothing more than a data layout, plus the data itself, which is nothing new. Because XML is being pushed by so many software vendors as the way to exchange information, many of Nekema.com's trading partners are strong believers in XML. To implement an XML-based exchange scheme fully,

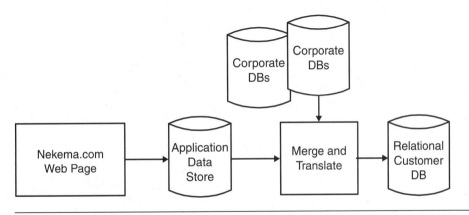

Figure 20-9 The final Nekema database design

Nekema.com has to develop a standard format for these exchangeable documents. Therefore, the metadata tags (their values and their order) are now in the process of being standardized for all trading partners.

Ideally, Nekema.com's XML document standard will be replaced by a standard that will apply for all industries. The hope is for XML standards that will address common functions (e.g., processing payments). Unfortunately, most efforts seem to be addressing industries (e.g., chemicals, retail). Nekema.com realizes that an XML endeavor is not going to be simple to design, implement, and maintain.

Note: This case study was submitted by Daniel C. Hayes, vice president, and Ho-Chun Ho of Nekema.com. Used with permission

The determination of the proper metadata solution *must* be based on individual metadata requirements. "Silver bullet" technology solutions are often selected, however, based on their alleged capabilities. In fact, many organizations tend to retrofit these capabilities into their final requirements. Nekema.com began the process of selecting a metadata solution with a heavy leaning toward marketplace solutions. During the rollout of the selected metadata solution, it realized that XML in and of itself would not solve their overall requirements.

In the next few chapters, we will see metadata solutions implemented in a variety of platforms with a variety of architectures. While exploring them, we must keep in mind the reason that implementations are chosen, and how that reasoning affects the end result.

Part V
Sample Metadata Solutions

It's time to see some live examples. We begin this section with a case study. Although it is fictitious, most of us will be able to identify with it wholeheartedly. It is entitled "A Typical Metadata Disaster."

The chapters that follow the case study are not fictitious. They represent actual implementations that have been altered slightly to meet the needs of the case study. Some of these chapters are quite technical in that they contain actual code and refer to system calls and vendor APIs by name; they have been labeled technical at the left on the first page of the respective chapter. Don't feel threatened by the label; the chapters will give you a solid idea of what implementation of each metadata solution involves.

None of the solutions illustrated in these chapters is intended to be portrayed as better or worse than the others. Each implementation has its advantages and disadvantages, and the real situation should be the determining factor in deciding whether a particular solution meets the needs of an organization. Also, the solutions are intended to represent today's metadata solution options, but clearly do not represent all available software products.

The following metadata solutions have been illustrated:

- A centralized metadata repository
- An integrated repository architecture
- An information directory
- Metadata interexchange
- A standalone metadata store
- An enterprise portal

Chapter 21

A Typical Metadata Disaster

As metadata savvy as we all are at this point, it never hurts to solidify our terminology, theories, methodologies, and step-by-step implementations with live examples. Part V of this book does just that. We begin by describing real metadata problems gleaned from actual clients' experiences. This chapter describes the details of the organization's environment, from both an operational and a metadata perspective.

In the case study presented in this chapter, an organization is already dealing with multiple metadata stores. As a means of organizing the application development process, a decision was made to acquire an integrated application development environment—one tool that could handle application development from soup to nuts. The acquired tool was selected based on its functionality and suitability to the organization's procedures. As many readers already have experienced, what should be used and what is actually used are often two different things.

The remaining chapters in Part V show various ways to handle the realities of this situation, all actually deployed. The variety of implementation strategies is closely linked to the scope and coverage of each depicted metadata solution. Each solution addresses all or portions of this chapter's typical metadata disaster.

As Chapter 20 explains, determining the right solution is often the most difficult aspect of a metadata solution implementation. Continue reading to glean the details of this pre-metadata solution environment. At the end of the chapter is a list of issues to consider as you read forward and consider the sample solutions.

Tools, Tools, and More Tools—Case Study Begins

The organization that strives to solve its internal metadata problems typically starts by buying new and slick off-the-shelf metadata solutions. These products, usually part of a packaged "metadata solution environment," come with their own sets of interfacing tools. Unfortunately, there is usually nothing new in the functionality of these tools, but the fact that metadata can be shared among the tool's components makes these products an easy sell. As a result of the recent product acquisitions illustrated in this case study, a new environment exists, as illustrated in Figure 21-1. The following functions can now be satisfied (or partially satisfied) as follows:

- *Application development tools.* Differences in terms of target platform each still require a specific tool. For example, mainframe development can be accomplished only with the originally installed PC-COBOL software based on its in-house customization, which now permits direct interface with the mainframe program library.

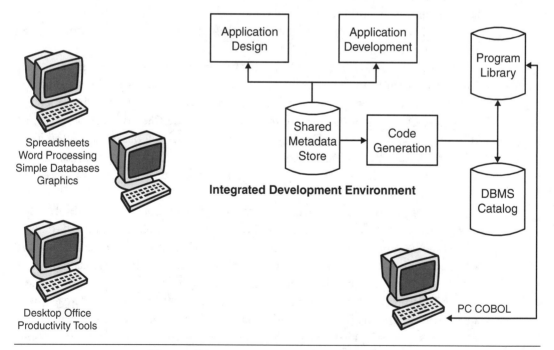

Figure 21-1 *The latest IT tool inventory*

- *Data-based decision support tools.* Existing desktop office support tools are still used to analyze production data in spreadsheets and local databases. Newly acquired office productivity tools allow the displaying of graphic results, such as pie charts, three-dimensional graphs, and bar charts.

- *Process and data modeling tools.* Originally performed within desktop support tools, new modeling tools within the new integrated development environment allow relationships between data and process models and their associated components, as well as reuse of certain modeling components. These models, used for application design, can be versioned when they are included as part of a versioned document created by a desktop tool as well as within the specific modeling tools.

All IT employees have their favorite ways of doing things. Some are quite impressed by the newly acquired environment and its associated software, but when push comes to shove, they are often most familiar and comfortable in this environment with existing desktop tools. Therefore, they put a substantial amount of application design information in text documents that contain embedded graphic models as opposed to using the newly acquired modeling tools.

Objectives, Objectives, and More Objectives

The acquisition of these new products and environments was based on the need to satisfy a recently mandated business objective. A short while ago, upper management met with IT executives and mandated the development of a strategic plan. In this document, which would be closely monitored once completed, each IT initiative, both existing and planned, would have to relate to one or more of the firm's business objectives. In addition, all IT initiatives would need to be scoped out in detail, with phased time, cost, and task allocations. The preparation of this plan included a meeting of all IT project managers to prioritize and allocate project tasks as part of an overall IT strategy.

As a result of the strategic plan requirement, all application development tasks became part of a well-organized task hierarchy, which related programming tasks to application objectives to project objectives to IT objectives to business objectives.

In Figure 21-2, for example, note that the business objective *Maintain Market Position* eventually relates to tasks associated with a specific IT project, that

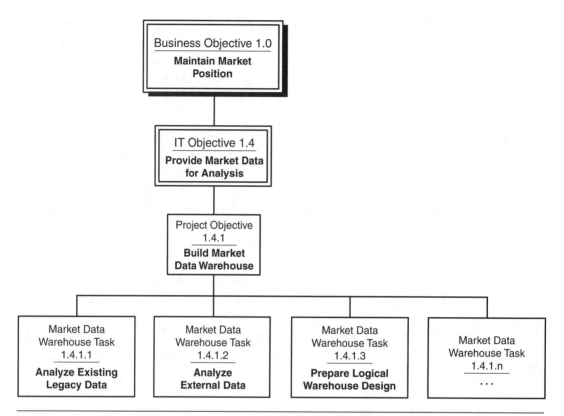

Figure 21-2   **A well-planned hierarchy of IT objectives**

of the *Market Data Warehouse*. In this organization, all IT initiatives were related to high-level business objectives *before* funding was approved.

An excellent strategy, if I must say so myself. Unfortunately, in this environment (as well as others), the people who are supposed to benefit from this objective-based approach (project managers on up) typically cannot answer these questions: "How do our developers determine what business strategy(ies) the IT initiatives are associated with? Do we all (developers, end users, project managers, executives) have access to the same objective/initiative links?" Did anyone even think of this . . . or better yet, is this something that we *want* everyone to have access to? In other words, has anyone done a full metadata requirements analysis, and where does objective-related information fit into it? During this evaluation, it was decided that perhaps some of the newly acquired tools had been acquired in haste, since those responsible for making the purchasing decisions did not consider the newly mandated need to relate IT initiatives to high-level business objectives, even though the initiatives were well known at the time of tool acquisition.

Continuing this true story, a metadata requirements analysis was then started, remembering our 5 Questions,[1] and it was determined, not surprisingly, that the broad business objectives were not the only ones that existed and had meaningful impact. In fact, in addition to the official business objectives, there were:

- *Departmental objectives*, which may or may not tie directly to those of the business
- *Project objectives,* which sometimes tie to those of the business (if the projects are IT projects), and sometimes tie to those of the department
- *Personal objectives,* by which all employees are measured during performance reviews

These objectives are stored in word processing–based text documents, on everyone's desktops. To clarify this case study from the point of view of our "situation," the author of these objectives keeps the document *only* on his or her desktop. Some departments require distribution of these documents, and if so, they are distributed as attachments to internal e-mail. So how was everyone supposed to relate IT initiatives to objectives given the actual workings of "management by objectives"?

Metadata, Metadata, and More Metadata

Continuing this situation's metadata requirements analysis, we have identified the need to track metadata about the following major categories within this identified scope:

- *Objectives*—business, project, and personal
- *Projects*—scoped initially to include IT projects only
- *Applications*—custom-developed software only

---

1. The 5 Questions is a trademark of and the questions and method are copyrighted by Database Design Solutions, Inc., Bernardsville, New Jersey.

- *Data stores*—with both physical and logical characteristics
- *Tasks*—the steps required to develop applications and/or their associated data stores

Metadata Requirements by User Category

Recall that, as discussed in Chapter 8, beneficiaries can be both people and tools. As a result of the metadata requirements analysis, we identified the following metadata beneficiaries:

- Upper management executives
- IT project managers
- Developers
- Database administrators
- Integrated development environment components, specifically the components used for application design and development
- Program library
- DBMS catalog
- PC COBOL installations

Table 21-1 lists the resulting metadata requirements by beneficiary category.

Metadata Flows

After assessing the metadata requirements by beneficiary category, the next step involved looking at the metadata flow in order to "source" the metadata. As a result, the metadata of record was determined where necessary. Because the scenario in this case study involved many *potential metadata of records,* solutions in the next chapters are based on the elimination of conflict. Figure 21-3 shows the metadata associated with each node of the current objective and application development processes.

Table 21-1   Metadata Requirements by Beneficiary Category

Upper Management Executives	IT Project Managers	Developers
■ Business objective name ■ Business objective number ■ Business objective target completion date ■ Business objective responsible executive name ■ Business objective responsible executive title ■ Business objective associated project name(s) ■ Business objective associated project manager(s)	■ Project name ■ Project-associated business objective number ■ Project-associated business objective name ■ Project-associated business objective responsible executive name ■ Project-associated business objective responsible executive title ■ Project allocated budget ■ Project start date ■ Project target completion date ■ Project task(s) ■ Project task start date ■ Project task completion date ■ Project task assigned resource name(s) ■ Project task actual cost ■ Project design location (tool name) ■ Project design name (model name, filename, etc.)	■ Project name ■ Project manager name ■ Project task(s) ■ Project task start date ■ Project task completion date ■ Project task assigned resource name(s) ■ Project design location (tool name) ■ Name (model name, filename, etc.) ■ Project design component(s) ■ Project design component type (model, text specification, flow, hierarchy, display layout)[a] ■ Application name ■ Program name(s) ■ Data store name(s) ■ Data element name(s) ■ Data element characteristics ■ Data access procedure name(s) *continued*

a. Depending on the type of design component, specific metadata requirements exist. These have not been identified for this case, because at the time of metadata requirements analysis, there was only one application development tool for which metadata components had been identified. Developers agreed to use the tool's capabilities as a metadata requirements baseline since no formal methodology or set of design standards existed at the time of this analysis.

Table 21-1   Metadata Requirements by Beneficiary Category   *continued*

Database Administrators	Application Design Tool Component	Application Development Tool Component
■ Project manager name ■ Project name ■ Lead developer name ■ Data model name ■ Data model location ■ Data access procedure name ■ DBMS name ■ DBMS version ■ Data store name ■ Data element name(s) ■ Data element characteristics ■ Database name(s) ■ Table name(s) ■ Column name(s) ■ Index names (primary and secondary)	■ Model type ■ Model name ■ Model author ■ Model creation date ■ Model update date ■ Model component name ■ Model component type ■ Model component relationship(s) ■ Tool version ■ Tool component version	■ Design model type ■ Design model name ■ Design model author (userid) ■ Application component name ■ Application component creation date ■ Application component update date ■ Associated component name(s) ■ Tool version ■ Tool component version

Table 21-1   *continued*

Program Library	DBMS Catalog	PC COBOL Installations
■ Application name	■ Data model name	■ Tool version
■ Project manager name	■ Data model location	■ Program name
■ Project manager contact number	■ Data model last update date	■ Program creator (userid)
■ Application component (program) name	■ Data model author	■ Shared component name(s)
■ Application component (data store) name	■ Data model author contact number/e-mail	■ Shared component location(s)
■ Application shared component (copylib, class library, etc.) name	■ Data model type/tool used	■ Job name
■ Application shared component location	■ Database name	■ Application name(s)
■ Application version	■ DBMS version	
■ Application component version	■ Database creation date	
■ Application installed location(s)	■ Table name(s)	
■ Application/component/location relationship(s)	■ Column name(s)	
■ Application software/application type	■ Column type(s)	
◆ Data store/DBMS type	■ Index name(s)	
	■ Index type(s)	
	■ Physical allocation(s)	
	■ Stored procedure name(s)	

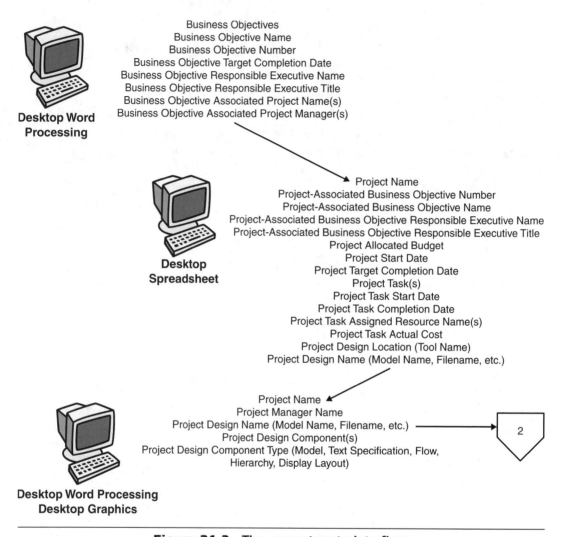

Figure 21-3 The current metadata flow

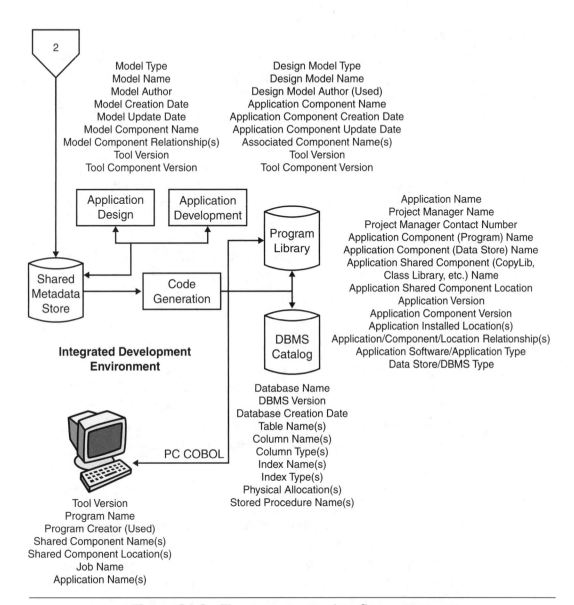

Figure 21-3 **The current metadata flow** *continued*

Identified Metadata of Records

Each solution in the upcoming chapters assumes a certain architecture. Because these architectures vary, the metadata of records have not been identified in this chapter. For example, some metadata solutions assume a centralized metadata store, whose contents most likely represent official metadata instances. These instances strive to *become* the metadata of records. Other metadata solutions accept the fact that metadata of importance exists in desktop publishing tools and may represent official metadata. In some of these solutions, this official metadata remains in the desktop tools, thus becoming a *set* of metadata of records, to some extent. Still others leave the metadata where it is, simply avoiding identification of the metadata of record.

The remainder of Part V illustrates practical means of solving the metadata dilemma depicted in this chapter. Although each solution is established to address this dilemma, all solutions have potential within every organization. Pay specific attention to the following qualities of each metadata solution:

- *Ease of implementation*. Can the suggested metadata solution be set up with minimal transition in this organization?

- *Scope of penetration*. Does the suggested metadata solution affect a restricted amount of metadata flow in this organization? How easy would expansion be with this type of arrangement?

- *Organization support*. How would the implemented metadata solution be supported in the current environment? What changes would be required?

- *Security*. Does the metadata solution protect important metadata? What user profiles will be necessary?

- *Metadata standardization*. Will the suggested metadata solution restrict metadata redundancy? How? Over what period of time? For what purposes?

- *Cost/benefit*. How expensive would the suggested metadata solution be to plan, design, and implement? What benefits would be immediate? What benefits would eventually result? When would you reach the break-even point?

- *Minimum and maximum functionality*. Does the metadata solution solve the immediate metadata problem? What other benefits does the metadata solution provide? Are they requirements now? Will these extras ever be requirements?

- *Technological effectiveness.* Does the metadata solution fit in with the organization's technical strategies? What is missing? What aspects of the solution are years ahead of this or your organization?

None of the solutions in the following chapters is necessarily better or worse than the others. As we have discussed, determining the right solution is a very customized process. As you proceed through the rest of Part V, consider where your organization meets our example.

Chapter 22

Metadata Solution 1
The Centralized Metadata Repository

The example provided in the previous chapter is a common one. Typically, metadata is scattered throughout an organization in a variety of formats—spreadsheets, text documents, databases, CASE tools, legacy applications, and so on. Not only is the data varied and distributed, but there exists a variety of user groups as well, each with its own needs and objectives—application developers, business analysts, database administrators, data modelers, among others.

The solution provided in this chapter focuses on an implemented centralized metadata repository. With the centralized metadata repository, all metadata of record is captured in a single data store. You can think of the centralized metadata repository as a "one-stop shop" where metadata is consolidated from many data sources to facilitate the processes involved in metadata management. This chapter illustrates an architecture that represents this shop as a distinct metadata solution that is accessed directly by all metadata beneficiaries through the repository software.

Figure 22-1 illustrates the architecture involved in this metadata solution using the Platinum Repository Open Enterprise Edition (PR/OEE) version 2.1. Metadata from numerous sources in the enterprise is imported into the metadata repository's metadata store, where it is transformed and managed for reporting and use by a variety of metadata beneficiaries, including the business

---

Note: This chapter was submitted by Computer Associates, Inc., Knowledge Management Division, Islandia, New York. Information and figures copyright © Computer Associates, Inc. Used with permission.

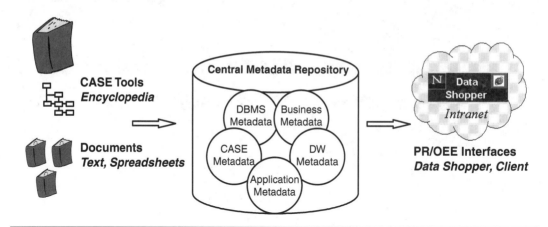

Figure 22-1 The centralized Platinum Repository Open Enterprise Edition architecture

users. All metadata beneficiaries retrieve and access their metadata directly through predefined OEE interfaces and templates.

The Interaction of Basic Repository Components

As discussed in Chapter 14, a metadata repository represents a set of distinct components. In the architecture illustrated in Figure 22-1, metamodels, templates, and utilities all play a role.

- *Repository metamodel.* The metamodel is the backbone of any metadata repository solution. This model must be broad enough to cover the wide range of tools and metadata sources as well as flexible enough to allow for additions and customizations where gaps exist. In our illustrated solution, portions of the deployed metamodel are depicted in Figure 22-3, later in this chapter.

- *Metadata store.* In PR/OEE, this metadata store can reside on any of three industry standard databases: Oracle, Sybase, or MS SQL Server.

- *Population tools/utilities.* In order to capture information from source systems, metadata information must be integrated into the metadata store.

- *Templates.* End users need an interface that allows them to easily find and understand the metadata information stored in the centralized metadata repository. PR/OEE provides two main user interfaces: Data Shopper for intranets, a Web-based tool, as well as the Repository

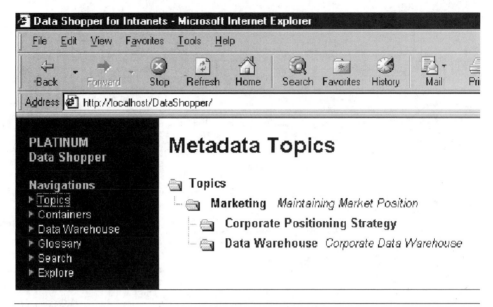

Figure 22-2   End-user access to the centralized metadata repository
via Data Shopper

Client, a desktop product. Both can be customized for various user
groups and both provide impact analysis and search capability. Figure
22-2 shows a screen from Data Shopper for intranets. Note that in this
example, information has been organized according to the organization's business structure. Other ways to categorize information are by
technology type, user group, and so on.

Suggested Metamodels

In the centralized repository metamodel, all source systems are mapped to the
same, common model. This single, integrated metamodel consists of several
interrelated submodels, allowing impact analysis from one model to the next.
Such integration facilitates the consolidation of disparate metadata as well as
the querying of the metadata by end users. Figure 22-3 shows a small subset of
the common metamodel. Oval constructs represent intersecting relationships,
which break up many-to-many relationships via the implementation of intersecting tables.[1]

---

1. See the Additional Readings section for resources about logical data modeling.

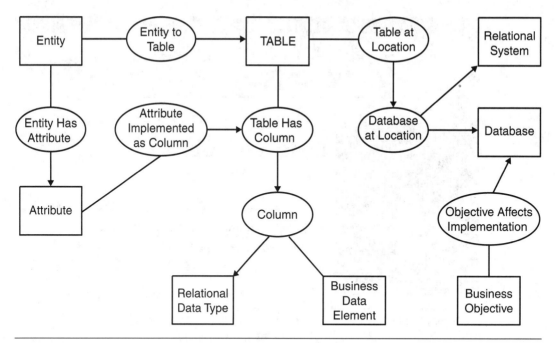

Figure 22-3 **Centralized repository metamodel**

The major PR/OEE metamodels involved in this scenario are:

- *Logical model metamodel.* This metamodel includes metadata from logical modeling tools, CASE tools, and even the metadata that is generally stored in most homegrown data dictionaries. Metadata objects describe entities, attributes, relationships, CASE model information, and so on.

- *Relational metamodel.* This metamodel includes metadata that can be captured from industry standard relational database management systems (RDBMS). Metadata objects describe tables, columns, indexes, databases, triggers, stored procedures, and so on.

- *Application metamodel.* This metamodel includes metadata for COBOL, JCL, and the object-oriented programming languages such as C++, Java, and Visual Basic. In addition, nonrelational databases such as IDMS can belong to this metamodel. Metadata objects describe program information, element and variable definitions, class definitions, job definitions, and so on.

■ *Data warehouse metamodel.* In addition to the metadata types represented in the relational and application metamodels, data warehouse-specific metadata is represented. This includes transformation logic, ETL statistics, fact and dimension table indicators, and star schema information.

■ *Business metamodel.* This metamodel contains information regarding business rules, project/organizational information, metadata ownership/stewardship, naming standards, acronyms, and so on.

Repository Utilities

Several PR/OEE utilities have been deployed as part of this metadata solution:

■ *Metadata extract, load, and maintenance.* The PR/OEE Population Center provides scanners that automatically extract metadata from a given source and populate the repository data store. For example, our organization in Chapter 21 would make use of a scanner for its DBMS systems, COBOL applications, text documents, spreadsheet information (extracted via flat file), and CASE models. In addition, the PR/OEE Client can be used for manual entry, manipulation, and organization of data. This interface could be used to enter metadata objects that are not covered by the base scanners, such as business objectives.

■ *Security.* The PR/OEE Security Manager is used to grant specific security privileges to repository users. Roles are associated with various portions of the metamodel and can be read/write or read only. For example, while the repository administration team may have access to the entire metamodel, business users may have limited rights only to element definitions and business rules.

■ *Metamodel customization.* The PR/OEE Extend Tool provides the ability to customize the repository metamodel to align the repository with the organization's specific metadata needs. For example, although business elements are captured in the base metamodel, a specific business objective object does not exist. By defining an objective as an object in the base metamodel, with attributes such as name, number, and so on, we can relate them to other metamodel objects, allowing for better impact analysis. For example, "What database applications are required to complete this objective?" would be a typical impact-analysis question.

■ *Change management.* PR/OEE provides tools to help manage the ongoing changes to metadata information. One such tool is a group of reuse rules that govern the repository update and loading process. Standard rule templates are provided for each automated scanner and the repository administrator can alter these rules to match the enterprise's business rules. The resolution of issues discussed in prior chapters is of paramount importance when metadata is being redundantly copied into a centralized metadata store, and these rules are essential to overall management of the metadata.

- *Glossary/standard name generation.* As members of the organization in Chapter 21 build the central repository, they are likely to discover business elements common to the majority of the applications. The process of metadata rationalization, which is discussed in a later section, helps provide naming conventions for these elements on both business and technical levels. To facilitate this, glossaries can be defined in the repository at the level of project, line of business, or enterprise to provide suggested business and/or technical names for common elements.

- *Repository unload.* Once the organization has loaded the repository, it should be able to unload the metadata in a useful form. PR/OEE provides several export options: DDL generation for RDBMS information, .ERX export for CASE tools, and copybook generation for COBOL applications.

Repository Templates

PR/OEE provides standard templates to organize the mapping of source metadata to the centralized metamodel.

- *Metamodel templates.* A standard metamodel is provided as a basis for mapping and storing the organization's metadata from a wide range of metadata sources. To simplify the management of these sources, the metamodel is logically divided into numerous standard templates: RDBMS systems, CASE tools, and so on. The metamodel templates can be used "as is" or as starting points for customization, as illustrated in Figure 22-3.

- *User interface templates.* As discussed in Chapter 14, templates are an essential means of representing metadata to each beneficiary category. Figure 22-4 illustrates the templates that relate to our illustrated metadata disaster. Implemented templates affect the access of metadata through both the PR/OEE Client and the Data Shopper for Intranet products.

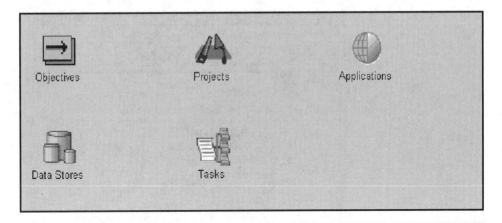

Figure 22-4   **Repository templates**

■ *Security templates.* Individual user groups require not only custom interfaces, but also custom security privileges. To implement various security profiles to meet the requirements of our illustrated example, PR/OEE provides security templates to establish such roles. These roles can be modified and augmented, as necessary. Figure 22-5 shows examples of security profiles that relate to our metadata disaster.

Repository-Based Processes

Metadata Inventory

Often the first step in metadata management is determining what metadata currently exists in the organization. With the use of its automated scanners, PR/OEE can extract information directly from the source systems to provide a metadata inventory.

Metadata Rationalization

Once the metadata inventory is in place, one of the most common processes facilitated by the centralized repository is metadata rationalization. This is the process of reconciling diverse instances of metadata to an organizational standard, or metadata of record. For example, in Figure 22-6, our metadata inventory found that different projects in the organization use a different naming convention for the same element, employee account number. One application uses the name *employee number* and another uses the term *emp_acct_code*.

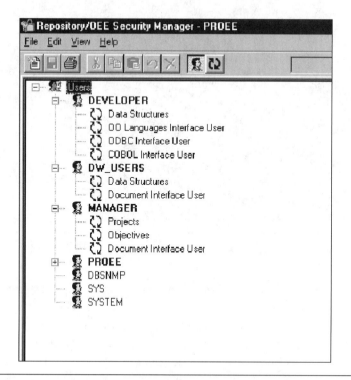

Figure 22-5   Repository security profiles

The information management team has determined that the common term *Employee_Acct_Number* should be used. This term is defined as a primary element within PR/OEE and used as a reference for future application development. This element is also linked to the existing naming conventions to facilitate impact analysis, which is described in the following section.

Change Management

Once we have established a metadata inventory and created a standard metadata of record, how do we handle changes? As described previously, reuse rules can be defined in the repository to implement these business rules and objectives. It is essential that the centralized metadata repository now become part of the metadata creation and management process.[2]

The centralized metadata repository solution can be used to solve the enterprise-wide metadata management problem outlined in Chapter 21. Inte-

---

2. Metadata management responsibilities are discussed in Chapter 29.

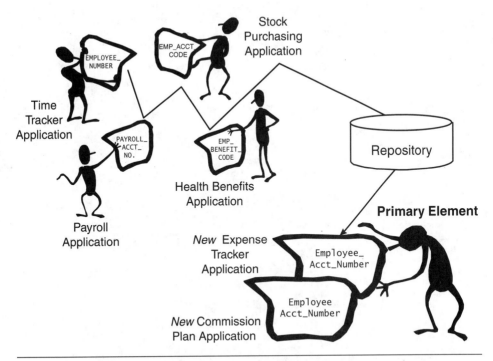

Figure 22-6 Data standardization and rationalization—
a metadata repository-based process

grating the standalone islands can point solutions into one, manageable metadata store creating a reliable source metadata of record. Once this source has
been established, various user groups in the organization can make optimal
use of this information for impact analysis, application development, naming
standards enforcement, data rationalization, legacy system inventory, and so on.
No longer is metadata hidden in proprietary systems in the organization but
shared in a common, accessible interface.

Chapter 23

Metadata Solution 2
An Integrated Architecture

With integrated repository architectures, the overall metadata solution represents a unified set of software. Software that is "unified" shares an underlying metadata repository via either direct access or active updates. The solution illustrated in this chapter is a reporting-focused metadata repository that integrates other distributed and standalone metadata resources. The metadata illustrated in this chapter includes a scoped world of data in the implementing organization. The similarities between the case study in Chapter 21 and this implemented metadata solution make the environment well suited for representation.

Metadata Solution Scope

This metadata solution began in a data administration team. The intended audience for the first release was restricted to the data administration staff and its deployed set of tools.

Metadata Beneficiaries

The key suppliers of metadata were:

- Texas Instruments Cool:Gen Central Encyclopedia (MVS), the deployed integrated development tool
- Computer Associates' ModelMart, an integrated conglomeration of data and process models created with ERWin and BPWin. This implementation focused only on ERWin models.

■ Various DBMS Catalogs (IBM's DB2, Oracle, Microsoft SQL Server, Tandem), used to represent physical production databases

There were no project planning or project management metadata requirements addressed during this initial metadata solution implementation.

The Common Metamodel

As with the metadata solution depicted in Chapter 22, all common metadata was stored in a centralized metadata repository. This repository was custom developed and deployed using the SQL Server DBMS. The metamodel is shown in Figure 23-1.

Across the repository architecture, a full set of metadata existed. The overall metamodel was deliberately kept very simple, and the data structure represents the basic metadata semantics that have meaning to the data administration team. This metamodel is divided into three logical groupings, one for the overall enterprise, one for metadata associated with development modeling, and one for implementation specifics. It is interesting how the metamodel is broken down, as follows:

■ An *enterprise logical model* metamodel, which represents subject areas, each assigned to one logical entity. In this model, enterprise subject areas are stored. Business terms and synonyms are kept in this model also, which functions primarily as a glossary for all company data.

■ A *development modeling* metamodel, used to represent data models that preceded physical database implementation.

■ An *implementation* metamodel, used to represent physical databases from the point of view of DBMS instances.

The Enterprise Logical Model consists of information that is not development specific, primarily a three-tier Zachman-type[1] classification schema (SUBJECT_AREA), a list of common domain attributes (ATTRIBUTE), and the enterprise vocabulary.

---

1. The Zachman Framework is a trademark of IBM, Inc., and represents an organized categorization of system development processes and deliverables.

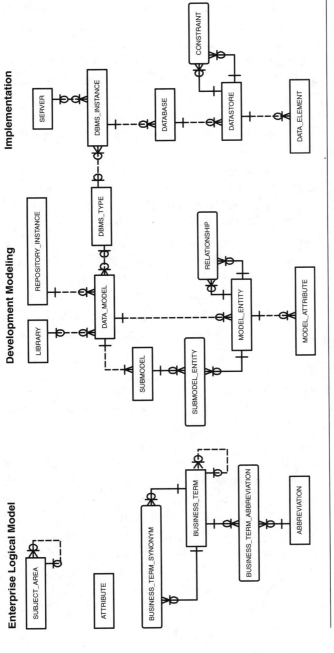

Figure 23-1   The common metamodel

Development Modeling consists of models created for specific development efforts. These are eventually migrated up to platform-specific enterprise models, with library-based separations. The two CASE tools used for relational modeling (ERWin and Cool:Gen) have strong logical/physical integration, which are also reflected in the metadata repository; for example, the MODEL_ENTITY entity has LOGICAL_NAME and PHYSICAL_NAME attributes. In this implementation, as with many, the distinction between logical and physical modeling has become blurred and each of the selected modeling tools has strong physical orientations.

Implementation consists of implemented, physical metadata scanned in directly from the RDBMS system catalogs. (For greater compatibility with non-relational platforms, the terms DATASTORE and DATA_ELEMENT have been used instead of TABLE and COLUMN.)

Linking the modeling and implementation domains was a key application requirement. A legacy data administration application did this successfully on the mainframe by cross-referencing physical names from the Cool:Gen Central Encyclopedia with the DB2 system catalogs. The new metadata repository has a similar capability through its ability to join MODEL_ENTITY.PHYSICAL_NAME with DATASTORE.NAME (and similarly on the attribute/column tables).

Enterprise Vocabulary

Above and beyond the full metamodel, the existing enterprise vocabulary is accessible via the implemented metadata repository. This list was maintained for many years as a basic list of standard and legacy abbreviations. Instances of this vocabulary are now populated directly into the Enterprise Model. Users of the metadata repository have the option of an enhanced search, which will automatically generate a search family of candidate vocabulary terms for a given string. For example, entering the token "CUSTOMER" will return its standard abbreviation "CUST," variations such as "CUSTOMERS," as well as legacy (known nonstandard) abbreviations (e.g., "CUSTMR), and synonyms ("GUEST"). All of these candidate tokens are assembled into a search family and presented to the user for confirmation of the final search parameters. Then, the actual metadata repository search is carried out using the search family.

The Metadata Solution Architecture

A three-tier, Web-enabled architecture resembles many data warehouses, with a batch ETL function populating the metadata repository independently of its presentation capability. A custom developed SQL Server database served as the centralized metadata repository, populated on a regular basis via scheduled batch refreshes (every two weeks). The architecture is depicted in Figure 23-2.

The central metadata store contained all common metadata, but also represented the only integrated view of its connections to the unique and specific metadata that remained in its source metadata stores. This metadata solution

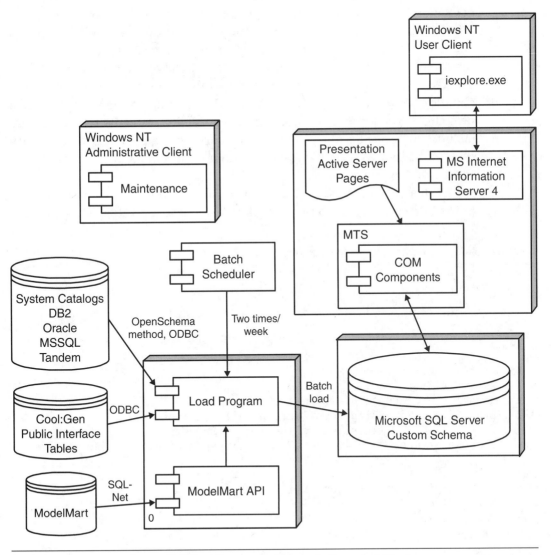

Figure 23-2 **The metadata solution architecture**

represents an integrated metadata solution architecture, since the central resident metadata is available to tools and software that lie outside the framework. In addition, the sources of metadata are well integrated with the central metadata store through automated refresh practices, as discussed later in this chapter.

Application Program Interfaces

The complexity of the common metamodel compared with its physical implementation in the underlying RDBMS system catalogs drove a strong technical requirement for simplified access. The average developer would have to understand metamodels and their relationship to underlying meta-meta constructs in order to query the contents of the ModelMart repository, for example. Writing direct SQL against this information store would have been very complex and expensive, and would have tightly coupled the repository load program to vendor-owned implementation details. Instead, the architecture includes tool-specific APIs, which can be called from any interfacing application, thus leaving the metadata knowledge requirement with the metadata administration group.

As illustrated in the sample code in Listing 23-1, the ModelMart API is used to read and return the contents of the ModelMart repository to requesting

Listing 23-1   Using the ModelMart® API

```
Sub Main()

'This proof of concept Visual Basic code prints all libraries, diagrams,
'entities,
'and attributes in a ModelMart repository to the Visual Studio debugger

Dim IServer As Server
Dim ISession As Session
Dim LoginString, ConcurrencyString As String
Dim libraryCollection, diagramCollection, entityCollection,
                    attributeCollection as Objects
Dim libraryReference, diagramReference, entityReference, attributeReference
                as ObjectReference

Const LibraryTypeCode As Integer = 2
Const DiagramTypeCode As Integer = 3
Const EntityTypeCode As Integer = 4
Const AttrTypeCode As Integer = 7

Set IServer = New Server
Set ISession = Nothing
```

```
Call IServer.Sessions.RemoveAll
Set ISession = IServer.Sessions.AddSession

LoginString = "UID=/;DSt=Oracle Vers. 7/8.xx;DSN=MY_TNS_NAME;MMM=x;"
ConcurrencyString = "OVL=YES;RSS=NO;"

'Log into ModelMart
ISession.Open(LoginString, ConcurrencyString)

'Get library collection
Set libraryCollection = ISession.Objects.Collect(, LibraryTypeCode)

'Loop through libraries
For Each libraryReference in libraryCollection
   Debug.Print libraryReference.Name

   'Get diagram collection for library
   Set diagramCollection = ISession.Objects.Collect(
       libraryReference.Handle, DiagramTypeCode)

   'Loop through diagrams
   For Each diagramReference in diagramCollection
      Debug.Print vbTab & diagramReference.Name

      'Get entity collection for diagram
      Set entityCollection = ISession.Objects.Collect(
          diagramReference.Handle, EntityTypeCode)

      'Loop through entities
      For Each entityReference in entityCollection
         Debug.Print vbTab & vbTab & entityReference.Name

         'Get attribute collection for entity
         Set attributeCollection = ISession.Objects.Collect(
             entityReference.Handle, AttrTypeCode)

         'Loop through attributes
         For Each attributeReference in attributeCollection
            Debug.Print vbTab & vbTab & vbTab & attributeReference.Name

      Next entityReference

   Next diagramReference

Next libraryReference

End Sub
```

software, including the refresh of the SQL Server metadata repository. Although the use of this API requires a sophisticated understanding of COM and object-oriented hierarchies, it turned out to be quite effective in representing the underlying metadata repository's contents and structure in one execution.

Batch Connectivity via Intermediate Tables

Because some APIs are not compatible with installed middleware, as in this case, the full architecture includes some batch extract files. The Cool:Gen access was accomplished through the vendor's Public Interface Tables. The underlying tables are then accessible via a standard ODBC (Object Database Connectivity) architecture.

Open-Schema Connections

Due to the complexity of DBMS catalogs, the development team chose to use Microsoft's ActiveX Data Objects' OpenSchema method as a means of populating the metadata repository. This method works across any ODBC- or OLE-DB–compliant database and returns consistent, standard metadata.

Using the Metadata Solution

A hyperlinked, Web-surfing navigational metaphor between the various objects in the model hierarchies and their physical implementations functions as the metadata repository front end. The sidebar shows a sample use case.

Maintaining the Metadata Solution

The key to the life of a metadata solution such as this one is its accuracy and relevance. The metadata administration group maintains this architecture via scheduled batch refresh policies, as mentioned earlier. More important is the ease with which the stored metadata can be accessed by components that are not part of the metadata solution architecture. The APIs form a key characteristic of this integration. As designed, they work consistently across all ODBC connections—the same code handles DB2, Tandem, and Oracle.

User opens DataStation, enters keyword "GUEST" for search.
System responds with "search family" containing all abbreviations, synonyms, variations, and related business terms. For example, GUEST has CUSTOMER as a synonym; even though GUEST is the approved business word, there is much data still named CUSTOMER. This, in turn, means that the following abbreviations all need to be searched:

GST   CUST   CST   CUSTMR

and so forth. DataStation makes this kind of painstaking research transparent.

User specifies that search is on entity (as opposed to model name or attribute).
System responds with pick list of entities that have any member of the search item's family in their name.

User chooses one entity to navigate to and review details.
System responds with details such as related entities, attribute logical names, parent model, and entity definition.

User "drills down" from entity into attribute detail.
System responds with details such as logical and physical names, attribute definitions, and parent entities in that model.

User requests navigation from modeled entity to corresponding implementation.
System responds with list of modeled systems that contain or access the information.

User selects one option (server name, instance).
System presents detailed view of implemented table, including information about server, database, and so on.

Chapter 24

Metadata Solution 3
The Information Directory

If it is not part of your immediate objective to integrate the various sources of metadata, or to determine which metadata is official, or even to begin identifying the future metadata of record values to avoid continued redundancy, perhaps you just want everyone to know what metadata exists. In a simpler sense, the real objective may be to know what *information* exists. For now, your best bet may be the development of an *active information directory*.

Information directories show us where information resides. They are quite valuable when the information is categorized into our own subject areas. Finally, they are almost indispensable when they actually retrieve the information based on these predefined categories and the associated selection(s). The functionality of an information directory typically stops there. In other words, once the metadata is located and retrieved, it is up to the directory's user to determine its usefulness and next steps.

Information Directory versus Enterprise Portal

These information directory metadata solutions have been likened to Web browsers, and in many cases have been renamed enterprise portals. I still choose to discriminate between the two, since information directories do not require Web browsers as part of their architecture. Today, this is perhaps the main difference, although functionally they are basically equivalent. They both have the objective of returning information based on particular metadata values. Differences rest with the following:

- *How the target information is categorized* (if at all), and what tools/software/procedures are required to find and access the information. Enterprise portals, for example, have a tendency to consider what they return to be multi-application in perspective; therefore, the information is often categorized as such.

- *What the metadata solution does with the target information* once it is located. In an information directory, location of the information is considered the metadata solution's objective and access is often an option, although today most solutions do open, or access, the located metadata and/or information.

- *The technical scope of all target information that can be located.* If the information to be identified by the directory's metadata has a prerequisite type or existence, it usually falls into the directory, rather than the enterprise portal, category.

The Directory Metamodel

Because the information directory is concerned primarily with the identification and location of metadata, by category, it is not necessarily focused on the elimination of metadata redundancy or the encouragement of metadata reuse. The metamodel of such a solution is concerned with all metadata required for:

- The categorization of a set of scoped information
- The association of these categories with such information
- The identification of the categorized information
- The optional access of the metadata-identified information

In general, the metamodel, illustrated in Figure 24-1, in support of all these functions is consistent, irrespective of the type of platform or tool in which the scoped information is located.

Populating the Directory

Because the directory represents a gateway (of sorts) to scoped information, the directory must be actively populated and remain accurate throughout its

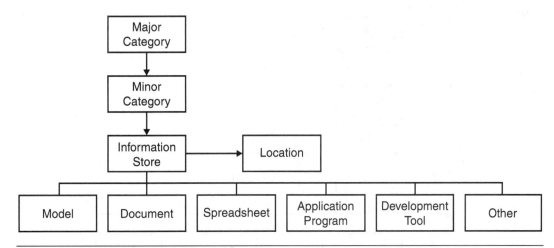

Figure 24-1 An information directory metamodel

existence. Depending, of course, on whether the directory retrieves or directly accesses this information, the active nature of the directory can be crucial in determining the directory's credibility. The population of this directory should really be looked at from two angles:

- *Business metadata population.* The creation and maintenance of the metadata associated with the categorization of the information being tracked and described in the directory
- *Location and accessibility of (physical) metadata population.* The creation, maintenance, and standardization of the metadata required to locate and optionally access the information represented by the directory

Because the metadata used internally by the directory is functionally separate from that which directory users see and are concerned with, its population usually takes on distinctly separate characteristics. Figure 24-2 illustrates how metadata can be perceived as having different "perspectives," each of which is essential to the directory's operation once combined.

Business Metadata Population

Applying the information directory solution to our case study implies a different set of metadata requirements by nature of the directory metamodel. However, this is not necessarily the case. The existing metadata requirements are still

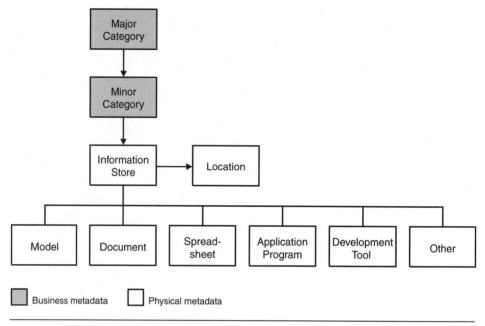

Figure 24-2 **The two-perspective directory metamodel**

applicable in most situations; they merely need to be reorganized or categorized to fit the directory perspective. Remember that the objective of the information directory is to *find* the information that our metadata beneficiaries
need, not necessarily to provide a fully integrated metadata solution. What is of
major importance now is (1) what we will be looking for and (2) where it
exists. The surrounding business metadata supports these directory objectives.

Consider the entities in our metamodel (Figure 24-2), and consider how the
identified metadata requirements should be used to populate this metamodel.

- *Major categories:* Objective, Project, Application, Information Store,
  (Model), (Design), (Task)
- *Minor categories:* Department, (Model), Component, (Type), Data,
  Process, (Information Store Type), Individual

Values that appear in parentheses are optional, depending on the focus of particular beneficiaries in your organization. For example, if a substantial number
of metadata beneficiaries will always be looking for models (i.e., they are not
necessarily familiar with the associated application, project, or information
store), then *Model* may be an appropriate major category.

Table 24-1 Drilling Down to Minor Categories from Suggested Major Categories

Major Category	Minor Categories
Objective	Company Name/Department Name/Project Name/Individual Name, Task Name, Deliverable Name/Type
Project	Department Name, Project Component Type, Individual Name, Model
Application	Application Component Type, Individual Name
Information Store	Information Store Type, Individual Name
Model	Model Type, Application, Project, Model Component, Individual Name
Design	Project, Application, Application Component, Model, (Type), Individual Name
Task	Deliverable Name/Type, Individual Name, Project, Application, Application Component Type

How will the values of these categories correlate within the planned directory metamodel? See Table 24-1 for suggested drill downs.

This table illustrates potential values that could be used to drill down to the actual information being sought via the directory. The population of this metadata requires a centralized administrator charged with standardizing these categories and determining the means with which to associate them to legacy and new information stores. In general, the amount of control over standardized values directly correlates with the usability of the directory throughout the organization. This statement applies whether the directory is centralized or distributed.[1]

In general, new information stores need immediate reflection in the directory. Depending on the types of information stores, direct connections to registries, DBMS catalogs, and other areas that log the existence of named information groups are required. As new in-scope information stores are created, they should be categorized and registered immediately.

Physical Metadata Population

Once major and minor categories are worked out, the associated information stores as well as the metadata required for the directory to identify them must

---

1. Part VI focuses on the maintenance of metadata solutions.

be acknowledged and populated. Realize that not all metadata needs to reside in this potentially redundant metadata store. Instead, the optimum situation might be, for example, pointers, or addressing information, to obtain that metadata elsewhere.

Following our two-perspective metamodel (Figure 24-2), we continue with the population of Information Store and Location details. Again, we revisit the metadata requirements as identified in Chapter 21, and consider where these metadata requirements fit in to the directory scheme. Remember, though, that because these requirements were organized by metadata beneficiary without respect for the planned metadata solution architecture, some of the addressing metadata that will be required by the directory itself may not have been directly mentioned. These requirements have been indicated in parentheses.

- *Information store*—Information Store Type (note subtypes in model), Information Store Location (note all "location" metadata below), Information Store "Contents" (in terms of named components), Information Store Version

- *Location*—(Tool Name), Tool Version, Tool Component Name, Tool Component Version, (Tool API Name), Database Name, DBMS Type, DBMS Version, Table Name, Column Name, Index Name/Type, Stored Procedure Name

For a directory to remain active, it should not be dependent on a manually triggered process for the update and population of required metadata. Most traditional directories have been replaced by Web browsers and other HTML-compatible technologies, which can automatically search predefined XML-compliant tags, for example, as a means of locating matched metadata values.[2] In the traditional sense, however, the population of required metadata in non-Web directories is often accomplished via reverse engineering tools, which read catalogs, registries, and other sources of specific metadata as a means of logging the existence of desired information stores. Modern tools allow the redefinition of these values during the scanning process so that compatibility with predefined tags is ensured. Again, the process is invoked manually and requires regularly scheduled updates to guarantee directory accuracy.

---

2. XML as a basis for a metadata solution is covered in the next chapter.

Directory Access

Most traditional directories are treated as custom applications in an organization. They represent a set of internally developed categorizations that are related to a scoped set of information stores. The directory itself becomes available on everyone's desktop as an internal application, usually distributed as a clone of a controlled master. Because the design is for access by individuals (as opposed to tools or applications), the directory's selection criteria are typically entered manually as selections from a preexisting list.

Marketplace tools are also available to handle the entire directory-based information access process. However, in most situations, these tools have their own metadata stores and associated metamodels. The populated metamodel components required to identify the existence of an information store must reside in the tool, and the tool does not usually open or access the metadata store directly.

The Web has changed the world of directories. In today's world of tags and search engines, directories are commonplace, and searches are based on the matching of a string with the contents of the target information store. For organizations that are considering traditional directories, however, this chapter illustrates a simple solution to information location.

Chapter 25

Metadata Solution 4
Metadata Interexchange

To conform to the fact that metadata exists everywhere, many solutions are moving toward the *exchange* of metadata as the main architectural quality of a metadata solution. In such a scenario, the metadata requirements analysis discussed throughout this book leads the metadata architect to a full metadata exchange architecture, which includes the following:

- A *common metadata store*, or the place where common metadata is stored, serves as the focal point for all metadata exchange; it represents the only place where a consistent representation of the common metadata exists.

- *Extract processes*, typically associated with various unique and specific metadata stores throughout the architecture, prepare metadata for translation by placing selected groups into an extract file, in many cases XML tagged based on a particular tool's metamodel.

- A *translation process* serves to translate extracted metadata from architectural components to conform to the overall metadata solution's common metamodel so that it can be passed to an optional *metadata staging area.*

- A *metadata staging area* holds uniform, delimited metadata in a common tagged order and format and passes it to the *metadata exchange mechanism.*

- A *metadata exchange mechanism,* often called the XML Parser, removes the XML tags from the translated metadata to allow its travel to and from the common metadata store.

A Common Metamodel

The metadata solution depicted in this chapter uses XML as the metadata exchange mechanism. Figure 25-1 illustrates the metamodel of the common metadata for this case study. This metamodel was created based on the requirements of all metadata beneficiaries identified in Chapter 21. Entities that are either in demand by all beneficiaries or required to link or relate to the specific and unique metadata requirements of other beneficiaries are combined to constitute the overall metamodel.

Entities in the common metamodel are identified via tags, which are then used to identify metadata stored in the XML documents that are exchanged among components. The instances of these tags correlate to the appropriate standard values in the organization. Typically these values are developed by a metadata management or administration function and are deployed as "standard" in order to facilitate the processing of exchanged metadata.

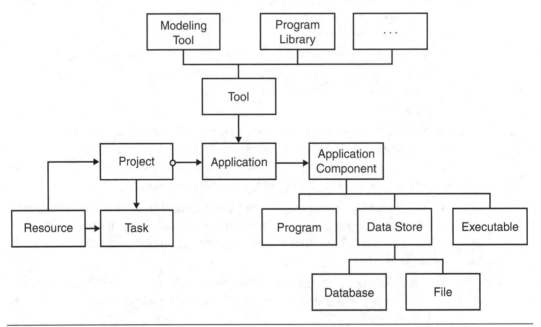

Figure 25-1 **The common case study metamodel**
for XML exchange

Standardizing Metadata Values

Probably the most essential characteristic for successful metadata exchange in an organization is the use of standard tags, in a standard order, with standard instance values. Because the tags correlate to common metadata (entities and attributes in the common metamodel), prerequisite standardization in terms of both value and usage is required once full metadata requirements analysis is complete. Looking at the common metamodel in Figure 25-1, it is clear that, based on their existence in the common metamodel, the following tags will become a part of XML-based metadata exchange throughout this metadata solution architecture:

- PROJECT
- TASK
- RESOURCE
- APPLICATION
- APPLICATION COMPONENT
- TOOL

These tags should be required in all metadata documents to be exchanged with the common metadata store. In addition, *standard instance values* should correspond to tag occurrences that are perpetuated (or can perpetuate) throughout the metadata solution architecture. Revisiting the case study metadata flow that we saw in Figure 21-3, we can easily ascertain in Figure 25-2 that standard values are needed for the following:

PROJECT—Most likely the values to be used for Project Name could correlate to the project approval/creation process, using corporate project names as a means of exchanging project-related information.

RESOURCE—With a focus on the human resource in this case study, current standard RESOURCE TYPEs would be required to indicate:

- PROJECT MANAGER
- PROGRAMMER
- MODELER
- Others, as they arise

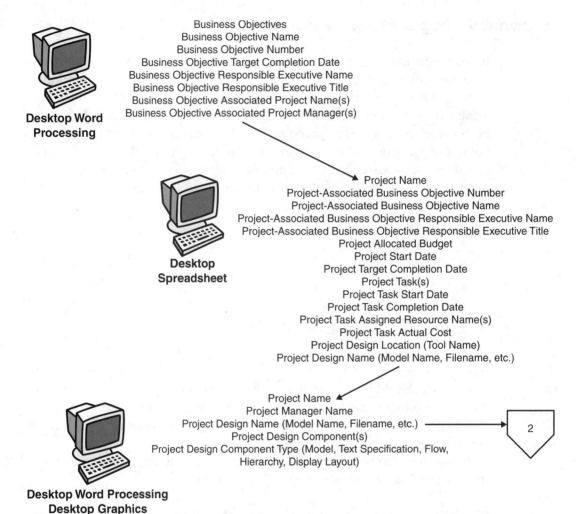

**Desktop Word
Processing**

Business Objectives
Business Objective Name
Business Objective Number
Business Objective Target Completion Date
Business Objective Responsible Executive Name
Business Objective Responsible Executive Title
Business Objective Associated Project Name(s)
Business Objective Associated Project Manager(s)

**Desktop
Spreadsheet**

Project Name
Project-Associated Business Objective Number
Project-Associated Business Objective Name
Project-Associated Business Objective Responsible Executive Name
Project-Associated Business Objective Responsible Executive Title
Project Allocated Budget
Project Start Date
Project Target Completion Date
Project Task(s)
Project Task Start Date
Project Task Completion Date
Project Task Assigned Resource Name(s)
Project Task Actual Cost
Project Design Location (Tool Name)
Project Design Name (Model Name, Filename, etc.)

Project Name
Project Manager Name
Project Design Name (Model Name, Filename, etc.)
Project Design Component(s)
Project Design Component Type (Model, Text Specification, Flow,
Hierarchy, Display Layout)

2

**Desktop Word Processing
Desktop Graphics**

Figure 25-2 The metadata solution flow, revisited

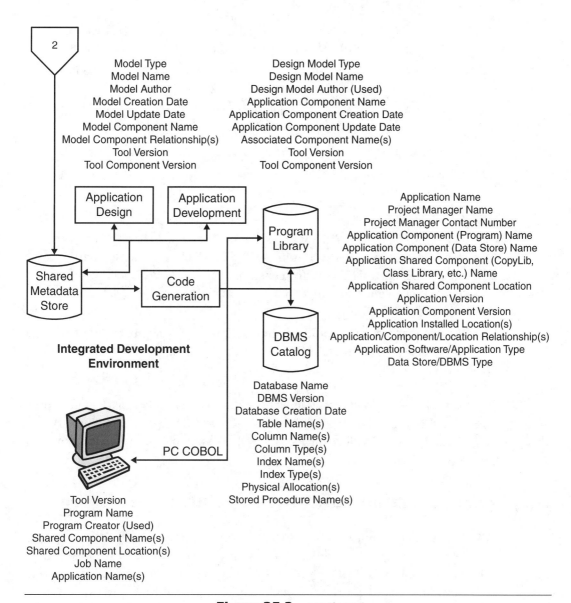

Figure 25-2   *continued*

RESOURCE INSTANCES—Need a standard format, and could be broken into LAST NAME and FIRST NAME, which can also be treated as "sub tags."

APPLICATION—As with PROJECT, should be tied to production application names and relate to codes used in the development process.

APPLICATION COMPONENT—Similar to RESOURCE, should have standard TYPES:

- PROGRAM
- DATA STORE*
- DESIGN*
- Others, as they arise

The COMPONENT TYPES with asterisks (*) can be broken down into standard subtypes. For example, DATA STORE already has standard types, such as DBMS and FILE. Within each of these types are specific values that can correspond to specific types of DBMS (e.g., ORACLE, SQL SERVER, and UDB).

TOOL—Standard values should equate to those tools that are part of the overall metadata solution architecture. Tool product names are usually used here.

Note that some metadata values have not been considered for standardization. PROJECT TASK, for example, is used only in the spreadsheet area of our metadata flow. If the values for PROJECT TASK are truly common, it is not clear at this point in our analysis.

Scoping the Metadata and Tools Architecture

The metadata exchange architecture is a simple one: Each metadata supplier and recipient uses XML-based Web transmission as its primary means of inter-component communication. Initial extracts, typically supplied by tool vendors, produce an initial extract file, which will eventually need to be translated to an XML document containing the tags that constitute common metamodel occurrences. In this architecture, these "translated" documents are held in an XML delimited metadata staging area before passing to an XML parser, which interprets and removes the XML from the metadata loaded document. Eventually, these occurrences are loaded into the common metadata store for direct extract via an organization's intranet, or to provide a link to metadata stored in another metadata solution component.

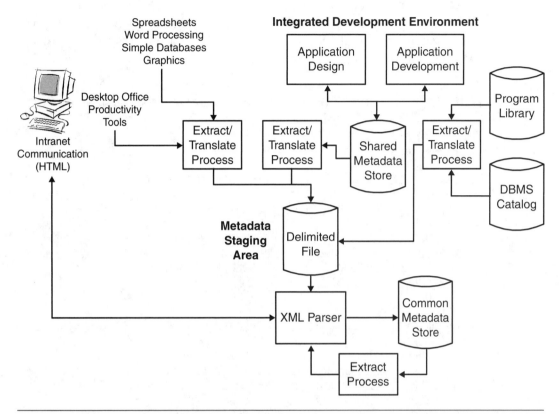

Figure 25-3 **The metadata solution architecture for XML-based metadata exchange**

As Figure 25-3 illustrates, the extract process associated with each metadata supplier and recipient delivers an initial XML delimited file, which is then translated into an entry in the XML staging area. The XML staging area contains uniformly represented XML documents, all compatible with the common metamodel. Once the standard XML tags and instances reside in the XML documents, they can be passed to the XML parser. This parsing will remove the XML and deliver the metadata to the common metadata store, or remove XML from the retrieved common metadata.

Metadata Source/Target Interface and Translation

The XML tags, as well as their translation, are key to this metadata solution architecture. Each extract process must deliver an XML document with set tags and the necessary standard values. These XML documents are then passed to a common XML Insert/Translation process. For example, Listing 25-1 presents portions of actual XML documents that could result from the depicted XML-based metadata exchange architecture.

Listing 25-1   Tagged XML documents used for metadata exchange

(a) Spreadsheet XML extract (by project)

```
<?xml version="1.0"?>
<PROJECT>
<PROJECT-NAME>Sales Forecasting</PROJECT-NAME>
<PROJECT-TASK>
<PROJECT-TASK-NAME>Project Management</PROJECT-TASK-NAME>
<RESOURCE>
<RESOURCE-TYPE>Project Manager</RESOURCE-TYPE>
<RESOURCE-FIRST-NAME>Jack</RESOURCE-FIRST-NAME>
<RESOURCE-LAST-NAME>Frost</RESOURCE-LAST-NAME>
</RESOURCE>
</PROJECT-TASK>
<PROJECT-TASK>
<PROJECT-TASK-NAME>SALECALC</PROJECT-TASK-NAME>
<RESOURCE>
<RESOURCE-TYPE>Programmer</RESOURCE-TYPE>
<RESOURCE-FIRST-NAME>Jill</RESOURCE-FIRST-NAME>
<RESOURCE-LAST-NAME>Frost</RESOURCE-LAST-NAME>
</RESOURCE>
<PROJECT-DESIGN-LOCATION>MegaTOOLS</PROJECT-DESIGN-LOCATION>
<PROJECT-DESIGN-NAME>Sales Forecast</PROJECT-DESIGN-NAME>
</PROJECT-TASK>
<PROJECT-TASK>
<PROJECT-TASK-NAME>SALESPROJECTION</PROJECT-TASK-NAME>
<RESOURCE>
<RESOURCE-TYPE>Programmer</RESOURCE-TYPE>
<RESOURCE-FIRST-NAME>Jill</RESOURCE-FIRST-NAME>
<RESOURCE-LAST-NAME>Frost</RESOURCE-LAST-NAME>
</RESOURCE>
<PROJECT-DESIGN-LOCATION>MetaTOOLS</PROJECT-DESIGN-LOCATION>
<PROJECT-DESIGN-NAME>Sales Forecast</PROJECT-DESIGN-NAME>
</PROJECT-TASK>
<PROJECT-TASK>
<PROJECT-TASK-NAME> Sales </PROJECT-TASK-NAME>
<RESOURCE>
<RESOURCE-TYPE>Modeler</RESOURCE-TYPE>
<RESOURCE-FIRST-NAME>Ann</RESOURCE-FIRST-NAME>
<RESOURCE-LAST-NAME>Frost</RESOURCE-LAST-NAME>
</RESOURCE>
<PROJECT-DESIGN-LOCATION> Mega-Modeler V3
```

```
</PROJECT-DESIGN-LOCATION>
</PROJECT-DESIGN-NAME>Sales</PROJECT-DESIGN-NAME>
</PROJECT-TASK>
<PROJECT-TASK>
<PROJECT-TASK-NAME>Customer</PROJECT-TASK-NAME>
<RESOURCE>
<RESOURCE-TYPE>Modeler</RESOURCE-TYPE>
<RESOURCE-FIRST-NAME>Ann</RESOURCE-FIRST-NAME>
<RESOURCE-LAST-NAME>Frost</RESOURCE-LAST-NAME>
</RESOURCE>
<PROJECT-DESIGN-LOCATION> Mega-Modeler V3
</PROJECT-DESIGN-LOCATION>
<PROJECT-DESIGN-NAME>Customer</PROJECT-DESIGN-NAME>
</PROJECT-TASK>
                        .
                        .
                        .
</PROJECT>
```

(b) **Application development XML extracts**

```
<?xml version="1.0"?>
<MODEL>
<DESIGN-MODEL-TYPE>PROGRAM</DESIGN-MODEL-TYPE>
<DESIGN-MODEL-NAME>SALES FORECAST</DESIGN-MODEL-NAME>
<DESIGN-MODEL-AUTHOR>FROSTJ02</DESIGN-MODEL-AUTHOR>
<APPLICATION-COMPONENT>
<APPLICATION-COMPONENT-NAME>SALECALC
                        </APPLICATION-COMPONENT-NAME>
<PROGRAM-LANGUAGE>C++</PROGRAM-LANGUAGE>
<ASSOCIATED-COMPONENT>
<TABLE-NAME>SALES</TABLE-NAME>
<TABLE-NAME>CUSTOMERS</TABLE-NAME>
<FILE-NAME>SALEEXT1</FILE-NAME>
</ASSOCIATED-COMPONENT>
</APPLICATION-COMPONENT>
<TOOL>
<TOOL-VERSION>MegaTOOLS V2.0</TOOL-VERSION>
<TOOL-COMPONENT> MegaADE V1.5</TOOL-COMPONENT>
</TOOL>
</MODEL>

<?xml version="1.0"?>
<MODEL>
<DESIGN-MODEL-TYPE>PROGRAM</DESIGN-MODEL-TYPE>
<DESIGN-MODEL-NAME>SALES FORECAST</DESIGN-MODEL-NAME>
<DESIGN-MODEL-AUTHOR>FROSTJ02</DESIGN-MODEL-AUTHOR>
<APPLICATION-COMPONENT>
```

```
<APPLICATION-COMPONENT-NAME>SALESPROJECTION
</APPLICATION-COMPONENT-NAME>
<PROGRAM-NAME>PROJECTEDSALES</PROGRAM-NAME>
<PROGRAM-LANGUAGE>C++</PROGRAM-LANGUAGE>
<ASSOCIATED-COMPONENT>
<TABLE-NAME>SALES</TABLE-NAME>
<TABLE-NAME>CUSTOMERS</TABLE-NAME>
<FILE-NAME>SALEEXT2</FILE-NAME>
</ASSOCIATED-COMPONENT>
</APPLICATION-COMPONENT>
<TOOL>
<TOOL-VERSION>MegaTOOLS V2.0</TOOL-VERSION>
<TOOL-COMPONENT> MegaADE V1.5</TOOL-COMPONENT>
</TOOL>
</MODEL>


<?xml version="1.0"?>
<MODEL>
<DESIGN-MODEL-TYPE>DATASTORE</DESIGN-MODEL-TYPE>
<DESIGN-MODEL-NAME>SALES</DESIGN-MODEL-NAME>
<DESIGN-MODEL-AUTHOR>FROSTA01</DESIGN-MODEL-AUTHOR>
<APPLICATION-COMPONENT>
<APPLICATION-COMPONENT-NAME>SALES</APPLICATION-COMPONENT-NAME>
<APPLICATION-COMPONENT>
<DATASTORE-TYPE>TABLE</DATASTORE-TYPE>
<TOOL>
<DESIGN-MODEL-TOOL>Mega-Modeler V3</DESIGN-MODEL-TOOL>
<DESIGN-MODEL-NAME>Sales</DESIGN-MODEL-NAME>
</TOOL>
</MODEL>


<?xml version-"1.0"?>
<MODEL>
<DESIGN-MODEL-TYPE>DATASTORE</DESIGN-MODEL-TYPE>
<DESIGN-MODEL-NAME>CUSTOMER</DESIGN-MODEL-NAME>
<DESIGN-MODEL-AUTHOR>FROSTA01</DESIGN-MODEL-AUTHOR>
<APPLICATION-COMPONENT>
<APPLICATION-COMPONENT-NAME>CUSTOMERS
                        </APPLICATION-COMPONENT-NAME>
<APPLICATION-COMPONENT>
<DATASTORE-TYPE>TABLE</DATASTORE-TYPE>
<TOOL>
<DESIGN-MODEL-TOOL>Mega-Modeler V3</DESIGN-MODEL-TOOL>
<DESIGN-MODEL-NAME>Customer</DESIGN-MODEL-NAME>
</TOOL>
</MODEL>
```

(c) Fully merged result

```xml
<?xml version="1.0"?>
<PROJECT>
<PROJECT-NAME>Sales Forecasting</PROJECT-NAME>
<MODEL>
<RESOURCE>
<RESOURCE-TYPE>Programmer</RESOURCE-TYPE>
<RESOURCE-FIRST-NAME>Jill</RESOURCE-FIRST-NAME>
<RESOURCE-LAST-NAME>Frost</RESOURCE-LAST-NAME>
</RESOURCE>
<DESIGN-MODEL-TYPE>PROGRAM</DESIGN-MODEL-TYPE>
<DESIGN-MODEL-NAME>SALES FORECAST</DESIGN-MODEL-NAME>
<DESIGN-MODEL-AUTHOR>FROSTJ02</DESIGN-MODEL-AUTHOR>
<APPLICATION-COMPONENT>
<APPLICATION-COMPONENT-NAME>SALECALC</APPLICATION-COMPONENT-NAME>
<PROGRAM-NAME>CURRENTSALES</PROGRAM-NAME>
<PROGRAM-LANGUAGE>C++</PROGRAM-LANGUAGE>
<ASSOCIATED-COMPONENT>
<TABLE-NAME>SALES</TABLE-NAME>
<TABLE-NAME>CUSTOMERS</TABLE-NAME>
<FILE-NAME>SALEEXT1</FILE-NAME>
</ASSOCIATED-COMPONENT>
</APPLICATION-COMPONENT>
<TOOL>
<TOOL-VERSION>MegaTOOLS V2.0</TOOL-VERSION>
<TOOL-COMPONENT> MegaADE V1.5</TOOL-COMPONENT>
</TOOL>
</MODEL>
<MODEL>
<RESOURCE>
<RESOURCE-TYPE>Programmer</RESOURCE-TYPE>
<RESOURCE-FIRST-NAME>Jill</RESOURCE-FIRST-NAME>
<RESOURCE-LAST-NAME>Frost</RESOURCE-LAST-NAME>
</RESOURCE>
<DESIGN-MODEL-TYPE>PROGRAM</DESIGN-MODEL-TYPE>
<DESIGN-MODEL-NAME>SALES FORECAST</DESIGN-MODEL-NAME>
<DESIGN-MODEL-AUTHOR>FROST102</DESIGN-MODEL-AUTHOR>
<APPLICATION-COMPONENT>
<APPLICATION-COMPONENT-NAME>SALESPROJECTION
                        </APPLICATION-COMPONENT-NAME>
<PROGRAM-NAME>PROJECTEDSALES</PROGRAM-NAME>
<PROGRAM-LANGUAGE>C++</PROGRAM-LANGUAGE>
<ASSOCIATED-COMPONENT>
<TABLE-NAME>SALES<TABLE-NAME>
<TABLE-NAME>CUSTOMERS</TABLE-NAME>
<FILE-NAME>SALEEXT2</FILE-NAME>
</ASSOCIATED-COMPONENT>
</APPLICATION-COMPONENT>
```

```
<TOOL>
<TOOL-VERSION>MegaTOOLS V2.0</TOOL-VERSION>
<TOOL-COMPONENT> MegaADE V1.5</TOOL-COMPONENT>
</TOOL>
</MODEL>
<MODEL>
<RESOURCE>
<RESOURCE-TYPE>Modeler</RESOURCE-TYPE>
<RESOURCE-FIRST-NAME>Ann</RESOURCE-FIRST-NAME>
<RESOURCE-LAST-NAME>Frost</RESOURCE-LAST-NAME>
</RESOURCE>
<DESIGN-MODEL-TYPE>DATASTORE</DESIGN-MODEL-TYPE>
<DESIGN-MODEL-NAME>SALES</DESIGN-MODEL-NAME>
<DESIGN-MODEL-AUTHOR>FROSTA01</DESIGN-MODEL-AUTHOR>
<APPLICATION-COMPONENT>
<APPLICATION-COMPONENT-NAME>SALES</APPLICATION-COMPONENT-NAME>
<APPLICATION-COMPONENT>
<DATASTORE-TYPE>TABLE</DATASTORE-TYPE>
<TOOL>
<DESIGN-MODEL-TOOL>Mega-Modeler V3</DESIGN-MODEL-TOOL>
<DESIGN-MODEL-NAME>Sales</DESIGN-MODEL-NAME>
</TOOL>
</MODEL>
<MODEL>
<RESOURCE>
<RESOURCE-TYPE>Modeler</RESOURCE-TYPE>
<RESOURCE-FIRST-NAME>Ann</RESOURCE-FIRST-NAME>
<RESOURCE-LAST-NAME>Frost</RESOURCE-LAST-NAME>
</RESOURCE>
<DESIGN-MODEL-TYPE>DATASTORE</DESIGN-MODEL-TYPE>
<DESIGN-MODEL-NAME>CUSTOMER</DESIGN-MODEL-NAME>
<DESIGN-MODEL-AUTHOR>FROSTA01</DESIGN-MODEL-AUTHOR>
<APPLICATION-COMPONENT>
<APPLICATION-COMPONENT-NAME>CUSTOMERS
                        </APPLICATION-COMPONENT-NAME>
<APPLICATION-COMPONENT>
<DATASTORE-TYPE>TABLE</DATASTORE-TYPE>
<TOOL>
<DESIGN-MODEL-TOOL>Mega-Modeler V3</DESIGN-MODEL-TOOL>
<DESIGN-MODEL-NAME>Customer</DESIGN-MODEL-NAME>
</TOOL>
</MODEL>
.
.
.
</PROJECT>
```

Consider the first XML document in Listing 25-1, Document (a). This document could represent the result of an extract process that expends all resources associated with a particular project (*Sales Forecasting*). Note the standardized RESOURCE TYPEs: Project Manager, Modeler, and Programmer.

The second XML document, Document (b), represents a tool-initiated extract process that exports all application components, again associated with a particular project. However, as in all multitool situations, our Application Development Tool does not use the term PROJECT, therefore, the ability to match based on PROJECT values is nonexistent. Likewise, the RESOURCE is not identified as such, and in fact, if we could assume the DESIGN-MODEL-AUTHOR to be a resource, the instance is not stored as a FIRST-NAME and LAST-NAME.

Evaluating the metadata in each tool is the only way to ascertain a true extract, merge, and translate process. This example matched on PROJECT-TASK-NAME and APPLICATION-COMPONENT-NAME to truly decide what sets of metadata could be combined without invalidating the overall common metamodel. The values that were used to compare and merge have been shaded throughout Listing 25-1.

It is interesting to note that a lookup table had to compare the DESIGN-MODEL-AUTHORs to the RESOURCE-FIRST-NAME and RESOURCE-LAST NAME combination. Also, note the problems that could arise when uppercase and lowercase values do not match. All these issues must be dealt with *before* an XML-based matching scheme is implemented.

Once the matching criteria are established, the two XML documents, each resulting from a tool-specific extract process, must be merged and/or translated to reflect the common metamodel. The third example in Listing 25-1, Document (c), reflects the translated result. Note that a combined set of tags, PROJECT-TASK-NAME and APPLICATION-COMPONENT-NAME, formed the matching criteria within a project. This assumes the need to define a project and its associated resources, by task, before the application design and development occurs in the tool of choice.

The values used to name the design models and application components *had to correspond directly* to the official spreadsheet values. It is important to reiterate that interproject standards for tags as well as tag values are crucial to successful XML-based metadata exchange. We did not originally see the need to standardize PROJECT-TASK-NAMEs, but further metadata analysis changed the initial plan.

Maintaining Standard Values

In order for translation processes to self-perpetuate, they access a database, or common metadata store, that contains standard tag instance values, ordered by tag value. In this way, as common tags are passed to the translation process, their associated instances can be looked up, rather than hard-coded in the translation process. The lookup tables should fall within the responsibility domain of Metadata Administration.[1]

---

1. Metadata administration is discussed in Chapter 28.

Chapter 26

Metadata Solution 5
A Standalone Metadata Store

Many organizations start metadata solutions by designing a simple standalone database. The architecture of this solution is typically quite simple—create a standalone application to collect, store, and distribute the necessary metadata. The distribution is done often by request. That is, a person who asks for the metadata can query the database directly, request a standard report, or perhaps receive an extract file. The designers of this solution typically are not very concerned with where the metadata goes. The major benefit of this approach is its obvious ease of implementation. However, the metadata store is not integrated with any of its metadata suppliers or recipients; the front end to this database typically stands alone. The primary downside to this approach is the lack of automated updates/inputs of metadata from interfacing tools via APIs or other direct connections. This, of course, could lead to an expanded metadata web.

Defining the Limited Scope

Limited scope implementations are typically associated with this type of standalone architecture. In the case study in Chapter 21 most, if not all, metadata beneficiaries will be retrieving some aspect of their metadata requirement from this implemented solution. However, the full metadata requirement for

---

Note: Portions of this chapter were contributed by Linh Nguyen, Consulting Associate, Database Design Solutions, Inc., Bernardsville, New Jersey.

some beneficiary categories may require going directly to the metadata source. In essence, there is no intertool metadata exchange or connectivity in a standalone metadata store.

Regardless of a limited architectural scope, the metadata solution must be able to store the metadata and provide a means to maintain and access that data. The standalone metadata store in and of itself is typically passive, in that it is manually maintained. The solution depicted in this chapter was built using Microsoft Access. It incorporates all the metadata required by all beneficiary categories and provides a front-end tool for current and future maintenance through its forms and reporting capabilities.

Designing the Metamodel

Analysis of the available metadata requirements reveals the relevant entities and their relationships. Based on the list of metadata requirements by beneficiary category, common sets of requirements can be grouped into entities. The next step is determining what relationships exist between these entities by drawing them in a model.

Figure 26-1 is an example of the resulting standalone metamodel. Realize that some relationships (e.g., *Business Objective to Project)* are optional. In other words, not all business objectives result in projects. Figure 26-1 also shows several subtypes (e.g., *ModelingTool, Data Model,* and *Program*). In these situations, information is common to all types of *Tools* (*Tool* is considered a supertype), yet depending on the type of tool (*Program Library, Modeling Tool,* etc.) specific types of metadata may need to be tracked.[1]

The illustrated metamodel is high-level in that it does not illustrate the attributes that are associated with each entity. Typically, the specifics of the model, including the primary and foreign keys, the nature of each relationship, and the attributes associated with each entity, are finalized in a modeling tool. This finalized model can then be used to generate the database. Figure 26-2 illustrates an example of one such populated entity with sample attributes.

---

1. See the Additional Readings for more resources on logical data modeling.

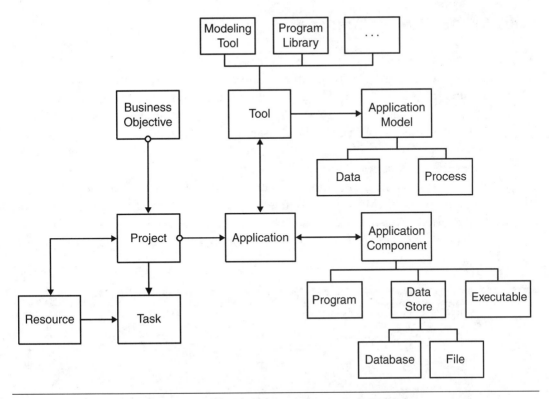

Figure 26-1 The standalone metamodel

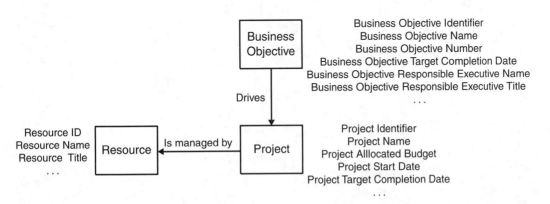

Figure 26-2 Sample entity-attribute relationships

Populating the Metamodel

Once all the entities, attributes, and relationships of the metamodel have been defined, the next step is to implement the physical metamodel as a database in Microsoft Access 2000. Many modeling tools can be used to generate a database schema for direct import into a Microsoft Access database. Figure 26-3 shows the CA ERWin tool about to generate the database schema. The database appears as seen in Figure 26-4. The metadata store is almost complete and is ready for data population.

Because most of the important metadata in our case study exists in text documents, multiple MS Access 2000 forms are created for manual metadata input. Formatted text, such as spreadsheets, can be loaded directly into the database. Again, this metadata solution is very simple to set up, and very simple to use for

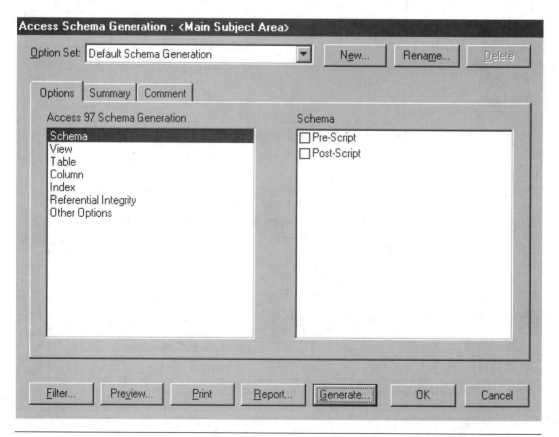

Figure 26-3   CA ERWin database schema generation into MS Access

Figure 26-4 Sample MS Access 2000 tables

metadata input. However, this type of implementation creates yet another place for existing metadata—perhaps this will become the official place, and the others will disappear. Issues surrounding this scenario are discussed in Part IV.

Figures 26-5 and 26-6 show the early developmental stage of the forms that will be used in the front-end application. Additional Visual Basic programming is required to relate all these forms into one usable application. Loading the metadata is performed via manual input from the created MS Access 2000 front-end screens and also through importing the Survey's associated MS Excel files using an MS Access import tool.

Preparing the Metadata Accessibility

Metadata accessibility is often a crucial concern in standalone metadata stores. Again, in this scenario, all interfaces with the metadata store will be through MS Access forms. Although easy to set up, this solution's architecture may not be on par with the other tools in use in the organization. Figure 26-7 illustrates the ease with which queries can be created. The architecture of this metadata solution is illustrated in Figure 26-8.

Figure 26-5 Creating MS Access forms

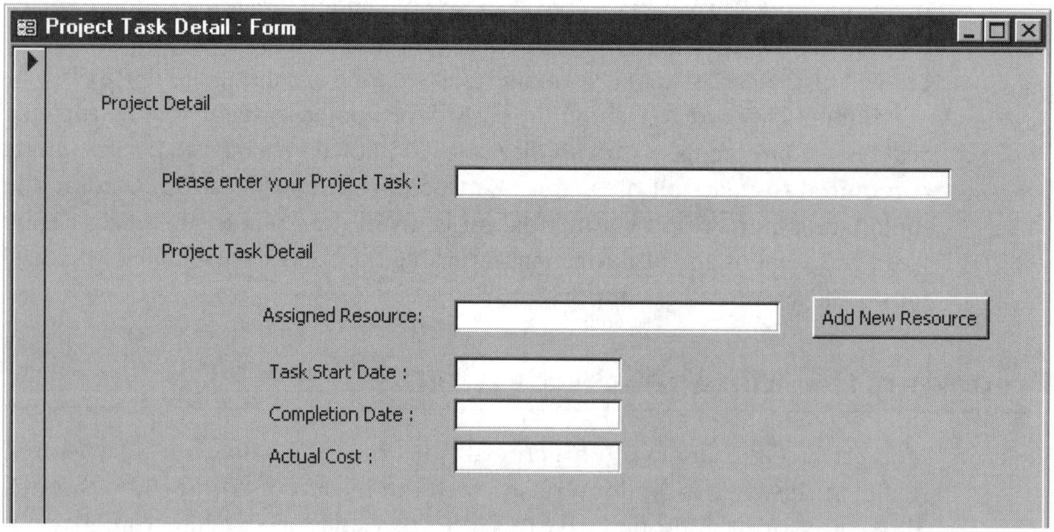

Figure 26-6 Designing the MS Access form interface

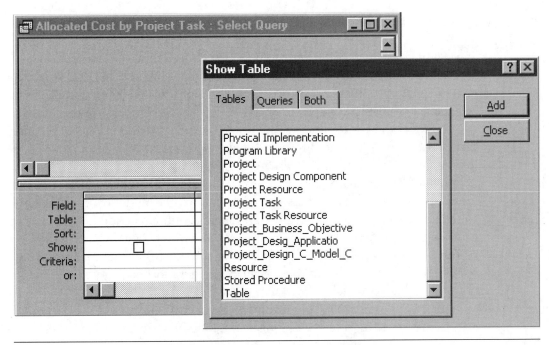

Figure 26-7 The MS Access query tool

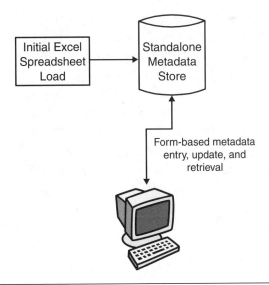

Figure 26-8 The standalone metadata store architecture

Maintaining the Metadata

Standalone metadata solutions often fall short over time due to their lack of active maintenance. To ensure their ongoing maintenance, the company appoints a Data/Metadata Steward in this example to take ownership of the metadata store. The MS Access 2000 database is housed locally on this individual's desktop and procedures are set up so that all subsequent IT Department projects are communicated to her. Regular updates/reviews are expected to guarantee the integrity and reliability of the metadata store.

General maintenance responsibilities include the manual addition of the metadata associated with all subsequent new projects and any other changes to metadata such as cost and resource allocation updates. Additionally, as the business requirements evolve over time, the Data/Metadata Steward would be responsible for implementing extensions to the metamodel and subsequently revising the relationships in the model. Many defunct metadata stores began with these plans.

Small scope metadata management can be adequately handled with a standalone metadata solution as long as the following situations are true:

- The source of all metadata is directly tied in to the metadata store on a regular, active basis.

- The metadata solution administrator is aware of the metadata's travels. Once extract requests start arriving, it should be time to consider a more integrated metadata solution architecture.

- The community of metadata beneficiaries does not exceed a number that can be managed easily by one administrator. Typically, this is one organization with limited scope metadata coverage (e.g., the definitions of data in a limited set of application databases).

- The metadata beneficiaries are read-only beneficiaries, so they are not creating the metadata as part of their daily routine.

Chapter 27

Metadata Solution 6
Building an Enterprise Portal

Another metadata solution approach focuses on the *accessing* of outside metadata using the metadata *within* the metadata store of the solution itself. In this scenario, the common metadata store is actually more of a meta-meta store because it tracks the location and access procedures required to get to the metadata stores that reside across the metadata solution architecture. This chapter describes the construction of an enterprise portal using the Meta-Matrix Enterprise Integration Server. The results of this implementation provide integrated access to metadata focused around all metadata beneficiary requirements: the objectives, projects, applications, data stores, and tasks that were identified as part of our typical metadata disaster in Chapter 21.

The enterprise portal approach uses meta-metadata to access the metadata based on where the metadata resides. In other words, the metadata remains *in its actual physical location*. It is unlocked and made available to each beneficiary *without moving or copying*.

Product Architecture

MetaMatrix is an integration platform that logically integrates all the information assets of an enterprise by capturing descriptive metadata. This metadata is then used to retrieve and process the actual information instances. Because our

---

Note: This chapter was originally submitted by Randall Hauch, Michael Lang, and Brad Wright, MetaMatrix, St. Louis, Missouri. MetaMatrix information and figures copyright © 2001 by MetaMatrix, Inc., New York. Used with permission.

metadata solution requires the integration of metadata stores (as opposed to data stores), the data that would be integrated by MetaMatrix in this case study is actually metadata. MetaMatrix hides the disparate nature of the metadata that resides in the various metadata stores across the metadata solution architecture by providing a single, unified point of access to all modeled metadata. It does so by creating a virtual database—a logical database that can be queried as a single entity even though more than one physical data source may be involved in the query. This virtual database should be considered a metadata gateway.

As discussed in Chapter 15, the metadata gateway, or portal, must understand each type of metadata, where it is housed, and its relationships to the metadata that resides in the other metadata stores. The metadata gateway lies between the various metadata solution components and the actual metadata stores, and therefore becomes an abstraction that remains accurate even when changes or additions are made to the underlying metadata stores. Figure 27-1 illustrates the overall intertool architecture.

The MetaMatrix Content Integration platform consists of the following subproducts:

- Metadata Modeler
- MetaMatrix Server
- MetaMatrix Console
- MetaMatrix Viewer

We will discuss the first two because they relate specifically to the case study.

The Metadata Modeler client application is used to create the models of metadata used by the server. The models of metadata are stored in a metadata repository, a proprietary database schema installed with the MetaMatrix server that can be installed in a number of common commercial relational database management systems. The Metadata Modeler application can import metadata from several types of sources and can also be used to create and modify metadata manually for data sources for which there is no metadata in an importable form. More important, the Modeler is used to create relationships among metadata of different sources that are semantically or literally equivalent. This latter function unifies the metadata into a single enterprise metadata model.

The server consists of a set of components distributed across multiple processes that collaborate to provide client applications unified and homogenous access to the variety of disparate sources of metadata. These components are designed to be scalable and fault tolerant and provide clients with uninterrupted and high-performance functionality.

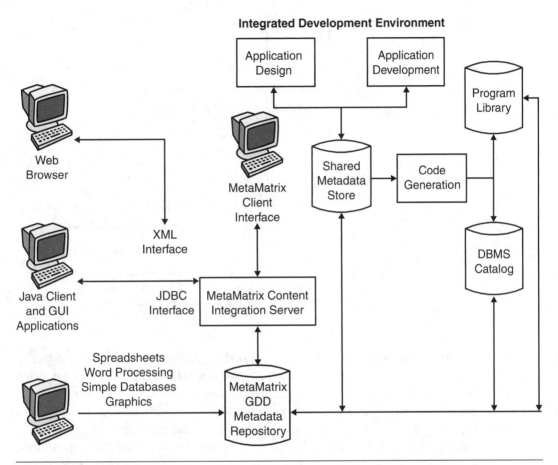

Figure 27-1 The MetaMatrix Content Integration server architecture

The server makes use of connector components that are responsible for managing connections with the metadata stores, translating requests for information to a source-specific protocol, and translating the response. MetaMatrix offers several connectors, including those for relational (JDBC-compliant) database management systems, for various live feeds, and for structured files. However, the server was designed so that creating custom connectors to communicate with other data stores is straightforward and requires a minimal amount of development.

The server's *query engine* is responsible for parsing, validating, planning, and executing the query requests submitted by clients. The query engine uses its own metadata to understand each type of portal-accessible metadata, where

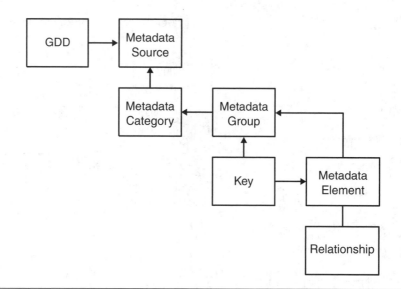

Figure 27-2 The MetaMatrix metamodel

it is stored, how it can be accessed, and the relationships to the metadata in other sources. Queries are specified through an SQL-like query language. Each valid complex query is then broken into atomic queries that involve a single metadata source. During query execution, the atomic queries are submitted to the appropriate connectors (and ultimately to the metadata stores) with as much processing as possible forwarded to the data store to allow optimized access in the store. Finally, results from multiple atomic queries are then joined to create a single result that is sent back to the client application.

The Portal Metamodel

To achieve content integration the MetaMatrix server makes use of metadata residing in a *Global Data Dictionary (GDD)*. The resident metadata describes the content sources that the server is integrating into a unified whole. Metadata in the MetaMatrix GDD is organized according to the MetaMatrix *metamodel*[1] depicted in Figure 27-2.

---

1. The MetaMatrix metamodel describes data sources, data categories, data groups, and so on. However, since we are integrating metadata as opposed to data (in this book), the entities have been appropriately renamed for clarity.

The MetaMatrix Global Data Dictionary consists of a collection of logical sources known as *data sources,* renamed in this diagram to *Metadata Sources*. Because we are integrating a series of metadata sources, these "metadata sources" are in fact *metadata stores.*[2] Metadata describing a metadata source is organized into *metadata categories* that may contain other nested metadata categories, or *metadata groups*. A metadata group represents a collection of related metadata similar to a table in a relational database. Each metadata group contains *metadata elements* that represent atomic units of information provided by a metadata source. Each metadata group may optionally have a set of *keys* and the relationships between metadata groups are stored in the *relationships*.

Applying a Portal to the Typical Metadata Disaster

A portal is being developed to provide visibility into the currently isolated metadata sources that were depicted in Figure 21-3.

Step 1: Modeling the Metadata Sources to MetaMatrix

The first step in building this business portal is describing the metadata sources involved to the MetaMatrix metadata repository. This is necessary before the MetaMatrix server can access the metadata residing in other metadata sources, and it is accomplished using the MetaMatrix Modeler. In our scenario, the sources are depicted in Figure 27-3 and include: word processing files, spreadsheets, and an integrated development environment repository. Because the first two sources cannot provide their metadata directly, the metadata identified for business objectives and projects must be captured using the MetaMatrix Modeler. However, since the integrated development environment uses a shared relational database as its store, the project design metadata can be imported directly into the MetaMatrix Modeler via the processing of extract files. After each source has been modeled, relationships can be created to associate information in the different sources. The result is a single interrelated metadata model of all the sources defined in our scenario.

Using the metadata modeled for our metadata sources, the MetaMatrix server can provide a single point of access for all metadata located throughout the metadata solution architecture.

---

2. As discussed in Chapter 7, one person's data is another person's metadata. MetaMatrix, like most portals, typically is used to integrate disparate data, but can be used to integrate disparate metadata.

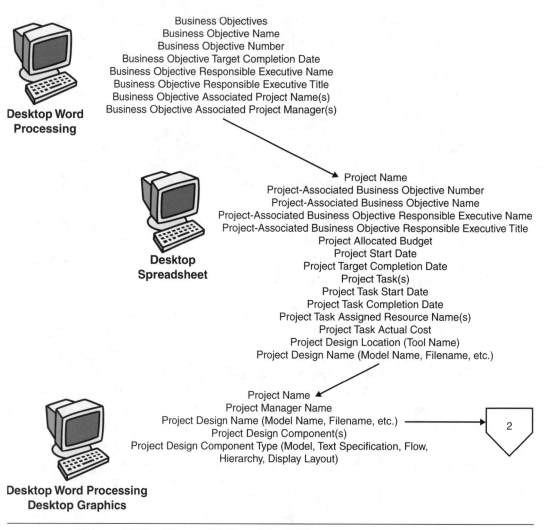

Desktop Word Processing

Business Objectives
Business Objective Name
Business Objective Number
Business Objective Target Completion Date
Business Objective Responsible Executive Name
Business Objective Responsible Executive Title
Business Objective Associated Project Name(s)
Business Objective Associated Project Manager(s)

Desktop Spreadsheet

Project Name
Project-Associated Business Objective Number
Project-Associated Business Objective Name
Project-Associated Business Objective Responsible Executive Name
Project-Associated Business Objective Responsible Executive Title
Project Allocated Budget
Project Start Date
Project Target Completion Date
Project Task(s)
Project Task Start Date
Project Task Completion Date
Project Task Assigned Resource Name(s)
Project Task Actual Cost
Project Design Location (Tool Name)
Project Design Name (Model Name, Filename, etc.)

Project Name
Project Manager Name
Project Design Name (Model Name, Filename, etc.)
Project Design Component(s)
Project Design Component Type (Model, Text Specification, Flow,
Hierarchy, Display Layout)

2

Desktop Word Processing
Desktop Graphics

Figure 27-3   **Figure 21-3 revisited: The current metadata flow**

Step 2: Deploying MetaMatrix Connectors

Once the physical sources that are to be accessed by the MetaMatrix server have been modeled in the metadata repository, the server must be configured with *connectors* that use MetaMatrix metadata to retrieve metadata from the sources. Connectors are plugged into the server via a connector framework.

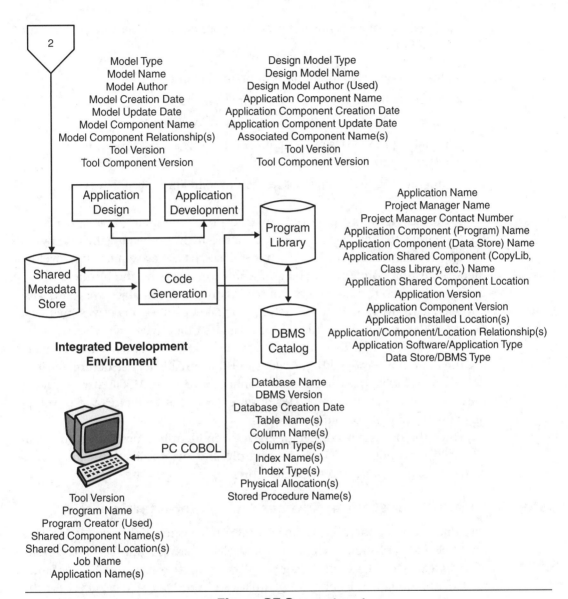

Model Type
Model Name
Model Author
Model Creation Date
Model Update Date
Model Component Name
Model Component Relationship(s)
Tool Version
Tool Component Version

Design Model Type
Design Model Name
Design Model Author (Used)
Application Component Name
Application Component Creation Date
Application Component Update Date
Associated Component Name(s)
Tool Version
Tool Component Version

Application Name
Project Manager Name
Project Manager Contact Number
Application Component (Program) Name
Application Component (Data Store) Name
Application Shared Component (CopyLib,
Class Library, etc.) Name
Application Shared Component Location
Application Version
Application Component Version
Application Installed Location(s)
Application/Component/Location Relationship(s)
Application Software/Application Type
Data Store/DBMS Type

Application Design

Application Development

Program Library

Shared Metadata Store

Code Generation

DBMS Catalog

Integrated Development Environment

Database Name
DBMS Version
Database Creation Date
Table Name(s)
Column Name(s)
Column Type(s)
Index Name(s)
Index Type(s)
Physical Allocation(s)
Stored Procedure Name(s)

PC COBOL

Tool Version
Program Name
Program Creator (Used)
Shared Component Name(s)
Shared Component Location(s)
Job Name
Application Name(s)

Figure 27-3   *continued*

To construct our business portal, five connectors are required to access the modeled metadata:

- Business objective definitions contained in documents
- Project definitions contained in spreadsheets
- High-level project design contained in documents
- Detailed project design contained in the integrated development environment repository
- Program catalogs contained in the program library repository

If the development environment and program catalog repositories are JDBC compliant, they can be accessed via the JDBC connector included with the MetaMatrix server. The three other sources, however, require the development of custom connectors. The connector for accessing the business objectives would open the document containing the business objectives and, with knowledge of the document structure, retrieve business objectives metadata described by the metadata model for business objectives. Likewise, the connector for accessing project definitions would open the spreadsheet containing the definitions and, with knowledge of the spreadsheet structure, retrieve project definitions. Creating custom connectors for the MetaMatrix server is performed using a Connector Development Kit that facilitates the development and testing of custom connectors.

Once the necessary connectors have been identified or created, they can be deployed using the MetaMatrix console, and any application can retrieve metadata in the connected metadata stores via the MetaMatrix server.

Step 3: Query the Metadata Sources Using MetaMatrix

The final step in constructing our portal is to develop the portal itself. This might be accomplished in a number of ways and using a number of technologies: Java Servlets, Java ServerPages (JSPs), or Microsoft Active Server Pages (ASPs). All, though, will submit SQL queries to the MetaMatrix server for the necessary metadata and will use the metadata returned to construct the stream of dynamic HTML. In the case of servlets or JSPs, the queries could be submitted to the MetaMatrix server via the server's Java API. In the case of Microsoft ASPs, the queries could be submitted to the MetaMatrix server via the server's XML servlet API. Regardless, the MetaMatrix server will present a consistent, unified virtual database to the portal.

Our portal in this scenario supports, among other things, the ability to identify the business objectives for a given project. The person using the portal enters the project name and the portal application retrieves the related business objectives using MetaMatrix. Since the MetaMatrix server presents the involved metadata sources as a unified source, all the information necessary to display the business objectives for a project can be retrieved via one query to the MetaMatrix server without regard to the disparate nature of the underlying sources. This query could be as follows:

```
SELECT BusObjectives.BusObj.Name, BusObjectives.BusObj.Number,
       BusObjectives.BusObj.TargetDate
FROM BusObjectives.BusObj, ProjDB.Projects
WHERE BusObjectives.BusObj.Number = ProjDB.Projects.BusObjNumber AND
      ProjDB.Projects.Name = 'Business Objective Portal'
```

Using the metadata, the MetaMatrix server can identify that this query involves more than one source and can construct and execute the necessary individual source-specific queries to retrieve and join the metadata. The portal application simply constructs the single SQL query, submits it to the MetaMatrix server, and then processes the resulting XML response. Using XML parsing or translation technologies such as XSL, the portal application could parse the XML response and generate the desired HTML stream that contains the dynamic content.

Part VI

Maintaining the Metadata Solution

We've implemented our metadata solution. We've established an administrative function and assigned technical metadata solution support. We are right on top of our metamodels and we continually evaluate the needs of the metadata beneficiaries. We have a phased implementation plan in place with enough to keep us busy for the rest of our corporate careers. We're finished. Or are we?

What is a metadata solution today must also be a metadata solution tomorrow. In order for this to happen, the software and metamodels are truly only one aspect of the solution. The other, and perhaps most important, part is the metadata itself.

Ensuring the life of a metadata solution requires more than the technical prowess to keep it alive and accessible in the organization—it also requires a persistent desire of the beneficiaries to keep after it. This desire is based on your ability to supply something they want—solid, consistent, and reliable metadata. Most metadata solution designers and developers separate themselves from this responsibility. Yet, as we discussed, good metadata is a prerequisite to a good metadata solution. It is time to realize that this common sense rule never goes away.

The final section of this book discusses the ways to keep a metadata solution alive. It begins by discussing *metadata responsibilities*—who, why, and when do these responsibilities take effect? After assigning the responsibilities, we discuss how to ensure the perpetual life of metadata. Finally, we will truly be finished when all readers are convinced that *metadata is no longer a runner-up.*

Chapter 28

Metadata Responsibilities

*Just because you don't announce a
plan doesn't mean you don't have one.*
—Herb Kelleher, EVP
Southwest Airlines Co.

Who wants to be responsible for metadata anyway? The intellectual challenge
clearly rests with the analysis and integration of the metadata world, not with
defining *what* metadata needs to be tracked, in what format, and for what reasons. Remember: A metadata solution that has no useful metadata is in demand
as much as a data warehouse that has incorrect data (and I know many of you
know exactly what I mean!). More important, just because you cleaned up the
metadata that you have now doesn't mean it will remain clean and accurate, or
that new metadata that arrives will be clean and accurate. Consider the need
for a plan, but consider the damage you can do by making the plan's execution
a hardship.

IT and End Users' Responsibilities

The delineation between Information Technology and the so-called end user is
not nearly so thick and rigid as it once was. Today many end users function
quite well without the Information Technology professional. In fact, the portions of their business days that run smoothest are often those that do not
involve the use of an application or database that was built by IT professionals.
The metadata and data disasters in many organizations have some roots on the

---

Note: Portions of this chapter were contributed by Patricia Cupoli, Database Design Solutions,
Inc., Bernardsville, New Jersey.

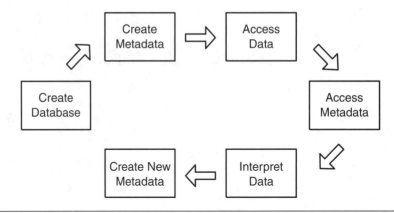

Figure 28-1   Metadata and data: the vicious cycle

IT side. The business community of end users, being forced to deal with the ambiguities and inaccessibility of the information created by their IT groups, has moved more to prebuilt software packages . . . and the software vendors are anxiously waiting to serve them.

Based on the increasingly overlapping nature of information-related responsibilities, metadata accountability has become even more blurred. In most organizations, the creation and maintenance of metadata has no official sponsor. Yet few people realize that the vicious cycle created by this haphazard metadata ownership perpetuates the need for metadata.

Figure 28-1 illustrates the vicious cycle of data/metadata relationships. Typically, a new data store (or database) is created, and often immediately afterward, some data-describing metadata is also created. As the data is accessed, and perhaps not understood, the created metadata is also accessed as a means of clarification. In most situations, this metadata does not meet the mark, so new metadata is created, often representative of a particular perspective and stored in a private stash. The cycle continues and the metadata web self-perpetuates.

Enterprise-Level Metadata Responsibilities

To prevent the ambiguity and conflict that results from multiple metadata efforts, an organization needs a good metadata perspective. The role of the so-called corporate metadata management function can evolve as the metadata solution evolves, with complementary scopes and architectural impact. As a common metamodel is created, its components should correlate with required metadata, *from that point forward*. In other words, as the beneficiaries create the world that the metadata is describing, the metadata should also be created.

Creating metadata should not be equated to the old ways of required system documentation. Instead, it should reflect the fact that much metadata is in fact created eventually. The change must take place on the application time line to result in truly usable metadata. For an enterprise to benefit, the process that aids this result must not inhibit the application's or the data store's progress. Typically, the metadata's key values (standard or common instance values) are defined in advance, and used to correlate instances of the common metamodel with the world of information that is being described. These instances must be available for selection during the metadata creation process.

For example, consider an initial metadata solution that supports application development. Its primary objective is to allow easy selection of application components, including production data (once populated) based on predefined corporate or enterprise categories. In a development environment supported by tools, Table 28-1 indicates where enterprise responsibilities could fall out over the course of each application's delivery. We will revisit this example shortly.

Table 28-1 Sample Enterprise Metadata Responsibilities

IT Enterprise Efforts	Metadata Requirements	Primary Responsibility
Business process model	Identification and description of ■ Business functions ■ Business processes ■ Business activities	Business architects, systems analysts
Data model and architecture	Identification and description of ■ Subject areas ■ Entities ■ Relationships ■ Attributes	Data architects, data analysts
Database design and database architecture	Identification and description of ■ Physical database characteristics ■ Table definitions ■ Column definitions ■ Primary keys ■ Foreign keys ■ Indices	Database administrators
Technical architecture	Identification and description of ■ Hardware ■ Software ■ Network configuration	Technical architects

To satisfy the responsibilities identified here, a metadata management function would be responsible for developing standard:

- *Business functions*—corporate roles that are assigned to specific suborganizations. Examples include accounting, sales, and building maintenance.

- *Business processes*—specific tasks that result in the update of a data store of some type. They are subcomponents of business functions and can be associated with one or more business functions. Examples include hire, pay, purchase, and order.

- *Subject areas*—major data categories that usually equate to components of an enterprise data model. Examples include Product, Facility, Organization.

- *Entities*[1]—logical groupings of data (e.g., a person, place, thing, or event) about which characteristics are collected. Examples include Employee, Department, and Building. Typically entities used throughout an organization are standardized and named in a metadata management function. All entities relate to a subject area as either a subtype or a more specific classification.

- *Attributes*—named characteristics of entities. Most organizations require standard names for attributes that must exist in common entities. Metadata management standardizes the names of these attributes, as well as provides common values and formats. Examples include Social Security Number, Product Name, and Employee Start Date.

- *Hardware*—physical network components deployed throughout an organization. Examples include servers, printers, and routers. Metadata management would standardize the identification of these components in terms of their names and attributes.

- *Software*—named applications, either purchased or internally developed. Examples include accounting systems, decision support systems, and desktop software packages. As with hardware requirements, the metadata management organization would standardize the identification of software in terms of its names and attributes.

---

1. See the Additional Readings section for sources of information about logical data modeling.

Project-Level Metadata Responsibilities

Once the common metadata requirements and their associated standard values have been identified, project-level metadata access can result. Each project must be associated with one or more of the predefined enterprise metadata standard instances, and must also define complementary project-specific metadata instances in support (or eventual support)[2] of the common metamodel.

In many companies, the business analyst and project manager conceptualize the project with business management, develop a project statement and project objectives, and obtain approvals. The project manager then identifies project tasks and resources in order to prepare a project plan. Together they prepare project schedules and budgets. They communicate with the project team and project sponsors constantly throughout the project. The project managers update the project plan based on status. These documents are sources of metadata or descriptive information. If the metadata solution is set up to handle project management, then project management has the primary responsibility to create, update, and delete these sources of metadata.

Project requirements are investigated during the analysis phase. These requirements have descriptive metadata associated with them—whether it is a business process model, data model, or data flow diagram. The metadata requirements include such examples as model name, definition, model type, and model author. The technical architects are working on a project-related tool architecture that is descriptive and should be documented.

The data analysts develop a detailed logical data model in the design phase and they or the DBAs develop the first cut of a physical relational or dimensional model. Links between the logical and physical models are developed here. Either the data analyst or the business analyst is determining the end-user metadata needs that must be accessible and whether a specific reporting tool will be involved. The developers are constructing applications and components, as well as implementation and test plans. Database administrators create and tune the database. Business users conduct the testing and assist with the cutover to production. All of these tasks create *and* require metadata.

The project manager is keeping a close watch on the project and its readiness for production and is in communication with many groups. The metadata

---

2. Because the common metamodel may represent only portions of one metadata beneficiary's metadata requirements, full project metadata requirements might exceed those of the common metamodel.

that relates to the overall project remains accessible and is updated as necessary. In Table 28-2 the responsibilities of each participant are illustrated.

Table 28-2 Metadata Creation Responsibilities by Source and Project Phase

Project Phase	Metadata Sources and Requirements	Primary Responsibility	Metadata Practice: Create, Read, Update, Delete (CRUD)
Planning	Business objectives	Executive management	CRUD
	Project statement, project objectives	Business analysts, project managers	CRU
	Project scope refinement	Business analysts, project managers	CRU
	Project tasks	Project managers with team	CRUD
	Project costs and time estimations	Project managers	CRUD
	Project schedule, project budget	Project managers	CRU
	Preliminary project plan	Business analysts, project managers	CRU
	Project approval document	Business analysts, project managers	RU
Analysis	Hardware and software tool product evaluations	Technical architects	CRU
	Recommended technical approaches for project	Technical architects	CRU
	Project technical architectures	Technical architects	CRUD
	Project requirements descriptions ■ Functional requirements ■ Presentation ■ Client reporting	Business analysts, systems analysts, developers	CRUD
	Project requirements descriptions ■ Data transformation rules ■ Business rules	Systems analyst, business analyst, data analyst	CRU

Project Phase	Metadata Sources and Requirements	Primary Responsibility	Metadata Practice: Create, Read, Update, Delete (CRUD)
	Project requirements descriptions ■ Data ■ Metadata	Data analysts	CRU
	New subject areas, entities, and relationships	Data analysts	CRU
	Search for reusable data and metadata for project	Data analysts	R
	Data access rules	Business analysts	CRU
	Project business process models	Business analysts	CRU
	Swim lanes diagrams	Business analysts	CRU
	Context data flow diagram or data process flow diagram	Business analysts, project managers	CRU
	Project plan updates	Project managers	RU
	Project communications	Project managers	CRU
	Logical data model and metadata for entities, attributes, data domains, primary key(s)	Data analysts	CRU
Design	Review tool approaches	Technical architects	RU
	Validation questions for logical models	Data analysts	CRU
	Source-to-target data mappings (for data warehouse)	Business analysts, data analysts	CRU
	Data sources documentation, metadata definitions	Data analysts	CRU
	End-user metadata directory	Data analysts, metadata analysts	CRU
	First-cut physical data model or warehouse dimensional model	Data analysts, DBA	CRU

continued

Table 28-2   Metadata Creation Responsibilities by Source and Project Phase
         continued

Project Phase	Metadata Sources and Requirements	Primary Responsibility	Metadata Practice: Create, Read, Update, Delete (CRUD)
Design *(cont'd)*	Link logical model to physical model	Data analysts, DBA	RU
	Test plans, implementation plans	Developers	CRU
	Conceptual and detailed designs	Developers	CRU
	Project plan updates	Project managers	RU
	Project communications	Project managers	CRU
Development	Referential integrity constraints	DBA	CRU
	DDL	DBA	CRU
	(Warehouse) load procedures	Developers	CRU
	Data transformation, rules procedures (warehouse)	Developers	CRU
Development, testing	Performance benchmark	Developers	RU
	Production readiness	Project managers	RU
Implementation	Systems components	Developers	RU
	Data structures and DDL generation	DBA	RU
	Project plan updates	Project managers	RU
	Project communications	Project managers	RU
	Project documentation	Project manager and team	CRU
Ongoing support	Approved production data elements and associated metadata changes	Data analysts	RU
	Logical data models	Data analysts	RU
	Program changes	Developers	CRU

Project Phase	Metadata Sources and Requirements	Primary Responsibility	Metadata Practice: Create, Read, Update, Delete (CRUD)
	Integrated application logical data model with enterprise data model	Data analysts	RU
	Data and metadata standards, policies, procedures	Data analysts	CRUD
	Technical architectures	Technical architects	CRUD
	Database changes	DBA	CRUD

End-User Metadata Responsibilities

End-user analysts are consumers of certain metadata in any environment. They use metadata for querying, navigating, and reporting. Some of these end-user analysts have been known to create their own metadata to use in a local reporting tool.

End users in some organizations may be responsible for metadata through a data/metadata steward role and/or participation in systems development. They are a source of definitions that represent what the data really means and how it should be modeled. They also keep a watchful eye on the quality of data and metadata and provide feedback to the appropriate groups.

Many developers of metadata solutions tend to trivialize the role of the business user. Because the design and development of metadata solutions require technical prowess, people who have their noses to the grindstone typically forget the importance of this key metadata beneficiary. Although it may be true that the end user may access metadata through a tool, instead of directly from a common metadata store of any type, the quality of the metadata is directly related to the amount of the end user's involvement during both enterprise metadata predefinition and project-level metadata supplementation. If our end users didn't understand what metadata was all about, they wouldn't be creating their own on a regular basis.

Suggested Organizational Structures

We have discussed many responsibilities that surround the planning, design, and implementation of metadata solutions. Many of them are intermingled throughout organizations. Because they are related yet quite different in terms of their individual responsibilities, we briefly review them here:

Data administration/management. This responsibility has been in existence for quite some time, stemming back to the 1970s when data dictionaries first became popular. These individuals typically handled the definition and control of data. In essence, they standardized data naming, developed and populated corporate data definitions, and as application development moved into the world of relational databases, they became responsible for the development and/or review of logical data models. Because the data management function does require the creation of data-oriented metadata, many organizations assign metadata management responsibilities to data management professionals.

Metadata management. A relatively new responsibility, having originated during the last five years in response to the demand for data warehousing.[3] The management of metadata involves participation in metadata requirements analysis, as discussed in Part II of this book. However, the development and maintenance of all metamodels—common, unique, and specific—are usually *not* handled by this function, particularly when *tools* form a part of the metadata solution. Finally, the development of metadata standards, as discussed in this chapter, is a key responsibility in this area. This function determines the standard metadata instances (enterprise or corporate values, as discussed earlier in this chapter), as well as the types of metadata to be collected at various points in the application lifecycle.

Metadata solution administration. Often called repository administration, this function is quite technical. It is responsible for the design, development, and support of the full metadata solution. Because the requirements of this role include the *ability to think like a tool*, development experience is a must. These individuals develop the metamodels and participate in the metadata requirements analysis process. The maintenance

---

3. See the Additional Readings section for sources of information about data warehousing.

of the common metamodel, as well as the maintenance and expansion of the full metadata solution, fall within this function's responsibility. The specifics of this role are discussed in Chapter 19.

Database administration. Technically sophisticated, database administrators create, monitor, and physically design production databases. There are DBAs for each installed database management system (DBMS), and they work closely with the development organizations by assisting them with database loading, access, and tuning.

Data stewards. Usually stationed in the business community, data stewards take responsibility for all data in a particular enterprise subject area (e.g., Product). They are typically the individuals who determine corporate definitions, and official data. Recently, data stewards have been getting involved with the identification of official metadata.

These functions are intertwined. In fact, many organizations have combined some of them into one role, often within the same organization.

Consider the way metadata relates to both data and the metadata solution over the course of its development. In Figure 28-2 the creators of the metadata solution are members of both the *Metadata Solution Administration* and the *Metadata Management* functions. Once a functional metadata solution environment is in place with corporate or enterprise standard instances of the

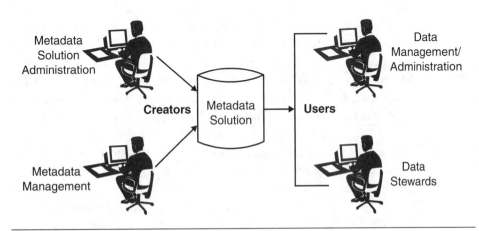

Figure 28-2 **The conceptual life cycle of metadata and data**

common metamodel, it is available for use by both *Data Management/Data Administration* and business area *Data Stewards.*

To perpetuate metadata's accuracy, a permanent organization or set of organizations must fulfill the roles that have been identified thus far:

- Data Management
- Metadata Management
- Metadata Solution Administration

Where do they fit in the organization? There is a strong belief that these responsibilities all belong to the IT organization. However, it should be refreshing to know that many end-user organizations have established fully operational metadata support functions focused on a limited scope metadata solution. We will review each option.

Metadata Support in IT

The most common way to assign metadata responsibilities is to keep them in the IT world. The most common means to create inappropriate metadata solutions is to ignore the business community. In light of these two statements, you should realize that end users *must* be involved, even if purely on a customer basis. All customers should have a say in what is being built or purchased for them.

Depending on the current setup of your IT organization, you could be extremely project focused (i.e., each application is its own organization with its own budget and management practices), somewhat infrastructure focused (i.e., there are standards and interproject organizations that support all projects, irrespective of budget), or totally customer focused (i.e., each end-user organization has an associated IT support function). Irrespective of the situation, metadata management and support *must* be interproject and intercustomer for it to be successful from both standardization and usability perspectives.

As illustrated in Figure 28-3, a separate organization, Metadata Solution Administration, handles all metadata standardization and definition as well as the overall design and support of the metadata solution (metadata solution administration). The illustrated scenario represents a project-specific organization with a separate infrastructure that handles all cross-project standardization and support. Although not illustrated, the end-user business community works closely with the Metadata Management organization to define requirements.

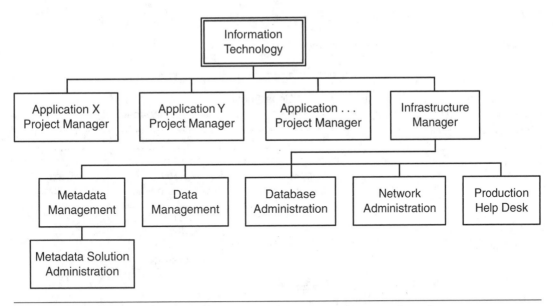

Figure 28-3 **The IT-based metadata support function**

End-User Metadata Support

Many business area functions have taken responsibility for their own data. Due originally to the proprietary or unique requirements of their business area, they established their own reporting databases, acquired their own software packages, and now, in many cases, are integrating all of these with their own metadata gateways or enterprise portals. Metadata has become a new but important functional responsibility in their organizations.

In a business area metadata management function, the scope of the supported metadata solution revolves around a standalone data warehouse or set of databases unique to that organization. It is common, however, for some aspect of this set of data to tie directly, via link or redundantly, to a corporate application or database. To complicate matters, purchased packages include their own metadata. Irrespective of the connection, the metadata that supports this organization focuses only on their definitions, their requirements, and perhaps their beneficiaries.

Figure 28-4 depicts a typical business area metadata management scenario. It is interesting to note that an IT organization does exist, and has a data management function. The business area also has a data management function, which probably focuses on data stewardship responsibilities—identification of

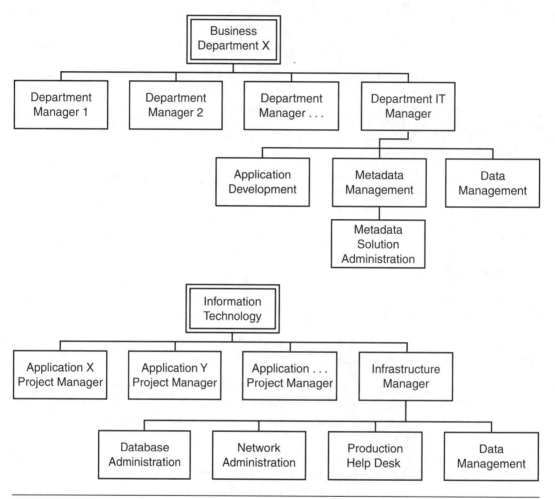

Figure 28-4   The business area metadata management function

official data, establishment of official definitions, and general support of data analysis. All these responsibilities are often handled in IT; however, in this scenario no metadata management function exists in IT.

Perpetuating a metadata solution requires perpetuating the metadata. The place that this responsibility should reside depends entirely on how other interproject resources are managed in the organization. The more centralized the responsibility becomes, the more standardized the metadata becomes. The more standardized the metadata becomes, the more successful the metadata exchange and portal-based metadata gateways are bound to be—everyone (software and people) will be speaking the same language.

Chapter 29

Ensuring Metadata's Livelihood

The fully implemented metadata solution represents a solid architecture from which metadata can be accessed. The full solution is to be used by metadata beneficiaries both within and outside the solution's world. The process presented in this book of implementing the full metadata solution began with an identification of all current and potential metadata beneficiaries. Each beneficiary was then analyzed in terms of its metadata requirements. Metadata requirements were analyzed from a "total beneficiary" perspective and organized into multiple metamodels. The common metamodel was used to begin the development of a full metadata solution architecture. Architectural requirements were then used to select and implement the "right" solution, which typically involved more than one metadata store.

To perpetuate the functionality and livelihood of any implemented metadata solution, a plan for maintenance and growth should be in place. Metadata solutions can grow or expand in several ways:

- *Functionally*, by increasing the roles played either by the overall metadata solution or by one or more of its metadata-supplying components
- *Deeply*, by covering a more intensive set of metadata in the same architecture
- *Widely*, by embracing more metadata beneficiaries with specific or unique metadata needs

A properly designed metadata solution does not require major revamping in order to accommodate expansion. The process by which to encompass extra pieces for existing metadata solutions is a smaller version of the initial process described throughout this book.

Adding the Functionality and Contents of Additional Metadata Stores

Metadata solutions are designed to be solid yet expandable. The practicality of initial implementations typically requires restriction of initial scopes to specific functional areas and/or metadata groupings. In other words, metadata solutions are designed to grow.

As illustrated in Figure 29-1, this initial metadata solution architecture depicts the separate storage of common metadata. Common metadata access processes are used by all components in the metadata solution architecture as the means of getting to metadata that is not common, which by nature of this architecture does not reside in the same metadata store but is kept where it is used. In a nutshell, this initial architecture resembles that of a preliminary enterprise portal.

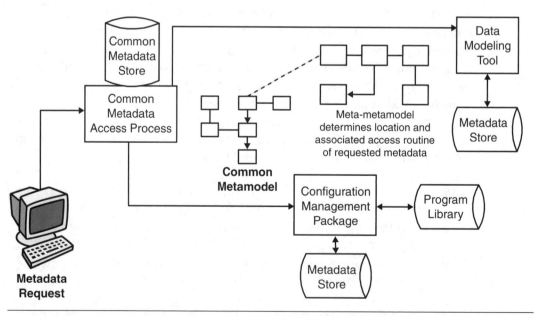

Figure 29-1 **The initial metadata solution architecture**

The delivered metadata solution was established to provide an easily accessible and metadata-based set of components to perform the following functions:

Logical and physical data modeling, for new and existing databases, based on the premise that logical definitions of data elements form the basis for data analysis once the logical data models are completed.

Application configuration management, focusing on the provision of an application component inventory. This aspect of the metadata solution serves as a connection between logical data elements and their physical implementations in application data stores *when the two metadata instances exist.* Minimally, people looking only for physical data element instances and aliases would be able to search the configuration management metadata.

In order to perform these functions, the accessible metadata spans the following metamodels:

Tool-based logical data modeling, focusing on the data modeling tool's specific metadata and its organization in the tool

Tool-based physical data modeling, focusing again on the same data modeling tool and the metadata associated with the physical database's representation of a particular logical data model, as well as the relationships between the metadata of the logical data model and the metadata surrounding its physical database implementation

Configuration management, as represented in the scoped *Configuration Management Package* to identify installed applications, components, versions, and their relationships

As is common with most metadata solutions of this initial magnitude, expansion will be required from both functional and metadata coverage points of view. Depending of course on the thrust of the organization (or suborganization) targeted by this *initial* metadata solution, the practical next steps could include any of the following:

Process modeling, potentially via another tool, with connections to not only the existing world of logical and physical data but also the existing physical configurations that are represented in the configuration management package

Directory-based information access, allowing access to physical data via standard terms and subject areas. These terms and subject areas may be represented in logical data models already described by the initial metadata scope

Data warehouse decision support, taking all metadata that focuses on data warehouse sources and making it accessible to end-user analysts who need to question the values in a production data warehouse

As the initial metadata solution grows, additional components become part of its architecture. Likewise, additional metadata beneficiaries, often metadata suppliers or recipients themselves, will continue to form part of the overall picture. Consider, for example, the type of analysis that would be required if we decided to include a data warehouse effort as part of our metadata solution architecture.

Additional Metadata Beneficiaries

As with initial metadata solution requirements, expanding a metadata solution requires us to list our additional metadata beneficiaries:

- Decision Support Tool
- End-User Data Warehouse Analysts
- Data Warehouse (potentially a specialized type of database, only if it has distinct metadata requirements)

Metadata Requirements for Additional Metadata Beneficiaries

Again, we need to consider the metadata requirements of these beneficiaries in comparison to those of our original beneficiary set. Are there any *new* metadata requirements? Are they unique to one or more of these new beneficiary categories? Are they so unique that *only* that beneficiary category requires them? Additional metamodels are often necessary when the range of new metadata falls beyond a manageable set of metadata elements. Minimally, new metadata requirements are related to existing common metadata to determine points of interface. Finally, each new metadata requirement is compared to that which is already a part of the metadata solution to determine whether it is a new requirement, or merely another name for one that already resides in the architecture. When metadata redundancy exists, an assigned metadata of record is required.

Consider the new requirements listed in Table 29-1. Clearly, some of the additional requirements appear for the first time (e.g., Report Name, Report Column Calculation, Report Display Type, Data Element Source Data Store, Data Element Transitional Procedure Name). Other additional requirements may be variations of existing metadata, as Table 29-2 shows.

Table 29-1 Analysis of Additional Metadata Requirements

Metadata by Official Source			
Data Modeling Tool	**Configuration Management Package**	**Program Library**	**Common Metamodel**
Data Modeling Tool Name	Project Name	Application Name	Tool Name
Data Modeling Tool Version	Project Manager Name	Application Type	Tool Version
Data Modeling Tool Userid	Job Name	Application Version	Tool Userid
Logical Data Model Name	Job Creation Date	Application Last Update Date	Entity Name
Logical Data Model Creation Date	Application Name	Program Name	Data Store Name
Logical Data Model Creator	Application Version	Program Version	Data Store Type
Entity Name	Program Name	External Component Name	Attribute Name
Entity Definition	Program Version	External Component Version	Data Element Name
Attribute Name	Program Component Name	Data Store Name	Application Name
Attribute Definition	Program Component Type	Data Store Type	Program Name
Relationship Name	Program Component Version	Data Element Name	
Relationship Type			
Primary Key Name			
Alternate Key Name			
Foreign Key Name			
Domain Name			
Domain Values			
Physical Data Model Name			
Physical Data Model Creation Date			
Physical Data Model Creator			
DBMS Name			
DBMS Type			
DBMS Version Number			
Database Name			
Database Creation Date			
Table Name			
Column Name			
Index Name			
Index Type			

continued

Table 29-1   Analysis of Additional Metadata Requirements   *continued*

Additional Metadata Requirements		
Decision Support Tool	**End-User Data Analysts**	**Data Warehouse**
Decision Support Tool Name	Data Element Name	DBMS Name
Decision Support Tool Version	Data Element Source Data Store	DBMS Type
Decision Support Tool Userid	Data Element Source Data	DBMS Version
Decision Support Tool User Name	Element	Database Name
Report Name	Data Element Transitional	Table Name
Report Creation Userid	Procedure Name	Column Name
Report Creation Date	Data Element Definition	
Report Column Name	Data Element Derivation Rule(s)	
Report Column Definition	Data Element Owner	
Report Column Calculation		
Report Display Type		

Table 29-2   Comparing "New" Requirements to Existing Metadata

"New" Metadata Requirement	Existing Variation
Decision Support Tool Name	Tool Name
Report Column Name	Data Element Name[a]
Data Element Source Data Store	Data Store Name
Data Element Source Data Element	Data Element Name

a. Further data analysis would be required to draw the conclusion that one is a variation of the other. If some elements are created solely for their display on a report (i.e., they are not physically stored elsewhere), then this conclusion may not be accurate. See the Additional Readings section for books about data warehouses.

These conclusions can be based only on an analysis of the metadata instances. In fact, it may be true that Data Element Source Data Stores are Data Stores, but it may also be necessary to track an additional relationship (Source), which is not contained in our metadata solution.

Keeping the Architecture in Place

After a complete metadata analysis for all additional beneficiaries, new metadata sources and recipients are identified, and each must be tied to the common metadata in one way or another. In our example, there are several connection points to the existing common metadata, so there is no need to expand that area of the metadata solution. Flexibility in the original design almost guarantees a connection at one of these points:

- Data Store Name
- Attribute Name
- Data Element Name
- Application Name
- Program Name

Furthermore, at the meta-meta level, instances are added when new metadata sources become part of the overall metadata solution. As discussed in Part III about meta-meta land, these instances are typically associated with specific types of metadata.

The revised metadata solution architecture now contains data warehousing–specific metadata components.

As illustrated in Figure 29-2, the *Decision Support Tool* now participates as a metadata solution component. Most of its metadata requirements are specific in that they relate only to reports generated by the tool itself. These will remain in the metadata store of the decision support tool. Other metadata requirements, however, most notably the metadata that surrounds the data warehouse implementation, will require access to the full architecture via the *Common Metadata Access Process.*

As metadata solution architectures are expanded, it is essential that each additional "point" on the line receive an honest assessment:

Is this additional point going to create a metadata web? That is, will the addition of this metadata store make it confusing, if not impossible, to determine which metadata means what? Typically, this issue is addressed via access routines specific to metadata beneficiaries. Keep those who know their metadata as it is from accessing other metadata that could confuse their perspectives. More important, keep them from *creating* metadata that could add redundancy (of course, this theory assumes that *their* metadata is not dangerously off, and that their metadata store can be controlled via security levels). Eventually, the *best* metadata wins in this situation . . . but how metadata wins this prestigious label is part of a planned metadata release process.

Is this additional point capable of receiving metadata from other points in the architecture? In the ideal metadata solution world, the metadata of

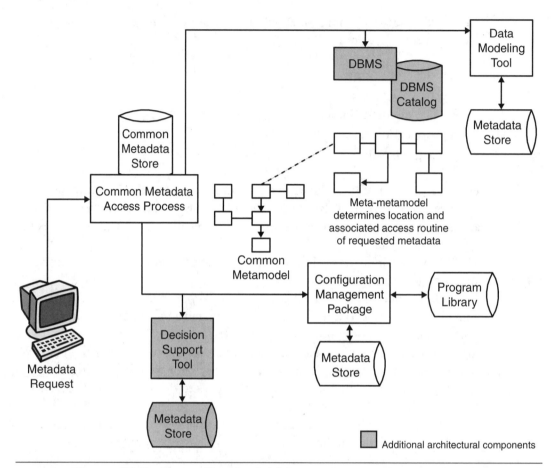

Figure 29-2   Expanding the initial metadata solution architecture

record is propagated. Unfortunately, not all vendors like the idea of receiving things from other vendors' products, although the world is changing, as discussed when we addressed metadata standards.[1]

Is this additional point capable of supplying metadata to other points in the architecture? Minimally, new points should be able to exchange metadata with other components of the metadata solution architecture. At worst, the exchange process is quite clumsy (e.g., getting extracts). At best, exchange takes advantage of newer on-demand technologies (e.g., XML, API-driven access, etc.).

---

1. Metadata standards are discussed in Chapter 16.

Is this additional point going to do more harm than good? Herein lies the rub. If you don't like the answers to the preceding questions, then perhaps this component should remain an outsider . . . at least until the answers change!

Phased Implementation

Performing required analysis *before* the adding of components to a metadata solution architecture ensures a phased implementation. Often, the best of solutions is short lived as a result of its initial success. As contradictory as this may seem, once the well-planned and successful initial metadata solution architecture is released, everyone else in the organization wants to get on the bandwagon. If they are interested only in receiving metadata, as they typically are, then their metadata request may need further analysis.

What will the proposed architectural component do with the new metadata, once received?

- Where will it be stored?
- Will it be supplied to other metadata recipients?
- Will it be merged with existing metadata to create quasi-redundant metadata?
- Will it simply be referenced in a read-only fashion?

How often will this "new" metadata be needed by the potential component? What means of access will be used?

In what format, if any, must the metadata be received?

Evaluation of these metadata recipient issues can lead to restriction of the initial metadata distribution and/or access in order to continue quality control of the metadata solution. The result is a *phased implementation*.

Consideration of the effects of adding a metadata solution component would guide architectural expansion to be phased as follows:

First release—the addition of all receipt-only metadata solution components. Metadata distribution to these components must be on a regular or demand basis to ensure the accuracy of their overall metadata perspectives. Received metadata should originate from common metadata stores and should be based on the metadata-of-record instances.

Second release—the addition of any receipt-only metadata solution components that will provide additional functionality and/or supplemental metadata depth to the metadata solution as it existed. These architectural
components will either use existing metadata to support additional roles
or contain additional metadata that will enhance the overall metadata
solution. Addition of functionality and metadata requires new beneficiary-
specific analysis. This analysis should focus on not only the metadata in
the new component but also the necessary bidirectional connections or
interfaces between the new component and the overall metadata solution. Depending on the volume of additions in the second release, it may
be necessary to prioritize the rollout of components in this group.

Third release—All metadata solution architectural add-ons that bring with them
additional metadata beneficiaries with unique or specific requirements.
These are requirements that cannot be met earlier and, therefore, should be
postponed to this last phase of metadata solution enhancement. These beneficiaries and their associated requirements will require full analysis and
most likely require the addition of common metadata interfaces, security-
based displays, and component-specific access requirements.

Revising IT Processes

In addition to the analysis associated with the planned and controlled expansion of a metadata solution, the role of the overall solution in an organization's
processes is always the most important perspective under which metadata
should thrive. Simply stated, metadata must continue to support the organization in a positive way as the metadata solution expands—and the metadata
solution needs the support of complimentary IT processes.

If the metadata solution evolves into the only place where internal and
external beneficiaries can determine the definition of a data element, then it is
essential that this role continue as data is created and acquired and also as data
is discontinued. During the days of the "old school philosophy," this was the
responsibility of a data management organization. In today's world of metadata
solutions, this should no longer be viewed as a responsibility, but as the joint
result of the metadata solution's involvement in any IT process surrounding
the maintenance of its associated metadata. It is not necessarily a bad thing to
have many hands in the pot, but if each hand changes what another hand created, then some process streamlining may be required.

Constant evaluation of metadata flows is the way to identify process redundancy or conflict. As a metadata solution architecture expands, revisit the flow of metadata as it was composed by the immediate metadata beneficiaries throughout the organization. If stumbling blocks or multidirectional forks multiply exponentially as the depth and width of the metadata solution expands, consider evaluating the processes that use or create the metadata of interest.

Successful metadata-based IT processes make the use of metadata solutions a benefit, not a hardship. Metadata that is immediately accessible should help, not hinder. Finally, the metadata should be of such quality that it *could* be used over and over again in such a manner that it makes no sense to recreate it.

Chapter 30

Metadata Is No Longer a Runner-Up

Concern should drive us into action
and not into a depression.
—Karen Horney

Complicated? Too much work? Not worth my time? The world of data has always been complicated. What is considered data today was clearly inconceivable just a short time ago. The more data we deal with, the more metadata we deal with. The more metadata we deal with, the more we need a metadata solution.

Many metadata publications address the *future* of metadata as one of metadata standards and plug-and-play metadata gateways. Fortunately or unfortunately, we are already experiencing the future. Many of the solutions addressed in this book represent standards-based metadata exchange (e.g., XML in Chapters 15 and 25) and portal-based technology (in Chapters 24 and 27). It is time to prepare our metadata, our metadata support, and our priorities for a true metadata solution.

Current Tasks to Ensure an Organization's Metadata Readiness

Before anyone rushes to start the implementation of a new technology, its impact on "the way things are" right now must be evaluated from the following two perspectives:

Note: Horney quote (in *Self-Analysis,* New York: Norton, 1970) from *The New York Public Library Book of Twentieth-Century American Quotations.* Copyright © 1992 by The Stonesong Press, Inc., and The New York Public Library. Used with permission.

1. How the technology will improve "the way things are"
2. How "the way things are" must accommodate the new technology

The two circumstances are reciprocal. As you prepare to implement a metadata solution, the organization should begin to plan for its infiltration. Begin by establishing solid, desirable metadata. This task should start now, and focus on the eventual role of metadata with the aid of an implemented metadata solution.

Identify

Decide what metadata needs to be tracked, irrespective of the metadata solution plans. As we have discussed, full metadata requirements analysis unveils the metadata that is in demand. You must be ready to accommodate minimally the common aspects of these requirements, or the common metamodel. Begin a metadata management function now and assign it the responsibility of metadata requirements analysis. Chapter 19 provides a simple starting point for identifying basic required metadata.

Standardize

Once identified, common metadata must be standardized as much as is reasonably possible. Will *Name* always be called *Name*? Will it sometimes be called *Identity* and other times be called *Title*? In today's world of metadata webs, the answer to questions like these is Yes. Within your organization, you can begin by agreeing in principle to a standardized term for all common metadata. This term will represent the official occurrence, or the metadata of record.

Proliferate

Once metadata is identified and standardized, it is time to see that it is deployed. The first aspects of deployment require the availability of standardized metadata instances. Good metadata values are meant to be shared.

Achieving these initial tasks makes an organization ripe for metadata impact. Common metadata translates into a set of common tags used to identify metadata instances that might be exchanged among metadata beneficiaries. Today's XML documents thrive on the existence of standardized tags. The more these tags appear throughout the organization, the less translation and merging will be involved as you implement more and more of a metadata-triggered search-and-retrieve solution.

Short-Term Metadata Objectives

Upon achieving the identified metadata preparation, focus your metadata objectives on six-month achievable milestones:

- Include the identification and reuse of standard metadata as part of development and delivery of all new information. As the need for new information arises, make sure that the populated common metadata is used to determine whether the need is real.
- Scope metadata requirements around information delivery to support the 5 Questions:[1]

    1. What data do we have?
    2. What does it mean?
    3. Where is it?
    4. How did it get there?
    5. How do I get it (Go get it for me!)?

- Establish a minimally focused metadata solution to support the above for new (scoped) information delivery.[2,3]
- Formalize the support of the initial metadata solution by creating a proper metadata solution administration function.

Short-term metadata objectives should span from six months to one year before completion.

Long-Term Metadata-Based Goals

Once a functional metadata solution is in place and a fully operational metadata management activity is properly pursuing its livelihood, the management of an

---

1. The 5 Questions is a trademark of and the questions and method are copyrighted by Database Design Solutions, Inc., Bernardsville, New Jersey.

2. "New" information delivery refers to the delivery of information in a new package or from a different perspective. The information may already exist in the organization.

3. "Scope" can refer to a defined set of source information, a defined set of tool suppliers or recipients, or a defined set of metadata beneficiaries, as discussed in Chapter 11.

organization's metadata becomes part of an overall strategic initiative. Likewise, the metadata solution increases substantially in scope by accommodating more architectural components and their associated functionality. Common metamodels may grow in depth; more specific and unique metamodels[4] will become part of the metadata solution architecture. The creation and access of information, regardless of its type, should become more and more metadata-based.

- *Standardized metadata should become a routine aspect of all information creation.* Via the use of an active metadata solution, it will be impossible to create new information or information derivatives without creating the required metadata. The metadata solution will function invisibly, much like today's file management systems, which require the creation of standardized filenames and types before a file is known to the operating system.

- *All information access should be the result of browserlike metadata-based searches.* The same metadata that is automatically created will be used as a primary search-and-retrieve criterion when information is required.

- *Industry standards should have a positive impact on developed metadata solutions.* Metadata exchange standards will be formalized by industry as well as by functional metamodel. Vendor products will have no choice but to support these standards and, therefore, integrate with the existing metadata solution fairly easily.

- *Sharing and exchanging metadata between and among organizations should be standards based.* Purchased information will include predefined standard metadata in support of international standards. Metadata solutions will automatically support this exchange via standard metamodels.

- *The need for common metadata stores should decrease exponentially as common metadata exchange standards and associated metamodels are deployed and accepted.* Over time, metadata requirements analysis will eventually be a task left to the standards committees. These groups will define the metamodels that reflect requirements in certain industries, software product categories, and information exchange formats. Our strategic metadata solution architecture will be

---

4. Common, unique, and specific metamodels are discussed in Chapter 9.

able to accommodate a generic metadata transfer mechanism, based on the flexibility of our component-based metadata architecture.

Business Strategy and IT Collaboration

We have already seen the handshake between Information Technology and Business Strategy. Appointments of Chief Information Officers began the partnership that changed IT's role from reactive to strategic support. Organizations realized during the 1990s that their largest assets were derivable from the data they already have. Unfortunately, they were unable to get to this information on demand.

Having realized the importance of stored information in determining business strategy, businesses moved to the Web as a means of collecting even more information. Who visits our Web pages? How many Web page visitors actually purchase a product? Are existing customers moving to e-commerce transactions? What is the difference between the traditional customer profile and the new electronic customer? To answer these questions, we must start with metadata: What data do we have? What does it mean? Where is it?

For perhaps the first time, business objectives are being incorporated into an organization's information till. The case study in Part V reflects "A Typical Metadata Disaster" and some evolving solutions, many of which address the incorporation of objectives into the metadata solution's contents. Aligning business strategy with Information Technology requires such an approach:

- Define corporate objectives.
- Plan objective accomplishments via approved initiatives.
- Relate initiatives to their IT rollouts:
  - ◆ Specifications
  - ◆ Design models and their components
  - ◆ Applications and their components
  - ◆ Data stores (databases, data warehouses, etc.)
  - ◆ Stored information
- Populate various metamodels along the way.

The collaboration of IT results and the business initiatives that drive them guarantees information on demand, as long as the metadata is maintained and accessible throughout the rollout.

If Not Now, When?

It is always easier to wait for that silver bullet. Vendors take advantage of our desire to find the perfect off-the-shelf metadata solution by constantly offering *a piece* of the overall solution. True metadata-based information on demand requires the definition of a metadata-based set of processes. The acquisition of a tool in and of itself will not ease the information blockage that most organizations face. The time for full metadata initiatives is now.

Everyone talks about how the Web is changing the way we do business. Few people, however, consider the impact that an internationally accessible set of software can have on internal information-based processes. Without considering metadata and its relationship to the categorization and definition of information, the information will never become available on demand. Many people choose to wait for formalized standards-based metadata definition, but waiting could work only if it were possible to freeze information creation until the perfect, all-encompassing standard arrives. If we don't start working now toward information on demand, when will we profit from its existence?

Appendix A

Glossary

Active in development   A metadata solution state that guarantees its involvement in at least one aspect of the development process. This state is used to ensure the accuracy of the metadata solution's contents.

Active in production   A metadata solution state that requires full dependency on the metadata solution as an information gateway. When the metadata solution is not available, no one can access anything in its scope of coverage.

ADE   (Application Development Environment)   The collection of processes, data, software, and tools used during the definition, design, and creation of a resulting set of computer programs and databases that mechanize or enhance a set of business activities.

ANSI   (American National Standards Institute)   An early IT standards agency sponsored by the U.S. government.

API   (Application Program Interface)   A common subroutine or set of program code that can be called from applications as a means of accessing contents in a metadata store or other database

Application blinders   The inability to see beyond an immediate need when determining metadata solution requirements.

Attribute   A named characteristic of an entity; see *Entity*.

Batch   Application processing that occurs outside the main application as a separate procedure. Batch processes are typically initiated manually or scheduled to run on a regular basis.

Beneficiary   A person or tool that supplies or receives metadata.

Business rules   Statements that refer to what can and should be done (within an application), so that from the point of view of a newcomer, all undocumented facts surrounding a business or business process will become accessible and will help explain the processing in an application.

CASE (computer-aided software engineering)   The philosophy that encourages the standardized capture of the application development process by documenting the application from conception through coding in a reusable, accessible automated tool; any software product that helps to implement the preceding philosophy.

CIO (Chief Information Officer)   The executive responsible for the IT organization.

COM (Common Object Model)   A software architecture jointly developed by Digital Equipment Corporation and Microsoft which standardizes software components for optimal reuse.

CORBA (Common Object Request Broker Architecture)   The overall OMG framework that supports application development with standard reusable objects and interfaces.

CRUD (Create, Read, Update, and Delete)   Standard database transaction types, which indicate the type of impact on resident data.

Common metadata   The category of metadata that is wanted, needed, and used by all metadata beneficiaries.

Common warehouse model   A specification that was initially developed by a multi-organization effort to standardize the metadata associated with data warehousing. The model encompasses XML (Extensible Markup Language), XMI (XML Metadata Interchange), and UML (Unified Modeling Language) and represents a common data warehousing metamodel.

CWM   See *Common Warehouse Model*.

Data   Instances of characters; raw facts or values that must be combined with metadata to become information. See also *Information; Metadata*.

Data administration   See *Data management*.

Data management   A function, typically dedicated to an organization in IT, responsible for maintaining, cataloging, and standardizing corporate data. Responsibilities may include the creation of an enterprise data model, the definition of corporate data standards, the review of application data models, and the development and maintenance of data dictionaries. Originally known as data administration, works very closely with database administration.

Data mart   A data store that represents an aggregation of select data from one production database for read-only decision support. In well-planned data warehouse architectures, it can be viewed as a subset of the overall data warehouse.

Data model   a graphic representation of a set of data and its interrelationships. Data models can be logical or physical (see Logical Data Model, Physical Data Model) and can be depicted in a variety of formats and methodologies, included E-R, UML, and Object-Oriented.

Data staging area   An intermediate set of cleansed, organized, and transaction-level data that is typically held for load into one or more data warehouses.

Data warehouse   An aggregation of production data extracted from multiple operational data sources and translated to meet the needs of enterprise decision support.

Database administration   An organization within IT that is responsible for the definition, monitoring, and tuning of physical databases and their associated DBMS software.

DBA (database administrator)   An individual in the database administration organization who is responsible for the creation, modification, and tuning of physical database structures.

DBMS (database management system). Database software such as Oracle and DB2.

DDL (Data Definition Language)   Standardized query language constructs used to set up individual databases by entering their physical requirements into a DBMS catalog.

Dictionary   Vendor-supplied or custom-developed databases that track user-populated data element definitions and their occurrences across an organization's applications.

e-commerce   The practice of conducting business over the Internet via the capturing of a company's Web page–initiated sales transactions.

Encyclopedia   Internal databases that store information tracked, developed, and maintained by a predefined set of single-vendor tools.

Enterprise model   An integrated view of multiple applications, or application perspectives. Generally speaking, they represent a bigger picture than single application, functional, or database depictions.

Enterprise portal   A metamodel-based gateway to a set of defined objects or information. They contain information categories, locations, and specific access paths.

Entity A person, place, thing, or event about which we store data. Used as the main component of logical data models in the E-R (entity-relationship) approach.

Entity-relationship modeling A data modeling methodology that shows defined entities and their relationships. An example would be the depiction of "Customer" *buys* "Product," where Customer and Product are both entities, and *buys* is the relationship that ties them together.

E-R See *Entity-relationship modeling.*

ERP (Enterprise resource planning) A category of off-the-shelf software packages that span the functionality of more than one enterprise business function and share a database.

Expert systems Applications that capture rules, both predecessor and concluding, so that they can conclude results based on a set of conditions.

Extension Changes, additions, and deletions to vendor-supplied metamodels.

Extract A set of data that is pulled from a main data source or tool.

FE (front end) The parts of an application that are seen by the business user as the primary interface. They typically run on a workstation and are used for query and update purposes.

GUI (graphical user interface) A front end that is represented by icons, pictures, symbols, and other nontextual components.

IDL See *Interface Definition Language.*

Impact analysis Metadata solution queries that show all contents that would be affected by a particular change, by returning all related metadata solution components.

Information A combined set of character group instances, typically collected into a predefined context, which when processed in a specific specialty creates a fact and/or statement of discovery.

Information directory A type of metadata solution used in the data warehouse environment and others to track (warehouse) data element definitions and their locations. Many directories are custom developed.

Information on demand The ability to search for and retrieve information based on the use of standardized metadata.

Instance data Described by a metadata value (see *Metadata value*), and input into a receiving tool, application, database, or simple processing engine. If the metadata value is Total Sales, then associated instance data could be $45,000,000.

Interface Definition Language   An OMG standard for defining CORBA-compliant interfaces.

Intranet   An internal network of connected processors built using Web protocols. Access is restricted to internal organization employees.

IRDS (Information Resource Dictionary Standard)   An original ANSI sponsored standard that addressed the requirements of early repositories and metadata solutions.

IRM (Information Resource Management)   A subprofession of IT that focuses on the administration, standardization, and distribution of data and information in an enterprise.

IS (Information Systems)   The corporate organization responsible for the planning, development, implementation, and management of computer resources, both hardware and software.

ISBN (International Standard Book Number)   The main identifier used by the U.S. Library of Congress to identify published books.

ISO (International Standards Organization)   An organization responsible for establishing software certification requirements.

IT (Information Technology)   The newly adopted name of an organization's IS department; See *IS*.

JAD (Joint Application Development)   A popular requirements gathering process that involves collective questions and answers from technical developers and the targeted business users, often led by a facilitator, or methodology-trained session leader.

LDM   See *Logical Data Model*.

Legacy   A computer application and associated data developed during a period of previously popular technology, often not documented.

Logical data model   A view of data and its inherent relationships that depicts the functional use of data despite its physical implementations. Data models can be developed using relational (E-R) or object-oriented (O-O) methodologies.

Metadata   The detailed description of the instance data; the format and characteristics of populated instance data; instances and values depend on the role of the metadata recipient. Examples of metadata include filenames, data element definitions, data element names, lengths, program names, and so on.

Metadata architecture   A logical spread of metadata sources and beneficiaries.

Metadata construct   The generic name of the metadata of interest; translates to either an attribute or a metadata component. Examples include Data Element, Data Element Name, Entity, and Model.

Metadata framework   An organizational set of metadata standards that cover the creation, storage, access, and update of metadata.

Metadata of record   The official source value of a particular metadata element; required in order to prevent or eliminate metadata webs.

Metadata requirements   The needs of all metadata beneficiaries and metadata solution components expressed in terms of metadata, metadata access, metadata solution functionality, metadata storage, metadata display, and overall metadata solution security.

Metadata solution   An organized and integrated set of related metadata, logically connected but often physically separate, with common access points and methods.

Metadata solution architecture   An organized set of interfaces depicting all metadata components, their associated beneficiaries, and the types of metadata transfer occurring throughout the architecture; the required tool, application, package, and repository interfaces necessary to maintain an accurate set of metadata throughout the continuing execution of metadata-reliant processes.

Metadata value   The actual instance of a metadata construct. If a metadata construct is Data Element Name, then one of its metadata values could be Total Sales.

Metadata web   An uncontrolled replication and re-creation of metadata, often without a plan or strategy.

Meta-metadata   The descriptive details of metadata; metadata qualities and locations that allow tool-based processing and access; the basic attributes of metadata solutions.

Meta-metamodel   An organized model of meta-metadata that depicts the relationships among the various types of meta-meta constructs. Meta-metamodels typically represent *metadata solution* views in that they integrate various tool or application-specific metamodels. Metamodel components are instances of meta-meta constructs. See *Metamodel.*

Metamodel   The graphic representation of an organized set of metadata requirements, typically organized by any of the following perspectives:

- The metadata source (a tool, application, metadata store, etc.)

- The metadata's classification (common, unique, or specific) and associated beneficiary category
- The metadata's usage (e.g., a particular development methodology)

Metamodel component   One entity or object in a metamodel, one box in the graphic metamodel representation.

Meta object facility   A specification developed by the OMG (Object Management Group) that addresses a meta-meta framework. MOF-compliant metamodels will be able to reside in the same physical metadata repository.

MOF   See *Meta object facility.*

MF (mainframe)   The most popular corporate computer processor of the 1960s, now considered "legacy" in many circles.

Normalization   The process of refining a database design so that each attribute in an entity depends entirely on the primary key and no other attributes.

Object Management Group   A standards committee established to develop independent software specifications based on an object-oriented component philosophy. Major efforts to establish standards include CORBA (Common Object Request Broker Architecture), MOF (Meta-Object Facility), and the CWM (Common Warehouse Model).

Object Orientation (OO)   The methodology of combining processes with associated data categories (classes) to ensure standard and reusable action/result combinations.

ODBC (Object Database Connectivity)   A standard means of database access adhered to by major DBMS vendors.

ODS   See *Operational Data Store.*

OIM   See *Open Information Model.*

Open Information Model (OIM)   A set of metadata specifications developed by the Metadata Coalition (MDC) geared toward standardizing the sharing of metadata between and among data warehousing products. The model was incorporated into the common warehouse model (CWM) when MDC merged with the OMG.

Operational Data Store   A captured set of transaction data that originates from a production application. Originally established as a means of saving transactions for historical analysis, the ODS does not result from major redesign or cleansing efforts.

OTS (off-the-shelf)   A common term for a purchased, prewritten, commercial software package, tool, or solution.

Passive repository   A standalone metadata solution that relies on manual trigger or update to remain current in terms of its contents.

PDM   See *Physical data model.*

Physical data model (PDM)   A model that represents an application-specific or tool-specific implementation of its logical data requirements.

Policy   Metadata solution-resident program code that is implemented, controlled, and executed by its software to perform a wide variety of services, including metadata validation and security checks.

Primary/secondary   Application architectures in which one processor serves as the main, or primary processor, and others function as subordinate, or secondary, processors in terms of overall application functions. Originally known as client/server processing.

Process model   A model of the processes in an application as well as their natural functional relationships; usually depicted in structured hierarchical diagram format. Process models often relate closely to physical application or tool-specific implementations.

Relational   A database design based on rows and columns (the relational model). The overall database contains a series of tables that can be joined via common data values in related columns.

Repository   An integrated, virtual holding area with vendor-independent input, access, and structure; used to directly store metadata and/or the metadata-based gateways to external metadata.

Repository state   A division of repository-resident or accessible metadata, usually based on a phase of application development (dev, tst, prd), but also definable by the repository administrator.

Reverse engineering   A process of reading legacy applications to obtain physical models. Typically, reverse engineering starts with the capture of physical definitions by reverse engineering products. The resulting physical models can then be refined and changed to support a newly engineered result.

RPC (Remote Procedure Call)   A set of program code that can be executed via an outside call.

Repository architecture   A modeled representation of the metadata repository and its relationship(s) to deployed applications, software packages, and development tools.

Specific metadata   Metadata that is preferred and required by one and only one beneficiary category. It is so precise that it originates from a source equivalent to the beneficiary category, often called *specialist* or *specialty* metadata.

SQL (Structured Query Language)   A standard set of commands used to access relational databases.

Submodel   A model that represents a logical grouping of a subset of a metamodel.

Subtype   A special class of entity that inherits the characteristics of the major, or parent, entity yet has unique attributes. An example is *Magazine,* which could be a sub-type of *Publication*.

Template   A repository-resident definition that controls the display, access, and processing of metadata solution resident (or accessible) information.

Transactional application   Custom software developed for the purpose of capturing process-based events, such as taking product orders.

Tunnel vision   The tendency to view requirements from the point of view of immediate needs and data sources without considering other individuals, data, or processes.

UML (Unified Modeling Language)   A standard means of specifying and representing models of software applications. The standard covers both model content and modeling syntax.

Unique metadata   The metadata is wanted, needed, and used by one beneficiary category (as with specific metadata), but it does *not* originate from the same architectural component that creates the metadata. The metadata originates from a different source, multiple sources, or in some cases, an unknown source.

VB (Visual Basic)   A popular client front-end development programming language.

XMI (XML Metadata Interchange)   A standard that allows the easy exchange of metadata between UML based modeling tools and MOF-compliant metadata repositories.

XML (Extensible Markup Language)   A subset of SGML (Standardized General Markup Language) for Web-based document transfer, which relies on common metadata markup. Developed by the W3C (World Wide Web Consortium), it relies on tags to describe the content that follows.

Appendix B

Additional Readings

Data Management

Brackett, Michael. *Data Sharing: Using a Common Data Architecture.* New York: John Wiley & Sons, 1994.

English, Larry P. *Improving Data Warehouse and Business Information Quality: Methods for Reducing Costs and Increasing Profits.* New York: John Wiley & Sons, 1999.

Inmon, William H., John A. Zachman, and Jonathan G. Geiger. *Data Stores, Data Warehousing and the Zachman Framework.* New York: McGraw-Hill, 1997.

Pascal, Fabian. *Practical Issues in Database Management: A Reference for the Thinking Practitioner.* Boston: Addison-Wesley, 2000.

Data Modeling

Carlis, John, and Maguire, Joseph. *Mastering Data Modeling: A User-Driven Approach.* Boston: Addison-Wesley, 2000.

Hay, David C. *Data Model Patterns: Conventions of Thought.* New York: Dorset House, 1995.

Muller, Robert J. *Database Design for Smarties: Using UML for Data Modeling.* San Francisco: Morgan Kaufman, 1999.

Reingruber, Michael. *The Data Modeling Handbook: A Best-Practice Approach to Building Quality Data Models.* New York: John Wiley & Sons, 1994.

Silverston, Len, Kent Graziano, and William H. Inmon. *The Data Model Resource Book: A Library of Logical Data and Data Warehouse Designs.* New York: John Wiley & Sons, 1997.

Data Warehousing

Adelman, Sid, and Larissa Terpeluk Moss. *Data Warehouse Project Management.* Boston: Addison-Wesley, 2000.

Dyché, Jill. *e-Data: Turning Data into Information with Data Warehousing.* Boston: Addison-Wesley, 2000.

Giovinazzo, William A., and William H. Inmon. *Object-Oriented Data Warehouse Design: A Star Schema.* Englewood Cliffs, N.J.: Prentice-Hall, 2000.

Inmon, William H. *Building the Data Warehouse.* New York: John Wiley & Sons, 1996.

Kimball, Ralph, and Richard Merz. *The Data Webhouse Toolkit: Building the Web-Enabled Data Warehouse.* New York: John Wiley & Sons, 2000.

Kimball, Ralph, Laura Reeves, Margy Ross, and Warren Thornthwaite. *The Data Warehouse Lifecycle Toolkit: Expert Methods for Designing, Developing and Deploying Data Warehouses.* New York: John Wiley & Sons, 1998.

Kimball, Ralph. *The Data Warehouse Toolkit: Practical Techniques for Building Dimensional Data Warehouses.* New York: John Wiley & Sons, 1996.

Enterprise Architecture

Boar, Bernard H. *Constructing Blueprints for Enterprise IT Architectures.* New York: John Wiley & Sons, 1998.

Cook, Melissa. *Building Enterprise Information Architectures.* Englewood Cliffs, N.J.: Prentice-Hall, 1996.

Goodyear, Mark. *Enterprise System Architectures.* Boca Raton, Fla.: CRC Press, 1999.

Spewak, Steven H., and Steven C. Hill. *Enterprise Architecture Planning: Developing a Blueprint for Data, Applications, and Technology.* New York: John Wiley & Sons, 1993.

Metadata and Repositories

Tannenbaum, Adrienne. *Implementing a Corporate Repository: The Models Meet Reality.* New York: John Wiley & Sons, 1994.

Object-Oriented Analysis

Binder, Robert V. *Testing Object-Oriented Systems: Models, Patterns, and Tools*. Boston: Addison-Wesley, 2000.

Booch, Grady. *Object-Oriented Analysis and Design with Applications*. Reading, Mass.: Addison-Wesley, 1994.

Brown, David. *An Introduction to Object-Oriented Analysis: Objects in Plain English.* New York: John Wiley & Sons, 1997.

Coad, Peter, and Edward Yourdon. *Object-Oriented Design*. Englewood Cliffs, N.J.: Yourdon Press, 1991.

Shlaer, Sally, and Stephen J. Mellor. *Object Lifecycles: Modeling the World in States*. Englewood Cliffs, N.J.: Yourdon Press, 1991.

Shlaer, Sally (Preface), and Stephen J. Mellor (Preface). *Object-Oriented Systems Analysis: Modeling the World in Data*. Englewood Cliffs, N.J.: Yourdon Press, 1989.

Process Modeling

Doumeingts, Guy, and Jim Browne, eds. *Modeling Techniques for Business Process Re-engineering and Benchmarking*. Boca Raton, Fla.: Chapman & Hall, 1997.

Barker, Richard, and Cliff Longman. *Case Method: Function and Process Modeling*. Reading, Mass.: Addison-Wesley, 1992.

Scholz-Reiter, Bernd, and Eberhard Stickel, eds. *Business Process Modeling*. New York: Springer-Verlag, 1996.

Systems Analysis

Blanchard, Benjamin S., and Wolter J. Fabrycky. *Systems Engineering and Analysis*. Englewood Cliffs, N.J.: Prentice-Hall, 1998.

Dennis, Alan, and Barbara Haley Wixom. *Systems Analysis and Design.* New York: John Wiley & Sons, 1999.

Kendall, Kenneth E., and Julie E. Kendall. *Systems Analysis and Design*. Englewood Cliffs, N.J.: Prentice-Hall, 1998.

Robertson, James, and Suzanne Robertson. *Complete Systems Analysis: The Workbook, the Textbook, the Answers*. New York: Dorset House, 1998.

————. *Mastering the Requirements Process*. Boston: Addison-Wesley, 2000.

Whitten, Jeffrey L., Lonnie D. Bentley, and Kevin C. Dittman. *Systems Analysis and Design Methods,* 5th ed. New York: McGraw-Hill Higher Education, 2000.

XML

Holzner, Steven. *Inside XML.* Indianapolis, Ind.: New Riders Publishing, 2000.

Finkelstein, Clive, Peter G. Aiken, and John A Zachman. *Building Corporate Portals with XML* (Enterprising Computing). Berkeley, Calif.: Computing McGraw-Hill, 1999.

Mohr, Stephen, et al. *Professional XML.* Chicago: Wrox Press, 2000.

Spencer, Paul. *XML Design and Implementation.* Chicago: Wrox Press, 1999.

St. Laurent, Simon. *XML: A Primer*, 2d ed. Alamonte Springs, Fla.: M&T Books, 1999.

Index

Also Available from Addison-Wesley

Data Resource Quality
Turning Bad Habits into Good Practices
By Michael H. Brackett
Addison-Wesley Information Technology Series

Written by a world expert in data resources, *Data Resource Quality* features the ten most fundamental and frequently exhibited bad habits that contribute to poor data quality, and it presents the strategies and best practices for effective solutions. With this information, IT managers will be better equipped to implement an organization-wide, integrated, subject-oriented data architecture and, within that architecture, build a high-quality data resource.

0-201-71306-3 • Paperback • 384 pages • ©2000

e-Data
Turning Data into Information with Data Warehousing
By Jill Dyché
Addison-Wesley Information Technology Series

e-Data: Turning Data into Information with Data Warehousing covers data warehousing and its surrounding technologies in a straightforward and engaging way, illustrating how companies are leveraging their data warehouses to serve a wide range of business needs. This book clearly lays out what business people should know about data warehouse implementation and the best techniques for evaluating and justifying new data warehouses and data marts.

0-201-65780-5 • Paperback • 368 pages • ©2000

The CRM Handbook
A Business Guide to Customer Relationship Management
By Jill Dyché
Addison-Wesley Information Technology Series

The CRM Handbook takes a cross-functional view of planning and implementing a CRM program from both technical and business vantage points. It includes a concise and easy-to-understand introduction to CRM and demystifies some of the well-worn buzzwords by putting them in the correct context. Real case studies of CRM successes and failures are used to cover the range of CRM applications, from sales force automation to helpdesk support, to marketing automation, to e-CRM, and beyond.

0-201-73062-6 • Paperback • 336 pages • ©2002

Data Warehouse Project Management

By Sid Adelman, Larissa Terpeluk Moss

Addison-Wesley Information Technology Series

Data warehouse development projects present a unique set of management challenges that can confound even the most experienced project manager. *Data Warehouse Project Management* addresses these challenges and provides a comprehensive roadmap to managing every aspect of data warehouse design, development, and implementation. Drawing on their extensive experience in the field, Sid Adelman and Larissa Moss point to critical success factors, reveal the many pitfalls to watch out for, and offer proven solutions that will enable you to put a successful data warehouse project into place.

0-201-61635-1 • Paperback with CD-ROM • 448 pages • ©2000

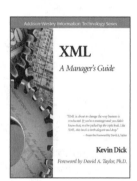

XML

A Manager's Guide

By Kevin Dick

Addison-Wesley Information Technology Series

This book serves as a concise guide for technical managers, as well as a starting point for developers interested in taking advantage of XML. It uses clear explanations of XML essentials as a foundation to demonstrate how this technology can substantially benefit your organization. Designed to let you access exactly the information you require, this book clearly delineates different paths through the chapters based on your needs, provides executive briefings for every chapter, and includes fast-track summaries of major points in the margins.

0-201-43335-4 • Paperback • 208 pages • ©2000

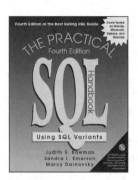

The Practical SQL Handbook, Fourth Edition

Using SQL Variants

By Judith S. Bowman, Sandra L. Emerson, Marcy Darnovsky

This latest edition of the best-selling implementation guide to the Structured Query Language teaches fundamentals while providing practical solutions for critical business applications. *The Practical SQL Handbook, Fourth Edition*, includes expanded platform SQL coverage and extensive real-world examples based on feedback from actual SQL users. The book begins with a step-by-step introduction to SQL basics and examines the issues involved in designing SQL-based database applications. It gives examples in SQL's most popular implementations from industry leaders, Oracle, Microsoft, Sybase, and Informix.

0-201-70309-2 • Paperback with CD-ROM • 512 pages • ©2001

Practical SQL
The Sequel
By Judith S. Bowman

Written by the co-author of the best-selling *The Practical SQL Handbook*, *Practical SQL: The Sequel* picks up where the first book leaves off. It goes beyond basic SQL query structure to explore the complexities of using SQL for everyday business needs. It will help you make the transition from classroom to reality, where you must design, fix, and maintain imperfect SQL systems. This book offers information, organized by use rather than by feature, for those who are working with SQL systems or are preparing to do so. Readers can turn to specific business problems and learn how to solve them with the appropriate SQL features. In particular, this sequel to *The Practical SQL Handbook* focuses on the real-world challenges of dealing with legacy systems, inherited problematic code, dirty data, and query tuning for better performance.

0-201-61638-6 • Paperback with CD-ROM • 352 pages • ©2001

SQL Queries for Mere Mortals
A Hands-On Guide to Data Manipulation in SQL
By Michael J. Hernandez, John L. Viescas

If you are accessing corporate information from the Internet or from an internal network, you are probably using SQL. This book will help new users learn the foundations of SQL queries, and it will prove to be an essential reference guide for intermediate and advanced users. The accompanying CD contains five sample databases used for the example queries throughout the book, plus an evaluation copy of Microsoft SQL Server version 7.

0-201-43336-2 • Paperback with CD-ROM • 528 pages • ©2000

Database Design for Mere Mortals
A Hands-On Guide to Relational Database Design
By Michael J. Hernandez

Sound design can save you hours of development time before you write a single line of code. Based on the author's years of experience teaching this material, this book is a straightforward, platform-independent tutorial on the basic principles of relational database design. Database design expert Michael J. Hernandez introduces the core concepts of design theory and method without the technical jargon. *Database Design for Mere Mortals* will provide any developer with a commonsense design methodology for developing databases that work.

0-201-69471-9 • Paperback • 480 pages • ©1997

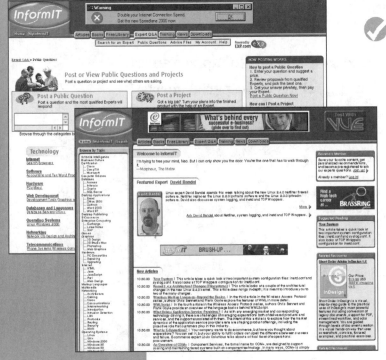